The Incomplete Circle

To Arlene, with many thanks for your contribution to this Book.
Ricky A.
19 Oct 2000.

The Incomplete Circle

Eric Atkinson, art and education

An exchange of letters, edited and introduced by

David Lewis

for Arlene, with greetings from David

Contributors:

Eric Atkinson
David Lewis
Norbert Lynton
George Hainsworth
Sir Terry Frost
Colin Phipps
John Davies
Peter Stead
Duncan de Kergommeaux
Stephen Joy
Fred Steinmetz
Arlene Kennedy

Scolar Press

in association with

The Volunteer Committee
of The London Regional Art and
Historical Museums, Canada

First published in 2000 by
Scolar Press
Gower House
Croft Road
Aldershot
Hampshire GU11 3HR
in association with The Volunteer Committee of
The London Regional Art and Historical Museums, Canada

Scolar Press is an imprint of Ashgate Publishing

British Library Cataloguing in Publication Data
A catalogue record for this book is
available from the British Library

Library of Congress Card Number : 00-105243

Standard edition ISBN 0 7546 0236 2
Limited edition ISBN 0 7546 0251 6

Produced for the publisher by
John Taylor Book Ventures
Faringdon, Oxfordshire

Designed by Peter Guy
Typeset by Tom Knott
Printed in Singapore

Ashgate US office:
Ashgate Publishing
131 Main Street
Burlington
VT 05401-5600
USA

ILLUSTRATION ACKNOWLEDGEMENTS

The editor, Eric Atkinson and the publishers wish to thank all those artists, museums, owners and copyright-holders who are referred to in the Acknowledgements and captions and who have kindly given permission for illustrations to be reproduced.

Illustrations of works by the following artists are copyright as follows:

Karen Appel © DACS 2000
Sam Francis © DACS 2000
Barbara Hepworth © Alan Bowness, Hepworth Estate
Roger Hilton © Estate of Roger Hilton 2000. All rights reserved, DACS
Piet Mondrian © 2000 Mondrian/Holtzman Trust c/o Beeldrecht, Amsterdam, Holland & DACS, London
Robert Motherwell © Dedalus Foundation, Inc/VAGA, New York/DACS, London 2000
Louise Nevelson © ARS, NY and DACS, London 2000
Ben Nicholson © Angela Verren-Taunt 2000 All rights reserved, DACS
Antoine Pevsner © ADAGP, Paris and DACS, London 2000
Kurt Schwitters © DACS 2000
Nicolas de Staël © ADAGP, Paris and DACS, London 2000
Antoni Tapies © ADAGP, Paris and DACS, London 2000
Alfred Wallis © 2000. All rights reserved, DACS

Contents

FOR MURIEL AND JUDY

Contributors

JOHN DAVIES and COLIN PHIPPS
are architects, and graduates from Leeds College of Art. Both were students on the Leeds Basic Course.

SIR TERRY FROST
is one of Britain's best-known non-figurative painters. His work is in many public and private collections in Europe and America. A Royal Academician, he was knighted in 1998.

GEORGE HAINSWORTH
is Professor of Fine Art, Design and the Built Environment at Leeds Metropolitan University, England. Educated at Leeds College of Art, the Slade, and the British School in Rome, in London he was awarded the Gulbenkian Scholarship for Sculpture. His paintings and sculptures have been exhibited widely and are in several public and private collections.

STEPHEN JOY
was Assistant Director of the Martha Jackson Gallery in New York, 1953–61, which thrust him into the centre of the New York art scene at its most powerful moment. Subsequently he was Director of the Dunkleman Gallery in Toronto, before joining Eric Atkinson on the faculty at Fanshawe and directing the Trajectory Gallery in London, Ontario.

ARLENE KENNEDY
is Director of the McIntosh Gallery at the University of Western Ontario. Educated at the Nova Scotia College of Art and Design, she is President of the Ontario Association of Art Galleries.

DUNCAN DE KERGOMMEAUX
is Professor Emeritus at the University of Western Ontario and is one of Canada's best-known abstract painters. Educated at the Banff School of Fine Arts, he was Director of the Canadian Pavilion Gallery at Expo 67. Widely exhibited, his work is in many public collections in Canada and the United States.

NORBERT LYNTON
is Professor Emeritus of the University of Sussex. He has taught at Leeds College of Art, Chelsea School of Art, London, the Open University, and the Royal College of Art, London. For many years he was a member of the British Council's Art Advisory Committee. His books include *Paul Klee*, *The Story of Modern Art*, *Victor Pasmore*, and *Ben Nicholson*.

PETER STEAD
was one of Britain's leading neo-plastic constructive artists until his death in December 1999. Two houses, designed in collaboration with the constructive sculptor, Stephen Gilbert, and built in Yorkshire in the mid-1950s, were the first industrial component houses in England.

FRED STEINMETZ
is Dean of Applied Arts and Business at Fanshawe College. A graduate in Radio and TV from Ryerson Polytechnic, he has been a director/producer and a consultant to the United Arab Emirates. In 1993 he received the Ruth Hancock Award of the Central Canada Broadcasters' Association.

Illustrations

Acknowledgments

The Volunteer Committee of the London Regional Art and Historical Museums in London, Ontario, has recognised for several years that in Eric Atkinson we have a unique artist and educator. We believe that his accomplishments should now be recognised by a wider audience. Through the initiative of one of our members, the late Mackie Cryderman, Eric Atkinson came to us in 1969, following a distinguished career in England, to take up the appointment of Chairman and later Dean of the Faculty of Applied Arts at Fanshawe Community College.

The idea of a book that would deal with the dual role of this remarkable man – artist and educator in two widely separated geographic centres, Yorkshire in England and Ontario in Canada – was first proposed by the late Jake Moore. The idea rapidly gained momentum. At first the book was thought of as a straight narrative. But as we got deeper into the project, the format of an exchange of letters, each dealing with a different facet, became increasingly attractive.

The Volunteer Committee is indebted first and foremost to Eric Atkinson for allowing us to explore his life, his approach to art education, and his art, in full and often hilarious collaboration. We are also indebted to David Lewis, not only for his contributions to the book, but for working with and encouraging each of our contributors. We are especially grateful to the following people for making the book a reality: Sean Atkinson, Brigit Atkinson, Tom and Penny Brown, Kelly Mancari, Woody Moore, and Ian and Flora Tripp, for their generous financial support; Shelagh Martin of the Volunteer Committee; and Barry Fair and Rebecca Boughner of the London Regional Art and Historical Museums.

We wish to thank our contributors, Professor Norbert Lynton, Peter Stead, Sir Terry Frost, Professor Duncan de Kergommeaux, Professor George Hainsworth, Stephen Joy, Colin Phipps, John Davies, Dean Fred Steinmetz, and Arlene Kennedy. We are grateful to John Taylor for his editorial supervision. We wish to thank Julian Satterthwaite and John Tempest for their help over a span of several months. We thank Lonnie Graham, Gino Lorcini, and William Kurylyk for their outstanding photography. We are indebted to the Director of the Carnegie Museum in Pittsburgh, Richard Armstrong, the Carnegie's Photography Department, Beth Levanti, and the Publications Department, Elissa Curcio, for their enthusiastic assistance.

We are also deeply indebted to Leonard Bartle and Professor Ron George at the National Arts Archives of the Lawrence Batley Centre at Bretton Hall in Yorkshire, England. Alex Robertson, Curator of Contemporary Art at the Leeds City Art Gallery, England, was unfailingly patient and helpful; and so too was Elizabeth Law, Collections Manager, Hartlepool Art Gallery, England. We wish to thank Dr Howard Rundle, President of Fanshawe College of Applied Arts and Technology, and Rona Slade, Associate Dean, Corcoran School of Art, Washington, DC. We are grateful to Sir Alan Bowness for permission to reproduce photographs of sculptures by Barbara Hepworth; to Celia Clear, Director of Publications, Tate Gallery, London; to Angela Verren-Taunt for permission to reproduce photographs of works by Ben Nicholson; and to Wendy Pasmore for permission to reproduce works and archival materials by Victor Pasmore.

Wilda Thomas
President, Volunteer Committee,
London Regional Art and Historical Museums

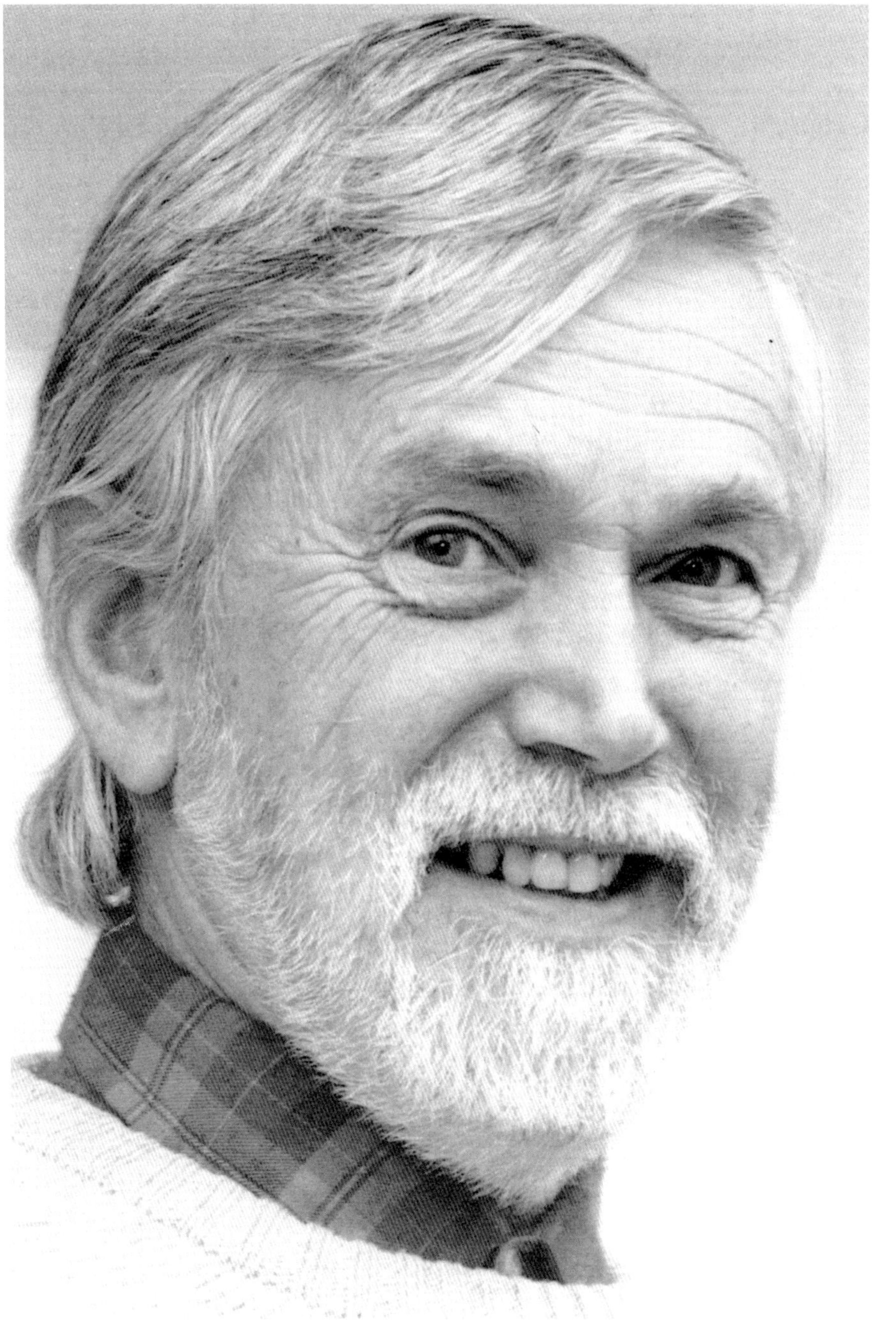

Eric Atkinson
(photograph: Gino Lorcini)

Introduction David Lewis

This is the story of a painter in the second half of the twentieth century. You will not, however, find his name, Eric ('Ricky') Atkinson, on the catalogue covers of prestigious art galleries in London, New York, Paris or Geneva. Not that he lacks a devoted following of collectors. The list of museums and public collections owning his work is respectably long. It is simply that this modest man, working as an artist in a suburban house in a provincial city in Ontario, is not an acknowledged star of the international set. Indeed, he is not even a household name in his native England – nor in Canada, his adopted homeland. Then why this book?

There are two reasons. First, here is a man whose life runs parallel to the lives of thousands of serious artists – painters, sculptors, writers, and musicians – who, by contrast with the international artistic élite, comprise the broad stream of our culture. The second reason is that, like so many of his contemporaries, he has been a teacher all his working life as well as an artist. But in his case, his teaching was not just a way of making a living while his creative mind was elsewhere in his studio. Throughout, he has played a central role in a revolution in art education which took a brief but robust form in Britain in the 1950s, and then crossed the Atlantic to Canada, in a broadened and maybe even more challenging form in the 1970s. Its impact was so potent that its ripple-effects are still being felt, and are likely to be revisited for years to come.

Simply put, the essence of the revolution was that the purpose of art education must be to discover and encourage creativity in every student individually. Obvious though this may seem, it ran counter to the practice of the time, which focused on the acquisition of skills – the transfer from teacher to student of the 'right' way to do things. And in opposing this, the revolution created controversy, and even bitterness.

Perhaps it is an over-simplification to talk about progressives and conservatives, or about liberals and authoritarians – but there certainly was an element of truth in such labellings at the time. The first group assumed that there is no right or wrong way in art. The second said that there is. The first believed that the courage to explore lies at the heart of art education, and that the essence of learning is to encourage every individual to make his own discoveries. The second asserted that the development of skills (the technical ability to draw and paint, to carve wood or stone, correctly) has to come before one can communicate. The first stated that it is a contradiction to set exams in art and offer diplomas of competence. The second not only assumed that you should, but conducted national exams and awarded national diplomas.

From such a simple parting of the ways, streams grew into rivers which flowed in two totally different and opposite directions. One group undermined conformity and the notion of a bureaucracy of educational standards by encouraging the river to flow where it would, the other reinforced the bureaucracy of art education, and encouraged the channelling of the river by enforcing national academic standards.

Ricky is a graduate of the Royal Academy Schools in London. A scholarship student, he went through the standard training of drawing from classical plaster casts, copies of the old masters, and life classes. His earliest paintings are representational. Born in Hartlepool, a port city in north-east England, his first two London exhibitions were of paintings of docks and cranes and merchant ships; nothing heroic, nothing complicated, no special messages, just the everyday working life of a seaport, directly and skilfully portrayed. The exhibitions were very successful. He could have gone on to be a succesful painter of realistic seascapes.

Instead, his life changed. And the change came with his first job. In 1956 he joined the faculty of Leeds College of Art at the invitation of the new head of its art school, Harry Thubron. As a recent graduate of the Academy Schools, one who knew the ropes, his task was to ensure that students passed the national examinations and got their National Diplomas in Design (NDD). But that was a subsidiary agenda. The real agenda was that Thubron was setting in motion in Leeds College of Art the most vigorous and radical departure in art education imaginable, and Ricky was to be his assistant.

Thubron sought to kick over the traces completely. He perceived the traditional methods of art teaching as a strait-jacket. Based on his experience with primary school children and their capacities for self-expression, he wanted to demonstrate a new approach to art education at the collegiate level. He strove to set his students a series of visual challenges and to encourage each one individually to make their own way, exploring and discovering as they went.

He built a team of artists around him, all strong personalities. But because of Thubron's energy and commitment they shared a common purpose. He rejected the notion of curriculum, or even stated theory. He saw these as the denial of open-endedness, and creativity as uncharted territory. He visualised points of departure, but refused to forecast where the journey might lead. He looked for beginnings, exploration, action, discovery, and self-discovery.

That someone like Thubron would come along and confront the establishment was inevitable. It had to happen, but its impact at the time sent shock-waves through the educational establishment. The revolution had to be snuffed out! But by the time the bureaucracy of the establishment, the regulators of education, and the administrators of budgets could take action six years had gone by and it was all over anyway. Perhaps it could not last. In all likelihood the episode was destined to burn itself out. Like many revolts, it was vigorous and confrontational, and then it was over almost as quickly as it had begun except for the memories and the impact. But it left its mark.

Thubron wrote nothing down. He perceived in definitions of what he was doing a new straitjacket. He was both right and wrong. He was right to see definitions as leading to curriculum and a new academicism. But he was wrong not to recognise that the consequences of his revolutionary ideas needed to be monitored so that they in turn could become the starting-points for new journeys.

Ricky was Thubron's principal assistant from the beginning to the end of the six years. It fell to his lot to preside over what was left of the revolution after Thubron's departure. But the revolution did not die. Ricky then took up an appointment in Canada, where he opened up entirely new fields of art education, until they, too, ran their course.

Running parallel with what happened in the studios of these colleges was the creative work of the teachers themselves – the painters, the sculptors, the constructors, the poets. This aspect is vitally important. Hence the parallel theme of this book, the art of Ricky Atkinson.

So how do we capture the spirit of what Thubron initiated – but without doing what he dreaded most, writing it down as an art historian might, or an art educator, as a definition and a curriculum? To quote a remark that the painter Ben Nicholson once made about art critics in a letter to me – 'they try to nail down one's magic carpet but magic carpets don't like being nailed down'.

After much discussion, we decided that the most effective way to explore the whole subject was by means of an exchange of letters between some of those involved. Letters, it seemed, would be a good vehicle. They are informal, and to an extent unstructured. And they reveal the writers as much as what the writers are writing about. The Leeds experience, and the later Canadian experience, have cemented friendships which have lasted through the years. We came from different backgrounds; and afterwards we went in other directions. Our letters are meant to recapture something of the ambience. After all, we were there. Maybe the art historians Ben referred to will read what we have written and will show us that the facts are not always right; but I hope we have kept our magic carpets flying.

Of course, events like the revolution in Leeds do not occur suddenly, just like that. A lot leads up to it. The first half of the twentieth century witnessed the most vigorous recasting of visual language and its purposes in the entire history of art. Running parallel were accelerating advances in science, technology and industry. In the minds of many thinkers there was an urgent need to bring art, science, and even social action together into a common arena of language.

By far the most influential of the efforts to meet this need was the Bauhaus in the 1920s. Put together by the architect Walter Gropius, its faculty in 1925 included an astonishing array of talents, artists, architects, and designers, including Paul Klee, László Moholy-Nagy, Wassily Kandinsky, Marcel Breuer, Lyonel Feininger, Josef Albers, and Oskar Schlemmer. Taking its lead from Cubism, and also from industry, the Bauhaus set out to challenge its faculty and students to discover a new language of synthesis based on primary elements.

> 'At the Bauhaus under Gropius the effort was made to unite art and industry, art and everyday life, using architecture as the intermediary....The principles of art were there for the first time translated into the field of education.'[1]
>
> 'It was an attempt to bridge the gulf between the world of the spirit and the world of everyday, between art and industrial production. The whole endeavour of the Bauhaus was to discover similarities between these two spheres and to make them generally known. To do this it was absolutely necessary to go back to first principles and to investigate the elemental nature both of art and of matter.'[2]

A basic course was set up by the Swiss painter, Johannes Itten. A sequence of exercises based on Cubism dealt with colour, plane, line, texture, space, movement, materials, and composition. Students then moved on to the more complex programmes of industrial product design and building design. To house the school Gropius designed his group of well-known steel, glass and concrete buildings. At the same time he was designing housing for industrial workers. He was an advocate of teamwork. Although his faculty included artists and designers with a broad spectrum of viewpoints, there was also a common collegiality between them and a common direction. At the core of the Bauhaus lay the theme that art and industry must come together to change the human condition, not just physically, but spiritually, to bring about a sense of wholeness, equity and unity in modern society.

But the impact of the Bauhaus is unlikely to have been so widespread if it had not been for the influence of its demonstrations, exhibitions and publications. From its workshops came a series of product designs with clarities of form which affected industries worldwide. Fourteen Bauhaus books, designed and produced by Moholy-Nagy, included *Cubism* by Albert Gleizes, *New Design* by Piet Mondrian, *Principles of Neo-Plastic Art* by Theo van Doesburg, *The Non-Objective World* by Kasimir Malevich, *Point and Line to Plane* by Wassily Kandinsky, *The New Vision* by László Moholy-Nagy, and *Pedagogical Notebook* by Paul Klee.

The Bauhaus was shut down by the Nazis in the 1930s.

'The fate of the Bauhaus (was) involved in a tragic contradiction. Nowhere else would the director of a state organisation have been permitted the freedom, given to Walter Gropius from the outset, to carry through such an uncompromising project and to call in the best talents from wherever they might be. On the other hand probably nowhere else would this have given rise to such violent opposition.

'It was sheer madness to jeopardise one's reputation and position by the appointment of such artists as Klee, Kandinsky, Feininger, Schlemmer and Moholy-Nagy as government servants in a state institution: artists whose significance was appreciated by only a very small circle and whose work and outlook excited the strongest expressions of outrage, abuse and detestation throughout Germany and even beyond its borders.'[13]

The general public in the 1920s, and the bureaucrats, hated the work of modern artists. Because people failed to understand the language or the messages of contemporary art, they felt insulted by it and ridiculed it. Not that the artists did not contribute their share of ridicule in return – especially the Dadaists, who made a point of insulting whoever and whatever they deemed to be bourgeois. It was easy, under these circumstances, to separate art from technology and industry. Ironically the notion of technology and industrial production being used to create social unity and economic growth – which lay at the serious core of the thinking of the Bauhaus, de Stijl in Holland, and Le Corbusier in France – was taken over as one of the cornerstones of Fascism in Italy, Nazism in Germany, and Soviet Communism. Through the 1930s each of these movements became increasingly nationalistic, militarist and oppressive, culminating in the outbreak of World War Two.

In the mid and late 1930s, one crisis followed another. Germany invaded the Saar, Austria and Czechoslovakia. The Spanish Civil War became a focus of young left-leaning English writers, among them Auden, MacNeice, and Orwell. Unemployed shipbuilders and steelworkers from Britain's industrial north and coal miners from Wales joined in hunger marches on Whitehall. As war became increasingly inevitable, a number of artists and architects fled from Europe to Britain and the United States, including Gropius, Mies, Breuer, Moholy-Nagy, Mondrian and the Constructivist sculptor Naum Gabo.

In 1938, in Chicago, Moholy-Nagy with the help of Gyorgy Kepes set up the Institute of Design to further develop the methods of the Bauhaus, and Mies became head of the School of Architecture at the Illinois Institute of Technology. Gropius collaborated with Maxwell Fry on several buildings in England, including a school at Impington Village, before leaving to take over the School of Architecture at Harvard.

Individual buildings in Britain by Wells Coates and Tecton (Lubetkin) made news and provoked controversy, and still remain classics sixty years later. Inspired by the Bauhaus, these architects also designed interiors, furniture, fabrics, and industrial products. A group of artists and architects came together to publish *Circle*, an international survey of constructive art, edited by J.L. (now Sir Leslie) Martin, Ben Nicholson and Naum Gabo.

In 1953, at a luncheon in honour of Gropius, the architect

Mies van der Rohe stood up and made a rare statement. 'The Bauhaus,' he said, 'was not an institution with a clear programme – it was an idea. The fact that it was an idea is the cause of the enormous influence the Bauhaus had on every progressive school around the globe. You cannot do that with organisation, you cannot do that with propaganda. Only an idea goes so far.'[4]

But the impact of 'the idea' on art education in Britain was minimal. Some teachers at the Euston Road School in London, notably Geoffrey Tibble, Rodrigo Moynihan and Graham Bell, flirted briefly with an abstract expressionism, but in effect it was as if all of the unrest and exploration of Cubism, Futurism, de Stijl, Dada, Surrealism, and Constructivism – to say nothing of the challenges of the political and social events in Europe and Britain – were of little account or relevance in art education.

Of course there was a committed avant-garde in Britain, artists such as Ben Nicholson, Henry Moore, Barbara Hepworth and others, and there were the critical writings of the philosopher-poet Herbert Read who championed them, but, like the poets and writers of the 1930s, they were young and easily marginalised from the mainstream of the British art establishment. Nevertheless, if we look back at what they were doing in the 1930s, we can see clearly why these artists preferred their relation to colleagues in Europe, to Picasso, Braque, Gris, Brancusi, Arp, Mondrian, and to international groups such as Abstraction-Création, and participated in exhibitions such as 'Thèse-Antithèse-Synthèse'. And we can also see that – in spite of the impact of the war on them – what these artists did after the war had its roots in their pre-war art.

The war came like a wall, cutting the British avant-garde off from Europe. They were not only deprived of seeing what their colleagues were doing, but even more important was their isolation from their thought. The war was of course physically devastating. Cities throughout Britain and Europe were laid waste by bombs. Millions died in air raids, on the battlefields, and in concentration camps. But the war was devastating spiritually also. The very technologies on which the social and economic future were to be built were now the agents of destruction.

In their isolation, several avant-garde British artists turned to nature, to the more permanent cycles of the seasons, not to escape, but to search for deeper, universal meanings, and to see the tragedy of war as transient, a terrible conflict that would pass. Their researches in the 1930s into pure pictorial and sculptural forms, shorn of external or figural references, were now combined with a concern for a human presence within rhythms and imagery drawn from the land. Henry Moore's sculptural vocabulary focused more and more on the human form perceived as bone and rock – the eternal cycle of life and death, subject to nature's slow erosions. In contrast, his air-raid shelter drawings perceived human life as frail and anonymous as cobwebs. In her own search for universal sculptural rhythms, Barbara Hepworth turned to the most elemental of natural forms, seashells and pebbles, and cast her human references in those simple and timeless contexts.

In a series of lectures given in 1947 and 1948, immediately after the war, Herbert Read diagnosed man's dislocation from nature as one of the key factors in human aggression. Speaking about the archetypal farmer, the man of the soil, he observed: 'Copulation, birth and death are no mysteries to him; they are not bedroom events – they are the daily substance of his life, the events which give rhythm to his existence. Man is, in a very real sense, part of the cosmic process.' And then he went on: 'I do not think that peasants are the only natural pacifists – artists and craftsmen, all who are engaged in the actual shaping or manipulation of materials, in what we call creative activities, lack any evident desire to give expression to destructive impulses.'[5]

Herbert Read, not surprisingly, came from a family of farmers in Yorkshire, just north of Leeds. After the war he moved back to Yorkshire – to Stonegrave, a working farm in the countryside of his childhood. Stonegrave, in turn, was not far from Castleford, where Henry Moore grew up in a coal-mining family, and close also to Wakefield, where Barbara Hepworth had her roots. And this countryside, with its rolling windswept hills, deep valleys with running streams, and compact tidy villages tucked into the contours, was a favourite area for Ben Nicholson, who went on drawing expeditions with his friend Cyril Reddihough. For all four, Moore, Hepworth, Read and Nicholson, the elemental and peaceful character of this land, moulded by millennia of wind and rain, summer sun and winter snows, and meadows under graze, similar in so many respects to Cornwall, provided a bridge between the 1930s and the post-war years of the 1950s, and set the war years, for all the horror, into perspective.

There began to emerge a contemporary sense of the

Englishness of English art, a connection to Turner, and Wordsworth, captured eloquently for a wide public in T.S. Eliot's 'Four Quartets':

> 'The end of all our exploring
> Will be to arrive where we started
> And know the place for the first time.'[6]

For the young artists of the 1950s the post-war years was also a period of personal discovery. Britain entered a period of social and economic, as well as physical, rebuilding. Being shut off from Europe affected not only the British avant-garde; artists and architects in France, Holland, Italy and Germany had suffered a similar isolation. Paris had to be rediscovered once more; cultural exchanges had to be rebuilt. The great pre-war artists, Picasso, Braque, Giacometti, Arp, Calder, and others emerged larger, it seemed, and more heroic than before, with new and vital works not yet seen. The same was true of the Constructivist artists like Antoine Pevsner. Then there were new voices, the Expressionist artists of the Cobra group, and a vigorous wave of new sculptors and painters from New York, David Smith, Robert Motherwell, Mark Rothko, Jackson Pollock.

By 1950 London had begun to hop with vitality. New galleries and dealerships opened, mixing international artists with British; and new British artists such as William Scott, Eduardo Paolozzi, William Turnbull, Robert Adams, and Alan Davie began to exhibit. Some of the younger artists picked up the challenges of the pre-war Constructivist artists and moved forward. A group of non-figurative painters and Constructivist sculptors formed around the painter Adrian Heath, including Kenneth and Mary Martin, Victor Pasmore, Anthony Hill and Terry Frost.

The impact was particularly clear in the case of Victor Pasmore, who was teaching at both Camberwell and Euston Road. At these two schools, like art schools all over Britain, students were required to pass standard courses in anatomy, perspective and geometric composition in drawing and painting. These were academic standards set in the nineteenth century; artists had to be trained in the disciplines of composition before they could develop their own statements. Although many of the students were ex-servicemen returning from the battlefields or, like Adrian Heath and Terry Frost, from prisoner-of-war camps, there was scant recognition of their need for self-expression, nor that the war itself, to say nothing of the extraordinary vitality of contemporary art in the last fifty years, would have any impact on the way art should be taught.

Not that the teachers were not serious artists. Part of the problem was that academic training so regulated the convention of art that it was difficult for artists to break the mould. The same convention also led to a public acceptance of what was permissible in art and what was not. For instance, Pasmore's colleague, William Coldstream took the academic exercises of the Euston Road School as his basis for a careful geometric and colour regulation of figurative compositions. But when, in 1947, Pasmore used similar disciplines as the basis for a sequence of Pointillist, Cubist and abstract compositions, he was regarded as a rebel. This development in Pasmore's work alarmed London's art world. But he pushed ahead, signalling his break from the figurative conventions of the Euston Road artists by holding an exhibition at the Redfern Gallery at the end of 1948 of his latest geometric abstract paintings and collages. What irked his critics was his abandonment of nostalgic views of the River Thames, with echoes of Turner and Whistler, in favour of totally abstract compositions that had no figurative references at all. And they failed to recognise that the basic organising principles of these paintings and collages were mathematical and compositional rules similar to Coldstream's. They also failed to recognise that the colours he worked with in the abstract paintings, the ivy greens, maroons, and mustard yellows were the colours he used in his landscape paintings and were also the colours of the Euston Road School.

However, it will not come as any surprise that Pasmore received understanding and support from Ben Nicholson, Barbara Hepworth and the younger St Ives artists. There he found that an easy relationship had been established between abstract painting and landscape. In the early 1950s he pushed on again, as Nicholson had done in the 1930s, by projecting the energy of abstract paintings into three-dimensional reliefs. He assembled constructions, using painted wood, metals and plastics.

The relation of these developments to the pre-war Bauhaus began to surface when Pasmore and Kenneth Martin became part-time teachers at London's Central School. Another development which related to the pre-war Bauhaus was a course devised in the early 1950s by Olive Sullivan at the Manchester School of Art. The atmosphere at the Central was experimental. William Johnstone, the principal, included Alan Davie, Eduardo Paolozzi, and other young post-war artists as part-time teachers. There Pasmore collaborated in establishing a foundation course based on abstract principles of geometry, space, and materials, influenced by Wassily Kandinsky's Bauhaus book, *Point and Line to Plane*, which had recently become available in an English translation.

And it is not surprising to find at this point that Pasmore became interested in the relation of art to industry, architecture and product design, thus picking up where the Bauhaus and *Circle* had left off in the 1930s. In 1953 we find him giving a lecture in Glasgow on 'Painting, Sculpture and Machine Technology', and in 1954 he accepted an appointment as Head of the Department of Painting, School of Fine Art, at King's College in Newcastle, which at that time was part of the University of Durham.

All of this is a precursor to the revolution in Leeds in the mid-1950s against traditional art education. But before we go to that, let us turn to another essential piece of the background. This concerns E. C. Gregory, known to his friends as Peter, head of the printing and publishing firm, Lund Humphries. Peter was a gentle man, deeply interested in the arts, and a friend of the artists. He had a beautiful private collection, put together, not as speculation, but through personal sensibility. I remember feeling that every object he collected generated a special energy and freshness – and gentleness. The mantel in his dining-room was presided over by a bright green frog – in the form of a lithograph by Picasso. At first you might have found the frog to be somewhat menacing until you realised that its face was benign and smiling.

Peter was sensitive to the interaction of art and industry, not through product design like the Bauhaus, but through culture, through the living presence of artists in a materialistic industrial world. He was aware that many of the best young artists needed to be relieved of financial pressure so that they could work. He looked at Britain's northern industrial cities and saw a cultural void. But he knew that there were always people – industrialists, doctors, university people – whose lives would respond to the presence of artists. One can only guess at how pleased he must have been with Pasmore's appointment to Newcastle.

Encouraged by his great friend Herbert Read 'to drop a little aesthetic leaven into the technological and materialistic ...'[7] world of one of these cities, and bearing in mind the Yorkshire roots of two of his favourite sculptors, Henry Moore and Barbara Hepworth, both of whom had trained at the College of Art in Leeds, he established the Gregory Fellowships in poetry, music, painting, and sculpture, and attached them to Leeds University.

With Pasmore's appointment at Newcastle, the Gregory Fellows in Leeds, and the presence of Herbert Read at Stonegrave, things began to move in the north. Enter now our final player, John Wood. John was one of those essential figures in this sort of situation, an administrator with a vision, the kind of man who could take two and two and make seven out of it. Perhaps that is not so surprising, since he was a linguist, a translator of Molière and Goethe, and as much a lover of music and drama as he was of visual art.

Our story involving John begins when he was in charge of further education in the northern part of Yorkshire. As you will see in Ricky's second letter, Harry Thubron was teaching in Sunderland. John saw what he was doing and put him as a teacher into a primary school in New Earswick. It was an experimental programme. John supplied unlimited paper, paint, wood, and other materials; and Thubron unlocked similar creative drives among the children of miners and farmers as Marion Richardson had demonstrated twenty years earlier. Then John put Harry into a Teachers' Training College in Scarborough, in collaboration with Pasmore, and with Ricky as one of his assistants. Same result. John, knowing Herbert Read's interest in art education,[8] took Thubron to Stonegrave. He also talked with Maurice de Sausmarez, an old friend of Harry's from the days when they were art students together; de Sausmarez was Professor of Art at Leeds University, and a member of the Board of Governors of Leeds College of Art. The result was that Thubron was invited to be Head of the School of Painting in Leeds College of Art, in 1956.

Ricky had graduated from the Royal Academy Schools in London in 1955. His career as an artist had already been launched. His first two exhibitions at the Redfern Gallery in London were successful. The Redfern was the gallery where Pasmore had exhibited his first non-figurative work. Ricky's training was traditional. He was fresh from the academic ropes. One of the conditions of Thubron's appointment was that his painting, sculpture and design students would take the National Diploma examinations. Thubron therefore turned to Ricky to ensure that the students would take life classes and pass their diplomas. This in turn opened the door for Thubron's creative Basic Course.

In Ricky's letters you will read that Thubron's invitation was not entirely by chance. Neither Thubron nor Ricky belonged to the London establishment. They were both from the industrial north, with all of its long and often raucous history of labour unionism and left-wing disaffection with Whitehall central government bureaucracy. Thubron's father and Ricky's father knew one another. Thubron taught Ricky's future wife, Muriel, at West Hartlepool. Ricky was one of Thubron's assistants at Scarborough. In Ricky's letters, and also in Norbert Lynton's, you will discern that although Thubron respected Pasmore, Thubron felt that he wanted his students to explore even more freely and creatively than Pasmore's basic course permitted.

Like Gropius at the Bauhaus, Thubron assembled a team of artists around him as teachers. Some of these he inherited. At first they were hostile, no doubt feeling uneasy and exposed by his apparent lack of structure or curriculum. But Thubron had a way of winning people around and bringing the best out of them. To these he added Ricky and Tom Hudson. But his most important assets were the Gregory Fellows, particularly the painters Alan Davie and Terry Frost, the sculptor Hubert Dalwood, and later Trevor Bell. And he was able to incorporate a distinguished local artist, Jacob Kramer. The presence of the Gregory Fellows gave him a special standing in the city. As artists they were nationally known. They exhibited and made news. They were colourful, maverick and outspoken. It was not long before the College of Art and the Gregory Fellows were the focus of vital exchanges between industrialists, politicians, and university intellectuals.

One of Thubron's strengths was that he did not expect his team to do the same thing he did. What he looked for was an acceptance of the general direction, and a sense of collegiality between his team members. He respected strongly held viewpoints, and encouraged argument. A case in point was his appointment of Tom Hudson to take over the machine shop which he had managed to set up through grants engineered by John Wood.

Hudson's love was the Bauhaus and the work in art education being done by Max Bill at Ulm. In the machine shop he was responsible for constructions, particularly using industrial materials, metals, glass and plastics, and he perceived these as carrying his students to the threshold, not only of product design, but of an understanding of the space-time considerations of architects. Pasmore's appointment as Consulting Director of Urban and Architectural Design for the new town of Peterlee acted as a strong confirmation of Hudson's point of view. Here was an artist working in equal collaboration with planners and architects, bringing aesthetic considerations of mass, scale, colour and proportion to an equal level with considerations of density, structure and budget. And Leeds College of Art was the beneficiary – for Pasmore was a frequent visitor.

It was perhaps inevitable that Thubron and Hudson would grow apart. Hudson's energy was intellectual, constructive and ambitious; Thubron's was sensory, emotional, subjective, lower in pace and more contemplative. Hudson wanted to build on Thubron's open-ended experiments to explore the meanings and ramifications of what was happening in the studios by involving other disciplines. He wanted to expose his students to discussions with visiting experts in psychology, anthropology, sociology, and art history. His intellectual questing and impatience chafed Thubron, who wanted to move forward more slowly, more subjectively. Thubron loved the accidental, particularly when it occurred in a structured situation – what Arp referred to as 'the laws of chance'. The result could bring, for Thubron, unexpected and exciting qualities. For Hudson such qualities provided an opportunity to analyse why they happened and what their significances might be. For Thubron, intellectual analysis killed the magic.

One can see Thubron's attitude clearly in his paintings of that period. Although their basis was often geometric – squares and circles – he would pile up his paint in layers until the canvas was rich and almost collapsing in its accretion of textures and physical presence. Harry liked artists. He respected people who lived their art and exposed their inner selves to the risks of language. While Tom was constructing intellectual experiments in the workshop, Peter Stead, as we shall see in his letter, ran an avant-garde private art gallery, the Symon Quinn, in Huddersfield, and was collaborating with the Constructivist sculptor, Stephen Gilbert, in synthesising art and design in the construction of a 'neo-plastic' building.[9]

In 1959 Richard Hamilton and Victor Pasmore arranged an exhibition called 'The Developing Process' at the Institute of Contemporary Arts in London, to demonstrate the basic courses in art education that were going on in Newcastle and Leeds. At first Thubron was enthusiastic, in part because of his friendship with Pasmore. But as the exhibition took shape, demanding the kinds of definition of purpose and meaning that Hamilton and Hudson wanted to demonstrate, Thubron's enthusiasm dimmed. He felt that definition would inevitably lead to system and curriculum, and the essence of open-ended exploration would be lost. In a sense he was right. Critics of the exhibition evaluated what the students were doing, not as explorations, but as finite art-objects.[10]

Ricky's painting underwent an enormous change in this period also. He came in as a representational painter of seascapes and docklands. Within three years he emerged as an expressionist abstract painter with a powerful connection to the landscapes of the dales and the north-east sea coast.

There can be no doubt that being with Alan Davie and Terry Frost on an almost daily basis had a lot to do with it. Terry's descriptions of walking through the snow-clad hills, or of fields plunging between granite walls into the valleys of the dales in the summertime, are clues to this transformation. And the iconography in Alan Davie's canvases – which at once link the realms of the imagination and the unconscious to the mysterious cyphers that are all around us and which we take for granted, such as the almost illegible names on rain-washed gravestones or the baffling marks of ancient cultures, the serpents of the Aztecs or the bird-emblems of the ancient Celts – these are cultural and iconographic echoes which have also continued to fascinate and haunt Ricky in his paintings to this day.

As we have pointed out, the Leeds experiment was, virtually by necessity, short-lived. There were a number of reasons for this, which are outlined in Ricky's letter on the subject (see p.83). One was the break-up of the team. In 1959 Maurice de Sausmarez moved to London. In 1960 Tom Hudson became head of Foundation Studies at Leicester College of Art. Frost, Davie and Dalwood all left, their tenures of the Gregory Fellowships having run out. And events in Thubron's private life led to his resignation in 1963. Perhaps the major underlying reason was the impossibility of keeping so much unstructured free-flowing creative energy at full throttle for longer than five or six years without it succumbing to repetition and formula.

Following Thubron's departure, Ricky became the interim head, and then the head of the Fine Art Faculty. There was no way he could repeat Thubron's success. He had to create his own way, by putting together a totally different team, and then, like Thubron, relying on the creativity and collegiality of each member to do their own thing. He was astonishingly successful, including an innovative and successful expansion into film.

But at a national level the challenge of the revolt that Leeds represented was causing a backlash. The Government set up two committees (the Coldstream and the Summerson) to report on the state of art education throughout Britain. The Minister of Education, Anthony Crosland, did not like what he heard. Both recommended greater autonomy for the art schools and less national bureaucracy. For a while the art schools were permitted to develop their own programmes. But then the recommendations of both committees were rejected. The drive to absorb the art schools into the Polytechnics, and to force foundation courses in painting and sculpture – adopted by several of Britain's schools in the wake of Leeds and Newcastle – to become thresholds to technology, entered into high gear.

Ricky was powerless as he watched the College of Art be absorbed, first into Leeds Polytechnic, and then into the University, thus losing for ever its independence. With a heavy heart he saw that the days of educational innovation in Britain were over, at least for the time being. There was small consolation in the realisation that the Bauhaus – after its short life of extraordinary creative and influential energy – had also been shut down.

In a despairing effort to reverse this trend, Patrick Heron created a national storm with his article 'Murder of the Art Schools' in *The Guardian* in October 1971, but to no avail. Recalling the battle this article engendered, Heron wrote in 1996:

> '... the amazing brilliance of Leeds, which I called "the most influential College of Art in Europe since the Bauhaus" in my "Murder of the Art Schools" article, and the quite dazzling multiplication of idioms and what one might call their endless interpenetration, had generated at Leeds an unprecedented inventive powerhouse on the national scene. It was an inventiveness so radical that one could not find two students there even doing roughly the same thing. An exhilarating creative energy was developed there, the influence of which cut through and across all accepted boundaries between art forms, idioms,

mediums. To such a profound extent was this the case that one could point, with undeniable logic, to the interdependence of painting, sculpture, ceramics, film, printmaking, spatial construction (even on an architectural scale), fashion, performance, and so on....'[11]

EMIGRATION TO CANADA

Ricky's decision to move with his family to Canada was made on the spur of the moment. By an odd coincidence Thubron was staying with him and his wife Muriel when the invitation came in 1968. 'If you don't take it, I will,' Thubron said.

As before, things don't generally happen just like that, out of the blue. The letter of invitation to Ricky to become head of a new school of fine art at Fanshawe Community College in London, Ontario, came from Peter Williams. Peter Williams had at one time been an assistant to John Wood, and was now the chairman of the Faculty of Applied Arts at Fanshawe. He knew Ricky and his work at Leeds well.

Meanwhile news of Leeds' reputation had reached several other countries. An exchange programme and exhibitions in Dortmund, Germany, were ongoing. Visits by teachers from overseas were commonplace occurrences. In 1967, an exhibition of work by the faculty and students of Leeds was put on by the English Speaking Union at the Corcoran Gallery in Washington, DC. This exhibition was seen by Mackie Cryderman, one of Fanshawe's board members. Mrs Cryderman, in turn, was involved in the art education of children and was deeply influenced in a well-known art education programme at Beal[12] by Marion Richardson and Herbert Read. She immediately recognised the underlying principles of Leeds, and became an outspoken advocate of Ricky's appointment to Fanshawe.

Ricky's arrival at Fanshawe came two years after Expo 67, but he was still able to ride on the upsurge of interest in the interrelation of the arts generated by that exhibition. The atmosphere was right for moving what he had been doing at Leeds to further stages of development. At Leeds he had appointed a strong faculty of professionals and visitors, including the Canadian artist, Robin Page. He had also produced at Leeds a wild and imaginative film, 'Musical', directed by the painter-photographer, Russell Platt.

Building on this experience, one of his first steps at Fanshawe was to set up a machine shop equipped with the latest technology. This allowed him, at one stroke, to defuse any anticipation that he might set up a traditional art school training in painting and sculpture, and instead it enabled him from the beginning to set about dissolving every traditional barrier between the disciplines by focusing on film, radio and television. In this way students entering the foundation course went through a seamless series of explorations, and were connected directly to the public in their own city.

The programme at Fanshawe and Ricky's reputation as an educator grew rapidly. He was appointed Dean of Fine Art at Fanshawe in 1972. He began to move the College steadily forward – as the Bauhaus had moved two generations before – into the then exploratory areas of media technology, production, television, advertising, and computerised design, all of which rely on interdisciplinary teamwork. His appointment of Tom Lodge, a nationally known producer, and Stephen Joy, a nationally known gallery director, to his faculty added a range seldom experienced in art schools before. His optimism at the prospect of art education in Canada being able to move these pioneering efforts forward received a further boost when Tom Hudson was appointed Dean of Instruction at the College of Art in Vancouver, British Columbia, in 1979.

All of this is reflected with great energy in the letters in this book. The sad thing is that in the 1990s Fanshawe's experimental programmes were faced with bureaucratic tightening and political control similar to those that Ricky faced at Leeds. These restrictions, and the loss of educational richness and freedom they have caused, are also reflected in the letters, leading one to assume that the time for revolt will come once again in the not too distant future.

On the plus side, Canada began to have a deep effect on Ricky's own painting. To understand the impact of Ontario we have to understand what he came with as a painter. Hartlepool, his birthplace, is a seaport on the north-east coast of England; and like many English towns its densely clustered buildings and intimate winding streets are tucked into the contours of hills around the harbour. It is the character of seaports that they are points of departure for the rest of the world; their mariners are adventurers setting sail to new horizons, enduring the perils of storms. The irony of Hartlepool is that throughout its history it has been the subject of attacks from the sea – the Danes, the Dutch, the Germans in World War One. So while there is a sense of adventure in the town, openness to the sea's space, there is also a defensiveness, a sense of inwardness and human vulnerability.

In one of his letters Ricky writes about growing up in World War Two, of attacks from the air, and the war at sea. He also writes about the ancient gravestones of Danish invaders, with their inscriptions so worn by time that they are indecipherable, markers of human transcience. Water, storms, the shaping of the land by water, the fascination of seafarers with wide horizons and endurance of storms contrasted with human frailty, these have been themes in Ricky's paintings from the beginning.

At first his language was representational. Ships in harbour were metaphors for dreams, for connection to the mysteries of faraway places; yet in Ricky's paintings the water is frequently flurried, a premonition of waves, and wind blows through the frailty of rigging. And then his paintings, at Leeds, became non-figurative. He learned from the Basic Course, side by side with his students. The canvas was an arena, a context, for playing out the *action* of his theme. His paintings were still concerned with the erosive action of water, with the action of land being shaped, with the movement of wind. But around him, now, the landscape itself was different. This was the country of the Yorkshire dales, where the uplands are moors and the almost vertical hillsides slide down into valleys where streams rush over dark rocks. So the space in his paintings is not horizontal any longer, but vertical; and he mixes sand with his paint to create a matt textural depth.

North America is a continent of invaders. Invaders – immigrants – bring with them scant baggage but long heritages, and with their heritages they create a new culture in a new land. Canada is no different. The Ontario Ricky encountered had a deep impact on him. Here was a scale so much vaster than anything he had previously encountered; a flat landscape so expansive that it flows from horizon to horizon, with Lake Huron as vast as an inland sea; and across this landscape-seascape roll huge storms with dark thunderclouds pounded by winds that seem to rotate with the rotation of the earth. And so, once again, his paintings change. But the themes are still the same; the frailty and transcience of human existence, and the markers of human passage being corroded into enigmas by weather and time.

1. *Space, Time & Architecture*, Siegfried Giedion, Oxford University Press, 1941, p.421.
2. *Walter Gropius*, Siegfried Giedion, Architectural Press, London 1954, p.27.
3. Op.cit. p.37.
4. Remarks by Mies van der Rohe in Chicago at a luncheon in honour of Walter Gropius on his seventieth birthday, 18 May 1953.
5. *Education for Peace*, Herbert Read, Routledge & Kegan Paul, London 1950, p.31.
6. *Little Gidding*, T. S. Eliot, Faber & Faber, London 1942, p.15.
7. Introduction by Herbert Read to the Gregory Memorial Exhibition, Leeds City Art Gallery, March 1960.
8. Several of Herbert Read's books deal with art education, notably *Education through Art*; *Education for Peace*; and *Icon and Idea*. Read wrote: 'We recognise an artist of some kind in every child, and we maintain that the encouragement of normal creativity is one of the essentials of a full and balanced development of the personality.' 'The Education of Free Men', in *Education for Peace*, Routledge and Kegan Paul, London 1950, p.91.
9. See Peter Stead's letter, p.103.
10. In 1981 an exhibition at the Institute for Contemporary Art in London, drawn from the British Art and Design Education Archive at the University of Liverpool, was organised by David Thistlewood. This was accompanied by *A Continuing Process*, by David Thistlewood, ICA, London 1981, which includes a compelling description of Tom Hudson's approach to art education, pp.38–41. It should be noted that Thubron declined to participate.
11. Preface to *Patrick Heron on Art and Education*, University College, Bretton Hall, Yorkshire, England 1996, p.9.
12. See Arlene Kennedy's letter, p.149.

Letter 1 Eric Atkinson to David Lewis

March 1998

Dear David

Here is the letter I promised you about my early life and some thoughts about a variety of experiences that influenced me as a young painter.

I was born in West Hartlepool in July 1928, the only child of parents who had married in 1919 at the end of World War One. West Hartlepool was a Victorian development built as an annexe to the ancient seaport of Hartlepool to accommodate workers in the rapidly expanding shipbuilding industry. Old Hartlepool, magnificently situated on a headland projecting into the North Sea, had for centuries been a target for Viking raiders attracted by the rich plunder to be found within the grey walls of the old Abbey Church of St Hilda. Evidence of historical significance can be found throughout the old port. Roman and Celtic marks may still be seen on the old stones in the remains of the sea-wall and I own two Roman coins that I picked up on the beach during the 1930s. When I was growing up, the fortified town-wall of huge sea-etched stones surrounded the ancient harbour, crowned by a dense mass of houses and pubs sweeping round to a delicate tracery of brightly painted cranes piercing the skyline along the dockside. The old fishermen's crofts, handsome Georgian houses and Victorian homes edging the narrow streets, interspersed by elegant red brick buildings built in the Flemish style, are nearly all gone now, as indeed are the once thriving shipbuilding industry and the annual arrival of the herring fishing fleet, but they have been replaced by more modern buildings and other industries that have contributed to the renaissance of the Hartlepools.

My family connection with Hartlepool is through my maternal great-grandfather, Captain William Brough, a Master Mariner and deputy Harbour Master of Hartlepool. William Brough was born in Sunderland in 1804, and was descended from a long line of mariners and keelmen. His first ship, the *Isabel*, was built in Hartlepool and made its maiden voyage from there to Denmark. Captain Brough lived by the town-wall next to the old Whitby Hotel. The house has gone but the old town-wall still stands firm in defiance of the ravages of sea and storm. My paternal grandfather was a mining engineer known as 'Blaster' Atkinson because of his practice of sinking mining shafts using dynamite. He had won the Queen's Prize at Bisley for shooting when he was nineteen years of age and moved to Hartlepool from Scotland during the late 1890s. My father and his brothers were not very happy in Hartlepool because they

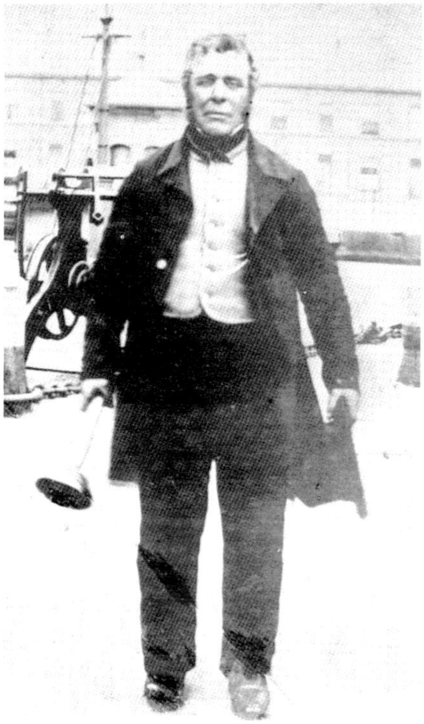

Captain William Brough,
deputy Harbour Master of Hartlepool,
*c.*1865

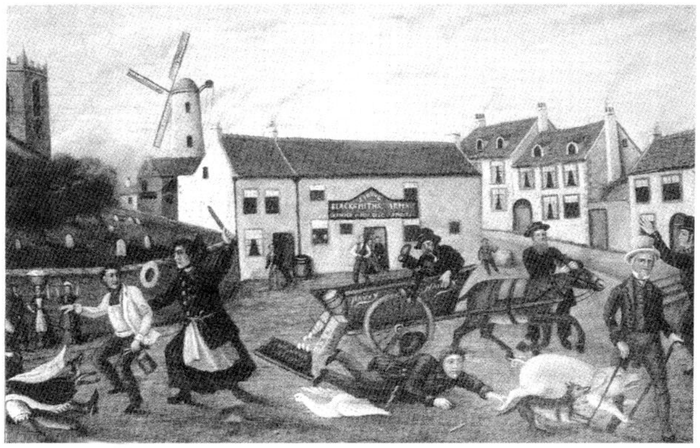

Navvy Nan
1857
*c.*30 x 50 in.
folk painting
collection: Hartlepool Art Gallery
(presented by the artist's mother)

were teased unmercifully at school – not surprisingly as they were sent there wearing kilts – and eventually my father ran away to sea. He rounded the Horn on a sailing ship, took part in rescue operations after the second San Francisco earthquake and was badly wounded at Gallipoli while serving in the Royal Navy during the disastrous campaign in the Dardanelles in 1915.

One of Captain Brough's sons, my maternal grandfather, was quite a character in old Church Street. A master tinsmith and lay-preacher, he owned and operated three shops in Hartlepool and Middleton. When Buffalo Bill Cody brought his Wild West Show to Hartlepool Town Moor my grandfather repaired several of his kettles and his children were given free tickets to the Show. My mother and her sisters had very happy memories of this unexpected treat as by all accounts Grandfather Brough was very tightfisted! When one of his shops was damaged during the bombardment of Hartlepool by German battleships in December 1914 he reputedly took his pet canary in its cage and the day's takings from the till and 'headed for the hills', leaving his wife and children to fend for themselves! He did, however, commission Mrs Vickery to make a copy of John Holmes' oil painting 'Navvy Nan' for his home in Middleton Road. This painting is one of the finest examples of naïve painting to be found in the north of England. As in an exuberant watercolour by Thomas Rowlandson, rowdy people rush to catch an escaping pig by its tail; full of gleeful pleasure and frolic it is similar to the paintings by the French painter Henri Le Douanier Rousseau whose fresh directness sprang from his uninhibited innocence. A love for the landscape and a respect for the sea and its changing moods seem to be in my blood, part of my genetic heritage, so I count myself fortunate to have spent my childhood in an area so visually satisfying to both.

My schooling came to an abrupt halt shortly after the outbreak of World War Two when our school was commandeered for use as an Army barracks, and although we had lessons twice a week at various teachers' homes survival became more important than education. Hartlepool had become the focus of enemy bombing sorties as large convoys of ships assembled in the natural basin outside the harbour before starting on their perilous voyages to Russia. We boys watched with fascination as the ships gathered in deep anchorage and frequently saw attacks by the Luftwaffe. How we cheered when an enemy plane was shot down! When the coastal bombing escalated, my parents decided to send me inland to stay with my Uncle John and his family in Coventry, little knowing that a few days after my arrival Goering and his Luftwaffe pilots planned to obliterate the city. After two days and nights in an air-raid shelter I emerged on 10 April 1941 to find the medieval centre of the city almost totally destroyed. I was returned to my parents in Hartlepool with all possible speed! I was thankful that I had been taken to visit the great Gothic Cathedral before it was demolished and years later I spoke to Sir Basil Spence about my experiences. He had come to Leeds to stay with his friend Maurice de Sausmarez and to give a lecture about his designs for building the new Coventry Cathedral.

Hartlepool had become an active centre in the war against Nazi Germany. The harbour was full of minesweepers, naval vessels and wonderfully camouflaged fishing boats bristling with machine guns. The night sky was often illuminated by a criss-cross web of tracer bullets, flecked with white puffs of smoke from anti-aircraft guns and occasionally by the more sinister flare of a dying aircraft as it began its fiery descent towards the inky black surface of the sea. Scenes captured so vividly by the wartime paintings of Paul Nash.

In 1943 I was a part-time student at the local College of Art. My parents, haunted by the spectre of joblessness during the depression of the 1930s, had articled me to a firm of local solicitors, but I pleaded to be allowed to try to become a painter so in September 1943 I enrolled as a full-time student at West Hartlepool College of Art. I also joined the local Civil Defence organisation as a messenger. The Civil Defence Headquarters was housed in an air-raid shelter in the grounds of Sir William Gray House and Art Gallery. We messenger boys slept in accommodation arranged for us in the Art Gallery until called upon to deliver messages to neighbouring air-raid posts during a raid. For these duties we were paid two shillings and sixpence a week to enable us to keep our bicycles in good working order. This princely sum soon melted away when I had to replace the front wheel of my bike after it had been shattered by shrapnel! Whenever I was on duty and there were no alerts I had plenty of time to study the paintings in the Gallery's Permanent Collection. The Principal of the College, George Webb, urged me to study the Pre-Raphaelite drawings and draughtsmanship of a local artist, Frederic Shields, but although I admired his technical dexterity I

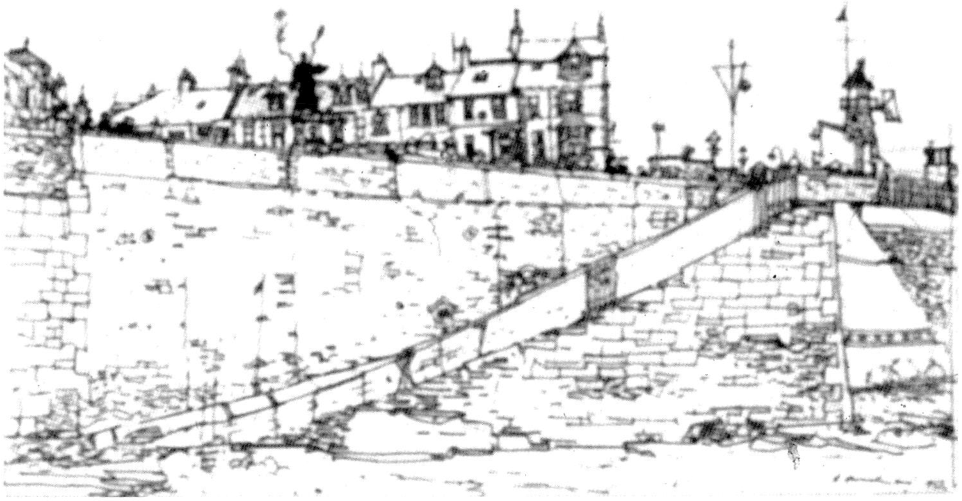

Eric Atkinson
Hartlepool seawall and memorial garden
1952
8 x 12 in.
pen and ink
collection: Brigit Atkinson

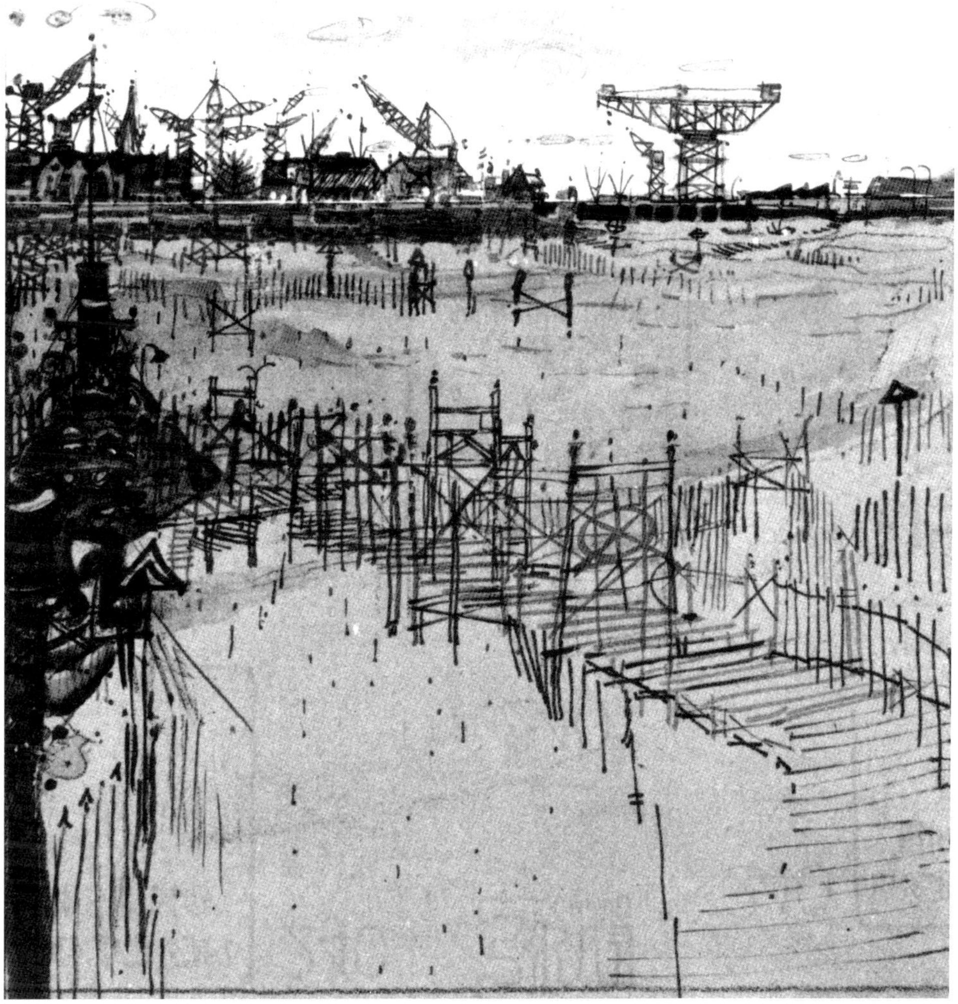

Eric Atkinson
Hartlepool, Durham
1954
6 x 6 in.
ink on sandpaper
collection: London Regional Art and Historical Museums, London, Ontario
(donated by Dr & Mrs R. Bull)

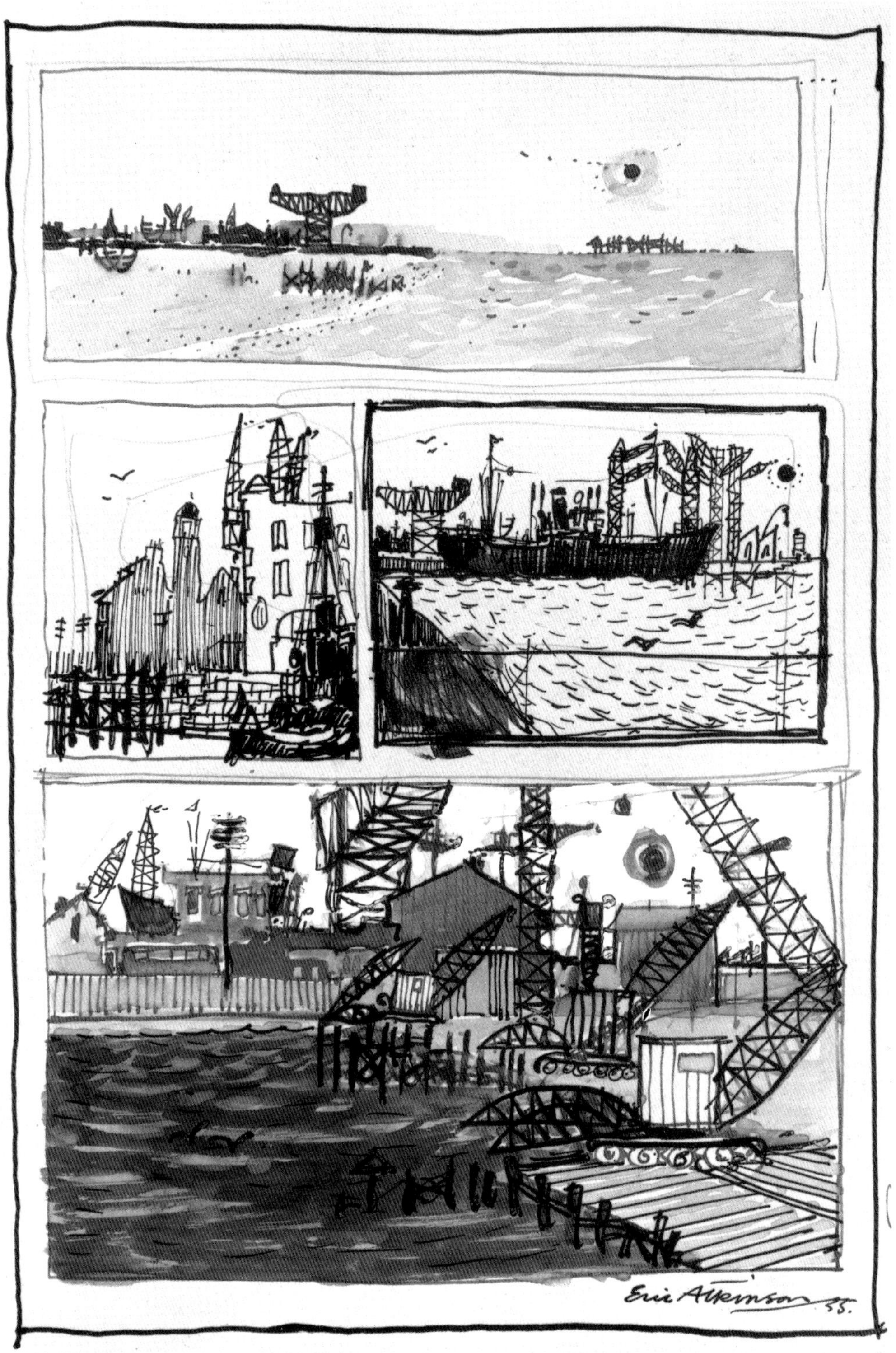

Eric Atkinson
Cranes, Hartlepool Docks
1955
30½ x 25½ in.
ink and gouache
collection: Jack Reading

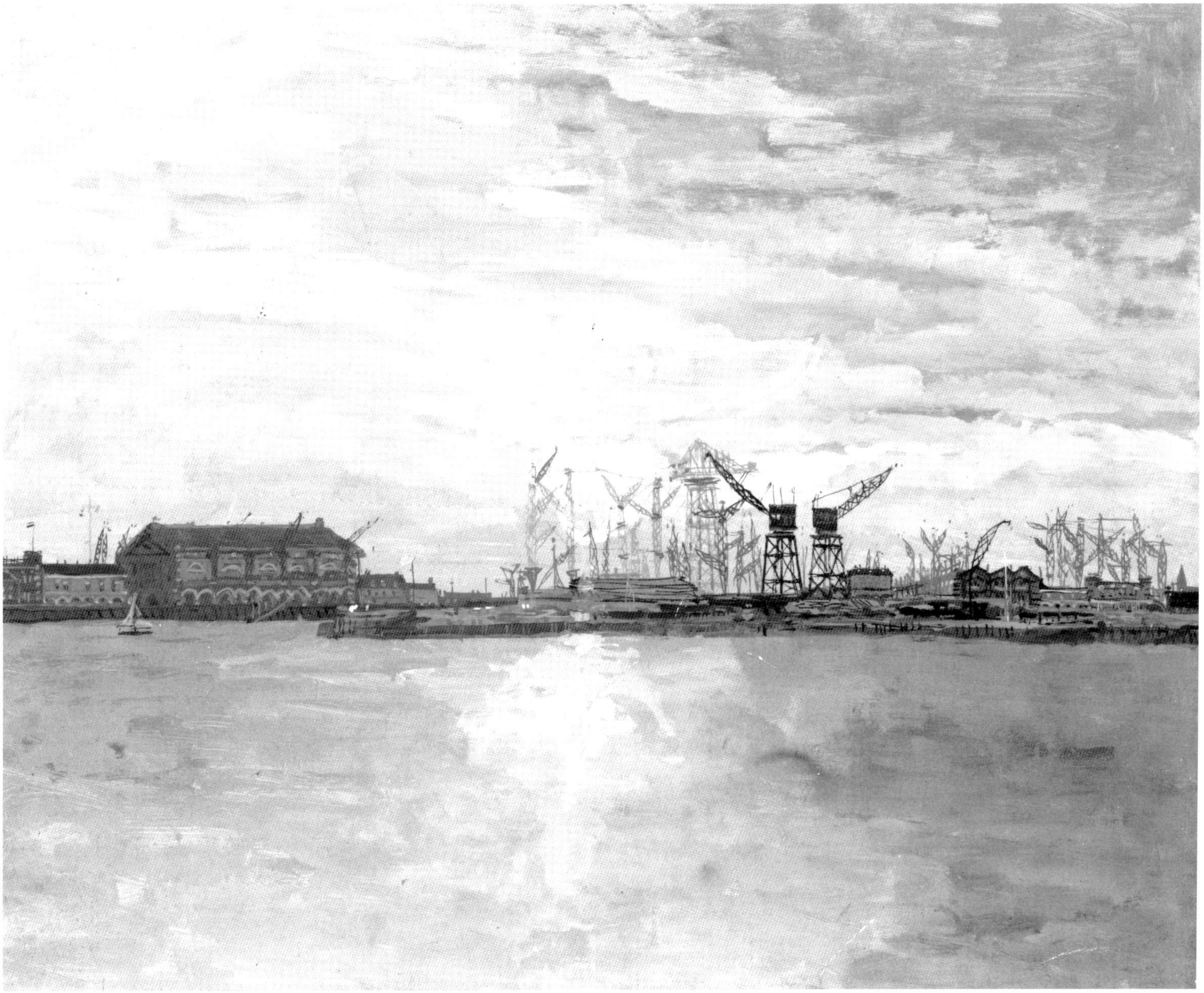

Eric Atkinson
Early evening, Hartlepool Docks
1953
28 x 36 in.
oil on board
collection: Leicestershire Educational Collection

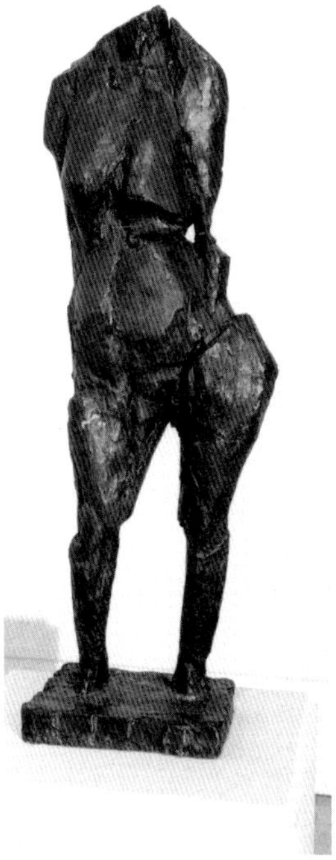

John Warren Davis
Standing Figure
1956
height: 38½ in.
bronze
collection: Leeds City Art Gallery

preferred the work of the Cornish painters, particularly that of Stanhope Forbes. Forbes had founded a School of Art in Newlyn that was the forerunner of the St Ives School. He also established links with a group of painters who worked at Staithes, a quaint fishing village on the North Yorkshire coast. I was a frequent visitor to Staithes as my mother had cousins living there. My relatives in Staithes owned several paintings of Saltburn, Staithes and Whitby by Rowland Hill that I liked very much and it was those paintings that initiated my love affair with the line.

About this time I met Henry Rushbury RA, an official war artist who had just been commissioned to make a series of drawings of Hartlepool Docks and Harbour. He requested the loan of an easel from the College of Art and I was asked by the Principal to deliver it to his hotel. I was delighted to meet an artist whose work I so greatly admired. He tipped me five shillings which endeared me to him even further and told me to draw … 'fill your sketch book laddie, there is so much here to record' and so I did.… I filled sketch book after sketch book with drawings and watercolours of the war-ravaged fishing port. Years later when I was a student at the Royal Academy Schools and Henry Rushbury was the Keeper of the Schools and one of my drawing tutors he recalled our earlier meeting and said gruffly 'glad to see that at least someone took my advice seriously!'

Frank Wood who taught drawing and painting at the College of Art was one of the very few tutors I encountered who truly understood Cézanne. He instilled in me a desire to understand what had happened to European Art during the years before the War. Those who did not share our experiences during the War cannot fully appreciate how isolated we were from information about art in Europe. There were compensations though … early in 1946 a fellow student and I cycled to Ambleside in the Lake District to visit friends who had been evacuated there from the Royal College of Art in South Kensington. They took us to meet a refugee from Nazi Germany, the artist Kurt Schwitters, and to see his master work the 'Merzbau'. This unique experience has grown in significance for me with the passage of time. We knew nothing of the Dada movement and very little about the pre-war Bauhaus so Schwitters' work was a revelation to us. To see found objects and scrap material incorporated into his collages with such skill was an eye-opener! Kurt Schwitters spoke good English and he insisted on showing

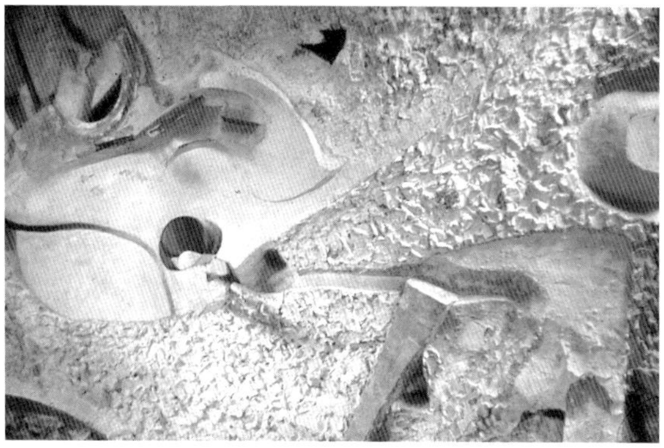

Kurt Schwitters
Merz Barn (detail)
1947

Nicolas de Staël
Study at La Ciotat
1952
12¾ x 18 in.
collection: Tate Gallery, London

us round his magnificent barn himself. He talked about the materials he used in his work and how they must be allowed to speak and reveal themselves to the spectator ... concepts quite new to us. He told me 'I am a painter, Mr Atkinson, but occasionally I like to nail objects to my canvas'. His words mystified me and I did not know what he meant until years later when I went to an exhibition at the Whitechapel Gallery of work by the American artist Robert Rauschenberg. Rauschenberg had been a student of Josef Albers at Yale and Albers had been a friend of Schwitters at the Bauhaus. I believe that my meeting with Schwitters was a turning point in my career when for the first time I realised that painting could take many forms and not confine itself to those encountered during my academic training.

Harry Thubron returned to teach at the College of Art in 1946 after spending four years serving in the Army. His enthusiasm inspired a generation of students at the College. My father, James Atkinson was friendly with Harry's father who owned a newsagents at the Dockhead and I had met Harry while he was home on leave in 1943. I was in Harry's drawing and composition classes, and he was my principal painting tutor until I was conscripted for military service in 1947. I met Muriel Ross, later to become my wife, in one of Harry's composition classes. She was one of the 'Middlesbrough girls', a group of students who travelled daily across the River Tees to attend West Hartlepool College of Art.

Muriel vividly remembers her first meeting with Harry Thubron in September 1946. 'Harry walked into a composition class wearing an ill-fitting demob suit ... it looked as though the suit was wearing him. It was the first time I had seen anyone wearing a nylon shirt with an attached collar. Harry talked about composition and drew diagrams on the blackboard to explain the basic rules of perspective. It was all completely over our heads. We were busy drawing compositions of labourers working on road repairs when Harry came up behind me, glared at my drawing and said "he looks like bloody old Molotov". In the evening drawing class Harry turned up wearing striped pyjama trousers tucked into sea boots, a navy blue "ganzey" (fisherman's sweater) and an RAF bomber jacket lined with rabbit fur which he wore inside out. He looked like a marauding viking. We hung on every word he said, not that we understood what he was talking about but we felt that we were finally at a real art school where teachers were expected and allowed to be eccentric.'

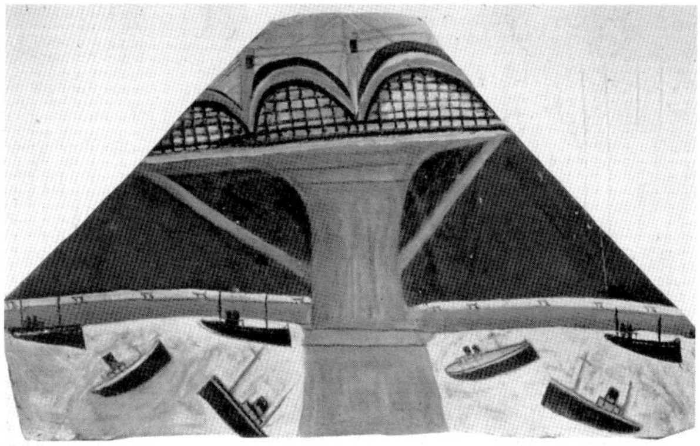

Alfred Wallis
Boats under Saltash Bridge
1940
c. 18 x 20 in.
oil on cardboard
collection: Mrs Warren Davis

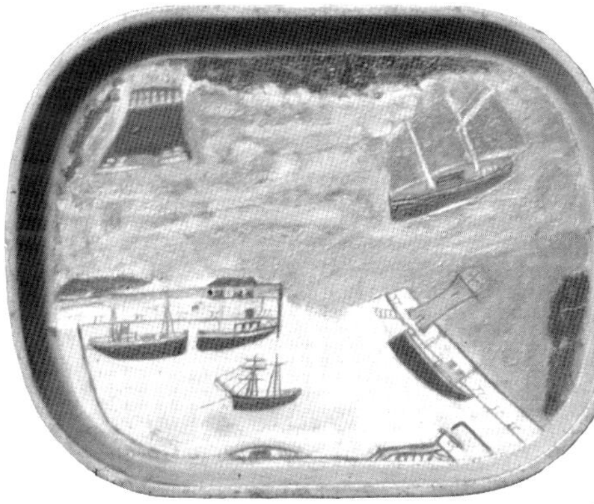

Alfred Wallis
Painted tin tray
1938
18 x 24 in.
collection: Mrs Warren Davis

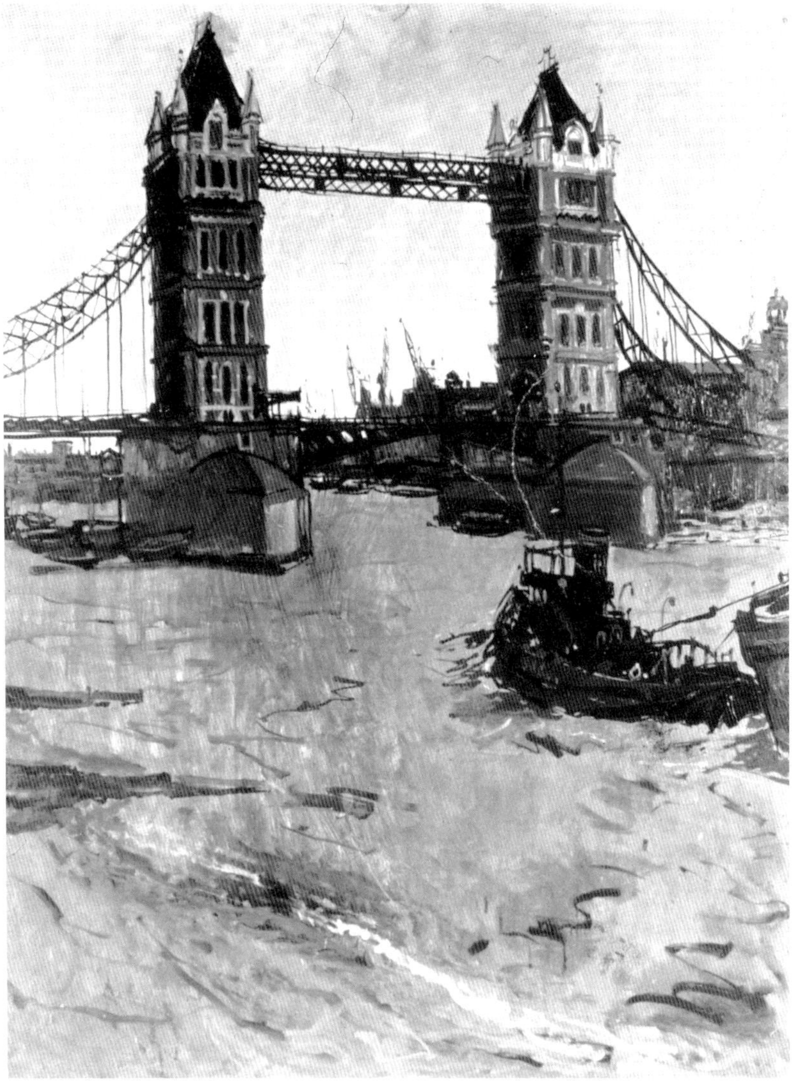

Eric Atkinson
Tower Bridge
1953
c. 36 x 28 in.
oil on board
collection: Government Art Collection

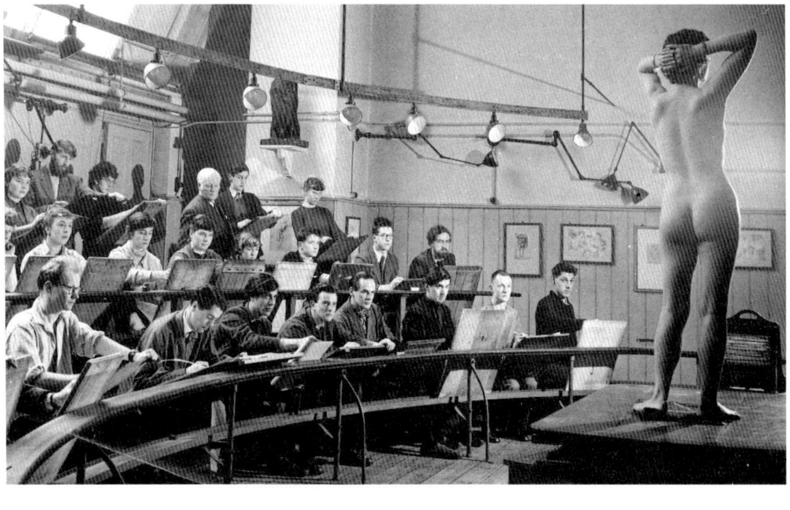

Life class, Royal Academy Schools, 1953
with Sir Henry Rushbury RA;
Eric Atkinson is in the front row, third from right

Whenever I came home on leave Harry exhorted me to continue drawing and painting. When I was released from the Army after nearly three years of compulsory service, Harry was instrumental in obtaining a scholarship for me to study at the Royal Academy Schools in Piccadilly. I was the first post-war student from West Hartlepool College of Art to be awarded a studentship to the Academy Schools and my acceptance opened the floodgates for future post-graduate applicants from the North.

In 1951 I was 'adopted' by the 'A Circle' (Art, Architecture, Antiques), a group of enthusiasts within the Headquarters of the Coal Board at Hobart House in London who met at regular intervals to attend lectures, concerts, plays, discussion groups and exhibitions. They decided to sponsor a student from a coal-mining area and endeavour to enrich his or her education while studying in London, in return for some lectures and demonstrations by the student and the opportunity to share the progress made by their protégé. It was a fine scheme in which everyone gained but sadly, like the Coal Board, it could not withstand the fiscal restrictions of the recession. When the 'A Circle' approached William Dring RA and asked him to recommend a student from a mining area who might benefit from their plan I was chosen as the first of their sponsored students. I shall be forever indebted to that small band of arts patrons who welcomed me with such enthusiasm. Two of them, Philip Gibbons and Jack Reading, became my first patrons and have remained lifelong friends. Members of the 'A Circle' came to all my early exhibitions and often showed their support by buying work ... they included me in their musical and theatrical outings ... most of which were beyond the financial reach of a student on a grant. For me ... and I hope for them ... their sponsorship was a resounding success.

Jack Reading, a founder member and secretary of the Society for Theatre Research, has recently donated his collection of my early work to the Hartlepool Art Gallery. Some of my theatre drawings (many made backstage at the Old Vic Theatre or at performances I attended with the 'A Circle') are in the collection of the Theatre Museum in Covent Garden. My love of theatre and my passion for the music of Henry Purcell owe their origins to the patronage of the 'A Circle'.

The exhibition of paintings by Nicolas de Staël at the Matthiesen Gallery in 1952 made a deep impression on me ... as it did on so many artists. I went to see it with Harry Thubron and saw Patrick Heron and William Scott there enjoying this remarkable artist's work. His canvases, saturated with Mediterranean light, were heavy with thick slabs of paint yet possessed all manner of subtle and sensitive gradations of colour within them. He used a palette-knife with the control of a master swordsman. It was the first time I had seen acrylic paint and gum used to build up a surface which was then cut and incised with skill and precision. The new materials de Staël used dried with greater speed than traditional oil and turpentine and enabled him to work quickly and directly ... rather as a typewriter assists a writer to communicate his thoughts more rapidly than a pen.

While I was a student I exhibited my work at every opportunity – at the Royal Academy Summer Exhibitions, the Leicester Galleries' 'Artists of Fame and Promise', mixed shows at the Irving Gallery, the RBA Gallery, the New English Art Club and the Contemporary Art Society. In 1953 I was asked to submit a painting for the 'Figures in their Setting' exhibition at the Tate Gallery and buoyed by favourable reviews and a newfound confidence I took a collection of work into the Redfern Gallery in Cork Street. The Directors, Harry Tatlock Millar and Rex Nankivell, liked my work and offered me a one-man show in February 1954 that would run concurrently with drawings in their lower gallery by the Welsh artist Ceri Richards as an 'Homage to Dylan Thomas'. I accepted with alacrity and dashed out of the Gallery before they could change their minds. I had met Terry Frost at the Leicester Galleries when I went there to see his show and he in his turn came to inspect mine. It was the start of a friendship that has spanned nearly fifty years. I was on a train travelling to Leeds in 1956 to begin teaching at the College of Art when I met Terry again and was delighted to learn that he was also bound for Leeds where he was completing the final year of his Gregory Fellowship in Painting.

In April 1954 Muriel and I were married in St Giles Cathedral in Edinburgh and left to spend our honeymoon in Italy. We were enchanted by the terraced hillsides of Umbria and the grand palazzos of Venice that seemed to have changed very little since they were painted by Canaletto. The Uffizi Gallery in Florence had just been re-opened after undergoing repairs and we spent several days feasting on its treasures ... making up for the long period of enforced starvation during the war. Our only other ex-

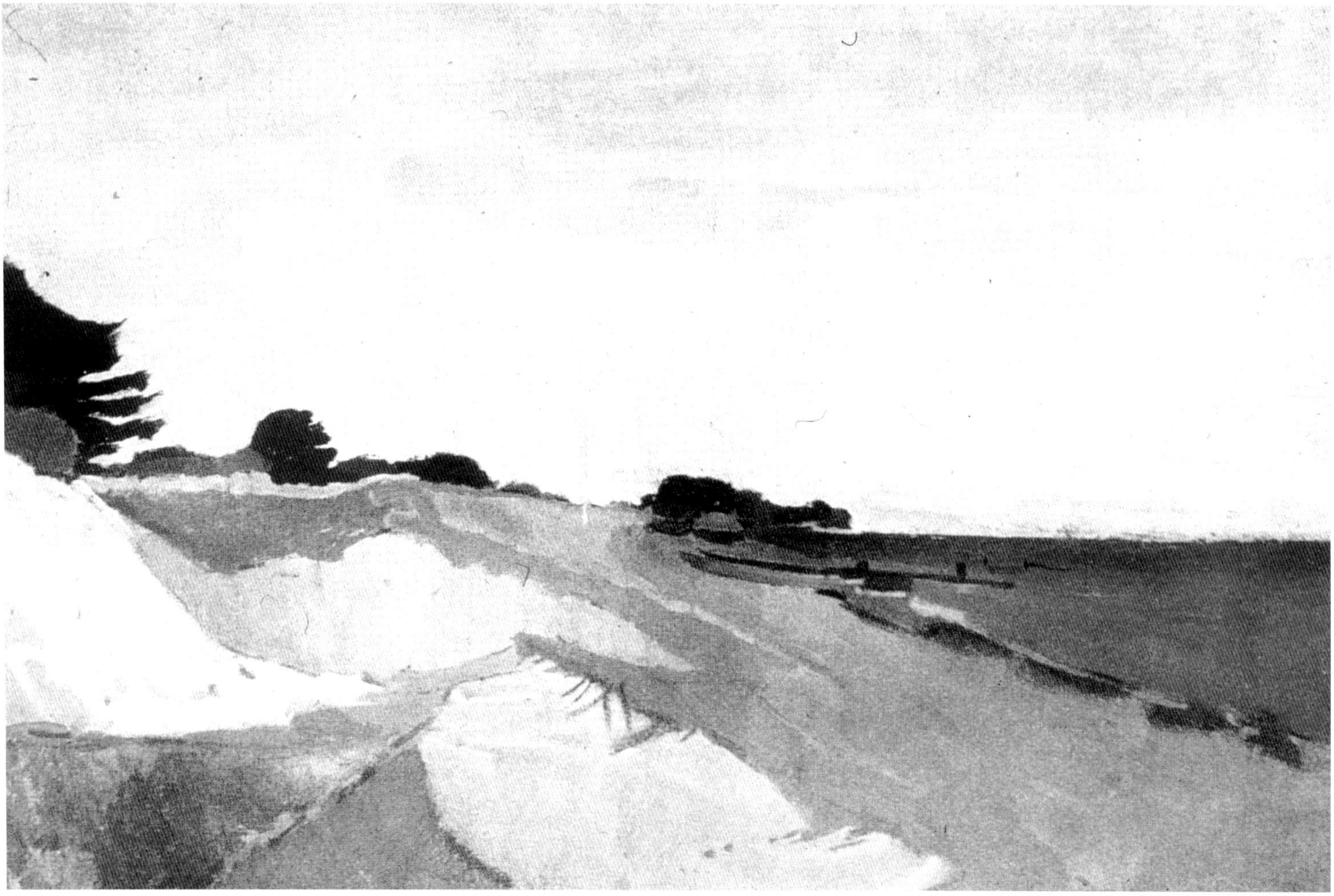

Eric Atkinson
Coast, near Aldwick
1956
20 x 30 in.
oil on canvas
collection: the late John Woods

perience of European galleries had been two years earlier in Paris where we had spent two brief weeks touring the museums and galleries. Perhaps the excitement of seeing the original works of art after having to rely on slides and photographs for so long is one reason I have always advised my students to try and seek out the real work and not be content with reproductions.

During that summer Muriel had been appointed as a lecturer at Bishop Otter College in Chichester and so we dispatched all our worldly goods to the left luggage office at Chichester railway station and left to spend the summer painting in France. On our return we found an eighteenth-century waterman's cottage to rent at Birdham Pool overlooking the estuary and close to the spot where Turner painted 'Chichester Canal'. Our guests from London arrived at weekends bearing small gifts of wine and pâté for their poor friends marooned in the country and on Sunday mornings I would take them across the field to visit our local shop. 'The Lock Stores', housed in an unprepossessing black Nissen hut, gave no hint of the gastronomic treasures to be found within its walls. Our astonished guests often returned to London carrying food and wines they could not find in the city! We owned no car at this point and ultimately the two-mile hike to the nearest bus stop proved too much of a struggle so we moved into Chichester itself.

I still had to complete a year of my five-year studentship and was travelling up to London three times each week. We rented a large Georgian house in East Pallant and I finally had sufficient space to set up my studio. We became very friendly with John and Ann Warren Davis who had met as students at Westminster School of Art before the war. John, a sculptor, was working in studios on their farm at Eastergate and we met often to talk about art and art politics. John and Ann owned some paintings by the Cornish 'Primitive' painter Alfred Wallis that I liked immensely and I studied them in great detail, marvelling at his simple and direct lines that resulted in such potent images. They introduced us to the wild, dramatic landscapes of South West Wales and we spent several weeks each year sailing with them, exploring the deep bays and inlets, steep cliffs and floating islands off the Pembrokeshire coast. John's native land made a lasting impression on me and I began a series of paintings of the Welsh Coast using thick acrylics and plaster. These summer journeys influenced John's work too and in 1958 we shared an exhibition at the Austin Hayes Gallery in York. Sir Herbert Read bought one of John's pieces and the renowned Yorkshire collector Ronnie Duncan bought some drawings. I sold three of my earliest 'storm' paintings. It was from this point that I began to record the atmospheric variations of weather on the landscapes of Pembrokeshire and Brittany and to use sand and acrylic to build up the physical texture of the paintings.

With love
Ricky

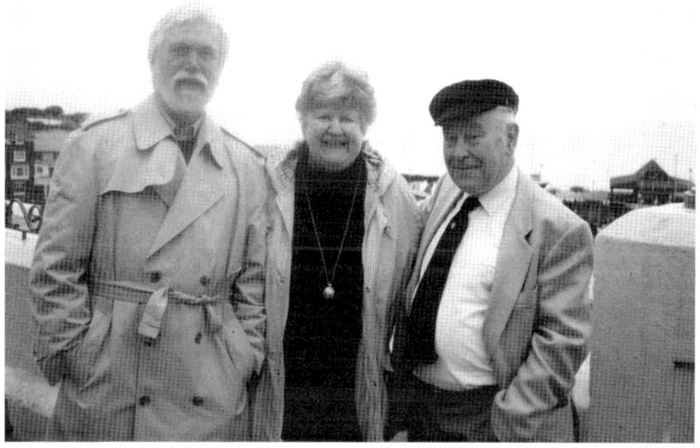

Muriel and Eric Atkinson with Jack Reading, Broadstairs, Kent, 1994

Letter 2 David Lewis to Eric Atkinson

Dear Ricky

Thank you for your letter. You ask what chain of events led to our paths crossing in Leeds in 1956. Was it by chance that at the age of thirty-four I'd enrolled as a first-year architecture student in the College of Art? No, of course not. Nothing is ever entirely by chance.

I remember parking my pea-green van on Woodhouse Lane in July 1956 and walking into Frank Chippendale's office. The architecture school was in an old church (should one say a 'converted' church?). I think his office was once the vestry. I explained that I wanted to become an architect. Chips, who was head of the school, had a curious way of smiling. One half of his mouth would curl upwards like a half moon while the other half stayed where it was.

'Why do you want to become an architect?' he asked; and then added quickly, 'nothing personal, of course.'

I explained that I'd been working with Peter Stead, a rare combination of artist and builder in the neighbouring town of Huddersfield. Peter also had an art gallery in that town, the Symon Quinn, devoted to showing contemporary art. He'd been collaborating with Stephen Gilbert, an English constructivist sculptor whose studio was in Paris, on the design of a house incorporating some of the ideas of Mondrian and de Stijl. The model of this house, I said, had been exhibited at the Salon Réalité Nouvelle in Paris and at the Stedelijk Museum in Amsterdam. I was planning to work with Peter and Stephen on further designs in an effort to bring this direction in architecture and art into a synthesis. If my explanation was unexpected, maybe a trifle baffling, Chips didn't show it. I added, a bit lamely, 'I want to learn to build'.

'We're starting an experiment this year,' Chips said. 'It's called the Basic Course. All the first-year students in the four schools in the college – the painters, the sculptors, the architects, and the designers – will be in one studio and in one series of lectures together.' The half moon rose on one side of his face. 'I take it you wouldn't mind being thrown in with a bunch of artists to begin with, would you?'

'No,' I said. 'Not at all.'

'The name Harry Thubron won't mean much to you, I don't suppose,' Chips went on. 'He's the chap heading it up. But we have other chaps joining him. Tom Hudson. Eric Atkinson. Norbert Lynton. Do any of these names ring a bell?'

I shook my head. The half moon hovered again.

'Herbert Read's behind it,' he said. 'And the Gregory Fellows, Terry Frost, Alan Davie and Hubert Dalwood will all be part of it. I'm sure these names are more familiar. We've decided to give it a try. Just to see if it works. Think about it. Then, if you still want to apply, you'll have to fill out the application forms. Let me know.'

Chips was right. The name Harry Thubron meant nothing to me; nor did Hudson, Atkinson or Lynton. But the other names did. I knew Herbert Read and Terry Frost from my St Ives years. I had known Alan Davie in London in the 1940s. 'Nibs' Dalwood was a more recent acquaintance. It sounded exciting.

Even so, several questions still remained unanswered. Why in my mid-thirties was I there in Leeds, in that school that had once been a church? How did I, a writer on art and architecture, come to be working with an artist- builder and a constructivist sculptor on colour-space experiments in the form of a house? How did Peter Stead come to be running an avant-garde gallery in a mill town in the industrial north?

Then there were other questions begging for answers too. Why was Herbert Read interested in the Basic Course, and a whole new way of art education at the college level? And why was it such a hot idea to have art and architecture students in the same studio, doing the same things, without differentiation?

To answer some of these questions, we'd have to go back a few years, to Cornwall.

The year was 1948. I was living at the time in a little granite cottage on a potato farm near Gurnard's Head, about five miles along the coast from St Ives towards Land's End. The cottage had no amenities. It had no running water – except during rain when the water from the hillside would cascade through the kitchen.

Above the cottage the hill rose up to a magnificent outcrop of granite rocks. From that high vantage point, one could imagine oneself as a seabird soaring over the green honeycomb of walled fields far below, and to the Atlantic Ocean's far horizon. After a day's work in the potato fields, I would take a book and find a grassy spot among those high-up rocks to shelter from the wind.

Britain was still trying to recover from the war. London and most of the industrial and seaport cities had been heavily bombed. Food, clothes, indeed most of the necessities of life, were rationed. So a handful of potatos from the fields were a godsend every day.

(right)
Barbara Hepworth
Pendour
1947–8
length: 28 in.
plane wood with
colour blue and white
collection: Hirshhorn
Museum, Washington

(below left)
Alfred Wallis
Boat enters harbour
*c.*1936
oil on wood board
collection: Mrs Warren
Davis

(below right)
Alfred Wallis
Boat and lighthouse
9¾ x 6¾ in.
collection: David Lewis

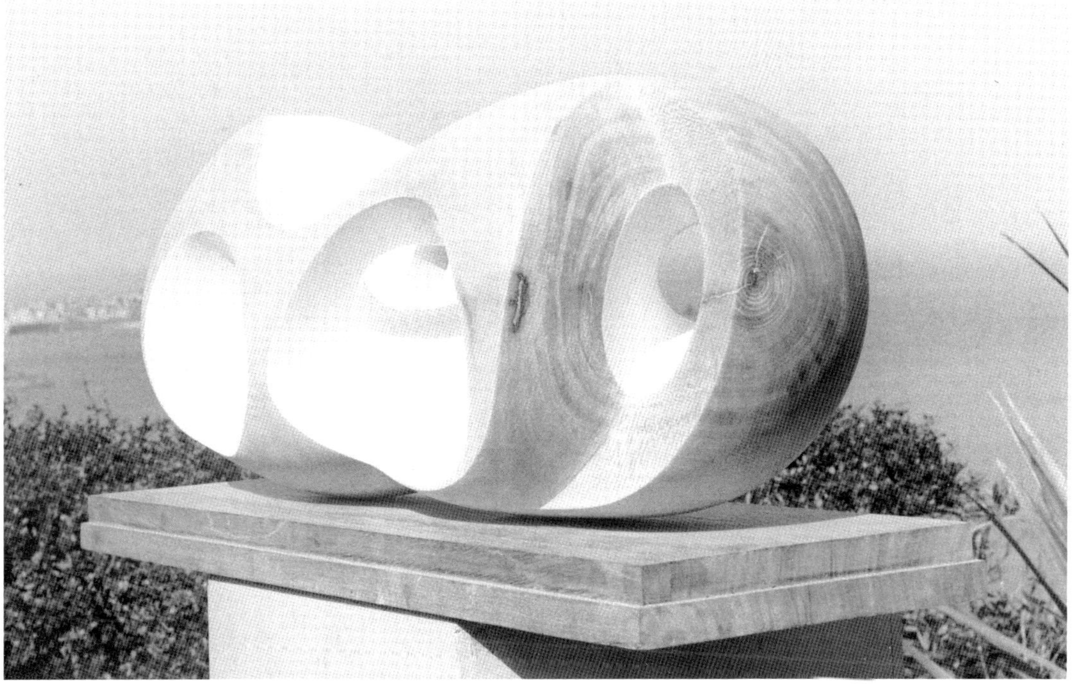

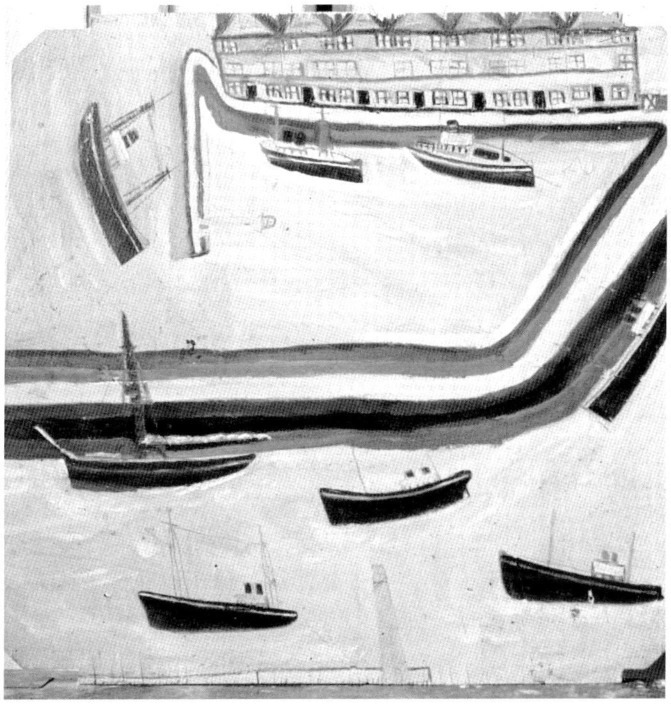

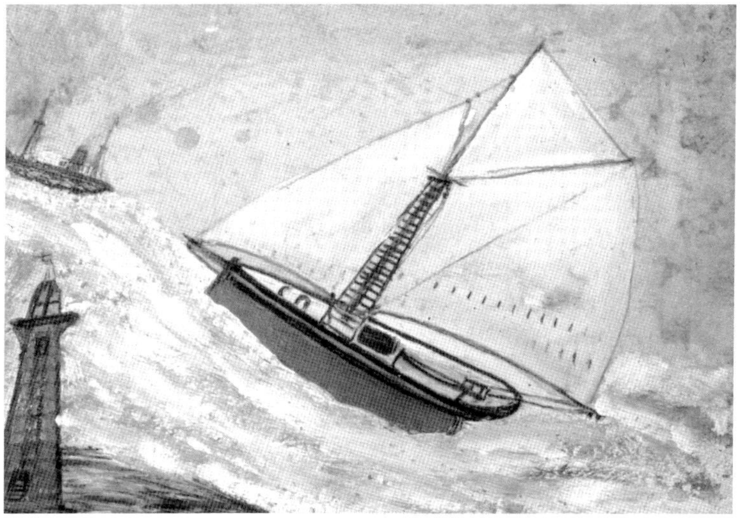

One evening I was in the pub at Gurnard's Head. Two men at the bar were discussing art. It seemed incongruous, but that's what they were doing. One of them kept looking at me as though I didn't quite belong. Somehow I managed to get into the conversation. The two men turned out to be young artists, Peter Lanyon and John Wells. 'My father,' I said, 'studied painting in Newlyn with Stanhope Forbes.'

Peter must have been standing down-wind from me. He suddenly said, 'Would you like a bath?'

And so it was that Peter Lanyon and his wife Sheila offered me two of the greatest of all luxuries – supper and a bath. On Friday evenings, twice a month, I'd walk along the cliffs to Peter's Attic Studio, perched on a high terrace overlooking St Ives, with its harbour filled with fishing boats, and the town on a spit of land between two sweeping beaches.

'Hey,' said Peter one Saturday morning, 'let's go and see Ben and Barbara.'

The previous night an Atlantic gale had raged and whined across the cliffs, and the sea as I walked along the tops of the cliffs had pounded on the dark rocks below. Now the air was calm as glass. The sun warmed us as we walked to Carbis Bay.

On the way Peter pointed out Little Parc Owles, where Adrian Stokes and Margaret Mellis lived, and the cottage where Naum Gabo and Miriam had lived until just a few months ago when they left to settle in America. For the first time I learned who they were. Peter made it seem as though Gabo's sculptures belonged to the air and the sparkling sea of that sunny morning. Then we came to Chy-an-Kerris, an undistinguished three-storey house built into the hillside below the street.

Standing on the pavement we could look down over the gate into a small paved yard where a woman was working on a sculpture with a fine rasp and sandpaper. 'That's Barbara,' Peter said in a stage whisper.

She wore a white cotton coat like a laboratory technician and she had her hair in a net. As we walked down the steps I was surprised to see how large and strong her hands were. With the palm of her hand she stroked the sanded surface of the sculpture as though it was a cat. We sat on the wall with our feet dangling and talked while she went on working and refining. The house had French windows opening on to the yard. Through the windows on the far side of the interior of the house you could see the sea, blue and silver in the sunlight and still heaving with laconic swells. The sculpture had an interior concavity which spiralled inside it and was painted pale blue. It made me think of the sea and the movement of the tides.

After a while Barbara went indoors and came out again with a plate of lunch, boiled potatoes, peas with a sprig of mint and a lamb chop. That chop must have been half a week's ration. She sat on the wall and talked with us while she ate. Then she drank her tea. She didn't offer us anything. Peter said he had to go. Just as he was leaving, a small man with a blue cotton cap and baggy trousers appeared at the French windows. 'Ben,' Peter said, 'I'd like you to meet David Lewis.' After a few moments, Peter left. 'You wouldn't by any chance like to play a game of ping pong?' Ben asked, his head tilted on one side.

He led me through the kitchen to an upstairs bedroom which had a large table in it. But instead of a net in the middle it had a twelve-inch plank perched horizontally on a pile of books. 'More fun than a net, my dear chap,' Ben said. 'You can bounce the ball onto the table over the plank in the ordinary way, or you can bounce the ball off the plank, or you can bounce the ball off the plank and onto the table.' 'Or,' he added as though in deep afterthought, 'you can miss them both altogether, and lose the point!'

We played game after game the whole afternoon. It got so hot Ben played in a singlet and I took my shirt off. He was incredibly fast. We laughed ourselves silly. Some of the games were close. But whenever I came anywhere near to winning, he'd find a way of temporarily modifying the rules. 'Let's say, for the rest of the game you can't smash.' Or 'let's say, only the person serving can win the next point'. And then he'd serve with an horrendous spin on the ball and collapse laughing.

The windows were open and we were glad of the gentle breeze from the sea. We could hear the whispers of the surf running up the beach and the cries of gulls. Between games I asked him about the small paintings propped up on the mantelpiece. 'That one,' he said, pointing to a small picture of a lighthouse and a boat in full sail rushing past it, propelled by a huge wave, 'is by an old fisherman called Alfred Wallis.'

It was the first time I'd heard of Alfred Wallis. 'He died a short while ago,' Ben said. 'In a workhouse. He was happy there. He was with old men like himself. Before that he lived in a little cottage on Back Road West in St Ives. Do

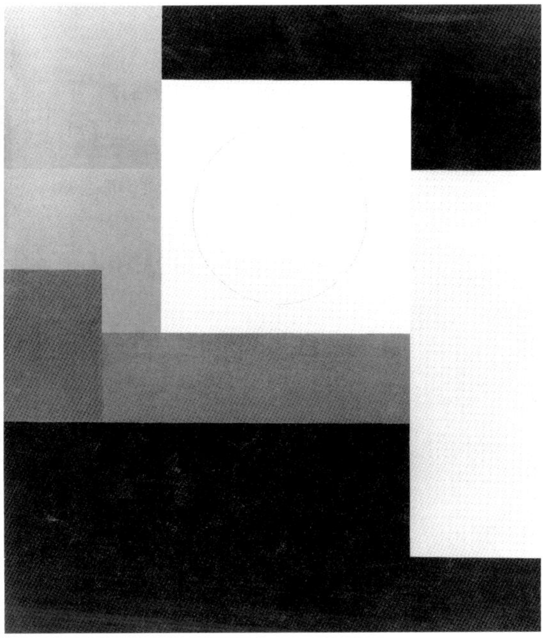

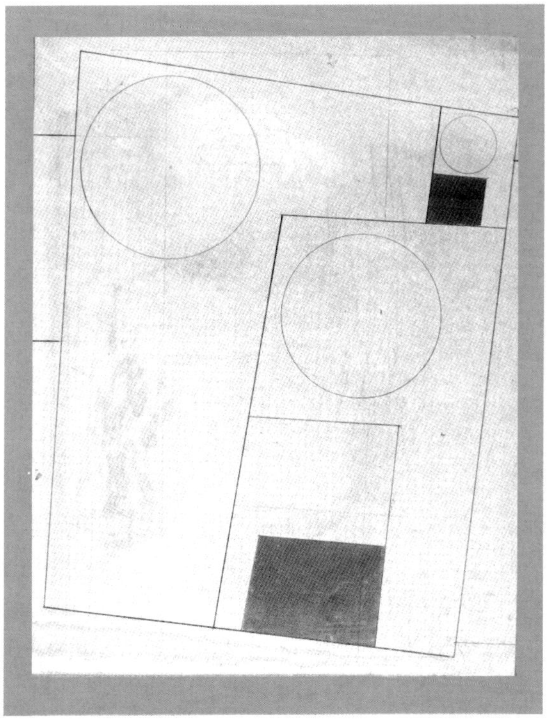

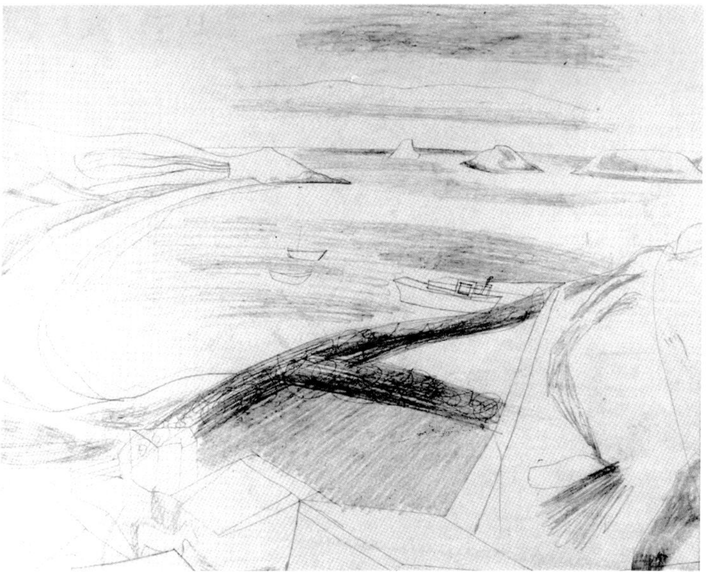

(top left)
Ben Nicholson
Painting
1940
16½ x 15½ in.
gouache
collection: Leeds City Art Gallery

(top right)
Ben Nicholson
White Relief, 1936
26½ x 36¾ in.
collection: Florsheim Collection, Chicago

(above left)
Ben Nicholson
August 1960 (3 circles and red)
13 x 11¼ in.
oil wash on board
collection: David Lewis

(above right)
Ben Nicholson
St Martin's, Scilly Isles
1952
12½ x 16 in.
collection: David Lewis

you know Back Road West?' I didn't. 'He painted every day. He was very reclusive. "I only paint what I know", he'd say. He used old scraps of cardboard that he'd scavenged out of rubbish bins. And his colours were leftover paints from the fishermen painting and caulking their boats at low tide.' Ben brought three or four more Wallis paintings from the next room and propped them on the mantel. 'Sometimes a scrap of cardboard might have an odd shape or a tear in it. Wallis would never try to change its shape. He'd just incorporate the shape as part of the painting. And he'd always use the colour of the cardboard as one of his colours,' Ben said. Then Ben added, 'What I especially like about his things is that they're not just paintings of ships and the sea. They're objects. Incredibly alive objects.'

There were other small paintings on the mantel and leaning against the wall. They had circles and squares drawn in pencil on textured backgrounds. One was simply brightly coloured rectangles. Suddenly I realised they were not paintings of anything, not even rectangles and circles. They were simply objects, precise as sharpened knives.

I saw Peter Lanyon quite often in those days. He drove a jeep at speed through the curving Cornish lanes as though he was riding a mustang. Between the high granite hedges on each side we'd get sudden and surprising flash-views of fields laid out like patchwork, and the sea.

We drove to Pendeen, where Peter described the tin mines, with their shafts cut through red rock and their galleries under the sea, and we drove to Portreath where the land, the sea, the harbour and the wind seemed encoiled in ever-changing rhythms of dance. When I first knew him his paintings were tightly wrought; but gradually they became more and more free, as though he was exploring the sinews of the land with wet rivers of colour and with the speed and intensity of our twisting and turning over the moors.

The following year I moved into St Ives and married the painter Willie Barns-Graham, and Peter was our best man. That was when I began to see Ben more often and to do secretarial chores for Barbara. Sometimes I'd stop in at the Leach Pottery for a game of cricket and a good argument over supper with Bernard and Warren and Alix MacKenzie about Eastern and Western ceramic traditions.

Ben got himself a small motor-cycle, and we'd pap-pap-pap up to the windswept moors, me on the pillion with Ben's drawing things strapped to my back, and Ben would draw the rhythms of the farms far below with wire-like lines, and he'd hatch the shadows as fierce black masses as though the graphite of his pencil were scraping into the paper. Willie and I even made a drawing expedition with him to the Scilly Isles.

Back in the studio, first at Chy-an-Kerris and then at Porthmeor, we'd look at paintings and white reliefs. The fact that the white reliefs had been made before the war, and the recent paintings explored a somewhat different pictorial language, made no difference. We'd discuss them side by side as objects.

For a while the white reliefs became especially important to me. They were simply a couple of squares and a circle. But the squares were never exactly square. Carved from boards of mahogany, the circles and squares were cut into the wood or raised in relief and painted white until they had the texture of plaster of Paris, so that with a sideways light their edges were either sharp white lines or soft shadows. Sometimes we'd sit in silence, and a cloud would pass over the sun and the white relief would soften; and then the sun would come out again, and the planes and edges of the relief would be sharp white once again.

I began reading whatever I could about the 1930s. Ben made me a present of his proof copy of *Circle*, the book he'd edited in 1936–7 with Leslie Martin, the architect, and Naum Gabo, the Constructivist.[1] I began to understand the international idealism which World War Two had shattered. Gabo's essay on 'The Constructive Idea' was particularly revealing. In it he wrote that the Constructive idea 'has revealed a universal law that the elements of visual art such as lines, colours, shapes, possess their own forces of expression independent of any association with the external aspects of the world'.

Patiently I read every essay and every quotation in the book. It didn't matter that it was only a black-and-white proof, and that many of the illustrations were smudged. I looked at every painting, every sculpture, every construction, every architecture and every piece of furniture.

I saw a common language in the paintings of Malevich and Mondrian, and in Aalto's houses and the town plans of Le Corbusier, and in Maillart's bridges which had the precision of a surgeon's tools as they spanned rivers and gorges in Switzerland. Looking at these objects, I understood the first words of *Circle*'s editorial: 'A new cultural unity is slowly emerging out of the fundamental changes which are taking place in our present-day civilisation'.

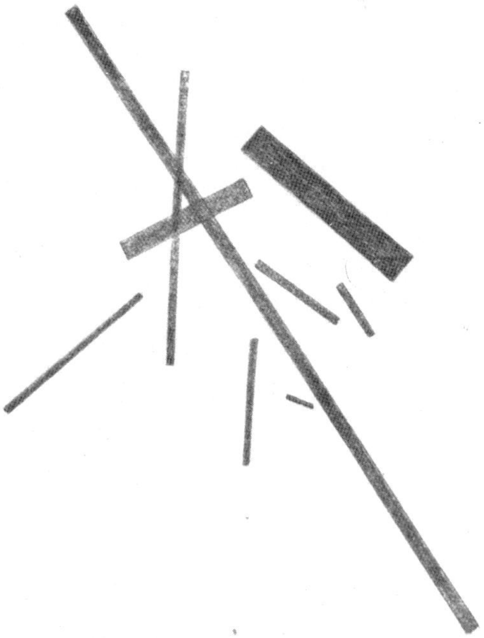

Kasimir Malevich *Suprematist Composition* 1914

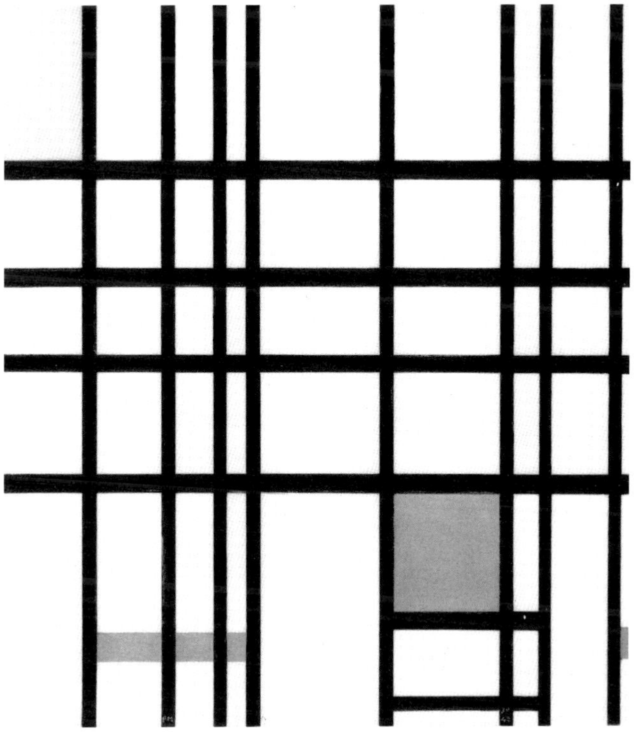

Piet Mondrian *Composition (Red, yellow and blue)* 1935 22 x 21⅝ in. oil on canvas collection: Tate Gallery, London

I was moved by the internationalism of the book. There were no frontiers. The paintings and sculptures, the buildings and the furniture, all seemed to belong together. They seemed to be metaphors of a determination which all these artists shared to evolve a society in which science, art and technology and an enlightened rationalism could come together and reconstruct our cities, and redistribute the world's wealth and resources, so that the disparities that divided classes and nations could be healed.

Looking back, Ricky, over the past forty-five years of almost continuous wars and human suffering, I ask myself whether I really was naïve to be moved like this. And does that make the thirty-two painters and sculptors, the twenty-nine architects, and the seventeen writers, from Russia, France, Holland, Switzerland, Germany, Belgium, the Baltic countries, and the United States, who were all drawn into the loose federation reflected in *Circle*, naïve too?

Around this time Willie Barns-Graham and I moved into 4 Teetotal Street, the middle cottage in a granite terrace in St Ives, just around the corner from Terry Frost and his wife Kath. Ben would pop in for lunch nearly every day, bringing his own hard-boiled egg and ryvita and a little piece of Swiss cheese. He explained Abstraction-Création,[2] and loaned me copies of *Axis*.[3] He gave me a copy of a book on Unit One;[4] and I read everything I could lay my hands on by Herbert Read.

When he spoke about the artists in Paris in the 1930s, and about how Gabo and Mondrian, and Gropius, Breuer, Mendelsohn and Moholy-Nagy had fled to London in the late 1930s under the gathering clouds of war, and when he spoke about the British artists and architects who were part of *Circle*, Henry Moore and Max Fry and Wells Coates and others – they became so alive for us in our little kitchen that we felt we knew them almost as well as he did.

There was clearly an extraordinary sense, not of an organised movement, but of the forging of an international language which individual artists respected and shared. I was especially interested in de Stijl. But Ben would always defuse the idea of movements and manifestos, and would talk instead about particular sculptures and paintings as objects which, because they were made by hand, carried the artist's language directly and personally without any critical intermediary. Or he would recount incidents that seemed to him to be, as he would say, to the point.

He told us how he and Barbara visited Brancusi in Paris, and how the sculptor had hand-carved the entire environment of his studio, his bake-oven and olive press, his bed, his doors and benches, and how he had sewn his own clothes and even his hat. Ben took with him a gift of those wonderful pencils painted in spirals like barbers' poles, in green and red and blue and white. Brancusi's eyes lit up when Ben rolled them across the table and the spirals spun. 'It must have taken you a long time to paint each one,' Brancusi said. 'No, I didn't paint them,' Ben replied, 'I bought them like that.' 'Oh,' said the sculptor, 'then I don't want them.'

He told us about how Mondrian had transformed his cheap rented rooms in Camden Town into an architectural space in which everything was in white and black and primary colours, chairs, tables and paintings, and how every object contributed to the serene equilibrium he'd made. Then he recounted how Mondrian had visited Ben's studio in Hampstead, which Ben had painted completely white. In that environment Mondrian was especially intrigued with the white reliefs, white on white. 'How do you like the studio?' Ben asked. 'Too much nature!' Mondrian replied, pointing to the topmost leaves of a chestnut tree just visible through the skylight.

I was fully aware – having lived through those years myself – that the 1930s also saw the rise of Nazism in Germany and Fascism in Italy, the Spanish Civil War, the Soviet purges, and the hunger marches from England's northern cities and the Welsh coal mines. Yet the *Circle* artists of the 1930s shared what Gabo in 1937 called an 'optimism about the final outcome, since we see that in the realm of ideas we are now entering a period of reconstruction'.

Then came the war. It shattered Europe's cities, raged through the deserts of North Africa, and engulfed the Far East. The very technologies that were thought to transform our societies were now the agents of destruction. Europe's intellectual life was decimated. The artists were dispersed and cut off from one another or went underground. Gropius, Breuer and Mendelsohn left London for America. Mondrian's studio in Camden Town was badly shaken by a bomb blast. He left late in 1940 for New York where he died in 1944. Urged on by Adrian Stokes and Margaret Mellis, Ben and Barbara left London for St Ives in 1939, taking their children with them. There they were joined by Naum and Miriam Gabo.

Communications were severed. Even London was increasingly difficult to get to. France, Belgium, Holland, Denmark, Norway, Poland and the Balkans were overrun. Russia invaded Finland, and until Germany attacked Russia no one knew which side the Soviets were on. Britain stood alone in Western Europe until Pearl Harbor when the United States entered the war. Night after night Britain's cities were bombed. The night sky was alive with searchlights and the glow of fires. The onslaughts on both sides were relentless and tragic.

Cornwall was tucked away, but far from being insulated. Margaret Gardiner has written eloquently in her book on Barbara about the deeply troubling moral and political dilemmas she brooded over as an artist, with long and often agonising quotes from Barbara's letters. [5]

However, the contrast between the intellectual pressures brought about by the war and the rhythms of nature seemed salutary, and gradually that contrast became reassuring. Below the cliffs the sea pounded the land with timeless rhythms, the wind whined over the moors, and tides shaped and reshaped the sand dunes. It seemed as though every day brought reminders of man's relation to permanent and universal rhythms, against which the horrors of war could be seen as transitory.

Unlike Barbara, I can't remember Ben ever talking about his paintings in terms of theory. He'd say, 'if the meaning of a painting can be explained in words, my dear chap, why paint?' Paintings and reliefs were objects made by hand. As objects they incorporated language. Visual communication was his interest. If you respond to the vitality of the object, its meaning will become personal to you. Paintings and sculptures were the arenas in which artists forged their visual statements. As the war became more intense, John Piper's paintings became dark and haunting; Graham Sutherland's imagery was spiked with thorns; in Henry Moore's sculptures, human form fused with the bones of the land.

Figurative images entered Ben's paintings soon after his arrival in Cornwall, and gradually invaded Barbara's sculptures too. But there was clearly no contradiction between these and the non-figurative or abstract works which were made parallel with them. In both cases, the human presence in the dynamic equilibrium of natural rhythms was the focus.

Ben gave me a book to read by the physicist A.S.Edding-

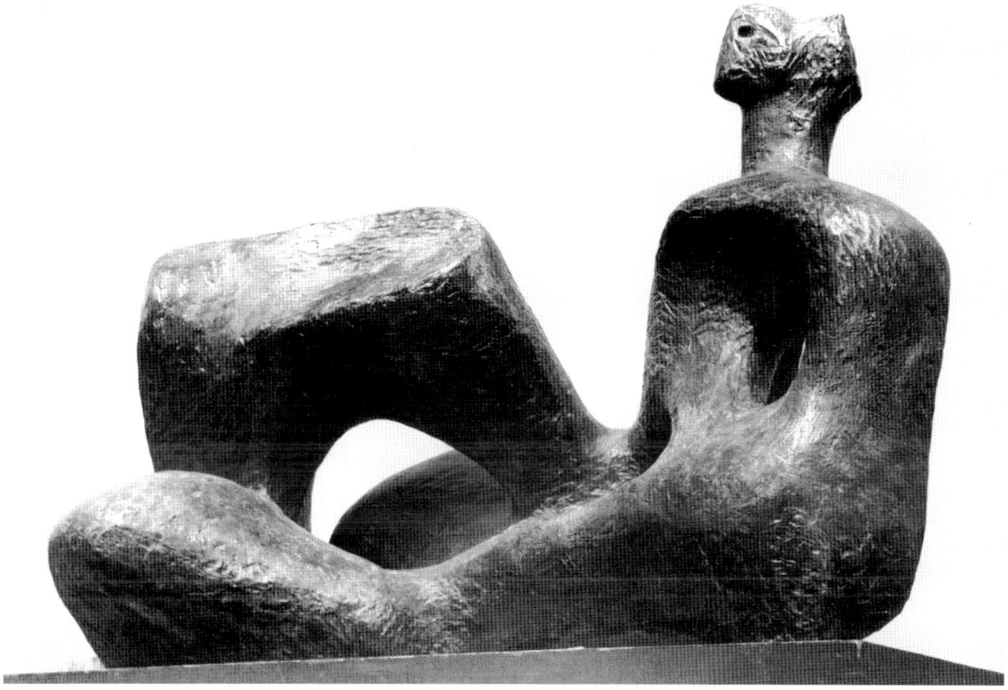

Henry Moore
Reclining Figure
1957
length: 7 ft 10 in.
bronze
collection: Museum of Art,
The Carnegie, Pittsburgh
(gift of G. David Thompson)

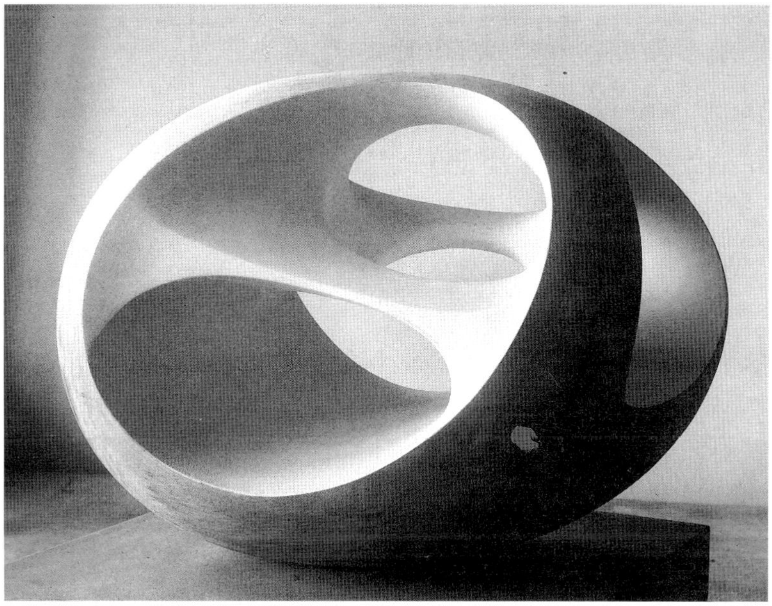

Barbara Hepworth
Oval Sculpture
1943
length: 16½ in.
plane wood with white
collection: Pier Gallery,
Stromness, Orkney

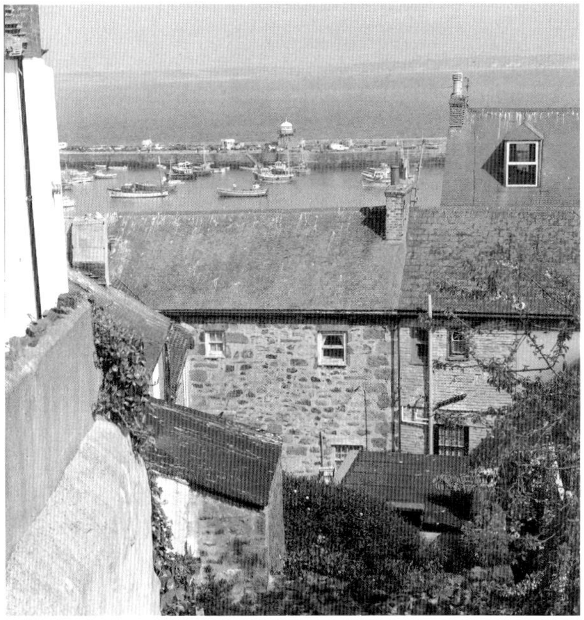

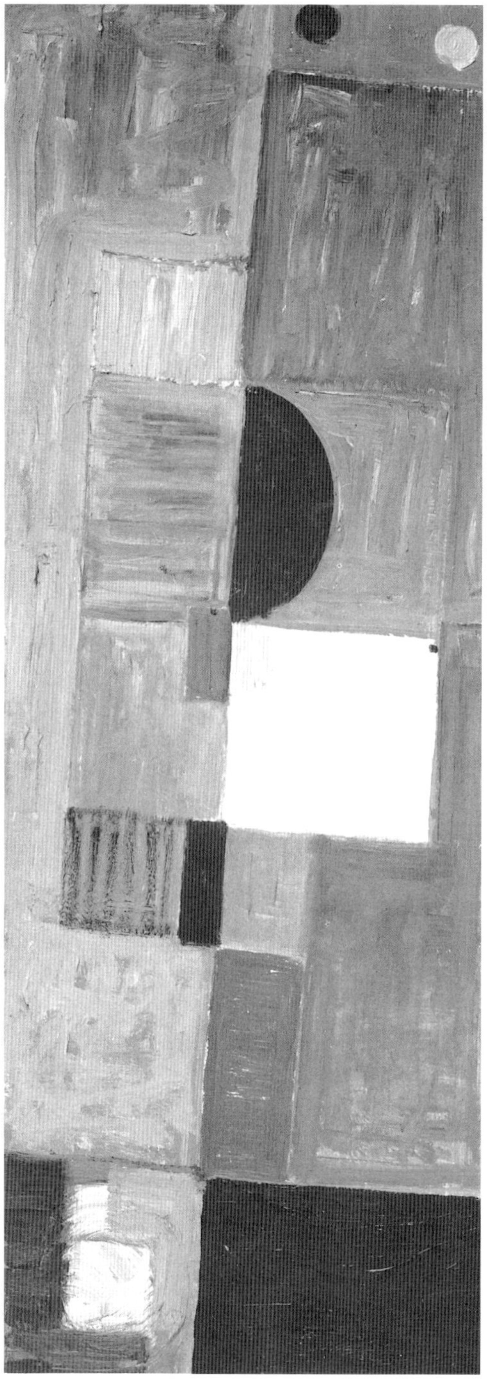

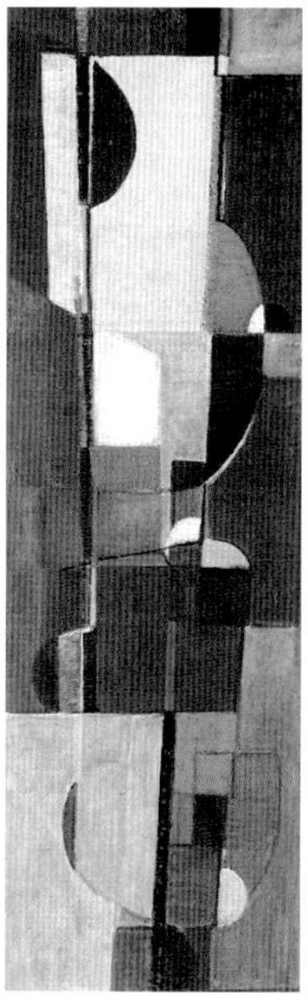

(above)
St Ives Harbour from Trezion
(photograph: David Lewis 1981)

(centre)
Terry Frost
Walk along the Quay (black, white and grey)
1948
24 x 10 in.
collection: W. Barns-Graham and David Lewis

(right)
Terry Frost
Walk along the Quay
1950
60 x 22 in.
oil on canvas
collection: Adrian Heath

ton, *The Nature of the Physical World.*[6] It was a reprint of Eddington's Gifford Lectures, delivered at the University of Edinburgh in 1927. Eddington spoke as a physicist and mathematician about the unity of nature, from the furthest reaches of space to the smallest molecules, but all the way through he reminds us that the only meaning the physical interrelatedness of nature has is in our minds and interpretations – in other words, a matter of language.

At the time I worked the breakfast shift at Rose's cafe on the harbourfront, and Terry worked the same shift at St Christopher's on Porthmeor. Terry and I would meet at about six before we went to our jobs, and walk along the harbour for a breath of fresh sea air. When the tide was out, the boats – painted black below the water-line and green or blue above it, with white trim and crimson keels – would be lying at odd angles on the sand. At other times, when the tide was in and the wind was blowing, everything would be in movement. Now the boats would be bobbing up and down and sideways, and their masts would be describing arcs in the air, and their ropes would be going slack and taut in turns, sometimes above the surface of the water and sometimes below it, and the reflections of the hulls in the water seemed like boats upside down to a point where you couldn't tell which was which, the boats below and the boats above – and then a breeze would ruffle the water like silver feathers and the whole scene would fracture into a thousand dancing shards, only to coalesce again.

At this period in his life Terry was still a student. Dependent on his ex-serviceman's grant, he was commuting back and forth to London to study at the Camberwell school. He talked quite a lot about the problem he was experiencing in fulfilling the requirements in the drawing and painting classes. In a taped interview with him in 1993 I reminded him of these early morning discussions. 'I was with a crowd of what I called "the Coldstream Guards". They hadn't got past Cézanne and they weren't going to. They were plumb-line happy, and you had to have everything on the Golden Section, and you have to have your chin in a chinstrap and everything had to be accurate. You couldn't talk about Cubism or anything like that. You mark on the floor where you're standing in relation to the model and where your feet are and where the easel is, and you can't make a mark on an ear without relating it across to the nose and so on and so on....' Terry liked to visit Victor Pasmore. He described how Victor was trying to break into abstract painting while

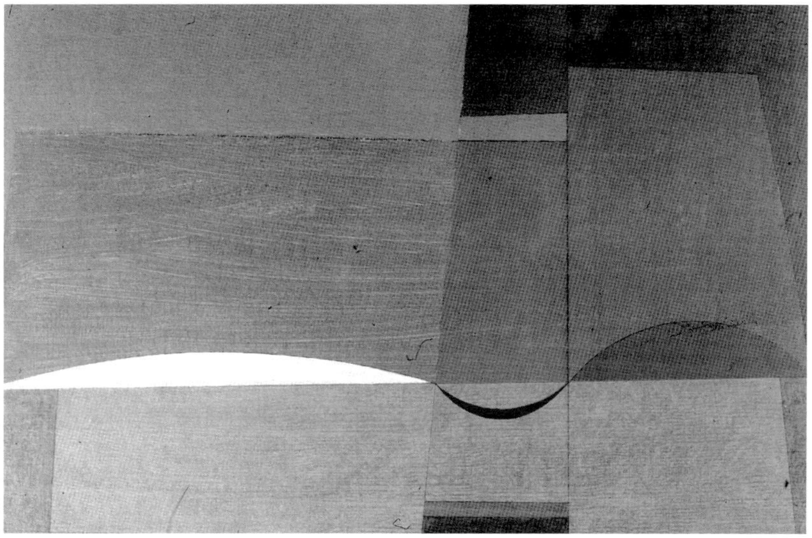

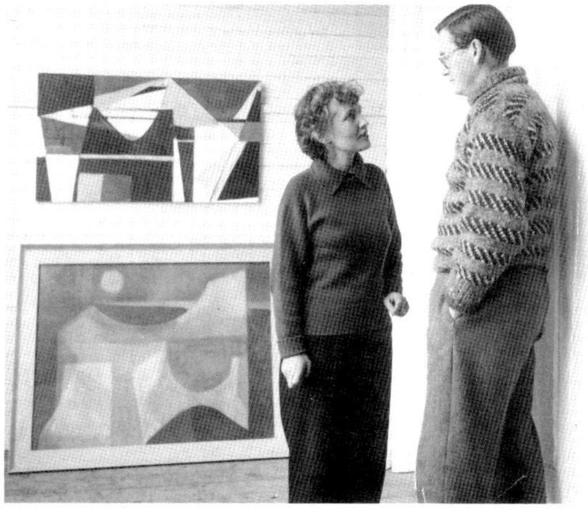

(above)
John Wells
Painting
1979
10 x 13½ in.
oil on board
collection: David Lewis

(right)
W. Barns-Graham and David Lewis, 1952

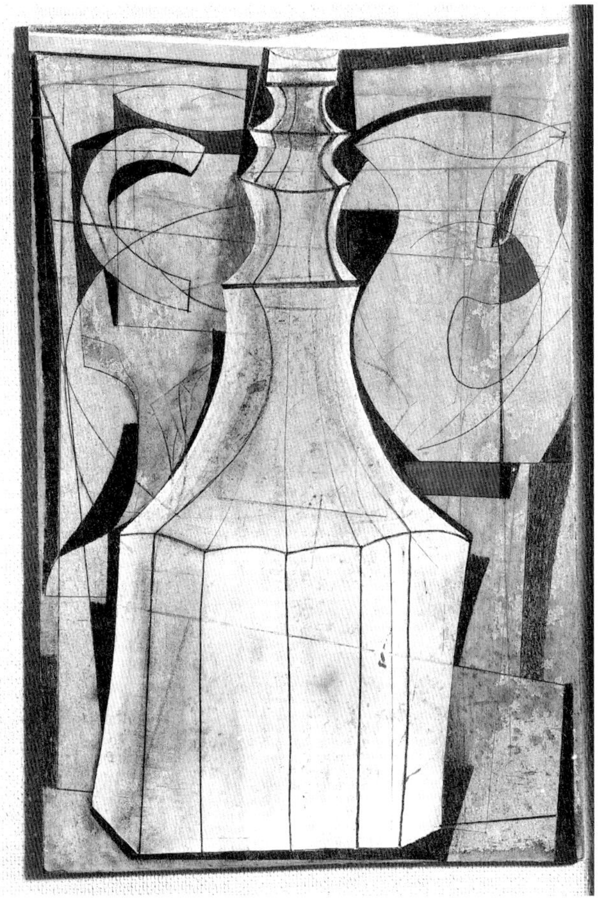

Ben Nicholson
February 14 – 49 (bottle)
1949
Private collection

retaining the underlying disciplines of geometric and colour composition.

Terry began a series of paintings called 'Walk Along the Quay' in which rectangles and arcs rocked back and forth up and down the canvas in syncopations of colour and texture. With my tips from Rose's I bought one of his sketches. When Ben first saw these paintings he was silent for a while, and then he said, 'Terry, you've got a theme that can last you a lifetime'. And it has. And thinking about that I recall what Ben had written about Wallis in *Horizon* a few years before: '... I remember one day he was complaining that he was short of some colours, and when I asked him which, he said he needed rock-colour and sand-colour, and I got these for him in the yacht-paint he was using.... Next day he made a new painting using, of course, rock-colour for anything but rock and sand-colour for anything but sand, and keeping to his usual small number of colours; and when I went out, having admired the colour of the painting, he said: "You don't want to use too many colours".'[7]

After Rose's I would open the doors to the Penwith Gallery mid-morning where I had the job of curator; and I would also work on an as-needed basis for Barbara, who by now had moved from Chy-an-Kerris to Trewyn Studio,[8] where one of my assignments was tracking down past sculptures which had never been catalogued. This gave me a wonderful opportunity to discover at first hand her journey from early figurative sculptures to the pure abstraction of the mid-1930s, the *Circle* years, and to the sculptures in the 1940s like the one I'd first seen her working on that morning at Chy-an-Kerris, which related to nature's rhythms. Although her drawings were the starting-points of ideas for sculptures, it was as if nature's corrosive agencies were themselves exploring the surfaces of woods and stones, smoothing them like sea-pebbles or hollowing them like caves or like the inner spirals of seashells.

At the Penwith I got to know the work of the younger artists as well. Perhaps the painter closest to Gabo was John Wells. His delicate paintings resembled Gabo's curvilinear transparent planes of plastic, but they were also rich in the moods of mists and sea and islands. In Willie's paintings, sea, sky and land became powerful interlocking masses. Terry's paintings, on the other hand, were robust and exuberant constructions of movement, texture and colour. It was as if he was painting his freedom after years as a prisoner-of-war.

Terry, John, and the sculptor Denis Mitchell, worked as I did for Barbara. Their job was roughing out her woods and stones. When I was working in the basement of her studio on my cataloguing, I could hear their laughter in the garden, and I could hear Barbara, who would have been inside her studio working on smaller pieces or on drawings, admonishing them to cut out the larking and concentrate!

Terry's studio was next door to Ben's.[9] Sometimes, when I visited Terry on my way to the Penwith, we could hear Ben's radio playing jazz, and we could hear his footsteps as he ambled to and fro, moving this and that around. And then suddenly the radio would be turned off and the silence seemed to become very intense, and we'd hear the scraping of razor blades on pigment-layered canvas – and we'd know that a new painting was evolving, and it would take him to a still-to-be-discovered destination.

Scraping – the physical action of making – was always a crucial part of Ben's way of working. Way back in the early 1930s, when Cubism opened new doors for him, painting and scraping and scumbling became the making of a physical object, a new reality in itself. Even his most severe works, the white reliefs, were carved and scraped. But now scraping was related to the land, to the erosion of rock, to the rhythms of winds and tides, to the textures of sand. And scraping was also the threshold of the creative process. As he worked away at layers of old paint, unexpected rhythms and textures would emerge, and the rhythms of working would set off taut lines and ambiguities of plane as if the painting was telling Ben precisely what it needed, like a pair of dancers. And colour would flash, like stabs of yellow gorse in the landscape, or the brilliance of blue sky in a break in the clouds, with the clarity of notes one finds in the music of Schoenberg or Bartók or Varèse. After a few hours he'd come looking for Terry and me. We would almost certainly be by this time in different parts of the town. Could we spare a moment to look at something? Then after we'd looked at the new painting in his studio he'd ask, do you think it's complete? Every painting was a journey, an exploration, a communication, a new self-realisation – both for the artist and for the person experiencing it.

When the war ended, a period of national reconstruction began. Aided by the Marshall Plan, the task of rebuilding the cities of Britain and Europe fell to the younger generation of architects and builders. Among the architectural leaders in London was J. L. (later, Sir Leslie) Martin, one of the editors of *Circle*. At first it was as if the principles of *Circle* could continue straight on, despite the intervention of war. Yet it was clear that things had changed. The artists and the architects of *Circle* were not the same artists and architects when they emerged from the war. In his Introduction to the 1982 exhibition of *Circle*, J. L. Martin remarked about two of *Circle*'s architects, Alvar Aalto of Finland and Richard Neutra of the United States:

> 'In retrospect we now know how Aalto's work rooted itself more and more deeply into the influences of landscape and materials that came directly from his own background and country. At another extreme we can see in Richard Neutra's work within industrialised technology the beginnings of an interest that has today transformed high technology into poetic expression.'[10]

One of the breakfast clients at Rose's was Theo Crosby, who was in St Ives on holiday. I don't think it was Rose's breakfast menu that attracted him as much as our waitress. Mary was a statuesque beauty; but as she didn't favour Theo with as much as a glance, I waited on him. When Theo wandered into the Penwith Gallery and discovered our mutual interest in the arts and architecture, and the fact that we were both South Africans, we became lifelong friends.

Theo was working for Max Fry and Jane Drew at the time. Shortly afterwards he became an editor with Monica Pidgeon of *Architectural Design*, and I began writing on art for him. Whether I was any good at it or not I don't know, but I tried to write about painting and sculpture from the inside – as explorations by artists I knew. Theo was a sculptor and writer as well as an architect. We were on the same wavelength. He was deeply committed to social issues and local urban contexts. He felt that technical specialisation threatened to separate architecture from art, to architecture's detriment. He loved the rich vocabularies of London's streets and street life, and he revered the physical quality of a work of art as much as its message. I therefore tried to describe the personal languages of artists rather than write as a reviewer or critic.

In 1950 plans for the 1951 Festival of Britain were under way. The physical size of the statements of Britain's resurgence was clearly symbolic. London's South Bank buildings with its Festival Hall were under construction. Large sculptures by Moore and Hepworth were commissioned

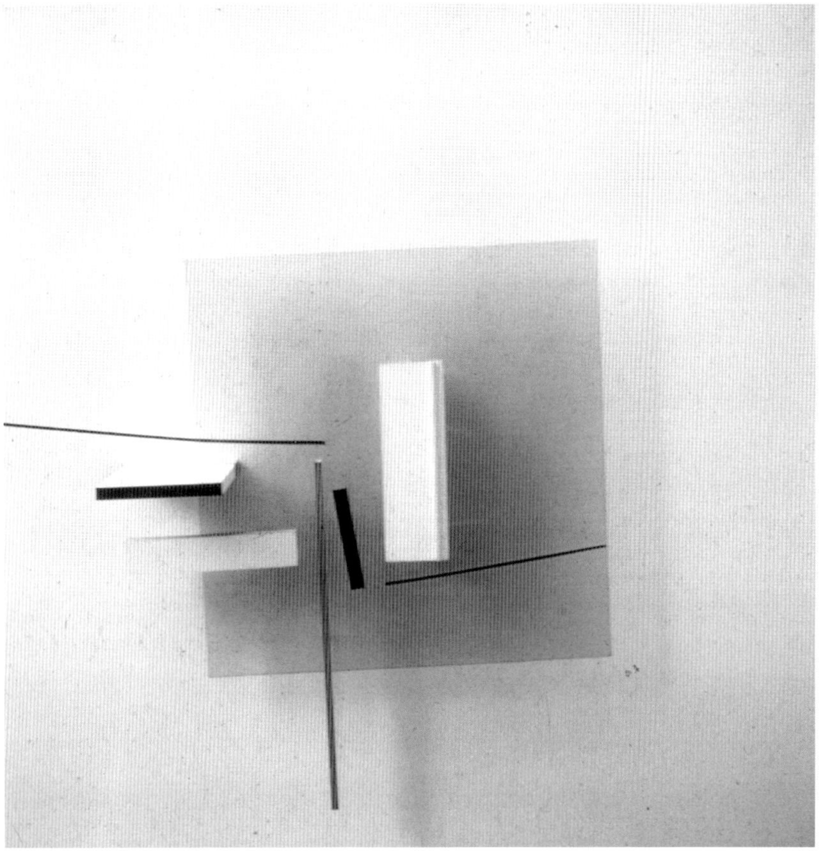

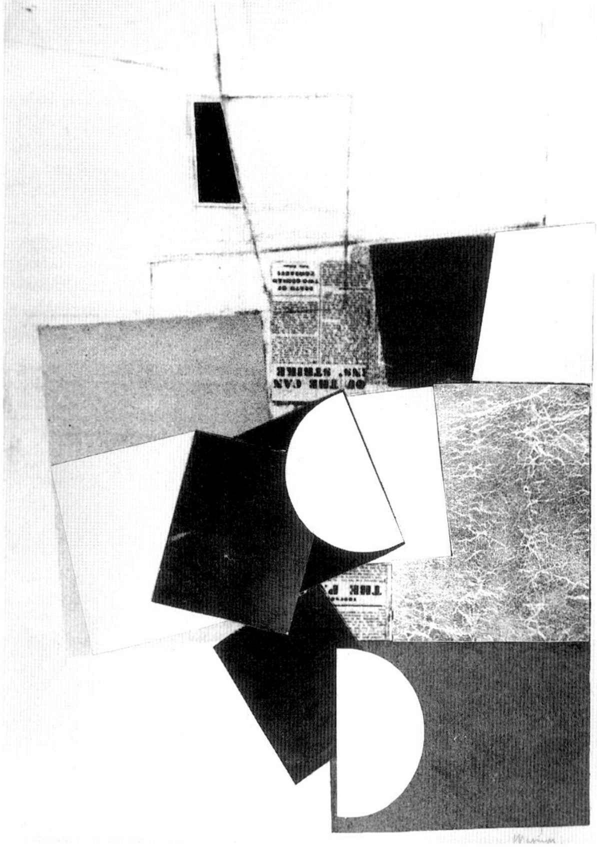

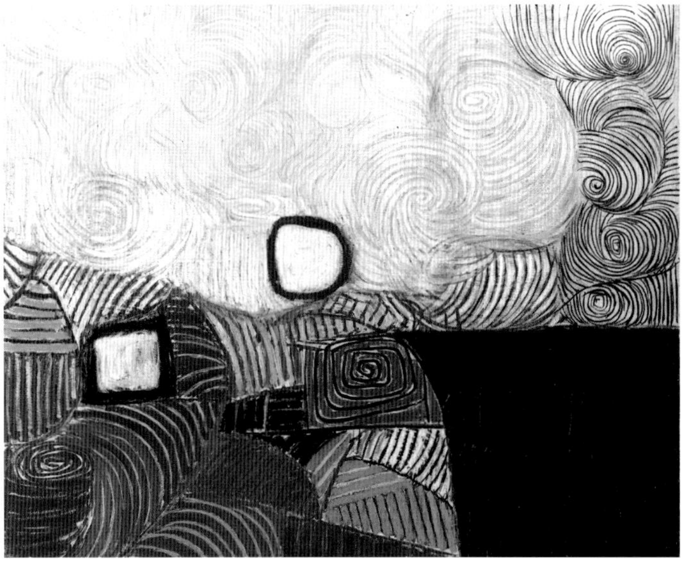

(above)
Victor Pasmore
Construction
1957

(above right)
Victor Pasmore
Collage
1950
24 x 16 in.
collage and photostat
collection: David Lewis

(right)
Victor Pasmore
Spiral Motif in Green, Violet, Blue and Gold: The Coast of the Inland Sea
1950
32 x 39½ in.
collection: Tate Gallery, London

among others. Exhibitions of extra-large paintings were planned. The Skylon became a symbol, not simply of a nation's resurgence, but of art and technology soaring together. New art galleries opened, with new dealers and artists. New names included Jankl Adler, Nicolas de Staël, Eduardo Paolozzi, William Turnbull, and William Scott. American artists, unknown before the war, entered the London scene, Francis, Kline, Gorky, Pollock, Rothko, and de Kooning.

The Institute of Contemporary Arts became a force. An early ICA exhibition, 'Aspects of Form', attempted to show that the forms and rhythms explored by artists have their roots as deeply in nature as they do in aesthetics, and suggested that the human need for aesthetics has its roots indeed in biological necessity. The sense that science and art are really two aspects of universal laws of form encouraged Herbert Read, in his preface to the book on the exhibition, to write about the mid-point in the twentieth century as 'an exciting moment in the history of human thought, and the paths that lead forward are bright with intellectual promise'.[11]

This same message was carried by the exhibition, 'Growth and Form', organised by Richard Hamilton as a tribute to D'Arcy Thompson, also at the ICA and opened by Le Corbusier. This exhibition demonstrated how forms in nature evolve from the endless striving for symmetry and balance in a world of change and challenge. As Thompson wrote, 'in every symmetrical system every deformation that tends to destroy the symmetry is complemented by an equal and opposite deformation that tends to restore it. In each deformation, positive and negative work is done.'

My range of friendships widened. Travel became easier. On visits to London I saw a lot of the painter-writer Patrick Heron and his wife Delia, and the sculptor Robert Adams and his wife Pat. Through Pat Heron I met the painter Roger Hilton, who at that time was quite unknown, and through Robert Adams I met the constructive artists Kenneth and Mary Martin. Roger Hilton, Willie and I travelled to Paris together. I met Brancusi, Arp, Corneille, Domela, Vantongerloo, Giacometti, Antoine Pevsner, and Stephen Gilbert. Constant (Nieuwenhuys) stayed with us in St Ives. I began writing for publications in other countries, including *Aujourd'hui*, *Domus*, *Casabella*, *Aut/Aut*, and *Arte Visive*.

In 1950 Barbara filled the British Pavilion at the Venice Biennale with sculptures, and I wrote the introduction to the catalogue. Through Barbara and Ben I got to know Herbert Read, the historian John Summerson, and E.C. (Peter) Gregory, a director of Lund Humphries. Each of these became important to me as my life began to turn more and more towards architecture. Willie Sandberg, the director of the Stedelijk Museum in Amsterdam, and the French writer Michel Seuphor encouraged my interest in de Stijl and Mondrian. I travelled to Holland to research Mondrian's earlier years, and subsequently wrote a short book on Mondrian, and another on Brancusi. In Utrecht I spent time with the architect Gerrit Rietveld in Mrs Schroeder's house.

In 1950 I met Victor Pasmore on his visit to St Ives to work with Ben on an exhibition at the Penwith. It was at the time of his spiral paintings and drawings. I remember watching him sitting on the black rocks of Gwithian, drawing the surges of the sea in black ink as bold and energetic spirals, and noticing how the white paper of his notebook became an equally powerful actor in his drawing with every additional robust black line he drew.

I began visiting him in his studio in Blackheath. His work was evolving from natural imagery to pure abstraction, as though he was laying bare the formal structures underlying natural appearances. He had followed a sequence of steps in painting, through Post-Impressionism, Pointillism and into Cubism. He made a series of Cubist collages, carefully organised with an underlying formal geometry of planes and textures. On one of these visits I bought one of these from him, which I still have on the wall of my dining-room here in the United States. He was just beginning to make constructions, feeling vindicated by Moholy-Nagy's *The New Vision* and by a book published in 1948 by an American artist, Charles Biederman, *Art as the Evolution of Visual Knowledge*. Biederman forecast that painting, which can only simulate space, would be replaced by constructions which project the colour-space language of art directly into the real space of architecture.

It seemed to me that Victor was never quite convinced about this. His constructions, although they were made of wood and plastic, always struck me as rectilinear paintings in three dimensions, rather than as architecture. I noticed that building designs in the late 1920s and early 1930s by Mies van der Rohe treated glass as a thermal but invisible box to be penetrated by planes as though it was non-

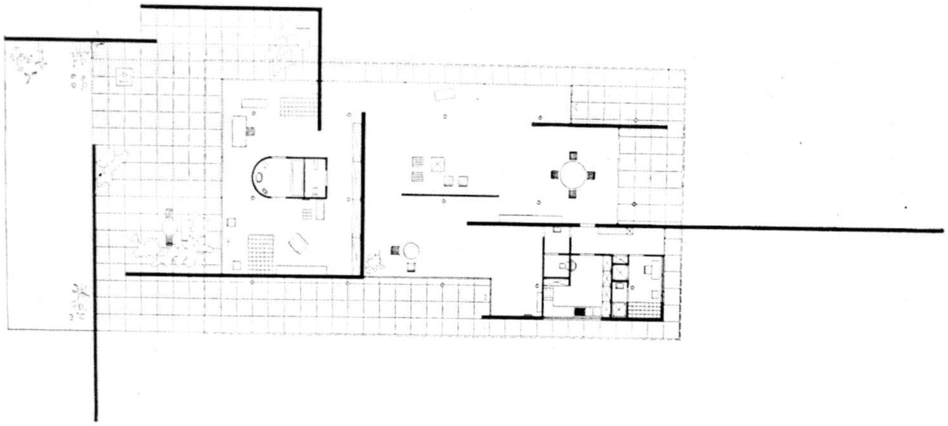

Mies van der Rohe
Plan for a house
1930
Berlin Building Exposition

existent. For example, the plan of the house Mies designed for the Berlin Exposition in 1931 could easily have been translated into a Pasmore-like relief in the 1950s. However, the colours Pasmore used (maroon, magenta, ivy green) seemed to be subject more to the internal demands of the relief as it was being made than to intellectual theory. Like Ben's colours, they seemed to be peculiarly English, related to the English landscape and to English lyrical traditions, particularly Turner. Nevertheless they carried Victor forward, not into building design but into collaborations with architects.

I had spoken with Rietveld about the use of colour in architecture, and about how colour could be integrated with the planes of walls and ceilings to define their spatial interrelationships. Primary colours plus black and white were of course the most powerful, and therefore the sharpest ones to use.

Difficult questions arose. Was architecture a sculpture for living in? Were constructions of the kind Victor was making part of an evolution, and destined to merge art with building design? Would artists become architects, and art disappear?

Questions such as these – and many others relating to the social roles of architecture – filled the conversations that Peter Stead and I had in the first half of 1956, culminating in my decision to enrol as a first-year student of architecture at Leeds College of Art, and become part of the inauguration of the Basic Course.

Well, my dear Ricky, that's it. You asked me to tell you how I got to Leeds. Don't say I didn't warn you that it would be a long story. Now it's my turn to ask you: how did you get to Leeds?

With love to Muriel
Yours
David

1. *Circle*, edited by J.L. Martin, Ben Nicholson and Naum Gabo. Faber & Faber, London 1937.
2. Abstraction-Création: an international group of abstract artists, centred in Paris, who published a journal in 1933, a forerunner of *Circle*.
3. *Axis*, edited by Myfanwy Piper, 1933–7.
4. *Unit One: The Modern Movement in Architecture, Painting and Sculpture*, introduction by Herbert Read, 1934.
5. Margaret Gardiner, *Barbara Hepworth: A Memoir*, Salamander Press, London 1982 (Reprinted by Lund Humphries, London 1994).
6. A.S. Eddington, *The Nature of the Physical World*, the Gifford Lectures at the University of Edinburgh, Cambridge University Press, 1927.
7. Ben Nicholson, 'Alfred Wallis', in *Horizon*, vol.vii, no.37, January 1943, p.51.
8. Barbara Hepworth moved from Chy-an-Kerris to Trewyn Studio in the heart of St Ives in 1951 when her marriage to Ben Nicholson broke up. The walled studio, with its exotic garden largely planted by the composer Priaulx Rainier, is now a museum administered by the Tate Gallery, St Ives.
9. Ben Nicholson occupied 5 Porthmeor Studios in 1951. This was a group of studios owned by the Arts Council. Terry Frost occupied no.4. Ben Nicholson's studio was subsequently occupied briefly by Francis Bacon, and then by Patrick Heron.
10. J.L. (now Sir Leslie) Martin, introduction to the catalogue of the *Circle* exhibition at Kettle's Yard Gallery, Cambridge 1982.
11. *Aspects of Form*, edited by Lancelot Law Whyte, Lund Humphries, London 1951

Letter 3 Eric Atkinson to David Lewis

June 1998

Dear David

Thank you for your letter asking me about the creation of the Basic Course at Leeds College of Art and how Harry Thubron came to choose Leeds as the proving ground for such a radical experiment in British art education. There is no simple answer as so much that happened was the result of chance meetings during a period in which the time was ripe for an explosive change of direction after the stagnation of World War Two. Before the war almost all art students were taught in ateliers where they received instruction from a master painter, sculptor or designer and where they faithfully reproduced work in the manner of their tutors while struggling to achieve their own individual style. The young men coming back from the war were eager to resume their education but their experiences had taught them to expect more from an education system that had not seen many changes since the 1920s.

As I told you in my previous letter I had been a student of Harry Thubron's at West Hartlepool College of Art from 1946 until I went into the Army in 1947. By the time I was demobbed in 1950 Harry had been appointed as Head of Fine Art at Sunderland College of Art and I, with Harry's encouragement, was on my way to London with a scholarship to the Royal Academy Schools. We did keep in touch and when Harry came down to London to visit the Galleries he usually stayed with me in my 'digs' in Brockley. I remember visiting the Matthiesen Gallery with him to see the Nicholas de Staël exhibition and the tremendous impact it made on both of us. That same year I was part of a three-man exhibition at the Irving Gallery in Leicester Square which was opened by Maurice Chevalier, and Harry, an avid fan, travelled down from Sunderland for the opening.

During the summer of 1953 a pivotal meeting took place in the North Yorkshire fishing village of Staithes. My aunt and uncle ran a small guest house, bakery and cafe in Staithes but behind the bakehouse was a large studio that had been used by Dame Laura Knight. I had gone there to work during the summer and invited Harry to join me. Maurice de Sausmarez, Professor of Fine Art at Leeds University, was also staying at my aunt's with a group of students. Harry and Maurice had known each other before the war when they were studying at the Royal College of Art. Maurice and I had both been invited by the Contemporary Art Society to submit a painting for their exhibition 'Figures in their Setting' at the Tate Gallery and were working on preliminary drawings, and Harry was completing a full-length seated portrait of me that he planned to send to the Royal Academy Summer Exhibition. (This portrait was accepted by the Academy but when it was returned Harry began to tinker with it, chopping large chunks off the sides and base but thanks to my wife the head and shoulders were rescued and still hang in our dining-room in London, Ontario!)

In between working sessions the discussions revolved round the opportunities for expanding and developing the art school curriculum. Maurice was very involved in planning new programmes for the Fine Art Department at Leeds University and Harry felt that he was just marking time at Sunderland repeating the same routine that had occupied him at West Hartlepool. These animated dialogues were the seeds that later germinated into the Leeds Basic Course. At that time all the art schools in Britain were subject to the National Diploma in Design, known as the NDD. Qualifying students submitted their work to be assessed in London by an appointed panel of examiners, largely Royal Academicians. During the 1950s James Fitton RA was chief examiner. Students were encouraged to imitate work by artists such as Walter Sickert or Victor Pasmore. Dark interiors, Euston Road style still lifes or romantic English landscapes. Art college curriculums completely ignored the revolution that had happened in European art during the first half of the twentieth century … a condition bolstered by the isolation of Britain from Europe during World War Two. But the Festival of Britain in 1951 opened a floodgate of new thinking about art and design. Major exhibitions of modern art were put on, Pasmore astonished everyone with his huge black and white abstract mural 'Spiral Motif' for the Regatta Restaurant on London's South Bank. For me, the change in Pasmore's work occurred in his painting 'The Inland Sea' in which he suppressed figuration in favour of revealing its abstract structure.

I first got to know Pasmore through Alan Reynolds and the Redfern Gallery in 1953 and I in turn introduced Victor to Harry Thubron. When Victor was appointed as Head of Painting at Newcastle, Harry invited Victor and Wendy, his wife, to run weekend workshops at Sunderland and that is when Harry really began to change and develop his views on art education. Pasmore's ideas about painting became a kind of mirror that reflected the changes in basic art education in Britain. As Victor himself said in his address at

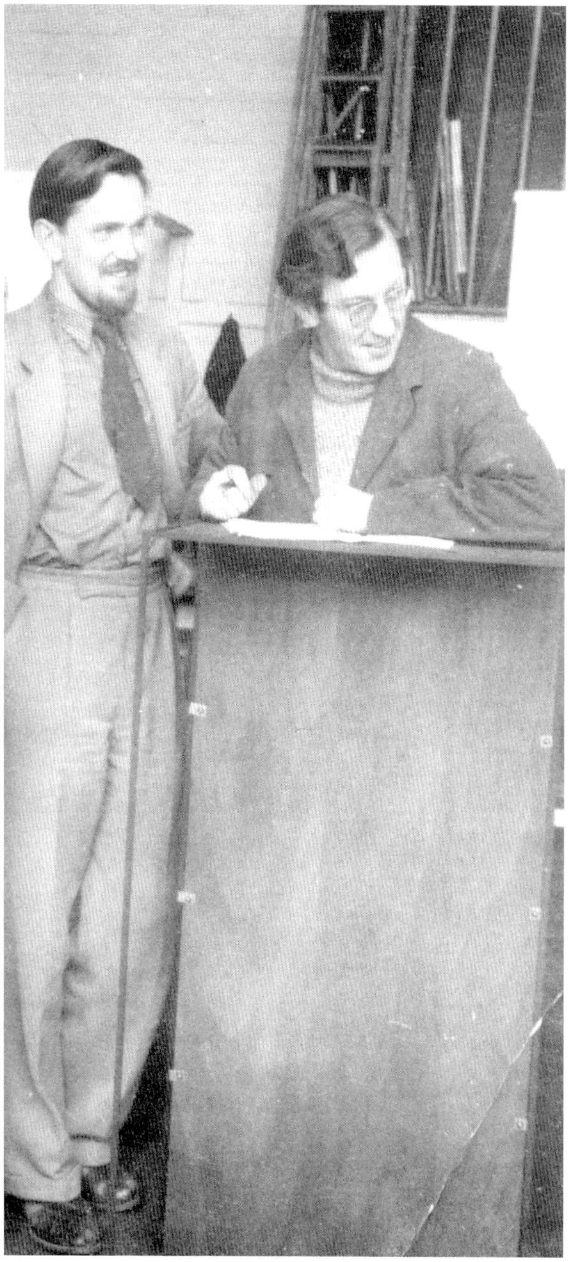

Ricky Atkinson and Harry Thubron
at Leeds College of Art, 1957

Bretton Hall in June 1993 when the 'Victor Pasmore Studios' were opened, 'in trying to meet this requirement in painting I turned to the example of the Bauhaus in Germany. The Bauhaus was not an Academy of Fine Art but an arts and crafts school in which diverse trades were taught. To unify this diversity a central course of studies was established under the direction of fine artists which included Paul Klee and Kandinsky. This course was abstract and as such concerned itself solely with the idea of "basic form". When I was appointed as Head of the School of Painting in the Fine Art Department of the University of Durham at Newcastle in 1954 I felt that something like this was necessary in Fine Art Schools now that painting and sculpture were becoming increasingly interdependent. In other words a new objective standpoint seemed to be necessary which was intrinsic. To meet these requirements I established an experimental course of studies in the painting school in which students were asked to develop independent images from basic visual forms and basic constructive processes and I reinforced this by holding large exhibitions of their work in the University Art Gallery.'

During 1954 several fateful meetings took place. John Wood, the enterprising Director of Further Education for the North Riding of Yorkshire, took his daughter Rachel to enrol as a painting student at Sunderland College of Art and met Harry Thubron. John Wood subsequently invited Harry to direct an experimental art programme for young people at the Joseph Rowntree Secondary School at New Earswick in York. He later introduced Harry to Herbert Read who was to become one of the most vigorous champions of the Basic Course and Harry renewed his acqaintance with Tom Hudson. Tom was Head of Painting at Lowestoft School of Art where my wife was also teaching. Tom had known Harry for some time and when Tom was demobbed from the Army and returned to resume his studies at Sunderland College of Art, Harry had assisted him in getting into the Courtauld Institute in London.

In February I had my first one-man show at the Redfern Gallery in Cork Street in London and Harry came down from Sunderland to pass judgement and we both went off to spend the weekend in Lowestoft. The main topic of conversation during that weekend revolved round the state of education in the art schools and how the necessary changes could be effected. How could students be given the basic grammar to understand abstraction and how could they

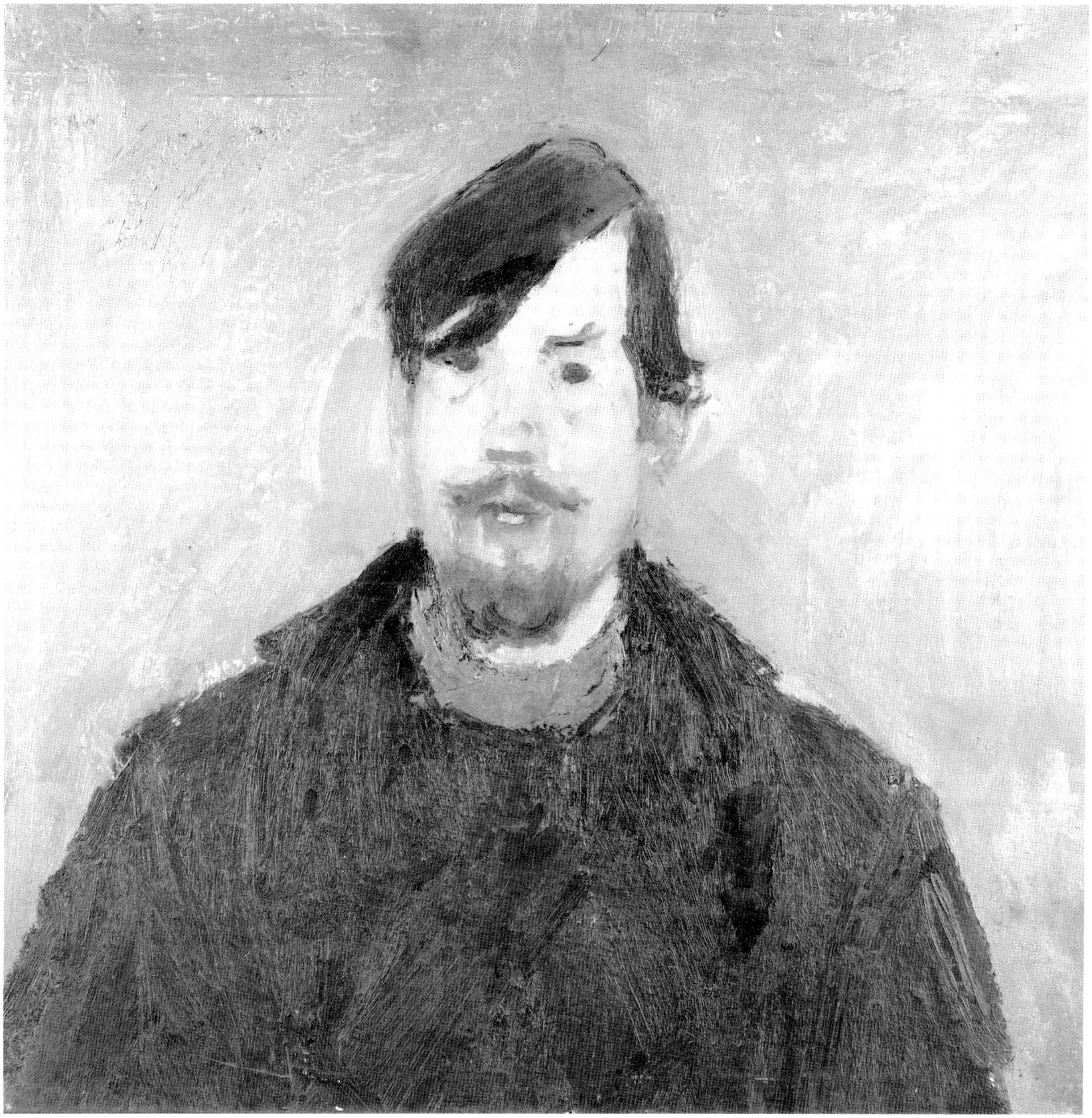

Harry Thubron
Ricky Atkinson
1953
27 x 21 in.
oil on board
collection: Muriel Atkinson

acquire the skills to deal with the new developments in technology without losing the expertise that was already at their disposal? Later that year Harry introduced some of his ideas to a group of teachers at a Summer School organised by John Wood in Scarborough. It was the first of many courses he was to direct there over the next few years with Wendy and Victor Pasmore and Tom Hudson. Early in 1955 Francis Helps retired as Head of Painting at Leeds College of Art and the Principal, Edward Pullee, with the support of Maurice de Sausmarez, Chairman of the Advisory Board, appointed Harry Thubron to fill the vacancy.

By the end of1955 my five-year studentship at the Royal Academy Schools had ended and I was actively searching for a teaching position. Two Scottish painters, Anne Redpath and William Gillies, who had liked my show at the Redfern Gallery suggested I should apply for a post at Edinburgh College of Art and I had been requested to present myself for an interview. The week before I was to leave for Scotland a telegram arrived from Harry asking me to apply for a vacancy in the School of Painting at Leeds the next day. Armed with my portfolio I travelled up to Leeds for the interview assuming that if I was unsuccessful I could carry on to Edinburgh as planned. Eric Taylor, the former Head of the Design School, had just been appointed to replace Edward Pullee (who had been appointed at Leicester College of Art) as Principal and so it was he who offered me the position as Lecturer in the School of Painting. After a brief telephone conversation with my wife (after all, Edinburgh was her home town!) I accepted. Three days later I found myself on the way to Wrea Head, near Scarborough to teach an extended workshop with Maurice de Sausmarez and a few weeks later I began teaching at Leeds College of Art ... it was the summer of 1956.

In 1956 Leeds College of Art was separated into five main schools – Painting, Sculpture, Design, Architecture and Teacher Training. Harry's objective was to organise an introductory course in primary principles that would gather students from all disciplines into an integrated whole. Although his initial programme did not encounter outright opposition there were several members of the Faculty whose reaction was lukewarm and uncooperative. Harry and I stayed with Maurice and his wife during that first difficult term and it was their support and encouragement that sustained us. The long and often heated discussions around their supper table which brought together so many enthusiasts from the University and from the City reinforced our belief that with sufficient persistence we could change the system. Frank Chippendale, Head of the School of Architecture, was an enthusiastic advocate for change and it was because of his willingness to participate that students were motivated to enrol in the School of Architecture. Norbert Lynton transferred from the Architecture School and undertook responsibilty for the History of Art Programme. Do you recall the lecture series on 'Modern Art' you gave at the City Art Gallery, David? These helped to finance your studies in architecture and you moved easily between the role of student by day and lecturer by night. These lectures, delivered to a standing-room only audience of students, faculty and interested members of the public opened my eyes to the paucity of my own art education. They sent me scuttling off to the library to read everything I could lay my hands on about Mondrian, Brancusi and the de Stijl movement in an attempt to fill in some of the gaps in my own knowledge. By the close of 1956 Tom Hudson had resigned from Lowestoft and accepted a position at Leeds where he assumed special responsibility for the Machine Shop.

Tom, Harry and I rented an apartment in Headingley initially just for the working week ... weekends were to be spent with our families. 'Raleigh Mews', conveniently situated opposite a fish and chip shop and adjoining a second-hand furniture store was accommodation at its most basic. What would our small group of champions think of the three prophets of the New Image living in a cold-water flat with no bath and an outdoor privvy? Baths (and often suppers) were generously provided by Terry and Kath Frost and by June and Frank Lisle who all lived close by. At this time Terry was Gregory Fellow in Painting and Frank was teaching at Bradford College of Art so supper was inevitably followed by long debates on the progress of the Basic Course.

During this gestation period the National Diploma in Design examinations were still in place and our students were expected to meet the National standards. My role was to ensure that they did exactly that. I became the bridge or liaison between the 'old' system and the 'new' one ... teaching drawing for the Basic Course students and directing the part-time programmes. Some of our most enthusiastic supporters were enrolled in part-time programmes. Benefactors like the late Rose and Bernard Gillinson opened their

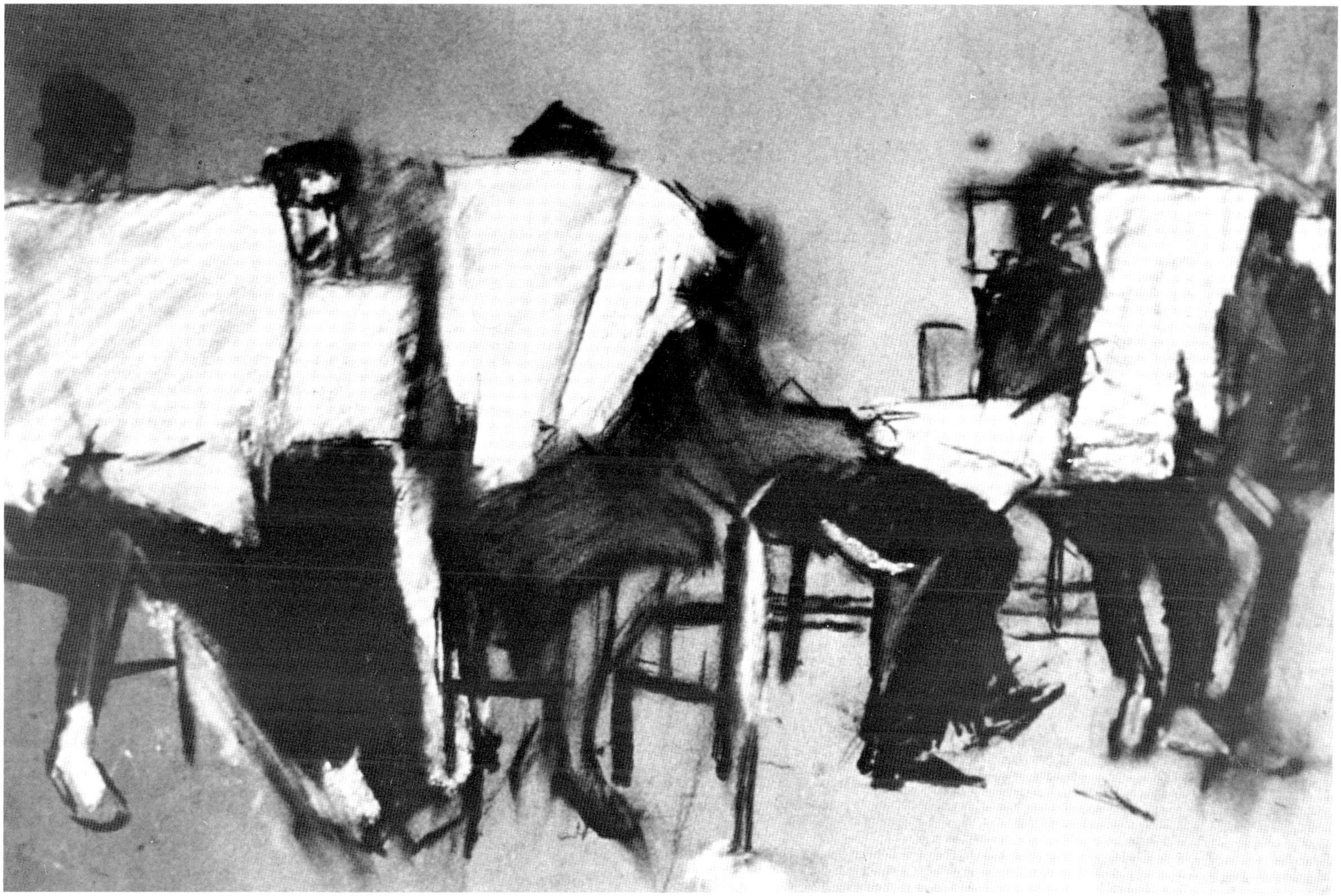

Eric Atkinson
Teaching drawing and figure composition, Leeds College of Art
1957
chalk and charcoal drawing
collection: Bretton Hall Archive, Wakefield

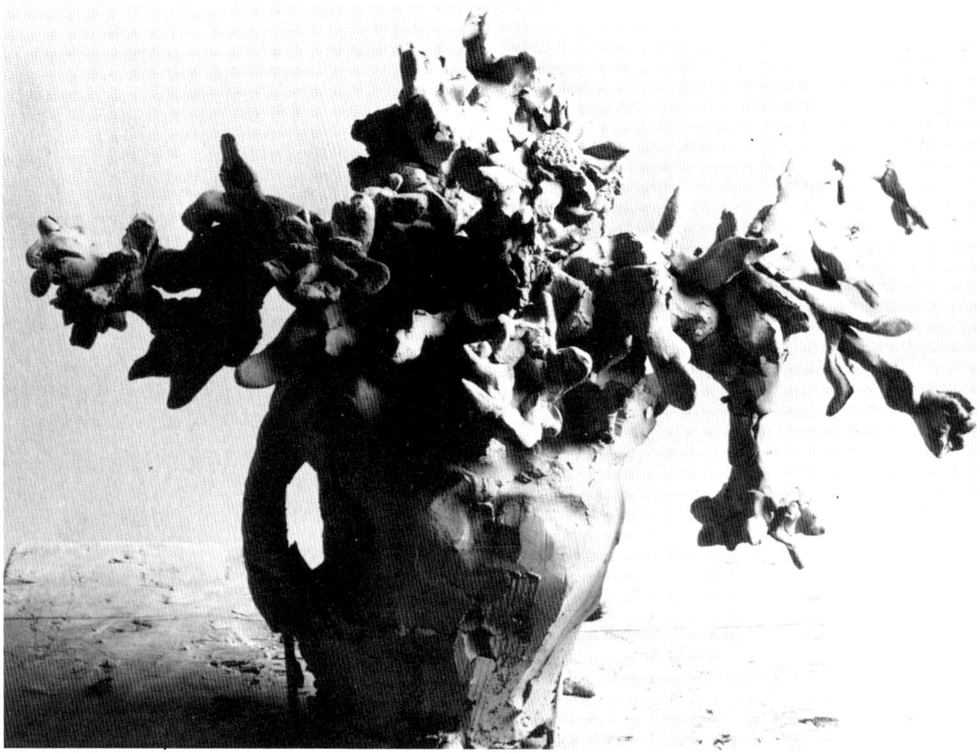

Student's project
Still Life, Flowers
1956
over life-size
modelled in clay
Basic Course, Leeds College of Art
collection:
Bretton Hall Archive, Wakefield

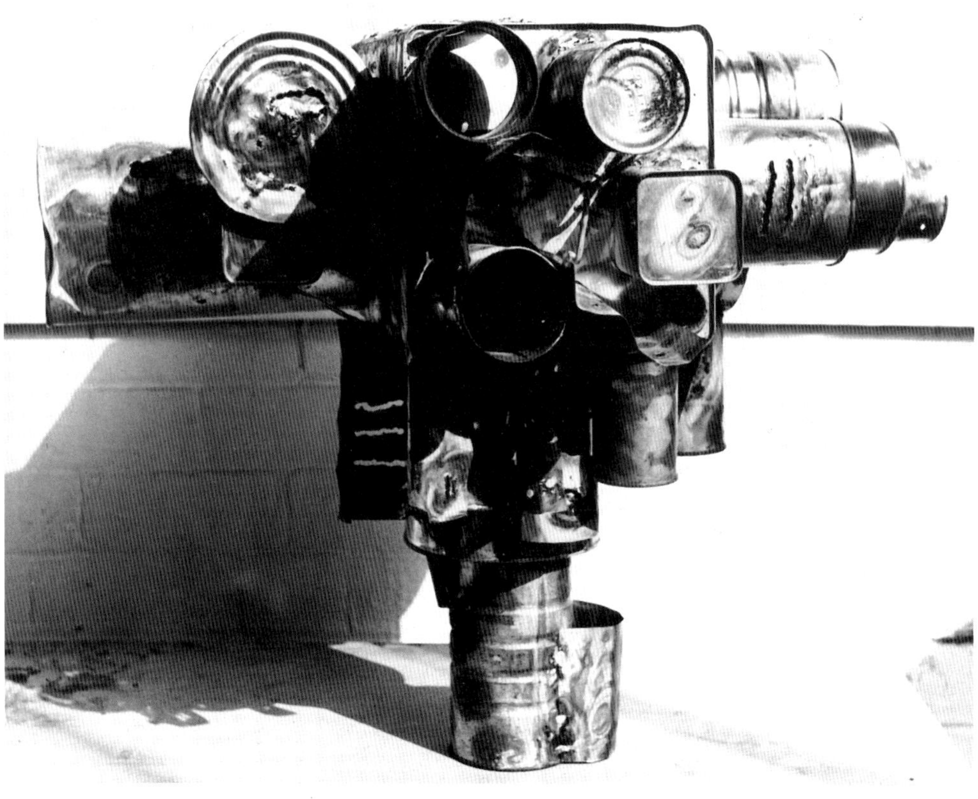

Tin-can sculpture
1956–57
Student's welding project
Basic Course,
Leeds College of Art
collection:
Bretton Hall Archive, Wakefield

homes to visiting artists, writers and politicians and by doing so helped to spread the word among those interested in the Leeds 'Experiment'. Throughout those early years we seized every opportunity to direct workshops and summer schools all over the North of England ably assisted by support from John Wood who had by then left the North Riding Education Authority and become Director of Further Education for Leeds. On one never to be forgotten occasion Harry and I arrived to direct a weekend course for the Northern Federation of the Arts at Lumley Castle in County Durham. We parked Harry's van at the front door and began to unload our cases and equipment only to be met by a very dignified butler who told us in no uncertain terms that we had come to the wrong castle and were expected at Lambton Castle across the river! We also ventured into South Wales and ran several highly sucessful programmes at the Barry Summer School under the direction of Leslie Moore, the ebullient Director of Further Education for Glamorgan. Often there would be vociferous opposition to the ideas proposed in the Basic Course. Teachers were especially resistant to change and did not welcome any proposed alterations to the 'status quo'; at one point we were branded as a 'nest of communists' … all because we advocated team teaching! Evidently cooperative teaching projects were viewed with deep suspicion and we were doubly damned because we also co-opted the Gregory Fellows in Painting and Sculpture (Terry Frost, Alan Davie and Hubert Dalwood) to teach at the College.

In 1959 the ICA Gallery in London mounted an exhibition 'The Developing Process' which showcased the work of students at King's College in Newcastle upon Tyne (the Fine Art Department of Durham University) administered by Victor Pasmore and Richard Hamilton and students from the Leeds Basic Course supervised by Harry Thubron, Tom Hudson, Terry Frost, Hubert Dalwood, Alan Davie and myself. Shortly after this Tom Hudson decided to leave Leeds and accepted the position of Director of Foundation Studies at Leicester College of Art.

John Wood organised an exchange exhibition between Leeds College of Art and the Werkkunstschule in Dortmund, West Germany in 1961. Sir Herbert Read wrote the foreword for the Leeds catalogue *Malerie und Plastik aus Leeds*. This initial exchange generated further visits between artists and educators from both cities. Gradually as more people began to understand what we were trying to achieve visitors from other schools began to appear on the doorstep at Leeds to look round. The British Council added Leeds to its itinerary for educators and artists from overseas and our first graduates were accepted for postgraduate courses in London. Of that first group of graduates in painting from the Basic Course in Leeds three postgraduates who were studying at the Slade School of Fine Art won prestigious awards in 1962 for sculpture: Chris Sanderson won the Prix de Rome, George Hainsworth won the Gulbenkian Scholarship in Sculpture and Barry Ward won the Abbey Minor Scholarship.

Encouraged by the success of our graduates and by the acceptance of our peers we embarked on a second Leeds Winter School in 1963 unaware that the group who had converged on Leeds in 1956 with such high hopes was to scatter once more and forge new allegiances.

Letter 4 Eric Atkinson to Norbert Lynton

Dear Norbert

I have just re-read the moving tribute you wrote for Victor Pasmore ... a sensitive appreciation of him as an artist and as a personal friend. Your recollections of your time as a student at a summer school directed by Wendy and Victor at Scarborough reminded me of the time we spent as colleagues at Leeds College of Art during the turbulent years of the first Basic Course. We recently received a charming letter from Wendy recalling the happy time she and Victor spent with us in Canada during the early 1970s. Wendy aided and abetted Muriel's purchase of a St Bernard puppy and she remembered Victor's horrified comment: 'Ricky ... look at the size of his feet!'

The Basic Course was an attempt to encourage students to discover their creative selves ... and as students living in the modern world they had to discover the past in terms of their contemporary world. This led to a unique way of teaching Art History (certainly unique in the 1950s) by going backwards in time so that everything was relevant to the exercises being developed in the studio. Could you share some of your own memories of that time?

The studio exercises were initially conceived to help students break free from the traditional transfer of skills method of teaching. They were basically an investigation of:

Mark
Line
Form and families of form
Colour and intensity of colour
Positive and negative
Space explored in plaster, wood and metal
Construction (both building up and carving down)
Materials (collage, assemblage and mixed media)
Machine shop practice
Relationship of all these components to one another.

As you may remember there was no set or structured curriculum. Harry Thubron adamantly refused to have anything written down because he felt it would promote academicism and stifle creative invention. No one knew (least of all the faculty involved) where these explorations would lead us. Anything and everything was possible in such a fluid situation that changed almost daily and developed organically and relied so heavily on random chance!

My task on the faculty was to act as a bridge between the old atelier system and the new explorations being developed in the studio. Never an easy task to be caught with a foot in each camp! Students however had to pass their National Diploma in Design examinations, or the whole of our experimental project would have to be shelved ... something that would have delighted a great many cynics.

Do you remember Harry asking with a wicked twinkle in his eye, 'What colour is an elephant's breath?' Or Terry Frost appearing one soft summer morning with an armful of brilliantly vivid roses and geraniums and asking the class to record 'forty-two reds ... every one different!'? Harry had borrowed Terry's copy of his cherished bible – a small and quite rare book on the geometry of perspective, and Terry never succeeded in recovering it. He finally gave up in his attempts when Harry told him that it 'was lost behind the grand piano' – and everyone knew that Harry didn't possess a piano, grand or otherwise!

I have had some correspondence with George Hainsworth who is still teaching in Leeds. We met him in Leeds City Art Gallery some years ago during one of our trips to Yorkshire. His reminiscences about his years at Leeds as a student and later as a young faculty member are very interesting and his observations on the viability of implementing such a programme in the light of today's educational climate are illuminating.

We read a review of a 'come-back' disc released by Eric Burden recently and that conjured up a few memories of the first Leeds College of Art Ball held at the Leeds Town Hall at which 'Eric Burden & the Animals' provided the music. Harry, in charge of the decorations and lighting, plunged the whole building (and most of central Leeds) into darkness, obliterating our vision of you dressed as Mephistopheles and Maurice de Sausmarez masquerading as Wyatt Earp!

Hoping to see you the next time I'm in London.
All the best,
Ricky and Muriel

Letter 5 David Lewis to Norbert Lynton

Dear Norbert

As you know, I was an odd duck in the Basic Course. I was thirty-four years old, and everyone else was eighteen or nineteen, and straight out of high school. There must have been sixty of us students in the College of Art lecture room promptly at 9 am on that first day of classes. We were all in our glad rags, sitting silent and respectful in rows in the raked auditorium. The boys wore jackets and ties, and the girls had skirts and blouses.

Eric Taylor, head of the College, came in and stood at the lectern to welcome us. I remember him as a man of slight build, with a little pile of curly brown hair on top of a long face. He told us we were going to be part of an experiment in education, a new departure; but he didn't elaborate. Then he introduced various faculty members. The only one I knew was Chips. It's always curious what things stick in one's memory while the rest disappears. I remember you being presented to us as an architectural historian who would also lecture on the history of art, and you stood up, young and pink-faced and self-conscious; and I remember some of the architecture faculty, Peter Savage, and a dowdy-looking woman called Mrs Blackwell, and Alec Lacy who wore a spotted bow tie.

Then we were all told to go upstairs to the big studio on the third floor. What a splendid room that was, with its huge windows and white walls and clean smell of fresh paint! Dutifully we stood in silence behind two rows of long bare tables. Of course we were silent; we knew none of our classmates. Was everyone else as nervous as I was, I wonder, not knowing what to expect?

After a few moments Harry Thubron came in, followed by Ricky Atkinson. Ricky cut a somewhat debonair figure, with his combed black hair and his black goatee and his correct neatly pressed clothes. Harry could hardly have been a greater contrast. He wore a dirty fisherman's jersey under an old tweed jacket, and dirty corduroy trousers, and huge labourer's boots with rubber cleats.

Harry had a way of pouting his lips when he talked, and he spoke rapidly with great enthusiasm. One had to watch out for flying saliva. He made a speech about how the purpose of most schools was to teach you the right way to do things, whether you were learning chemistry or engineering or philosophy – but not here! Oh no! You're in the wrong school, my friends, if you want to learn the right way to draw a plaster cast of a Greek discus thrower! In this school, if you learn anything at all, it'll be to find your own creative self. And his role, said Harry, would be to confront us with a series of challenges and explorations. He spoke about Cubist collages and Kurt Schwitters and about art made with odd pieces of torn newspaper and wallpaper and old bus tickets. He quoted Paul Klee's *Pedagogical Sketchbook*, and the bit about going for a walk with a line. I sometimes wonder what my classmates made of all this.

Of course, it being our first day, each of us had come in with sharpened pencils and sheets of white paper and erasers, and you could tell the architects from the rest by their rulers and celluloid triangles. But Harry strode over to a huge roll of plain newsprint, which he hoisted up and hurled with a resounding bang on to one of the tables as though he was an all-in wrestler, and he began to tear off sheets at great speed, talking all the time, while Ricky handed out the torn-off sheets and thick sticks of charcoal. Because they were ripped off, each sheet of newsprint had a pair of sharp parallel edges and a pair of ragged edges.

'Make a mark,' Harry shouted, spittle flying. 'Any mark! Don't be pussyfoot. Come on, make a really strong mark. Something you can be proud of. Now make another mark. Quick! And now a blob. A big black BLOB. Anywhere! And now find a way of relating those marks, first to one another, and then to the edges of your sheet. Good stuff, charcoal, gets all over your fingers. Don't be afraid of being messy. Now you, and you, and you, and you ...' he said, pointing to cowering students at random. 'Pin up what you've drawn, side by side, on that wall. Start telling us what you did.'

Some students had bold forms. Others were weak, as though they were uncertain or shy. It didn't matter to Harry. 'You! Describe what you did. Describe the relationships you drew. Don't be timid. Say what's on your mind. It's OK. Come on, everyone. Pitch in! Say how you react to what you see.'

I was reminded of sitting quietly behind Victor Pasmore at Gwithian, watching him make a spiral drawing in charcoal of sea-water swirling around the black rocks, and how each black line made the white paper of his sketchbook come more and more alive.

A few days later Alan Davie appeared. He was very thin and had a long wispy beard the colour of autumn grasses. It was nine in the morning, as usual, and we were all at our places behind the tables. 'I want you to make me something beautiful,' he said. He spoke with a Scottish burr. 'I want it

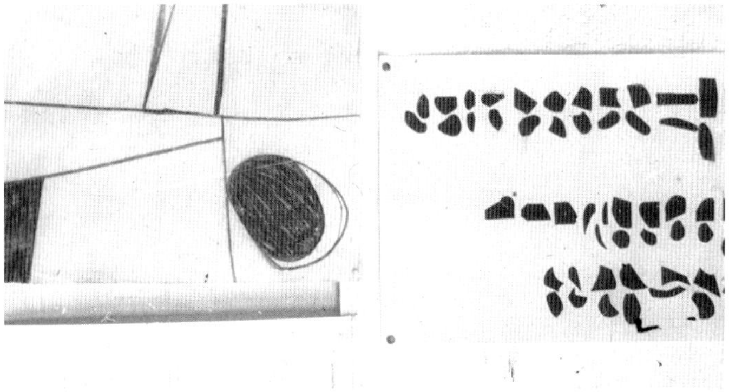

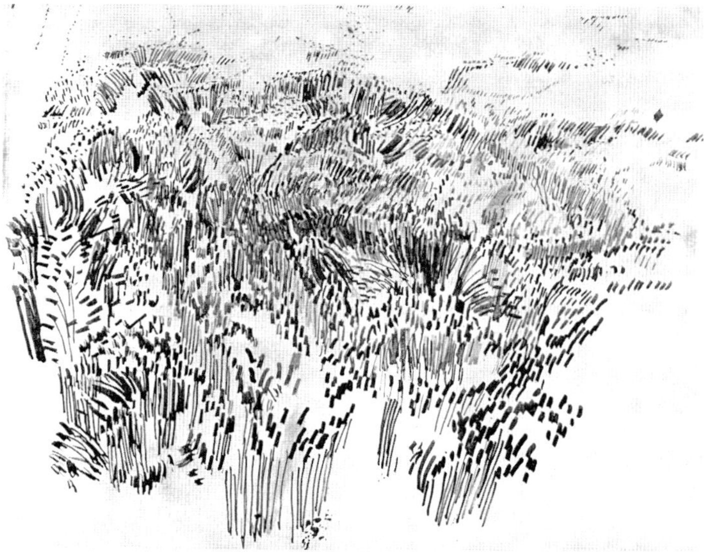

(above)
Harry Thubron
Families of forms
1956
Basic Course, Leeds College of Art

(above right)
Miles McAlinden
Drawing, blobs and lines as landscape
1957
Basic Course, Leeds College of Art

(far right)
Printing and
stamping marks
1956
Basic Course, Leeds College
of Art

(right and below)
Two versions of black and white curves
1956
Basic Course,
Leeds College of Art

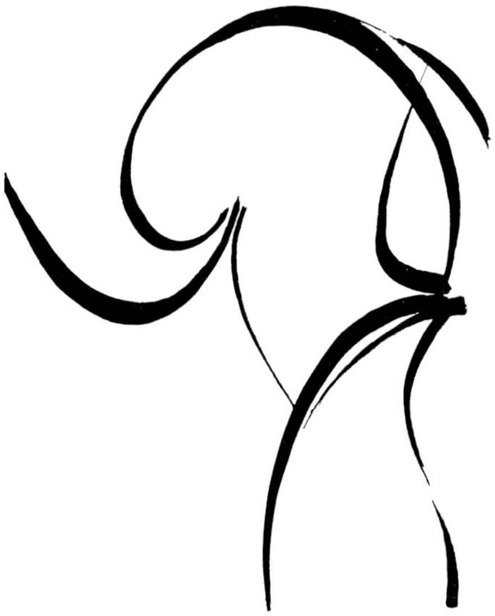

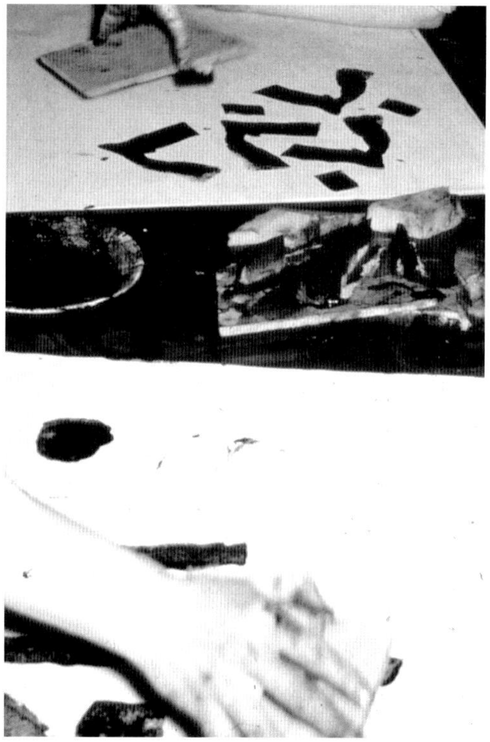

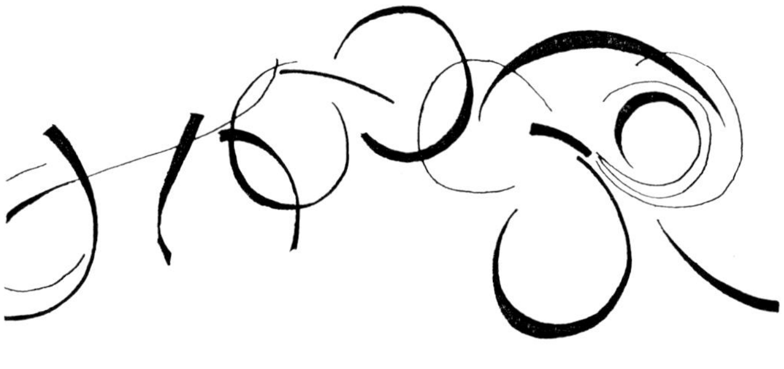

to be very, very beautiful. And I'll be back at five o'clock to collect the results.' The door closed, and he had gone.

We got to work with our pencils and small sheets of white paper. Several of the girls tried to draw a flower from memory. The girl sitting next to me was pretty. I didn't know her name. She had dark wavy hair that tumbled down to a white lace collar. I tried to draw her hair and her collar. We didn't talk to one another; we just worked. We did a lot of delicate shading and a lot of erasing. The results were ghastly.

The following day Alan Davie appeared again at nine in the morning. 'Today,' he said, 'I want you to make me something ugly. Filthy ugly.' And he was gone.

Well, that loosened us up alright. We really let fly. We tore our own huge sheets off that roll of newsprint. We used up the charcoal in no time. We scratched and smeared and stomped on each other's papers. We ripped and we glued and we poured ink and colours and we used white chalk, and we even incorporated string and wire and trash we found at lunchtime in the street, and anything else we could lay our hands on. We must have made a fair amount of noise. We certainly laughed a lot, but no one came in to tell us to calm down. There's nothing like making something ugly to get people laughing and yattering and knowing one another.

The next day several of the girls came in wearing one of their father's old shirts as a smock. I wonder why. Alan Davie made us look at the beautiful things and the ugly things side by side. It was quite an eye opener. It didn't take a genius to discover that the beautiful things were dead as door nails, while the ugly things had the richness of texture and movement and colour and mass and space, all amid the maze of accidents.

Harry told us to get rid of hard pencils and erasers and triangles and other instruments of restriction. Instead we were encouraged to use sponges and house-painters' brushes, and rags and brillo pads, and charcoal and black poster paint. We never knew what to expect from one day to the next. To us students it seemed as though the challenges Harry set us were at random. Looking back, we could see that they weren't.

Then Harry would have us spread out what we'd done on the floor. He would start talking about our exercises, getting more and more excited as he went on, discovering qualities in them that none of us who'd made these things expected. He reserved his cruellest words for examples of timidity or for what he perceived to be a lack of thought or exploration. Sometimes he'd see something in a drawing on the far side of the floor, and in his enthusiasm he'd walk straight across the drawings in between to get there, extrapolating as he went. The soles of his big boots would leave imprints, but we didn't care. It was all part of the spontaneity and discovery that everyone was engaged in.

As he spoke about what we'd done, he'd refer us to the work of various artists. His favourites seemed to be van Gogh, Cézanne, the Cubists, and Schwitters. To my first-year student colleagues most of this was a new, astonishing territory. Harry wanted to make your lectures, Norbert, come alive for us and be relevant to the things we were doing in the studio, and he wanted us to go to the library and to the City Art Gallery, and learn to look. He often referred, as I've said, to Klee's *Pedagogical Sketchbook*, not as a textbook, but as an example of how an immensely inventive person explored, going off in a new direction of graphic language almost every day. He wanted us to invent and explore.

One might say that if Harry represented feeling and spontaneity, another new member of the faculty, Tom Hudson, represented rational construction. Whereas Harry's chief reference was Klee, Tom's was Moholy-Nagy. Through Tom we had a go at designing furniture, made welded metal sculptures, made de Stijl type constructions, and worked in fibreglass.

The Gregory Fellows were frequent visitors. Terry enthralled us by describing the hills and dales of the West Riding with their black stone walls demarcating the meadows – as washing lines with clothes hanging out to dry; and then he showed us his 'washing line' paintings, and you could feel their physical presence. And Nibs Dalwood asked us to make huge balls of plaster of Paris, and use knife-blades and stems of weeds and lengths of furry jute-string and wire and corrugated carboard to press quickly into the surfaces before they dried so we could make lines and gashes of textured tension.

Terry came into the studio with geraniums and leaves and whatnot to demonstrate colour. He asked us to subdivide a board into small squares freehand, and then start with a blob of red. A primary red, in any one of the squares. Now add a tiny bit of yellow, and make another blob next to it. Now a bit more yellow and another blob. And so on, until

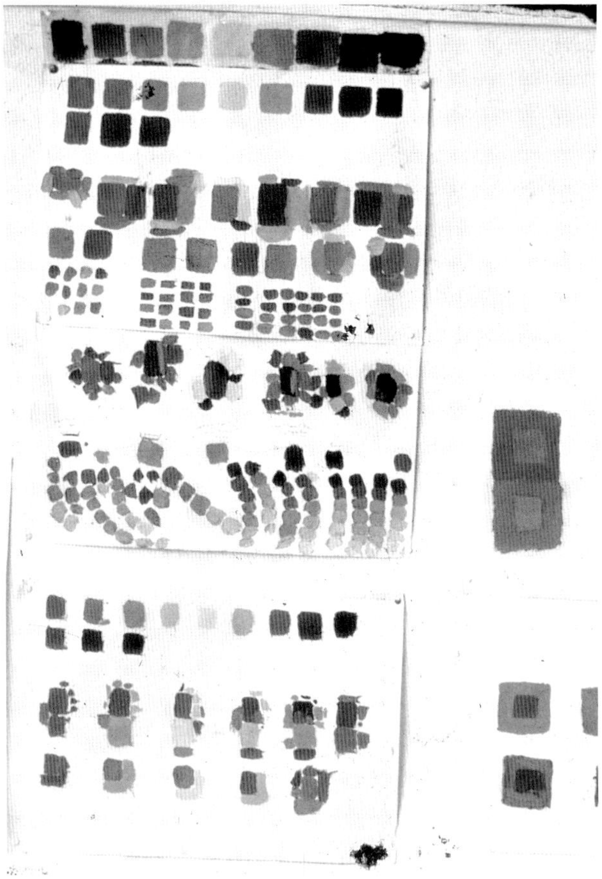

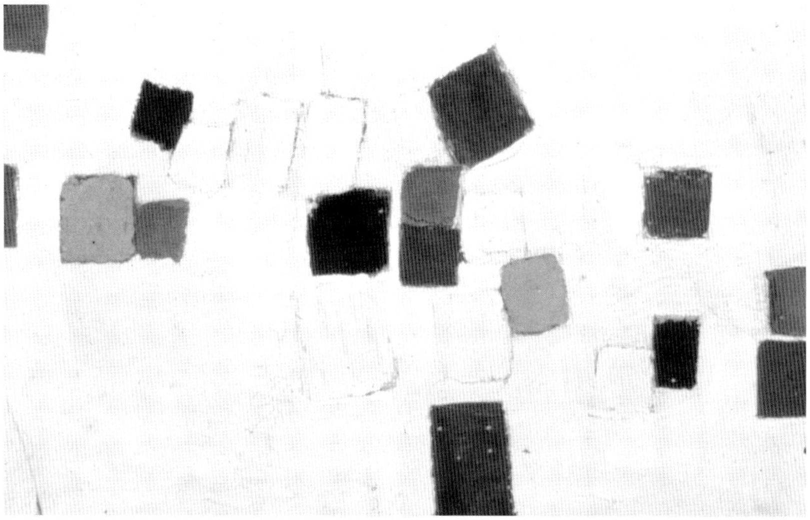

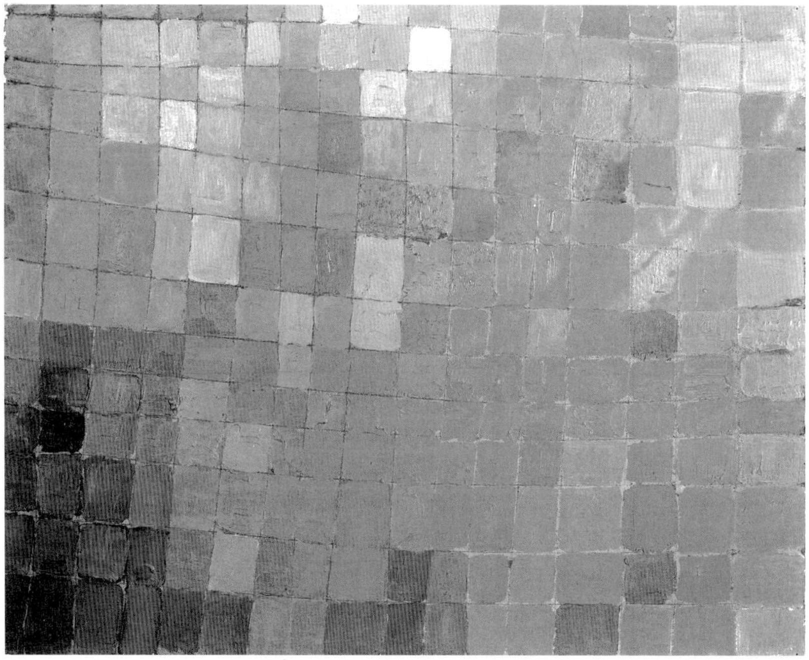

(above)
Harry Thubron and Terry Frost
Colour course
1958
Basic Course, Leeds College of Art

(above right)
Harry Thubron
Colour and space
1958
Basic Course, Leeds College of Art

(right)
Colour exercise in red
1956
Basic Course, Leeds College of Art

we built up red into orange into yellow as a series of blobs called the red-yellow range. Now the red again and add a blue, and build up the red-purple-blue range. And so on. Now take a new board, subdivide it again, and make a composition. But the point was that it wasn't theoretical or academic. None of that prism colour-spectrum stuff. It was all to encourage the personal discovery of colour. There was no right and wrong. If you were colour-blind or had only one eye it didn't matter. Whatever you did you were asked to explain and defend. I still have one of my red paintings.

I regret if I make it sound as if the Basic Course was unstructured. That's not so. It had a structure. But it was important for the students not to see what lay ahead. Harry refused to write out a curriculum. In his view if you articulated the structure of the course that lay ahead you undermined the adventure, the spontaneity, the exploration, the sudden insights of discovery, the creativeness, of both the students and the teachers. But you certainly could see the structure if you looked back. Then it was clear.

We progressed from line to mass, and from two-dimensional mass to three-dimensional mass, from black-and-white to colour. We moved from three-dimensional free-flow forms, not unlike the sculptures of Jean Arp, to forms whose disciplines responded to the uses and shapes of the human body, such as handles for opening and closing doors, and we studied how nature moulded pebbles or grasses or the eyes of insects. We moved from geometric drawings in perspective to building constructions in rectilinear and curving planes, some stationary on the floor, others suspended and in movement, others incorporating kinetic colour.

As I've said, every day was a new adventure, a new challenge. We explored two or three aspects of aesthetic adventure every week – not intellectually from the outside, but from within, by the actual making of it. Sometimes the noise of excitement in the studio was too great for me, and I couldn't concentrate. To get away from the hubbub I would retreat to the floor under one of the tables. There I could work unmolested. I always knew who was in the room from the shoes. Harry had his labourer's boots, Terry had big soft shoes, and Herbert Read's were always small and neat, highly polished and laced with precision.

We had life classes too. This was because the painting and sculpture students had to pass the NDD exams. Ricky was in charge – since he was such a recent graduate from the Royal Academy Schools. One of our models was Eddie O'Donnell, who was a well-known jazz musician. We loved Eddie. He had a sharp tongue for gossip. We'd meet him at the end of the day in one of the pubs for a beer. He was thin as a skeleton and when he modelled he wore a flimsy jock-strap that had the look of a much-used floor rag. We also had a female model who fancied herself in a silk gown as light as gossamer. One day the gown was missing. Harry had mistaken it for a paint cloth. Mostly we drew the models, not in traditional stationary poses, but in movement, and you may recall, Norbert, that we learned from your lectures about Duchamp's nude and Boccioni's bottle.

You also may remember that Jean-Paul Sartre and Existentialism were the rage at that moment; but Eric Taylor for some reason thought of Sartre as a purveyor of smut. He called us in to warn us not to read stuff like that. The same evening a group of us stood on the staircase outside his office and sang an imitation of the music-hall song that went something like this:

> O Monsieur Jean Paul Sartre
> Je ne suis pas votre tartre
> Qui promenade sur le Montmartre....

To this day I don't know if he heard us, or was even in his office at all. His door, somewhat disappointingly, remained firmly shut.

I was not on a scholarship until I got into my fourth year of studies, so I had to earn a modest income by teaching adult education classes in the evenings. I did a series of lectures on modern painting and sculpture, including Mondrian, de Stijl, Brancusi, the Constructivists and others, in the City Art Gallery in Leeds. I also taught at Wakefield Prison, where the secretary of my class was a prisoner by the name of Klaus Fuchs, the physicist who had given atomic secrets to the Russians.

Towards the end of the Basic Course Harry put on an exhibition in our studio. He mixed the work of us students with paintings, sculptures and constructions by Pasmore, Nicholson, Hepworth, Frost, Dalwood, Moore, Davie, Barns-Graham and others. It was a wonderfully alive and revealing show.

However, an embarrassing problem arose when Harry decided to paint all the walls white once again, and the floor black. The floor certainly needed to be painted as we'd

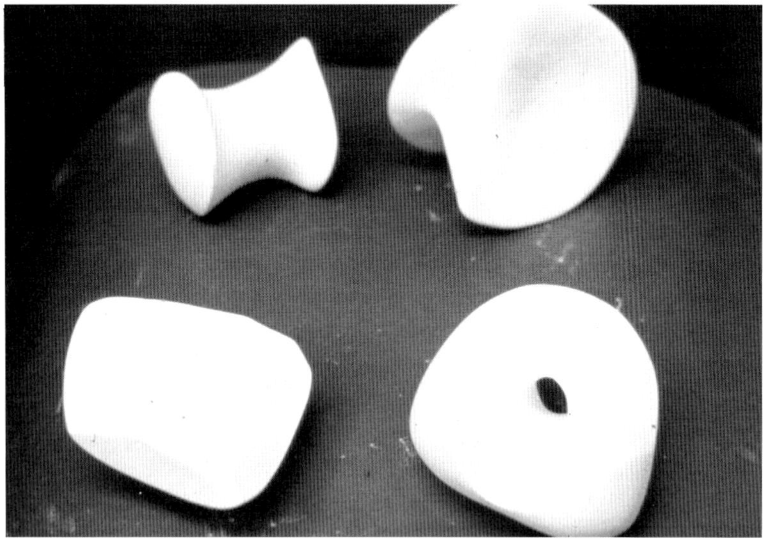

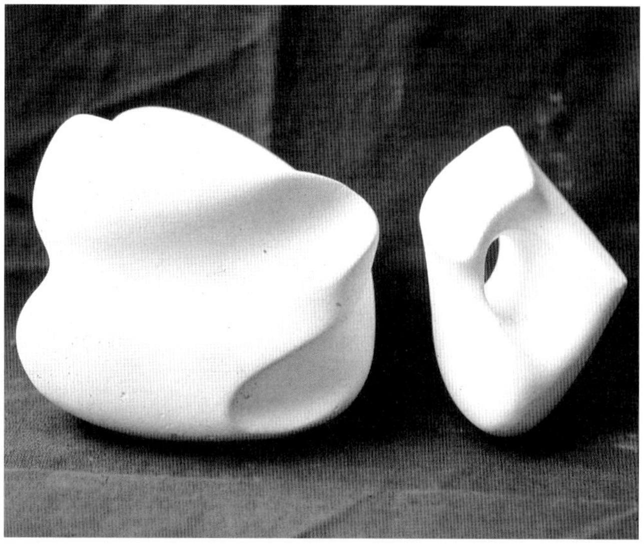

(above)
Basic sculpture for architectural students
Basic Course, Leeds College of Art

(above right)
Hand on sculpture
1957
Basic Course,
Leeds College of Art

(right)
Space frame construction
1957
Basic Course,
Leeds College of Art

(far right)
Aluminium sculpture
1957
casting project run by Hubert Dalwood
Basic Course,
Leeds College of Art

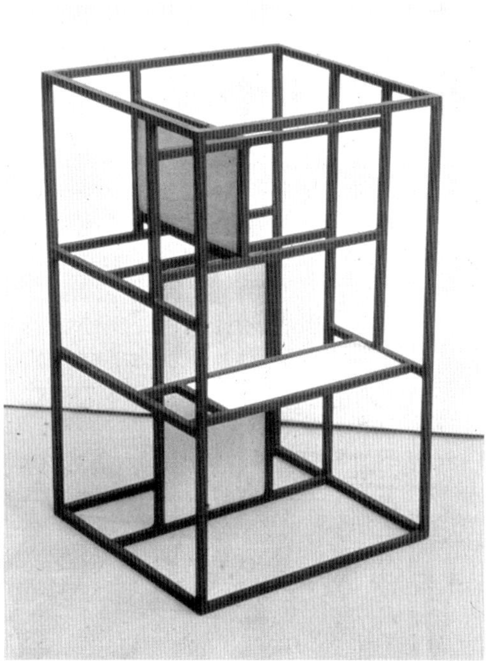

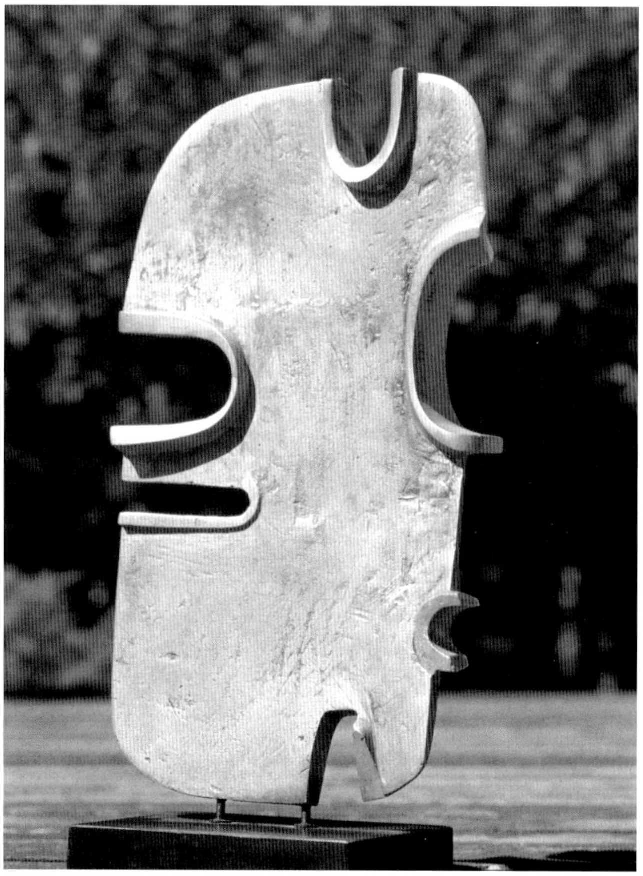

made quite a mess of it in the Basic Course. Characteristically he left the job to the last minute. So he settled on a quick-drying powder paint for the floor. But instead of mixing the powder with water, as the can instructed, he decided to mix it with turpentine to make it dry faster. It certainly did dry fast – so quickly that it reverted in patches to black powder like soot. Perhaps I should go no further than to say that Herbert Read, among other notable guests, came in a neatly pressed light brown suit, and Lady Read came in white shoes.

After my first term of living in a pathetic little upstairs apartment in Chapel Allerton, I found an old warehouse, which I bought for £700. You may remember it. It was in a small village called Little London, outside Leeds. The village had a pub, a couple of small grocery shops, and a sweetshop combined with a post office run by two ancient sisters who wore their hair in plaited coils over their ears like sleeping eels. Every cottage had a front garden filled with flowers, and boxed in by stone walls. In the warehouse I built a kitchen on the ground floor, a bathroom on the second floor, and skylights in the roof on the top floor, and with a group of architecture students I formed a commune, and that's where we lived and worked all the way through architecture school.

Every day the warehouse gang, as we were called, would cram with our drawings and books and models into the pea-green van and drive to Leeds. Ricky and Muriel Atkinson moved into the cottage two doors down from us. We had several guests who came to stay and lectured or performed, Theo Crosby, the architect Jane Drew, the composer Priaulx Rainier, and another composer, Cornelius Cardew. Cardew played compositions on a piano he'd altered with sponges and rubber bands, and included unorthodox 'instruments' such as pop-guns and wooden spatulas for thumping on pot lids, all of which would be conducted by him and performed by us in his concerts.

What did all this have to do with art and architecture? The short answer would be 'everything': but that isn't really an answer at all. Art and architecture are creative activities. They are languages, spoken differently by different people. How the Basic Course at Leeds affected the students who went through it is a question each person has to answer individually.

How did it affect me? Well, let me say, first of all, that I wish that every writer on art and architecture could go through it too, since you learn about using all of the senses (sight, touch, smell, taste, even sound) and about using of all your personal experience of living and all of your intellect simultaneously in making objects. There is no substitute for the insight this gives you into the actual workings of the creative process.

You learn to work in isolation and to work in teams. You learn to work with other people's agendas and foibles, with patience and impatience. As time went on, the dividing line between faculty and students eroded. Early on the students raised money to edit and publish a magazine, *Accent*. We reviewed buildings, industrial design and engineering (Nervi, Candela). In each issue we included reproductions of student paintings and drawings side by side with illustrated articles on internationally known artists. Peter Stead collaborated with me on an article about construction in colour, space and time. Here is a brief excerpt from something I wrote for the catalogue of Alan Davie's retrospective exhibition, organised by Helen Knapp at the Wakefield City Art Gallery, and reprinted in *Accent*.

> 'Alan Davie explained to me the other day how he made a series of bird drawings. He laid twelve large sheets of paper out on the floor and took a brush and a tin of paint and made a black circle on each sheet in sequence very quickly; and on each sheet the circle was slightly different in size and position. He did not have any image in mind, and the circle was merely a shape on each page – to which he now added two black lines. As he went along the "character" of each circle gave him the lead as to the black lines which each page needed, and the black lines gave him the lead as to the next shape needed, which was a diamond shape. The next shapes were two big black triangles; two smaller circles came next; and then herring-bone – a bird began to emerge, perhaps from the primal egg, a different bird in each case, twelve compellingly present, and in one or two cases, rather fierce birds.'

For me, my past experiences in Cornwall came alive every day I was in that studio. I understood physically what Ben meant when he created a 'ground' or a context for a painting, through layering veils of colour on a canvas, and then scumbling and scraping and eroding until a rhythm began to emerge and set in motion a flow of lines, textures and colours. I understood with my body as well as with my head what Brancusi had meant when he remarked that within

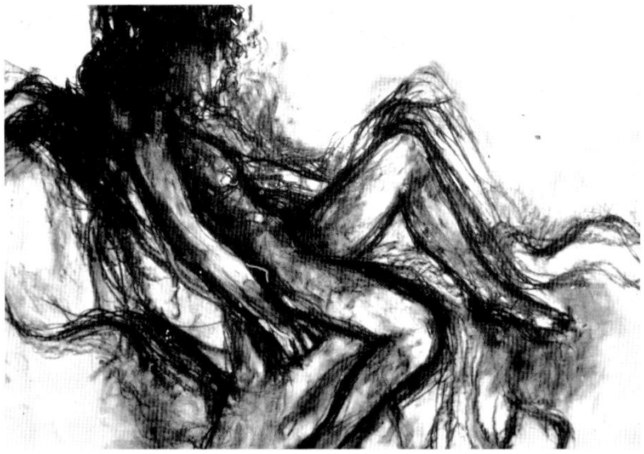

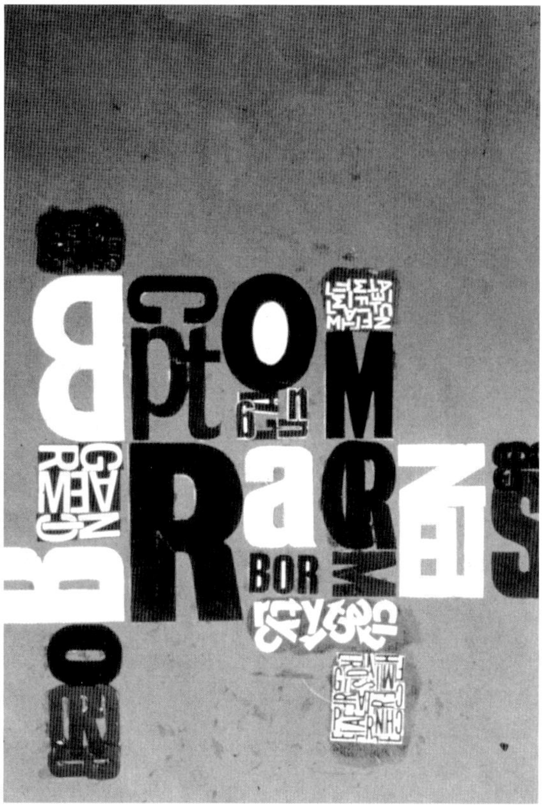

Model in movement,
1958–59,
Life class drawing, Basic Course, Leeds College of Art

(right) Graphic design,
1957,
Basic Course, Leeds College of Art

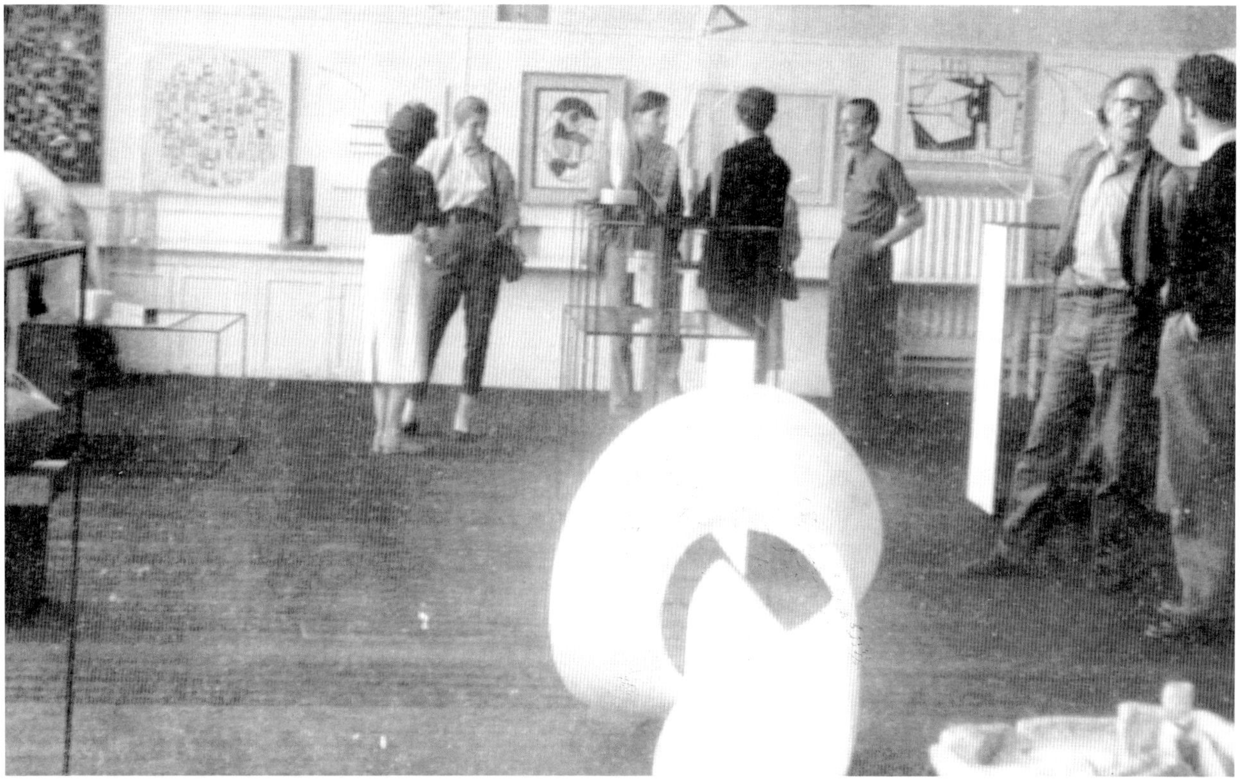

Exhibition of works by staff, students and invited artists at Leeds College of Art, 1957

Paintings on wall (*left to right*) by
Harry Thubron,
Victor Pasmore,
Wendy Pasmore,
Ben Nicholson,
Wilhelmina Barns-Graham,
with sculpture by
Barbara Hepworth
in foreground

Visitors (*left to right*):
Lady Read,
D Thubron,
Eric Atkinson,
Norbert Lynton,
Ron Holmes,
Terry Frost,
Barry Ward

every block of stone lay a sculpture waiting to be released. I understood how to hear the whispers of light and shadow caressing the inside of a Hepworth sculpture. I understood physically how Alfred Wallis, the untutored fisherman, would find a piece of cardboard in a dustbin in an alley behind a shop, and squirrel it home, and start with the shape and colour of the cardboard, and even its quality of cardboardness, and with his few bits of left-over boat paint; and how, before the morning was out, a storm had raged, and boats had found refuge in the nurturing harbour beyond the lighthouse; I understood all that.

Meanwhile I was working with Peter Stead and Stephen Gilbert on moving the constructive idea forward from art into domestic buildings, so that the spatial energy of de Stijl and Mondrian could be revisited in terms of steel and anodised aluminium and laminated plastics, and in terms of an actual site in rural Yorkshire. The sloping site of the Branch Lane house, outside Huddersfield, overlooked a wooded valley and meadows. Peter included me in the detailed problems of design and construction. It was an unforgettable learning experience. We visited factories together where aluminium siding and other components were manufactured. I did some illustrative working drawings for him. All this, in turn, gave me insights into what Victor Pasmore was doing at Peterlee.

And I was writing on art and architecture in international journals, and putting together a book on housing in Great Britain with HansMartin Bruckmann.

The impact of Leeds continues with me to this day. After graduating, and emigrating to America, I have, like Ricky and Harry and Terry, combined teaching with practice. Peter came with me for the first three years. Together we founded a firm called Design Collaborative. This evolved into Urban Design Associates. Today it is one of the leading firms in its field in the United States, devoted to working on those parts of cities in the most desperate need of attention and help. But in a real sense it's an extension into urban design of the lessons of the Basic Course, and of Ben's contexts, and of my collaboration with Peter and Stephen. Our efforts always begin with walking the streets, and listening to the people, and hearing the language of the city as it tells us about its history, its issues, and its hopes for the future. And then, and only then, do we nurture the birth of new designs to graft into the stems of the old.

It's odd, Norbert, sitting here in my library in West Homestead, which is part of Pittsburgh, and thinking back over thirty-five years about how far we all have come. The river below me has such a lovely American-Indian name, the Monongahela. About five miles below us it joins the Allegheny and forms the Ohio, and the Ohio flows into the Mississippi at St Louis, and the Mississippi, which starts off north of Minneapolis, flows on southward to New Orleans and the Carribean. This is such a huge country, and these rivers flow like lazy silver serpents across thousands of miles of farmlands and prairie, and through cities with beautiful names like Cincinnati and Memphis, and I find myself thinking about the steel mills that used to be below my window on the river banks, and about how they produced the steel which powered most of the American industries of the early twentieth century and set out the railroads which opened up the west, and I think of the incredible opportunity I have had to put into practice, in the dozens of cities and communities all over this continent which this activity spawned, the lessons I have learned, and how privileged I have been. Life goes on, and the circle is never complete.

With best wishes
David

Letter 6 Norbert Lynton to David Lewis

May/June 1999

Dear David

It seems like yesterday, though we're talking of more than forty years ago. Some of the details have blurred, probably were a bit vague even then, but the main events, the major facts are crystal clear. And will always be: you are asking me to recall one of the two or three great turning-points in my life. You remember Constable on his boyhood by the river Stour: 'these scenes made me a painter, and I am grateful'. Working with Harry opened my eyes, mind and spirit to art and, oh yes, I am grateful, more than grateful.

The moment was 1957. Since 1950 I had been working in the School of Architecture, part of the Leeds College of Art but a physically separate unit across the road and with little or no awareness of the Painting, Sculpture, Graphics and Furniture Schools in the main building. I was teaching French Renaissance architecture to a succession of young men, most of them recently demobbed and at first older than me, their eyes on getting their diplomas and out into an architect's office and not likely to get passionate about Philibert de l'Orme. A silly job in a pretty dreadful place, really, under a head who proclaimed that architecture had died when Georgian design went mercurial around 1780. He had other specialists teach Greek-and-Roman and Italian Renaissance; he himself taught English. His work as architect was risible: little stage-classical porches stuck onto cheap housing, for example. The architects on his staff went through teaching motions year after year, with no enthusiasm and little to offer. Peter Collins was an exception: a modern classicist, passionate about Auguste Perret's translation of the classical orders and Beaux-Arts planning into fine concrete buildings; I certainly learnt something from him. For the rest, I browsed busily through the *Architectural Review* in the library and sometimes felt I was the only one there with any interest in contemporary design.

Chance had dropped me into art history. At home there were a few art books and old, fairly banal pictures, but no talk or special awareness of art. We consumed music by means of the radio and occasional concerts: the great names from Bach to Brahms. I played the piano a bit at school. My seven years at an English boarding school (I arrived from Germany in 1938, aged ten) had protected me against any interest in art. The word wasn't mentioned, no art was seen, no art was committed. Culture was Eng. Lit. plus Gilbert and Sullivan. I sang treble, alto, tenor and bass in the church choir, Palestrina, Victoria, etc; the whole school sang Gregorian plainchant every Sunday: great experiences both. Altogether I loved that school but it taught me nothing about art, or life or the world.

Then Birkbeck College (University of London): evening classes and a day-time office job. But which course or courses to take? I had no clear notion who or what I might want to be. More Eng. Lit., more History? I signed on for a BA General degree programme no longer taught but perfect for someone as undecided as me. Those two subjects, plus what? Had there been a History of Music course I'd certainly have gone for that. Instead there was History of Art which could surely do no harm and someone called Professor Nikolaus Pevsner teaching it. I found myself in a dingy basement in Woburn Square and joining a small class looking at French Romanesque sculpture via those old five-inch slides, projected by Pevsner. This was 1945. In 1948 I emerged with my first degree, my first girlfriends, Nikolaus Pevsner as a friend, memories of Eric Hobsbawm as a vivid History lecturer (his colleagues warned me against his Marxism), and Nikolaus's suggestion that I should go to the Courtauld Institute of Art (also London University, but full-time) for two years, to do art history 'properly'. A tiny grant paid my fees. I ran into debt at home and into marriage at the Courtauld, and in 1950 had a second degree and was a certified art historian. The Leeds job came next: the Courtauld had noticed I responded to buildings and architectural drawings and put me forward for it.

The first years were grim. Next to no money, dispirited and distant colleagues, a city where the trams stopped running before the films finished. Frank Chippendale became head of the School of Architecture, bringing some life into the place and getting better work out of his staff. You know better than I what his School was like. I had made some personal contact with the art people across the road and knew that the head of painting was switching to a job in London. My first knowledge of his successor, Harry Thubron, must have come through Tom Hudson, who had arrived with Harry and with Ricky. Tom had been at the Courtauld for a while and greeted me as a sort of fellow-spirit. When the College art-historian-librarian departed, in 1956, Tom had me meet Harry and between them they arranged for me to inherit that post. A crisis delayed my taking it up: I got polio that summer, collapsing with it dramatically in St Ives where I was staying with the first painter I ever met, a young ex-Leeds lad called Trevor Bell. My wife was warned I might never return from the Truro isolation prison or would return severely paralysed. Nobody told me but I wasn't having it anyway, survived, slowly surfaced, had some expert physiotherapy in Leeds from the engaging Miss Bliss ('blissiotherapy'), and emerged feeling new, reborn, clarified.

At this point I started the new job, lecturing on the history of art A–Z and on modern art history from Impressionism on. At the Courtauld I had learned about Giotto to Tiepolo and Reynolds, more or less, so a lot of the A–Z was new to me, while the modern stuff was not only new but strange, enemy country. But I got to know Harry, Tom and Ricky. I spent a lot of time in the College studios, where Harry was teaching what others called the Basic Course. Students spent a lot of time drawing abstract forms and/or nature (sunflowers, honesty, etc) from close to. They worked with great intensity, looking hard, at things and at the marks made on the paper. Harry had a way of opening their eyes to the marvellousness of both. He responded with extraordinary alertness to how students reacted. Everyone was engaged in a process of discovery, and Harry was brilliant at charging it with energy and joy.

Tom, in many ways Harry's lieutenant, saw to the three-dimensional work for the Basic Course. This took some setting up, because it called for tools and machinery for working with metal and plastics. At first it was mainly building up and carving plaster, in what I came to recognise as a de Stijl way: quite a searching process for young students who had expected to be modelling heads. It took setting up also in the sense that it had to find some diplomatic accommodation with the Sculpture School where there had been no change of staff. Altogether the Harry group had swept into the College like a miniature mafia, determined to change things radically in the face of pre-existing colleagues wedded to very different habits. I was seen as part of that new-broom mafia, and remember how other colleagues seemed to be waiting nervously to see what would happen to them. What happened to several of them was that they got swept up in the mafia's wake, learnt a lot in a short time and found themselves both converted by Harry's enthusiasm and refreshed in their view of art, their teaching and their personal work. It was an entirely selfless mafia, bringing energy and high spirits to anyone not permanently blocked.

The local education officer, John Wood, a very bright and, when necessary, tough man, backed Harry to the hilt. There were many enemies in Leeds at first, and John's steadfast trust in Harry was essential. There were more and longer-lasting enemies in London. Work for the Intermediate exam had to be sent to London and assessed by Ministry-appointed old fogeys. In 1958 or 1959 the Royal Academician Arnold Machin, modeller of pretty terracotta figurines, failed the whole Leeds year. Previously he had passed work of much the same sort and level – decent figurative paintings to a centrally-set theme (a market square, a fairground etc), done under Ricky's guidance by students taking time off from their generally much more adventurous work. It was especially important on such an occasion to have the backing of Herbert Read, by then the recognised national champion of modern art and of art education. Herbert was warmly interested in, and spoke up for, what Harry was doing. Also he worked with Tom on annual exhibitions of schoolchildren's art, sponsored by a popular newspaper. There were informal meetings at Herbert's house, Stonegrave, and he visited the College.

The University of Leeds had the Gregory Fellowships, established by Eric ('Peter') Gregory, director of the publishers Lund Humphries: a sequence of painters, sculptors, poets and composers, each staying for three years or so. The music fellowship ended with the first incumbent: the music department, it seemed, found having a living composer (Kenneth Leighton) too disturbing. The whole University had little use for the artists. These felt rather isolated up the hill and soon came down it to the College of Art, finding that a much livelier centre than the University art department (studio work plus art history), then headed by Maurice de Sausmarez. And Harry, of course, drew them in, involved them. Thus Terry Frost and then Alan Davie found themselves teaching there part-time, and the sculptor Hubert ('Nibs') Dalwood. Maurice got involved in another way. He was a sensitive naturalistic painter and a gifted writer with a strong base in art history. He made himself a sort of chronicler of the teaching done by Harry at the College and during the various summer and winter schools Harry soon set up. The first of these was at Scarborough and was nominally run by Victor Pasmore, head of the art department at Durham University.

I was hungry for knowledge of modern art. Useful books and articles were extremely rare in those post-war years; some of what we would now think of as key areas of modern art history awaited discovery and research: Futurism,

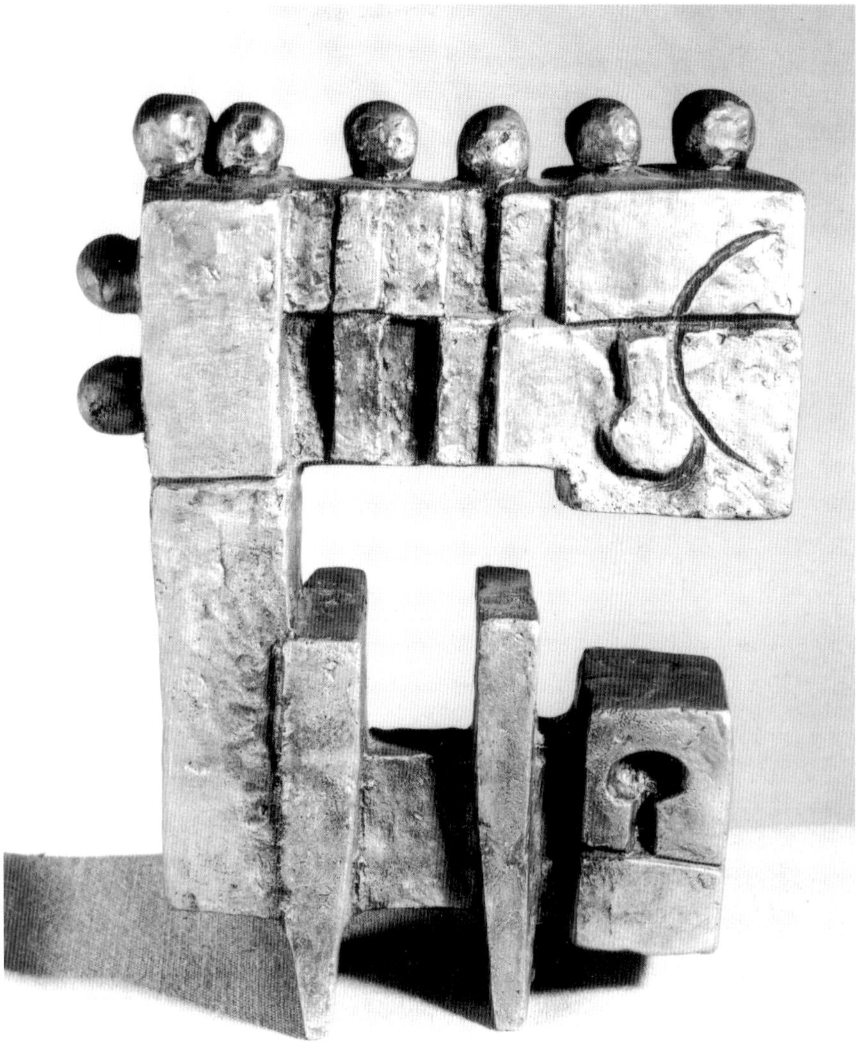

Hubert Dalwood
Object: Open Square
1959
16½ x 13½ in.
aluminium
collection: Leeds City Art Gallery

Dadaism, the Russians. Tom taught me a lot about the Post-Impressionists, Cubism and so on. Harry was passionate about 'Vincent' and about Klee. I could read German, and bought the original German version of Haftmann's *Painting in the Twentieth Century* (1955), two volumes, text and plates, full of stimulation in a way that no other general account has been since. That was for the library, but no one else wanted to use the text volume. I bought for myself the paperback of Felix Klee's selection from his father's diaries (1957). Klee remains a cardinal figure for me (a few years later I wrote a little book on him, making my own translations); through him I got very interested in the Bauhaus and started working seriously on that at a time when what one could read about the Bauhaus was seriously misleading. Information was very scarce, as you will recall; anything stronger than superficial thinking was rarer still. In fact, David, you provided me with an all-important stimulus. Do you remember? You lent me a slim Faber publication, perhaps twenty pages altogether, with ten tipped-in colour plates and an illuminating text by yourself, on ... Mondrian! Did I ever thank you enough? I had scarcely heard of him. I looked, I read, I looked again. I photographed the plates to make slides from them and a few days later gave my first lecture on Mondrian, who had become for me, even more than Klee, the gateway into modern art, the exemplum and guide who made all the doors open and the barriers drop away. Your little Brancusi book added to the permanent excitement soon after – both these great artists were after joy, weren't they? - but it was your Mondrian that took the new me into new realms and made me feel at home in this marvellous new world. The more I got involved in modern art, the deeper and closer became my attachment also to the past.

And of course Harry & Co. Harry and Tom would sometimes do lectures for me: Harry on van Gogh; Tom on the beginnings of Constructivism, naturally, but also very effectively on Toulouse-Lautrec (he could do a better Hollywood Toulouse than even José Ferrer). Harry made it clear to the students that the art history courses were essential, and the occasional essay-writing that went with them. I, probably the first art historian employed in an English art school, had the best possible support. Also from the authorities: the library grew from sad beginnings into a major, professional resource, run by a proper librarian and located at the heart of the College; I went on making, mounting and labelling the slides, building up a collection that had been tiny and had ended with Manet. I was encouraged to develop a freewheeling liberal studies programme by bringing in people from the University, lively individuals like E. J. Thompson, Alastair McIntyre, John Rex, who got paid peanuts and spoke brilliantly about ideas and the world.

Harry was inclusive and mobile where many others, not excluding radicals and reformers, are narrow and finite. You probably know that but a lot of people don't, still don't, and I'd like to stress it. He did not teach 'a Basic Course'. Maurice published a book, after observing Harry at the

College and at summer schools, and this seemed to be saying how to do it, and saying it in his name. Everyone buying it could have a go, and perhaps it did some good. Maurice was a sensitive man. But it certainly did not represent Harry in any serious way, and it turned into a series of recipes and instructions what in Harry's hands was always fluid, re-invented, open-ended.

A story to prove this point (and perhaps to show that I felt seriously engaged in Harry's work). In 1957 the work I saw in the first-year studios was black on white: charcoal or pencil or brush and wash on paper. During the summer vacation of 1958 I suddenly thought that this was not necessarily the way to start; it seemed to give black and white a predetermined, non-colour role. I rushed up to the studio on the first day of the new term to tell Harry what I had thought, if necessary to argue with him. I found all the first-year students working with colour. The point is that Harry never finalised his thinking. He also reacted with great alertness to the students, noting what brought out the right kind of attention, what seemed to dissipate energies, praising, stimulating, often marvelling himself at what he saw being done. We all felt that art was dawning, widening without confinement – not at all a closed system to be mastered, least of all a set of exercises each cohort had to go through.

Another story, to reinforce the point. In that summer of 1958 I had attended the Scarborough summer school. Victor was its leader, by age, experience and reputation. I was one of a large group students of varying status and ages but, unlike them, had gone just to see what would happen, what I might learn about this strange activity, with no thought of becoming an artist myself. Wendy Pasmore was there; she had a brilliant way of making clear the programme that Victor outlined to us every morning. Tom Hudson was there, supporting Harry in many ways, but Tom too was a great teacher. Victor had us all using black on white to develop from 'point and line to plane', echoing the Kandinsky book title (I don't think he had seen an English translation). I found that pretty exciting and began to see marks and shapes in relationship to each other, not just as separate things, and how small changes could have great effects. Colour we used only in our spare time; I remember Tom saying something encouraging when I had done a clumsy little painting in primaries. He and Harry both had substantial experience in teaching children and I reckon I benefited from the gentleness this bred in them. When Harry announced a year later that he was going to run a winter school in Leeds, focusing on colour, I signed up for that and so found myself for the first time trying to tune colours to one another in simple ways. One exercise was to adjust Windsor red, blue and yellow to give them the same visual weight; another was to mix them to make black and then add white and see which hue dominated the resulting greys. I found squeezing colours out of tubes and making a mess with them deeply frightening at first. I got over that and then it was as though my eyes were being peeled and I was seeing colour for the first time. I did those mixtures and kept adjusting them, again and again, to get the colour chord clearer and the grey greyer even though the tints were delicious. At the end of the day Harry looked at what I had done and praised my persistence. Yes, he approved of the colour adjustments etc I had made, but what did he really want me to notice after all that effort? 'Have you seen the amazing shapes you've been making?', he said; 'look at that, and that group there.' Joy, again, but the point is that he turned what had been a focused assignment, demanding all my attention, into an opening world of discovery and adventure. That duality has stayed with me ever since as a key factor in creative work. The next day we did 'discords', difficult to understand at first, thrilling to handle once one did, exciting to look at.

I have said already that all sorts of people came to the short courses. There are a lot of well-known painters around who'll tell you how much they got from them. Harry treated us all alike – beginners, stolid amateurs and established professionals; all of us were capable of doing things that interested him. Not that Harry was always happy with the way things were going; he was the first to sense any lack of drive or enhancement. I have known him be quite worried that a course seemed to be slackening off; his answer was to throw a spanner into his own works, introduce a contradictory element that could challenge the students even to the point of anger and resistance when things had been going so placidly. He was strong. The last thing he cared about was whether we loved him. We did therefore love him, individually and as groups. But then none of us came to play around. If Harry could annoy us at a particular moment, we soon saw the necessity for it. He wasn't there to win, except in the sense that he wanted us all to come away refreshed and recharged. College students, attending day after day, week after week, could of course be challenged and stretched in a developing way that could not be hoped for from a ten-day summer school, yet the all-together-in-one-boat intensity of the short courses was something quite special and amazingly productive.

Sometimes I would give talks with slides in the evenings. The better part of the evening would go to dancing to pop music on someone's tape-to-tape recorder. The Twist it was then; I became an expert by watching and imitating beautiful Sally Scott (where are you, Sally?). Try and believe that: on top of all this other personal and professional growth, me, aged around thirty-five, twisting by the hour to Dusty Springfield and Frank Ifield. That was the second highspot in my dancing career. The first had been much earlier, when I took fellow Birkbeck student Shirley to a 'hop' and impressed her with my quickstep after just one lesson.

Harry was of course conscious of the doubts and downright hostility expressed by the British world of art and education. In their different ways Victor in Durham and then Newcastle and Harry in Leeds were working a revolution from the bottom up. That needed both explaining and defending and there was some need for texts, in the general and the professional press, in reports to authorities, in exhibition catalogues. Victor could sometimes produce lapidary statements, worked and reworked as though each would be his last words. I remember us all, the Leeds group plus Victor, trying to get such a statement out of him and on to tape, but it was never quite right and he'd insist on trying again. Harry hoped that I'd be able to serve as a sort of PR voice, and indeed I did on a few occasions. I suspect I never got the message across as penetratingly as he hoped; I was too much the academic product for that. But he couldn't do it for himself because he was too much the other way. Everyone around him came to know Harry-speak though no one could imitate it – had to know it, in fact, because that is how he taught as well as chatted over a glass of beer. Some of the phrases surface still, forty years on: for example, about someone he didn't think too intelligent, 'he's as dim as a nun's nightlight'; or 'he's away with the pixies'. He laughed a lot, we all did. The language could be pretty coarse (I remember being shocked at first) but always expressively so. Tom, whose language was perhaps the roughest, could also make adroit formal speeches and, behind the scenes, good sharp jokes. He had a repertory of mocking impressions of, for example, Sir William Coldstream, painter, Professor at the Slade School of Art in London and incisive chairman of the committee appointed to review top-level art education in England and Wales at this time. (His committee did in fact make constructive and liberating proposals which, largely realised in the 1960s, made our art schools the envy of the world and vital art centres in a country otherwise devoid of them – until Conservative attitudes came to reign over us at the end of the 1970s.) Tom's mockery focused on the Coldstream painting method of slow looking and notating, particularly on the almost sexual urgency and desperate self-exposure necessitated by the first brushstroke; he called his performance 'The Rape of the Rectangle'. Ricky was a great fund of jokes, too.

I am probably not getting across the sense of effort combined with fun that teaching at Leeds then gave us. It was work and it was purposeful, ambitious even, but it was grim only when someone outside, like Machin, made trouble for us. Inside the College we were in pioneering high spirits.

Harry was a marvellous artist. Not many people knew this in his lifetime. He valued what he did, but he never promoted it. Teaching was his priority, though in fact a lot of time went into his own work even then, and much more after he retired. When I first knew him he was painting invisible landscapes, the best of them white on white, recalling winter scenes and revealing his love of whites. They could be very thick, these paintings, worked over and over. I recall a kid poking a bulge in one of them, during a Yorkshire Artists' exhibition at the Leeds Art Gallery, and dark green paint oozing out from it to make a fat line down the beautiful surface and drip on the gallery floor. I rushed to tell Harry of the disaster and he came to look. He laughed. 'That's fine,' he said, 'that's just what the bloody thing needed.' Soon he worked mostly with collage, using all sorts of found rubbish. Like Schwitters, some said, but not at all if one looked at either of them properly. Yes, Harry could be amazingly refined, quite oriental in his delicacy; he could also be rough and tough though never noisy for noise's sake. His use of found bits and pieces – rubbish of many sorts, from bits of discarded packaging to a tired old silk rose off someone's hat – was not polemical, any more than his use of white. He was not making a point with his materials, apart from the broad one of beauty being all around us and just needing to be seen and embraced. Later

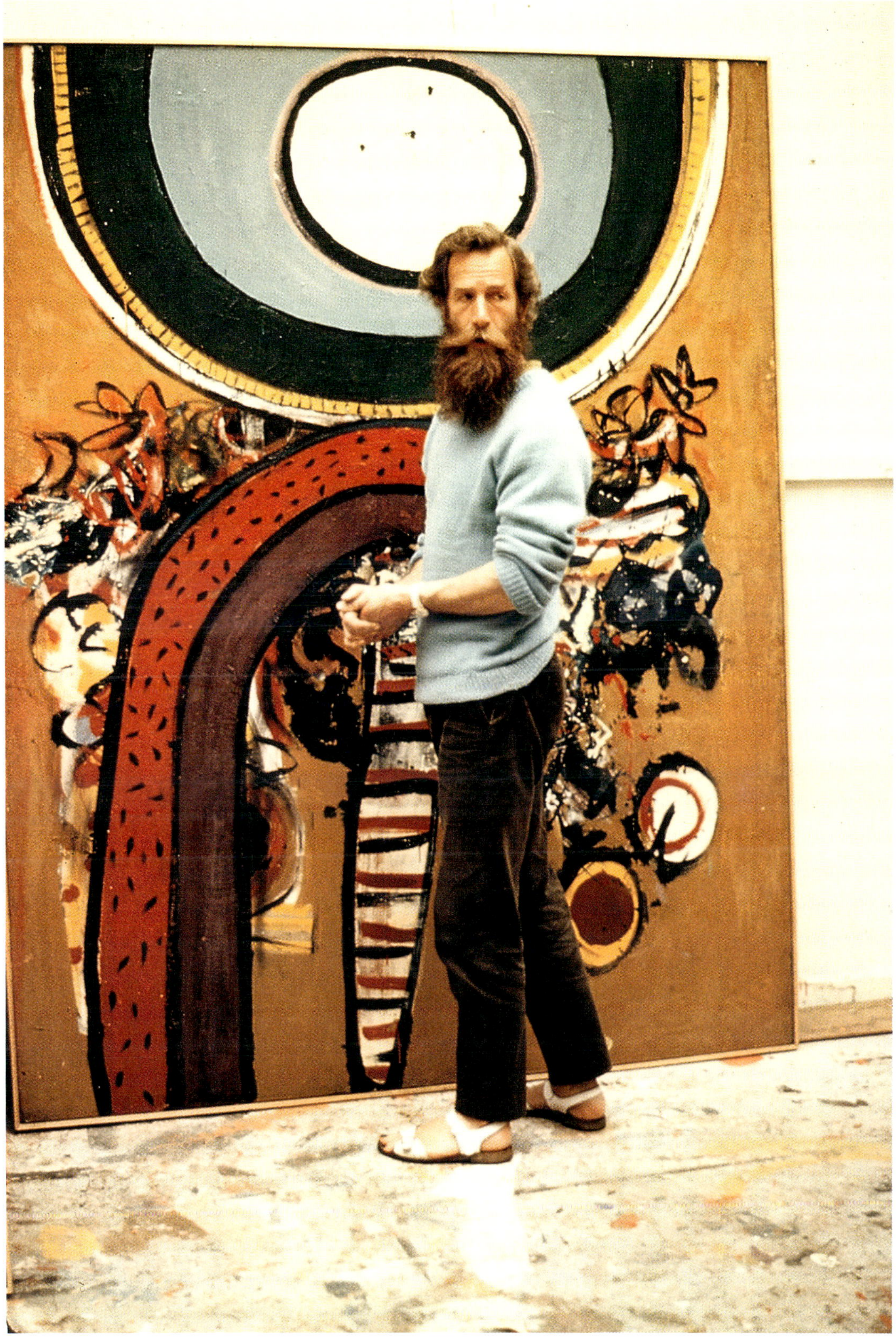

Alan Davie in the studio
at Leeds, 1960s

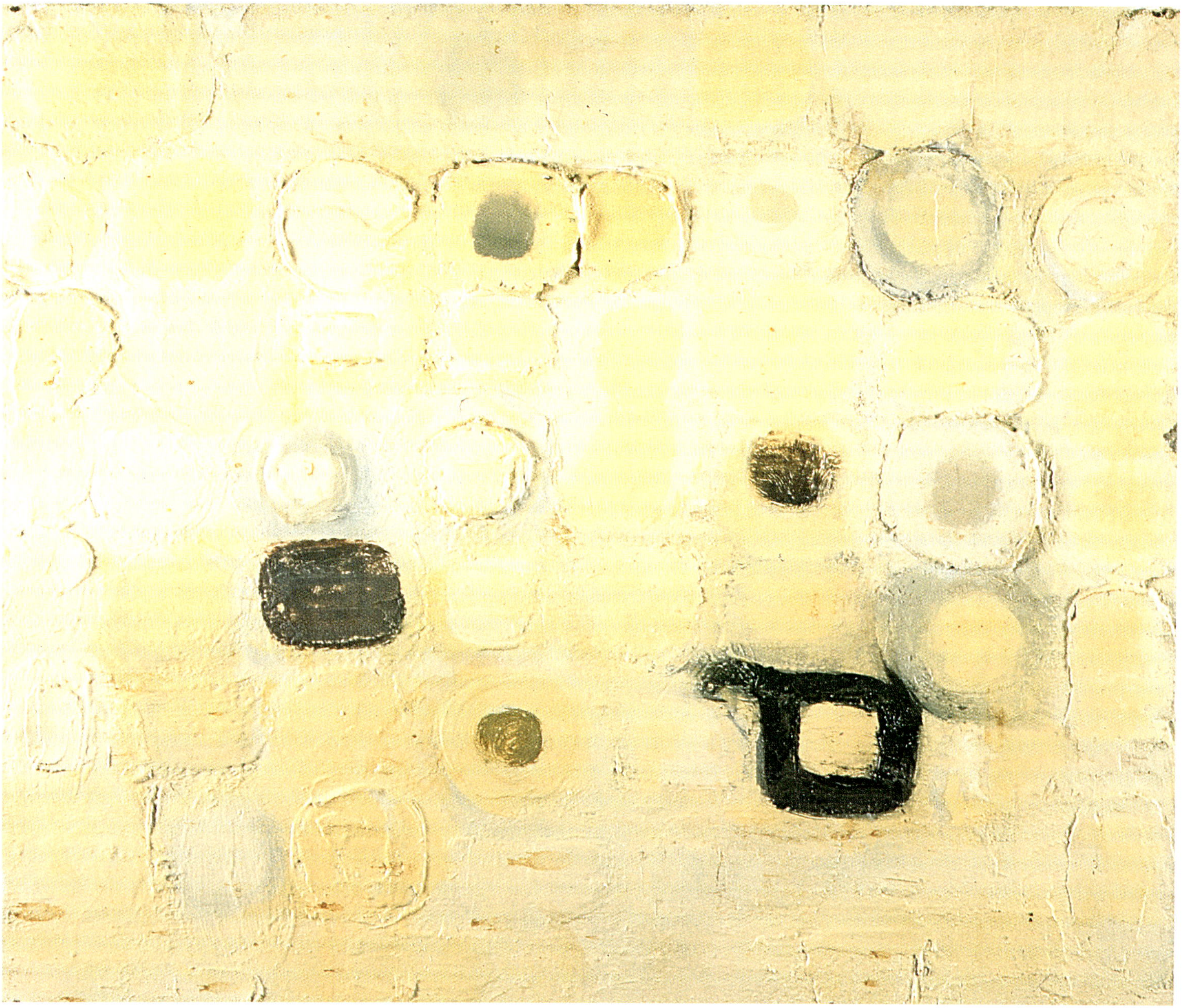

Harry Thubron
Family of Forms
1958
28 x 28 in.
mixed media on board
collection: Eric & Muriel Atkinson

Cloth sculpture project
student assessment exhibition
(3rd year Fine Art),
Leeds College of Art, 1968

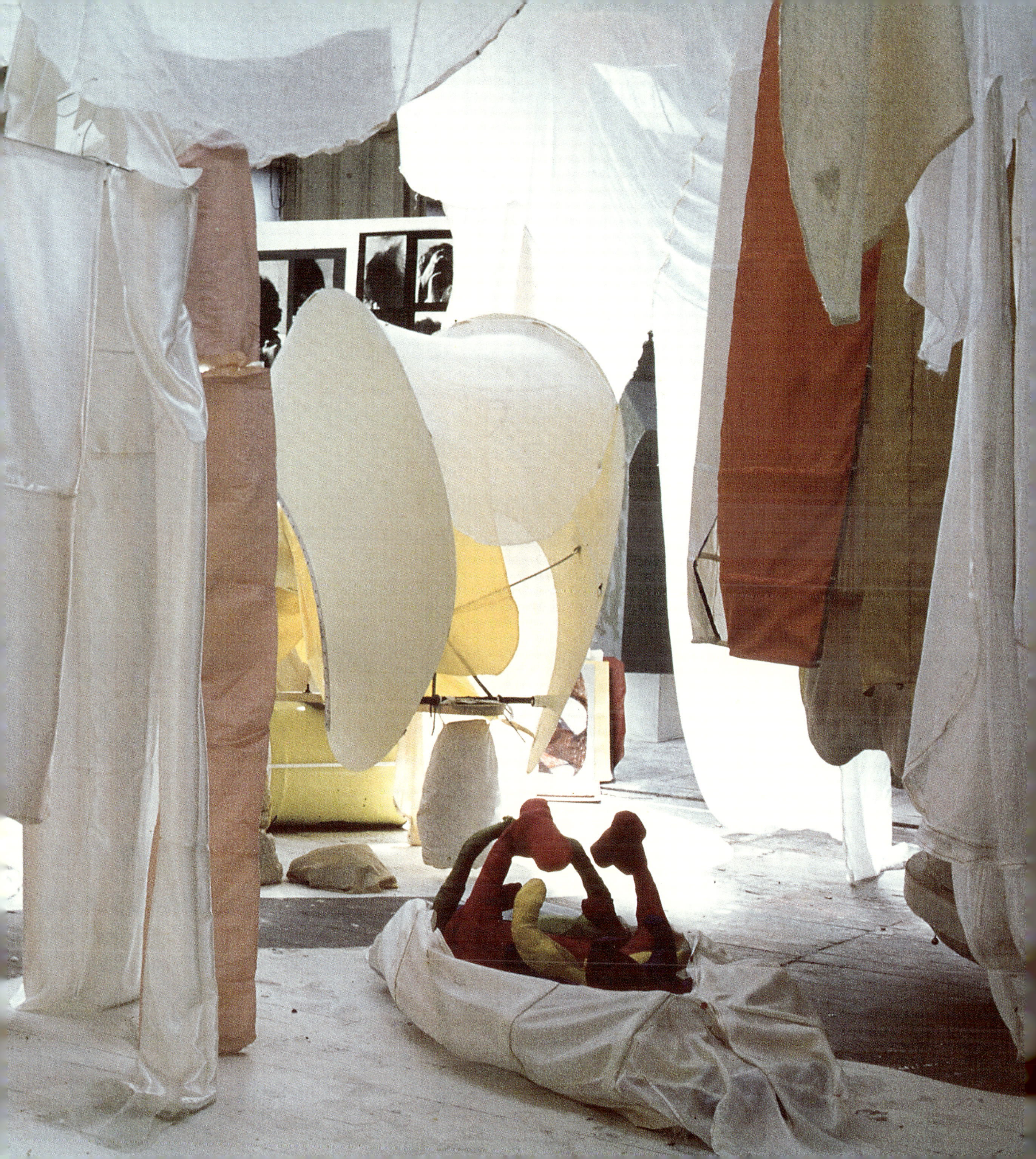

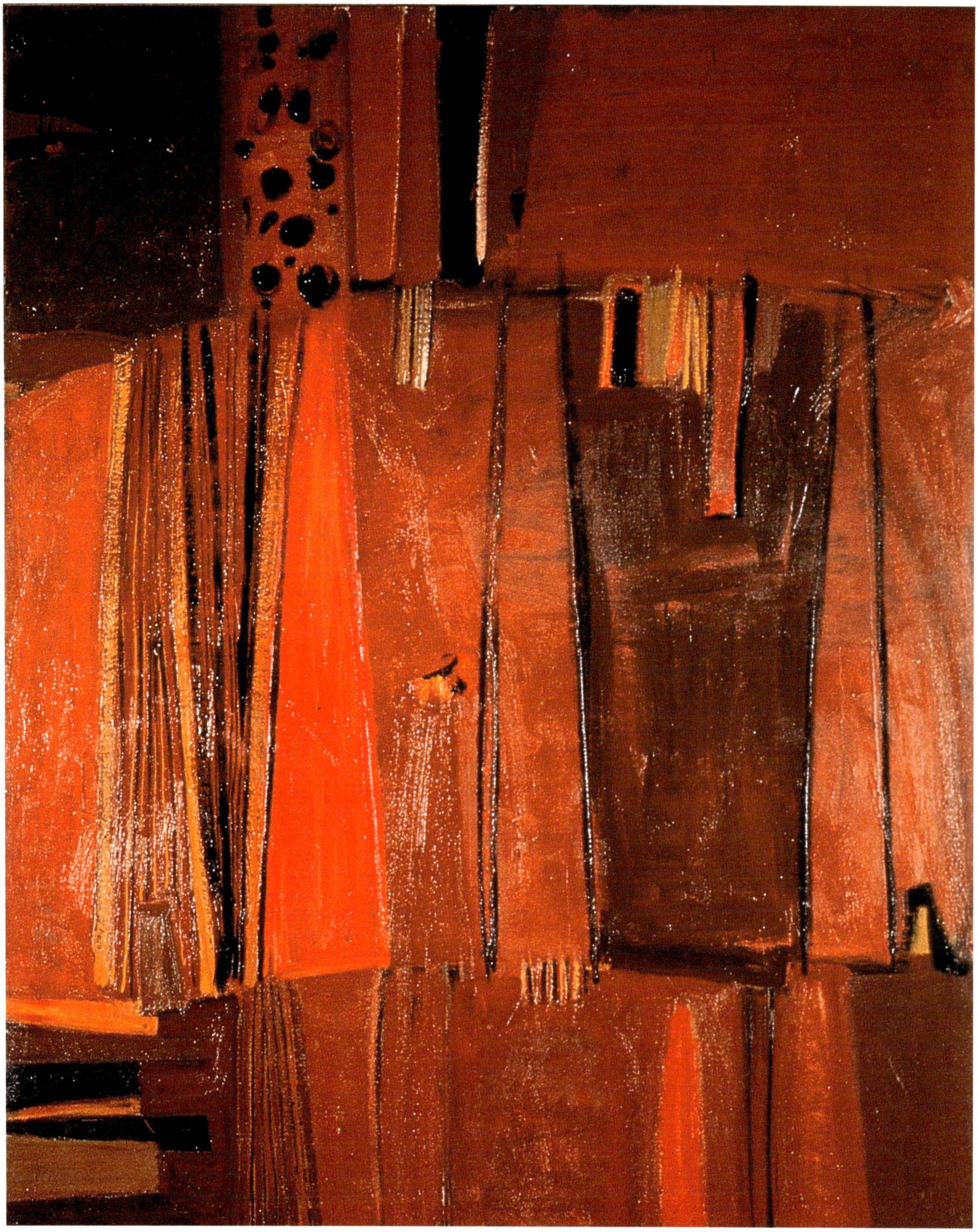

Terry Frost
Brown Verticals
*c.*1958–59
84 x 68 in.
oil on canvas
collection: Leeds City Art Gallery

1st year Fine Art Drawing Studio, with instructors David Wright and Tony McAulay, Fanshawe College, London, Ontario, 1980s

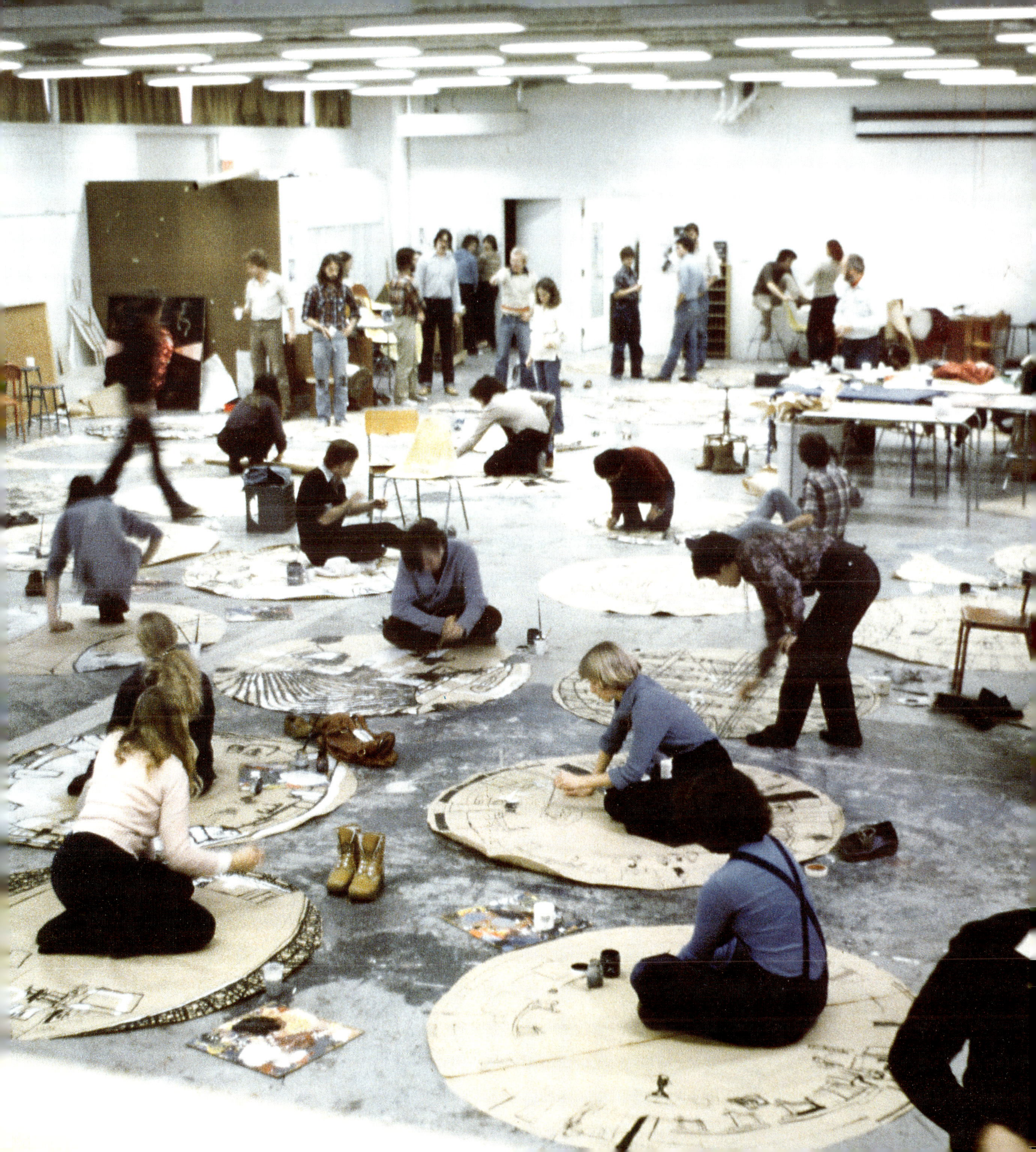

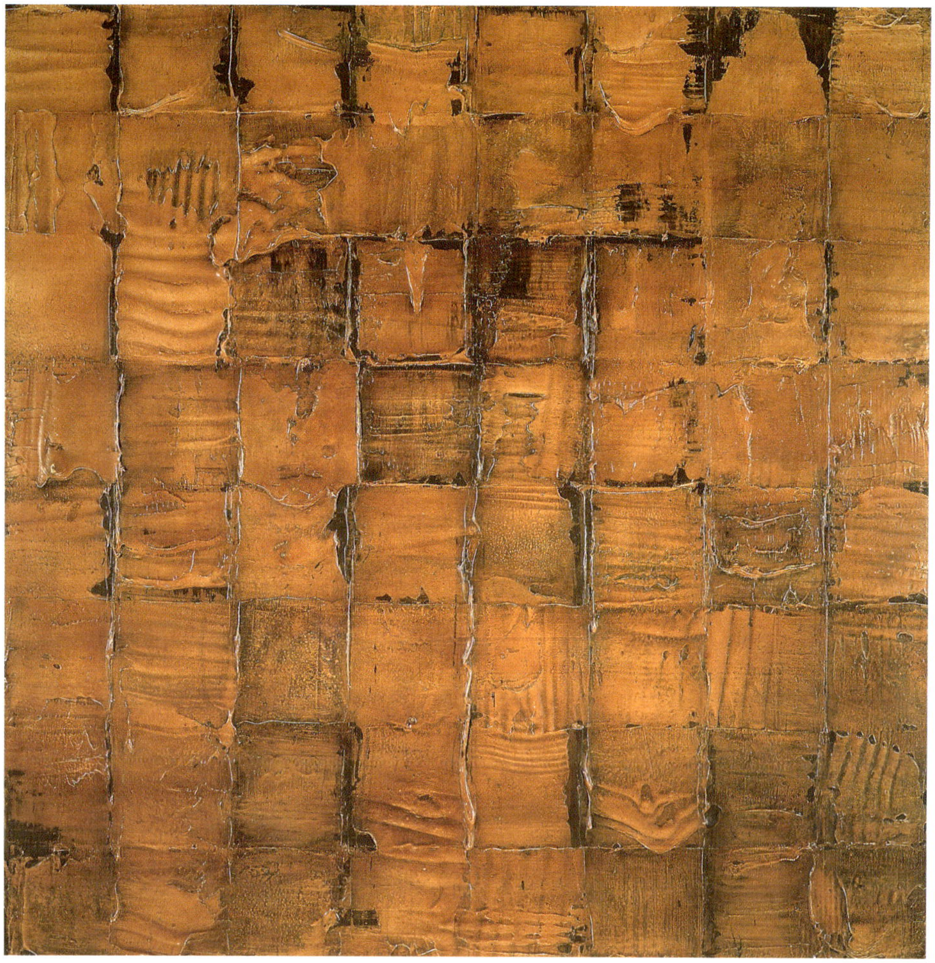

Duncan de Kergommeaux
Untitled 1–79
1979
87½ x 87½ in.
acrylic
collection of the artist

Peter Stead
House at Almondbury
West Yorkshire, 1959

Peter Stead
Construction
1957
steel, plastics, aluminium

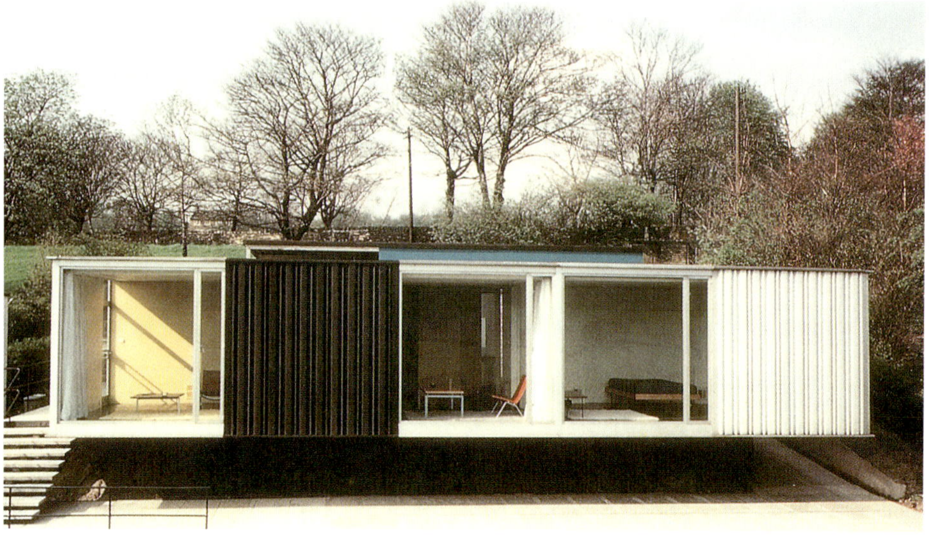

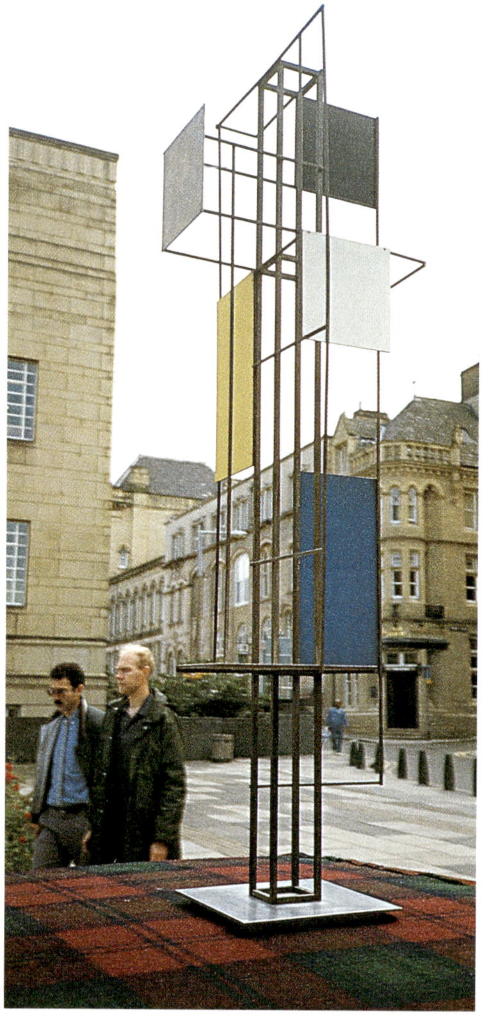

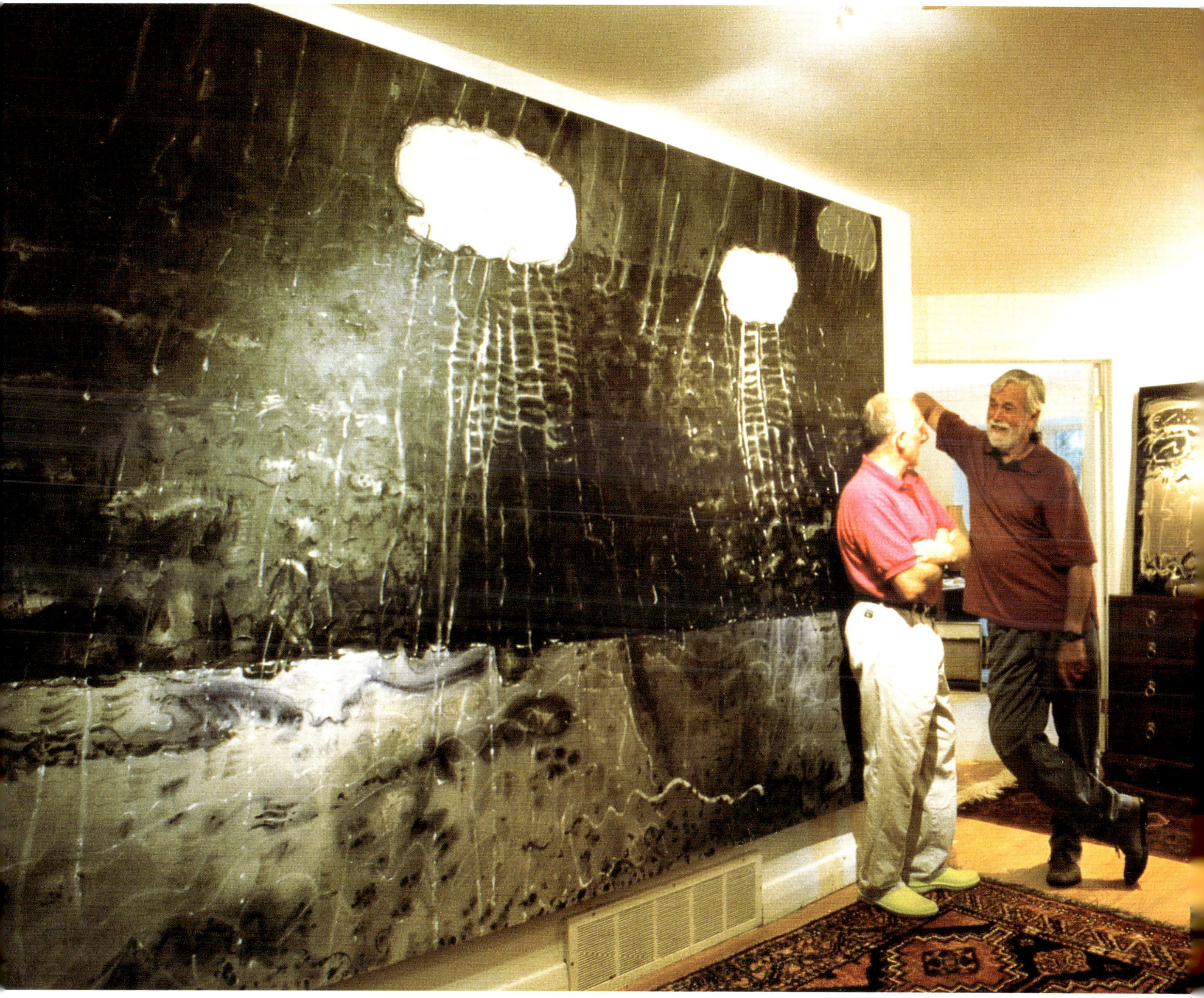

Eric Atkinson
Staircase to the Clouds (diptych), 1995, 80 x 112 in., acrylic and wax on canvas
collection: Kelly Mancari, London, Ontario
The artist with the owner at the latter's home

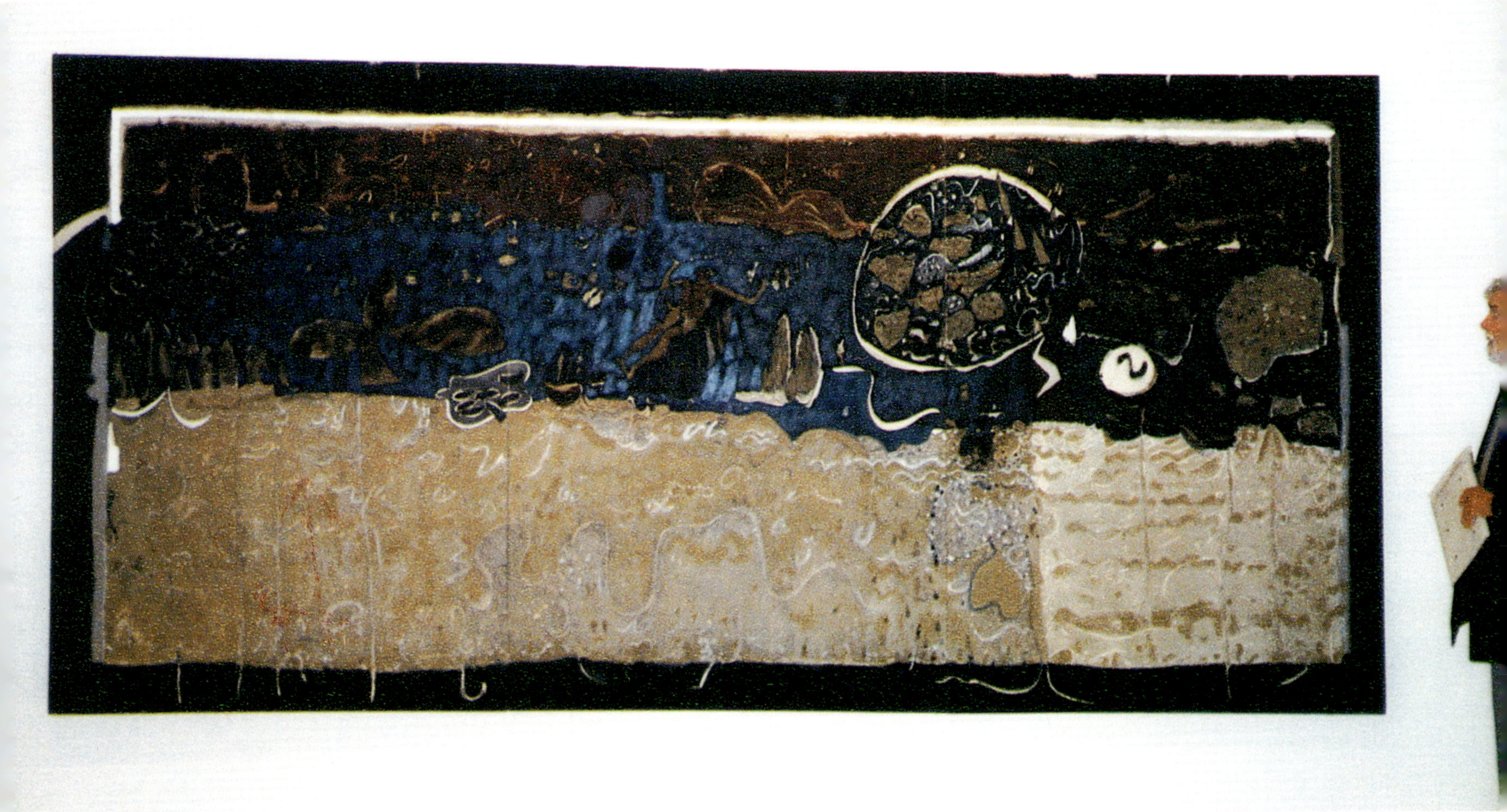

Eric Atkinson
Floating to Valhalla
1994
80 x 169 in.
acrylic and sand on canvas
With the artist

he gave me a low relief. I shall never tire of it. Rough though it is, it is also full of grace and restrained energies, more like Morandi than Schwitters. He constructed images, he carved and sometimes coloured what he called 'woods', some of them blatantly sexual. He made prints, large but concentrated one-colour forms on white, distantly descended from Matisse's blue figure cut-outs.

Harry never thought of art having to be abstract or figurative, and though he didn't insist on life drawing as an essential discipline he did get students at the College, and then also on short courses, to draw models moving around the studio. Terry Frost was using landscape experiences in his abstract paintings, those done in Yorkshire and those done in Cornwall, and I'd say these were his best paintings ever; Hubert Dalwood had been making figure sculptures but in the mid-1950s turned to abstract reliefs and free-standing forms that often still hinted at human anatomy; Alan Davie combined gestural marks with symbols and hints of body parts. I think that Harry's presence helped each of them do exceptionally good work in those Leeds years. Perhaps because of an intense awareness of Matisse that I recall striking us all, like a sunrise, after his death and especially the large and revealing memorial exhibition shown in Paris in 1956, Harry always knew that the figure had to come back into painting and play again its dominant role, but through new sorts of figuration. Though his own work always had a particular Harry character, whatever material or method he was working in – and there was irreverent humour in it, at times also something close to tragedy – he was, in his art as in his teaching, inclusive, catholic. Nothing had to be excluded on principle; nothing would be excluded that took his fancy. His work could be rumbustuous but it was never coarse; it was essentially elegant, subtle and economical.

Remember – who am I talking to? you know this at least as well as I, but people not around in the 1950s have no inkling of this – modern art was still enemy territory in England. The Institute of Contemporary Arts, founded in London by Herbert Read and others and from 1950-on located on a first floor in Dover Street, was a radical stronghold where twentieth-century art, and sometimes new art, sometimes also anti-academic art from all periods and places, could be shown and debated, as well as new architecture. In 1945–6 the Matisse and Picasso show at the Victoria and Albert Museum had released an amazing fury, mostly aimed at Picasso's awesome female figures: a pent-up fury, as though Picasso represented war and destruction, and drew to him all the English fear of having wool pulled over one's eyes. Do you know Lionel Lindsay's book *Addled Art*, about how ugly and evil modern art is, and how Jewish artists and dealers are behind it all. He was furious at seeing a book on Picasso in the window of a Paris gallery: blatant trickery to make people think that partly Jewish painter significant. That was published in 1946! In 1953 Trevor Bell, finishing at Leeds College of Art, had never heard of Picasso. A blockbuster Picasso show at the Tate in 1960 drew the first queues ever for a modern show and was received with some respect even by critics, but I know very well how he still had to be mocked by people at the top of our cultural institutions in the 1970s and 1980s. The new painting from America, you'll recall, met with general hostility at the end of the 1950s: the art of St Ives – Ben Nicholson, Roger Hilton, Terry Frost etc – rooted in landscape and nature's light, still had to be fought over. 'Bauhaus' was a negative term meaning 'intellectual' and therefore not artistic. Art was expected to be nice, to fit over one's mantelpiece and go with the curtains, and on no account frighten the horses. (You must remember the extraordinary broadcast speech made by that so-so painter of horses and English gentlefolk, Alfred Munnings, as president of the Royal Academy in about 1953, attacking anyone who could take Picasso seriously. Lindsay, by the way, wrote an admiring book about Munnings.)

It was natural, under those circumstances, for progressive artists to choose their positions and dig themselves in. That is what Pasmore seemed to be doing (he moved a lot subsequently), also Richard Hamilton, Tom Hudson, Terry Frost, Alan Davie etc, just as Ben Nicholson and Barbara Hepworth had to do in the 1930s before non-academic British art went Surrealist and Neo-Romantic. The point of all this is that Harry was never a this or a that artist, never a member of a group or a movement. His work might well have been better known if he had been. Quite the opposite: he looked wayward at the time, unwilling to commit himself to any of the parties in British art. Much of his work is abstract, but rarely entirely so; much of his work refers to the figure, but never unambiguously so. His paintings, in so far as I knew them, were never quite flat; his three-dimensional works could move towards what people call Constructivism and involve metal planes and lathe-turned forms but they were never Constructivist in spirit. I have

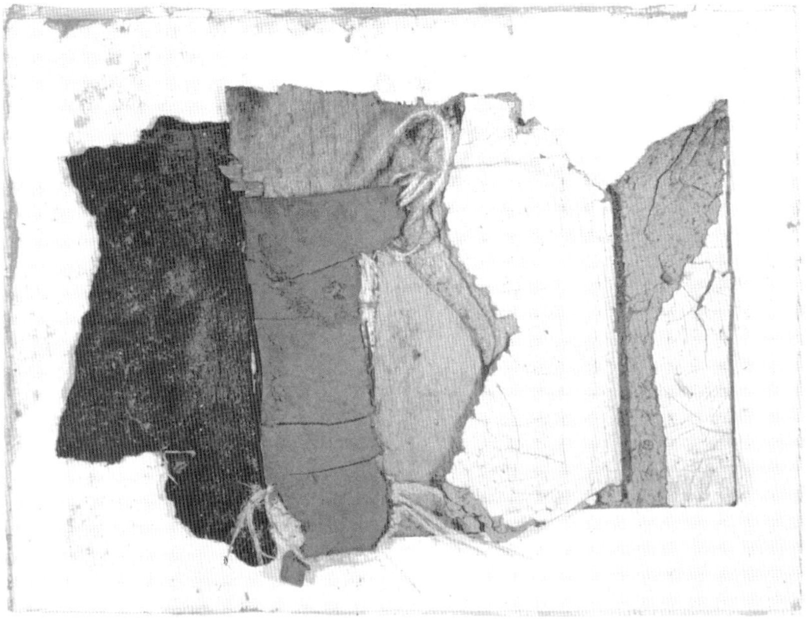

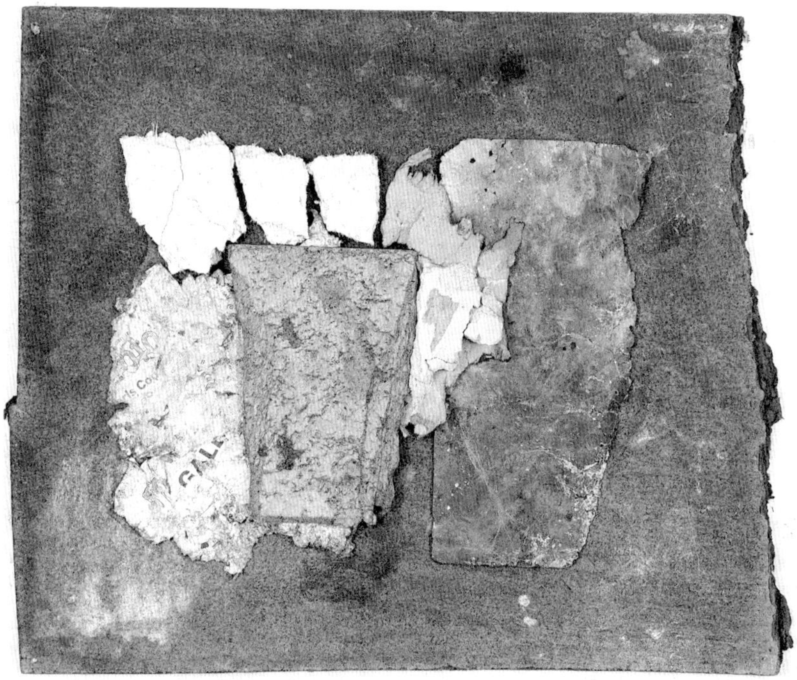

(top)
Harry Thubron, *Found objects,* 1976, 12 x 15 in., print, collection: Eric & Muriel Atkinson
(above)
Harry Thubron, *Painting relief,* 13½ x 17 in., mixed media, collection: Norbert Lynton

one such, a square relief in sheet copper with two domed forms side by side set into a square recess: title *Negress*, subject breasts. Of course, there they are, blissful presences. The point is that I was shocked when I first saw it, shocked by his implied ironic take on Constructivism, his seducing that high-minded, technology-eyeing art into such indulgent (and timeless) ways. Had Harry been a this or a that artist, with an 'ism' to his name and a brand-image, he could have shone among his go-ahead contemporaries. Had this witty and charming man minded his Ps and Qs, had he not been so fiercely opposed to all the attitudinising and art-politics he witnessed both as artist and teacher, had he screened his working-class status and done that advisable bit of sucking-up to the powerful in the English art scene, he could well have been received as a major artist and an inspiration *through his art*. As it is, many remember the great teacher and reformer of teaching; few looked at his art long enough. In this country you have to be famous before anyone will bother with you. In 1976 Harry had a one-man show at the Serpentine Gallery in Kensington Gardens: an enchanting exhibition in a delightful setting. It got little notice and few saw it. To its great credit, the British Council bought an admirable relief painting for its collection; I had some hand in that.

I often wish I had been able to do, and had done, more to promote Harry as artist. I don't seem to have a promoter's skills; also by then I was deeply involved in my work as professor at Sussex University, more or less out of touch with London. Harry was a great man, certainly one of the most important shapers of my life. But he was also a very fine artist, among the very best of his generation, to say the least. The same joy and dramatic adventures that made his teaching so extraordinary are in his art, are *concentrated* in his art. The world should be more aware of this, and grateful for it. Shouldn't we, couldn't we, do something about this?

All the best
Norbert

Letter 7 Eric Atkinson to David Lewis

September 1998

Dear David

As you are well aware, Leeds was not the only College of Art developing a Basic Course programme during the 1950s and 1960s but it was the programme we were most involved in and I helped to develop. In my last letter to you I intimated that disagreements had arisen between members of staff regarding the direction of the programme. Harry's philosophy was very different from that of Tom Hudson. Tom aligned himself much more with the structure of the pre-war German Bauhaus and to the programmes developed at Ulm under the direction of Max Bill. Harry was determined to keep the programme very fluid and analytical in character and vowed never to write a 'how-to-do-it' manual that could become a crutch for teachers unwilling or unable to strike out on their own. In retrospect it was inevitable that their two philosophies would conflict. Harry became very wary of Tom's Constructivist ideology and Tom felt that Harry's approach relied too heavily on chance or random theory. This dichotomy was solved when Tom accepted a position as Head of Foundation Studies at Leicester College of Art in 1960.

Changes were imperative if the programme was to progress beyond its inaugural stages and not remain trapped by its initial success. Several significant departures took place during the period between 1959 and the Leeds Winter School in 1963. Norbert Lynton, who headed the History of Art programme at Leeds, accepted a position in London. In 1959 Harry's old friend Maurice de Sausmarez resigned as Professor of Fine Art at Leeds University and moved to London, initially as Principal of the Byam Shaw School of Art (and later Head of Fine Art at Hornsey College of Art). Maurice sought to recruit me as his assistant and although the offer was tempting I decided to remain in Leeds. However, I did buy Maurice's house in Little London in Rawdon, a village approximately ten miles outside Leeds and so you and I became neighbours.

Little London, a cluster of millstone grit houses and cottages that had housed a weaving community during the last century, had been discovered by you some years earlier on one of your investigative expeditions. You bought the warehouse at the end of Lombard Street and were busy converting it into a dwelling for yourself and fellow students in the School of Architecture. Our house in Lombard Street became the centre of activity for many projects initiated at Leeds College of Art and a 'home from home' for visiting artists, teachers and students. We embarked on an ambitious restoration programme to modernise the house without endangering its character. We added a comforting Aga in the small kitchen I had panelled with pine boards and we gradually replaced all the window frames which leaked fearsome blasts of icy air into the house during the winter. We knocked down walls and removed the large and hideous Victorian fireplace that crouched in the living room. Of course we had hoped to uncover an elegant Georgian fireplace lurking behind it but alas we discovered not one but two more fireplaces hidden there … each one uglier than the last! In 1960 we opened up the top floor of the house, a large open space which had once housed weaving looms and I was installed in the studio of my dreams with magnificent views across the Aire Valley.

Lombard House was a great house for entertaining and we used any excuse to throw a party. Quite often the company would be joined by our two small children roused from sleep by the sounds of merrymaking floating up from downstairs. During one party for the external assessors just before Christmas 1965 our five-year-old son padded in and caught sight of Alan Davie, resplendent in a scarlet cardigan, sitting talking and stroking his long beard. Sean pounced on him with delight and demanded to know 'where have you left the reindeer?' Our daughter Brigit was much more reticent but startled overnight guests would often find her cuddled up fast asleep beside them when they woke in the morning. We were fortunate enough to be lent a collection of small works by the Cornish primitive painter Alfred Wallis. These were put on exhibition at Leeds College of Art and later at Bretton Hall where my wife was teaching. When the exhibitions closed we hung several of them on the rough white walls of Lombard House. Living with these paintings taught me a great deal about space and frequency … their simple but potent imagery became a major influence on my work. Another influence was Alan Davie's dictum. While he was Gregory Fellow at Leeds we journeyed deep into the Yorkshire Dales in his red Jaguar car. Alan was a passionate glider pilot and told me 'Laddie, you must look at the landscape from above so that you can exclude the horizon line and familiarise yourself with physical space'. A prophetic lesson indeed.

But to return to the changes that were taking place in Leeds. Harry lost another good friend and strong supporter of his programme when in 1957 Terry Frost, who had

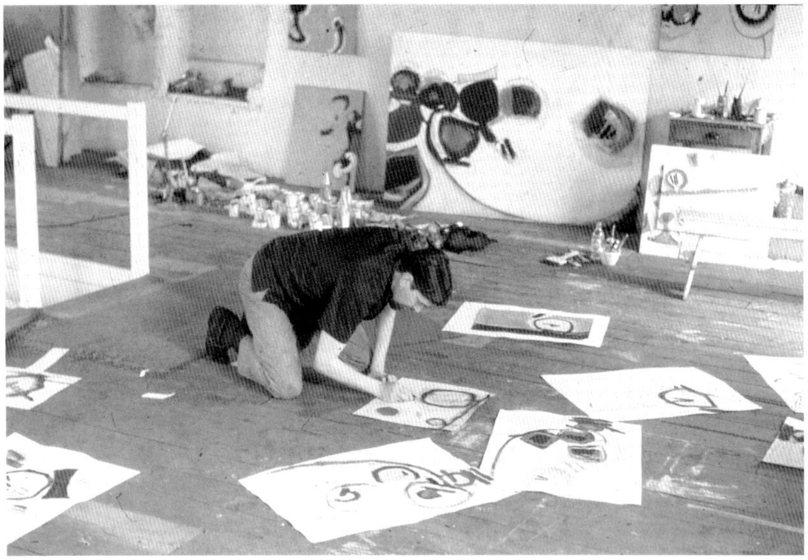

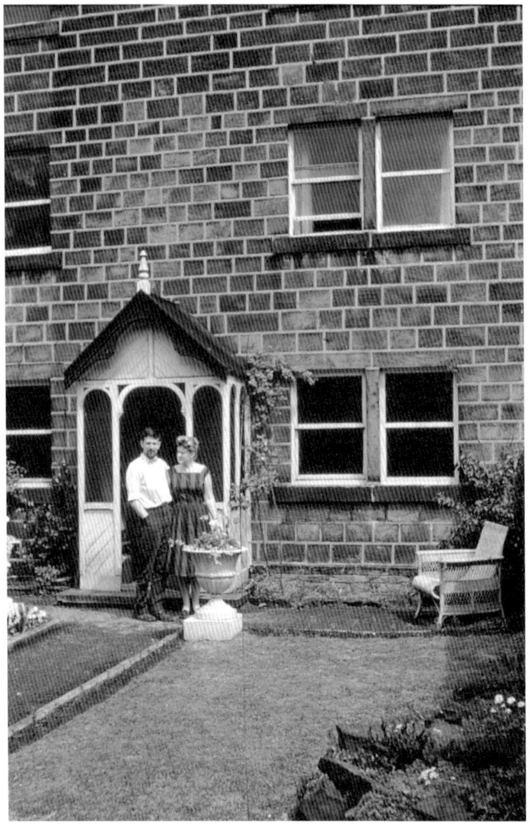

Ricky drawing in his attic studio, Rawdon, Leeds, 1962

Ricky and Muriel outside Lombard House, Little London, Rawdon, Leeds, 1962

remained in Leeds after his Gregory Fellowship was completed, decided to return to Cornwall. In 1964 Terry accepted a full-time teaching position at Reading University. Alan Davie, who had succeeded Terry as Gregory Fellow in Painting, was a stalwart supporter of the programme but his Fellowship too had run its course and he also left Yorkshire. Harry had succeeded in keeping the original team together for five years but he was becoming increasingly frustrated by the lack of official support for his ideas. In spite of the encouragement of politicians like Hugh Gaitskell and Dennis Healey whom he had met through Rose and Bernard Gillinson and the recognition of his work in the United States (where *The Education of Vision*, edited by Gyorgy Kepes of the Massachusetts Institute of Technology, was published in 1964, containing an essay by Anton Ehrenzweig that praised the work being done at Leeds), recognition at home seemed very slow in coming. To add to his frustration his total absorption in promoting the programme had been achieved at a terrible cost to his personal life which began to unravel in 1962.

In 1964 Harry showed his paintings at the Lord's Gallery in London and their favourable reception encouraged him to return to his studio. In ironic contrast to his life Harry's work at this time reflected a private world of absolute calm and zen-like meditation. He was deeply involved with the problems encountered in absorbing three-dimensional objects in a flat picture plane ... problems that would later engross the American painter Robert Rauschenberg. In 1964 Leeds City Art Gallery had mounted an exhibition of work by students and staff at Leeds called 'The Teaching Image'. This exhibition was critically acclaimed and received international press coverage but Harry had already made the fateful decision to leave Leeds and start a new programme at Lancaster College of Art where he would have more time to concentrate on his own work. This decision completely stunned the staff and although I had been acting as Head of the Painting School during the previous two turbulent years I was not alone in wondering 'where do we go from here?'

In 1964 I was asked by a Board headed by Eric Taylor, the Principal of the College of Art, and Quentin Bell, who had succeeded Maurice de Sausmarez as Professor of Fine Art at the University, if I would take over as Head of Fine Art. As Senior Lecturer in Painting I was well aware of the dissension within the College in the wake of Harry's apparent

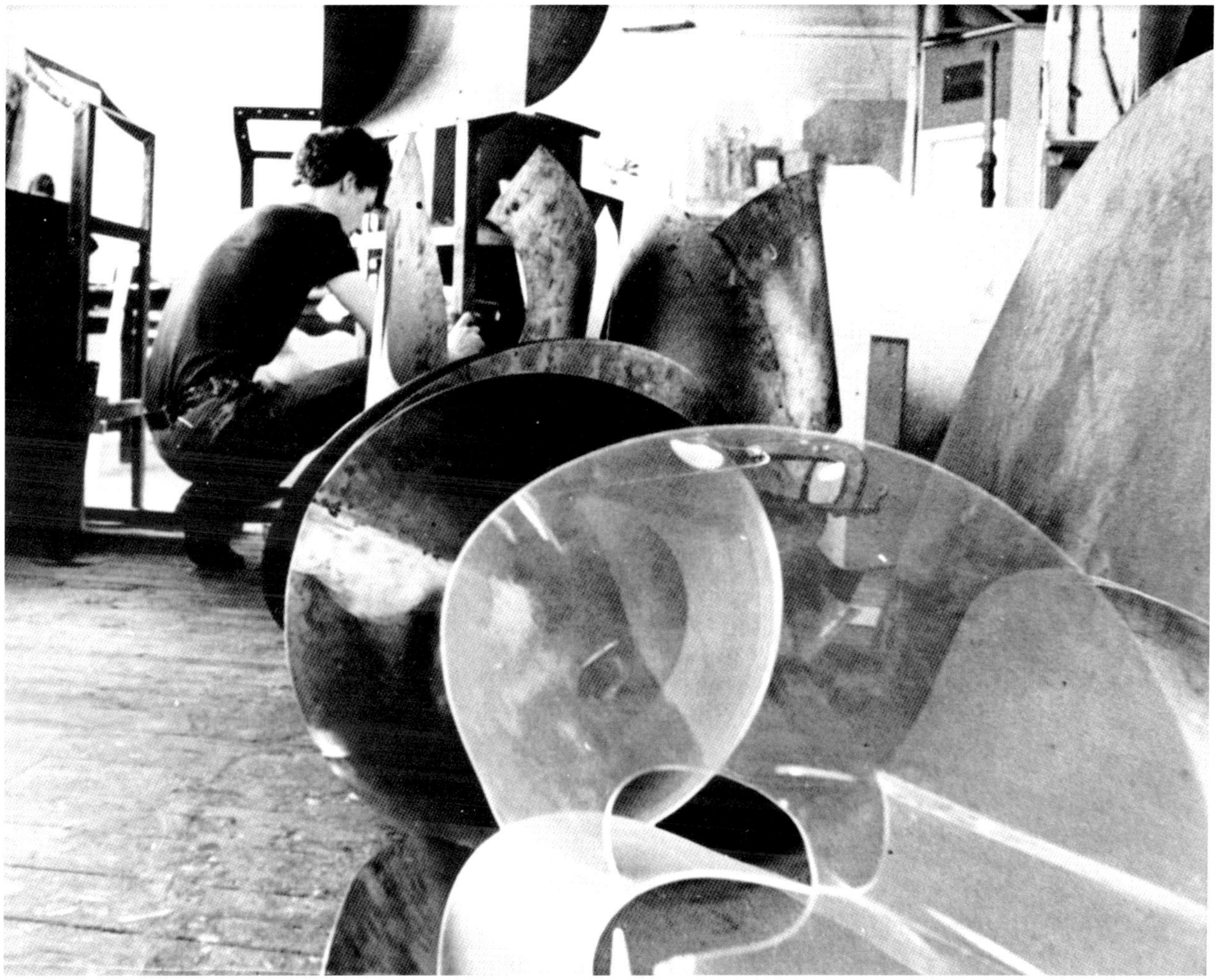

Sculpture studio, Leeds College of Art, 1964 (Metals, plastics, resins and vacuum forming)

defection and knew that it would be a formidable task to rebuild the morale of the department and continue to expand the framework initiated in the Basic Course. There was also the responsibility for the unknown demands of the new Diploma in Art and Design. This new degree programme (Dip AD) which granted Colleges some autonomy over their own educational programmes was the direct result of the recommendations proposed by a committee headed by Sir John Summerson in a report for the Ministry of Education. This report was intended to bring about changes in the curriculum that would put the Art Colleges on an equal footing with the Universities. Colleges were encouraged to develop their individual programmes, formulate their own methods of working and appoint their own external assessors. So it really was possible to challenge and change the system.

The first three years of the DipAD programme were not easy for me. There was some resentment when I stepped into Harry's shoes but by and large those who were not supportive either retired or found work elsewhere. Young and enthusiastic artists eager to help in shaping the new degree programme joined the Faculty and I was able to appoint

Alan Davie, the distinguished Scottish painter and former Gregory Fellow, and Kenneth Martin, the eminent Constructivist, to serve as our first external assessors.

The new DipAD in Fine Art focused on Painting and Sculpture. Our aim was to provide an environment that enabled students to recognise and to some extent realise their individual potential. My first act as the new Head of Fine Art was to tear down the wooden partitions that separated the School of Painting from the School of Sculpture so that there was an easy flow of ideas between the two disciplines and an unconstrained exchange of images between two- and three-dimensional undertakings. The materials might be different but the educational ideology was the same. Prints, Textiles, Ceramics, Plastics, Machine Shop Practice and Experimental Film-making all became extensions of equal concern to the degree course. My intention was to devise a constantly developing programme in which creativity was given priority. Imagination supported by relevant skills encouraged dynamic enquiries rather than predictable solutions. My philosophy was to gather together a group of equally talented people and encourage them to explore the possibilities in a pedagogical situation. Even strong individualists can find some common ground in the pursuit of excellence in education. In 1946 I had met Kurt Schwitters in the Lake District and vividly recalled his comment: 'Mr Atkinson, I am a painter but occasionally I like to nail objects to my canvas!' At the time I had not understood what he meant but as the degree programme took shape I realised that an essential component of the programme must include all manner of experimental concepts whether we understood them or not ... whether they were successful or not. So explorations using every available means of visual communication and new media became an essential part of the basic educational research programme.

Changes in the approach to art history (now renamed Complementary Studies) were essential if they were to complement and enrich the exploratory nature of the programme. A lecture series, often accompanied by intensive week-long workshops, was initiated that exposed the students to a wide variety of expert practitioners in a diversity of fields. As ever in an educational bureaucracy the greatest problem was stretching a limited budget to cover the expense of such a venture. I was very fortunate to have on my staff a sculptor, Harold Cove, who was a brilliant administrative assistant and always managed to find the necessary funding for a special project. His unfailing dependability gave me the flexibility to monitor the day-to-day running of the Department and to navigate it through the first three years of the DipAD programme. There were many days when I envied Harry Thubron painting in the peace and quiet of his studio.

Willy Tirr, George Hainsworth, Miles and Un McAlinden, David Seeger and Barry Ward were joined in the Fine Art Department by staff I appointed to expand the range of the Department. Among them were the painter Patrick Hughes, and Robin Page, a Canadian artist of great diversity and even greater controversy. Robin, a great bear of a man, was everyone's idea of a typical Canadian lumberjack, Russell Platt was recruited to start an experimental film unit, Ken Rowatt, a Constructivist from Nottingham, and Alexander Weatherstone, a contemporary from the Royal Academy Schools, came to teach painting and supervise student theses, the sculptor Glynn Williams joined us, and Roy Slade arrived to coordinate the fledgling Post Diploma programme founded by Tommy Watt who had recently been appointed as Head of Fine Art at Canterbury School of Art. Every member of Faculty canvassed their friends and acquaintances to come and discuss their work with our students. Among the visitors to the College were the American artists George Brecht, Walter de Maria and Yoko Ono, Scottish entrepreneur and gallery director Richard Demarco, musicians George Melly, John Tilbury and Cornelius Cardew, fibre artist Ann Sutton, sculptors Bruce Lacey, Denis Mitchell, Kenneth Martin, Bill Tucker and John Warren Davis, painters Patrick Heron, Trevor Bell, Alan Davie, Terry Frost, Richard Hamilton, Kate de Sausmarez, John Walker, Victor and Wendy Pasmore. Gallery directors Bryan Robertson and Jasia Reichardt, Director of the British Council Lilian Somerville, poets and writers, politicians and physicists ... anyone who excelled in their field was welcomed with open arms, open minds and occasionally frank and riotous discussion!

Exciting though this was the main emphasis of the Department was on studio activity. This could take the form either of individually set problems or group projects. Among the most successful of these was a first year project directed by Miles and Un McAlinden. The students were divided into eight groups of five and asked to design a tent which incorporated some unique expression of their personalities. During the month allocated for this exercise

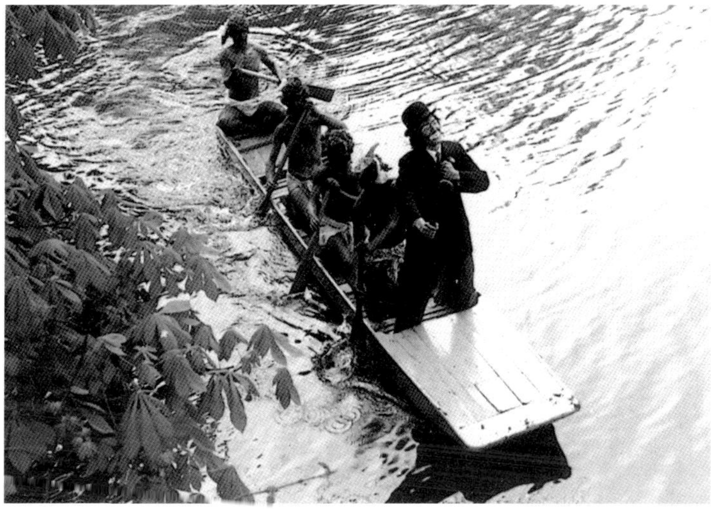

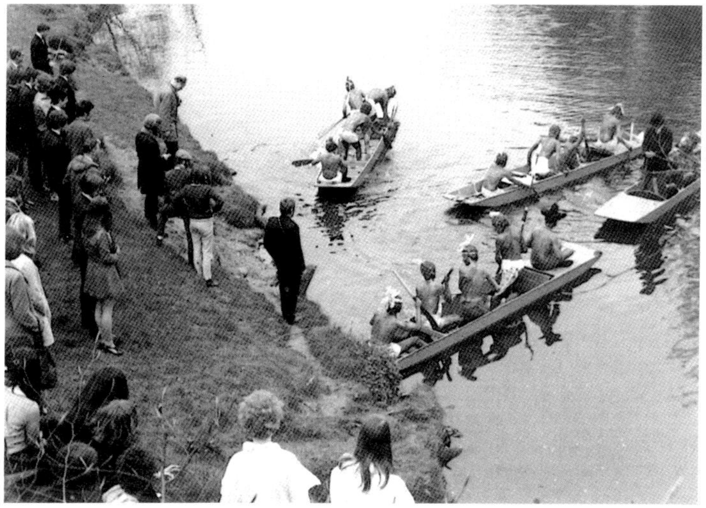

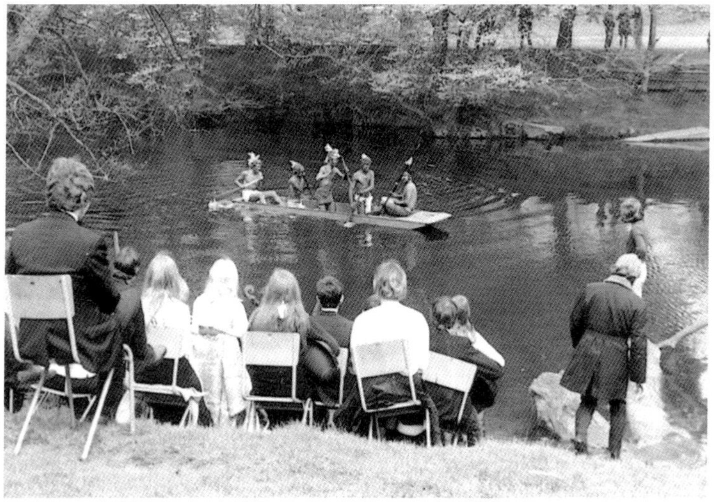

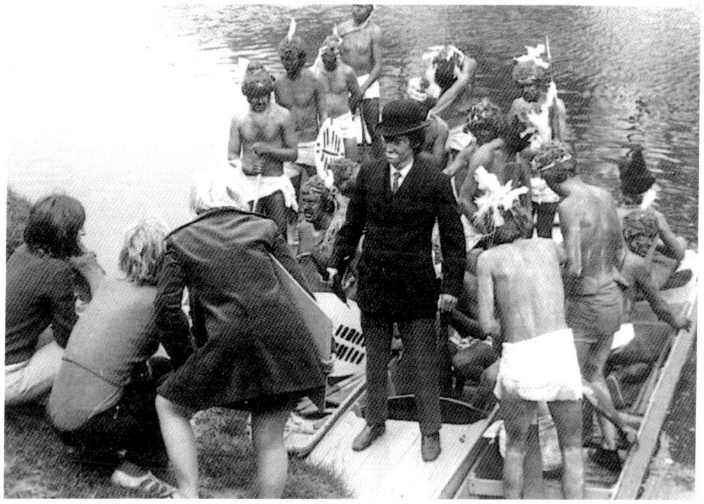

Film stills by Russell Platt for 'Musical', 1967
collection: Bretton Hall Archive, Wakefield

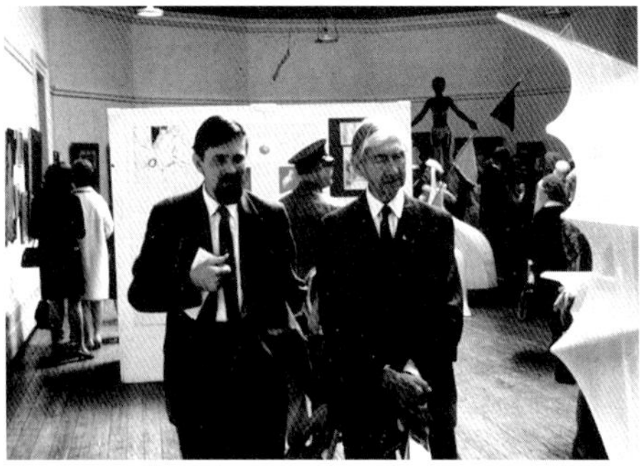

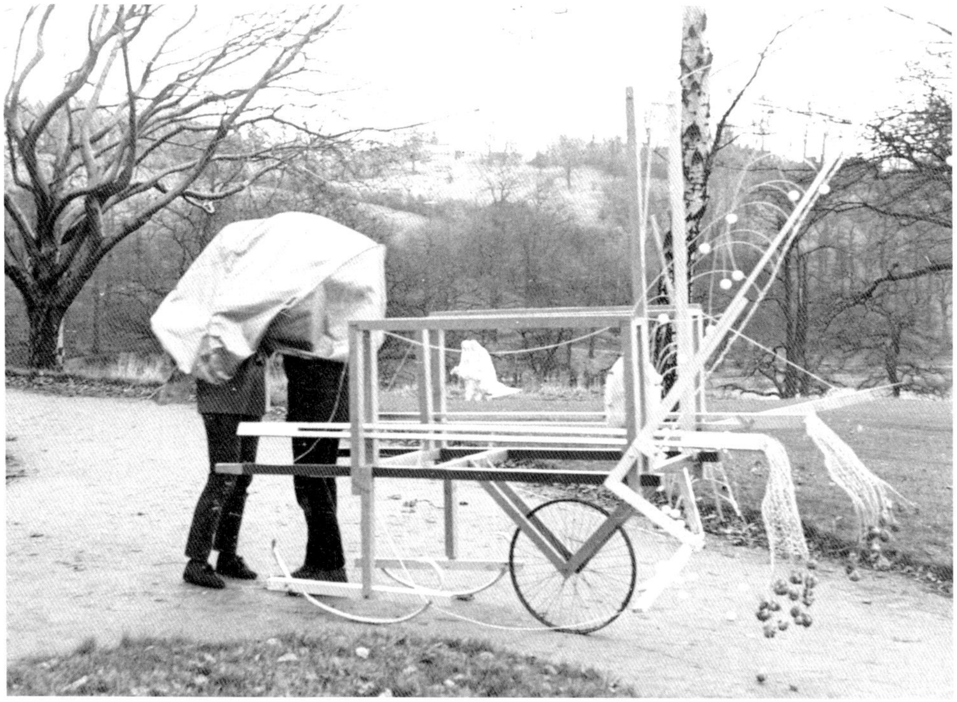

(above)
Sir Herbert Read and Eric Atkinson
at the Fine Art Diploma Show,
Leeds City Art Gallery, 1967

(right)
Film and sculpture project in a local park, 1968
(third-year DipAD students, Fine Art)
collection: Bretton Hall Archive, Wakefield

(below right)
Fine Art Diploma Show, Leeds City Art
Gallery, 1967

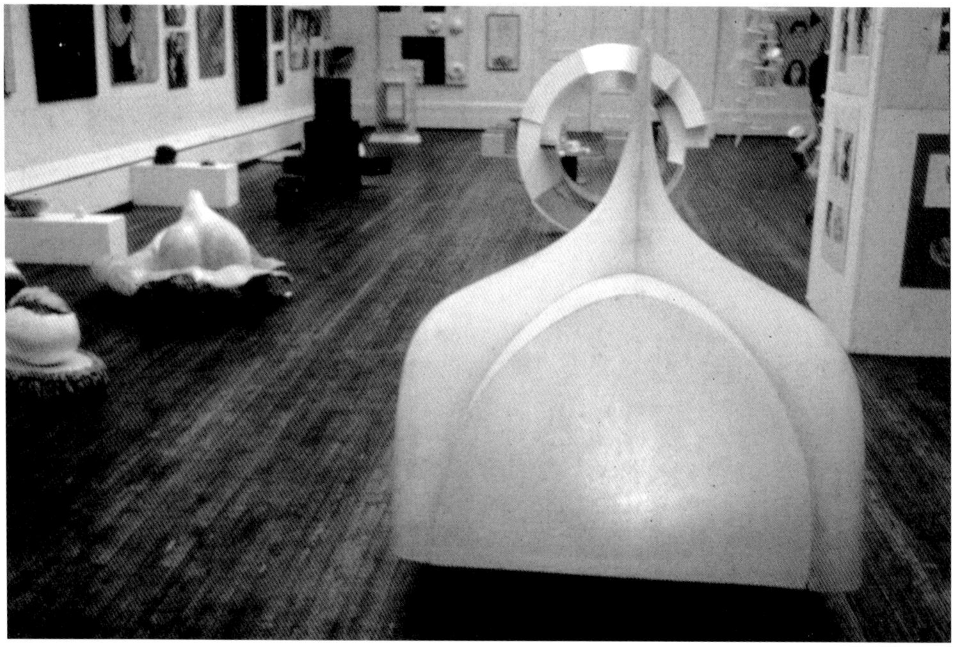

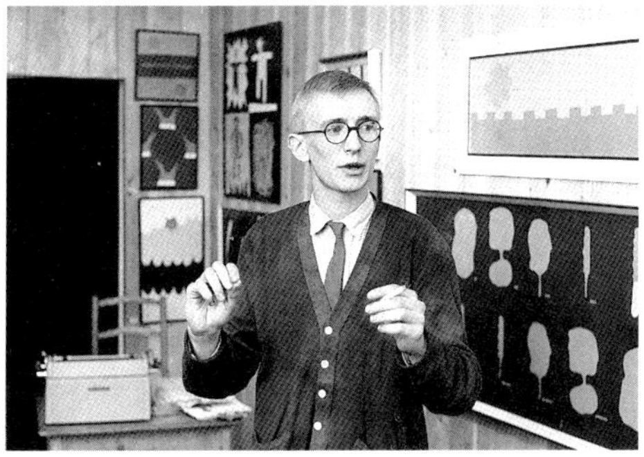

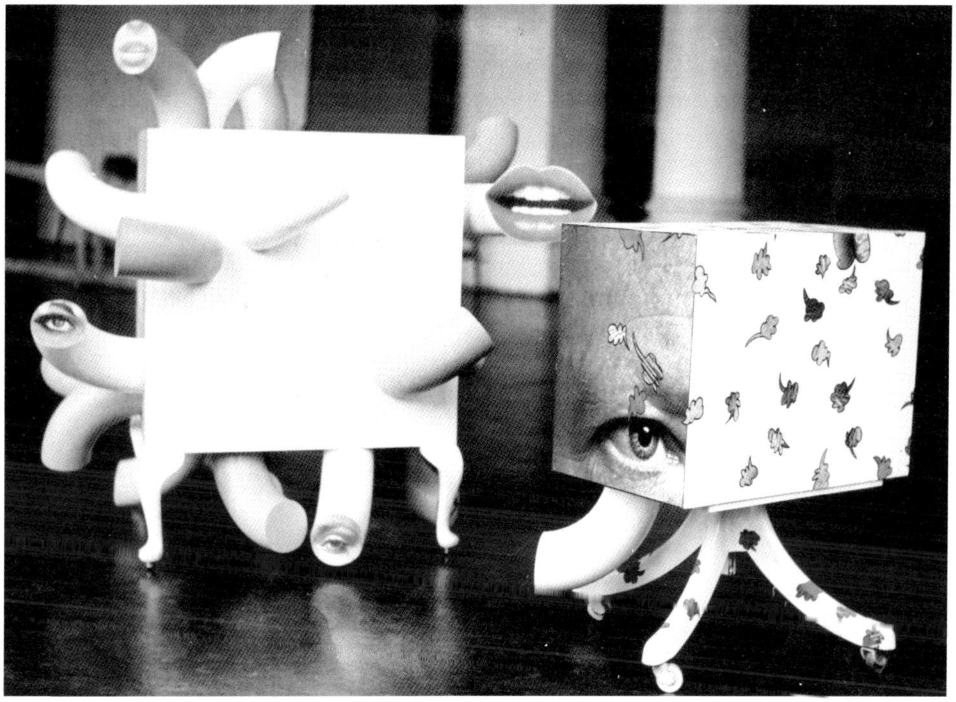

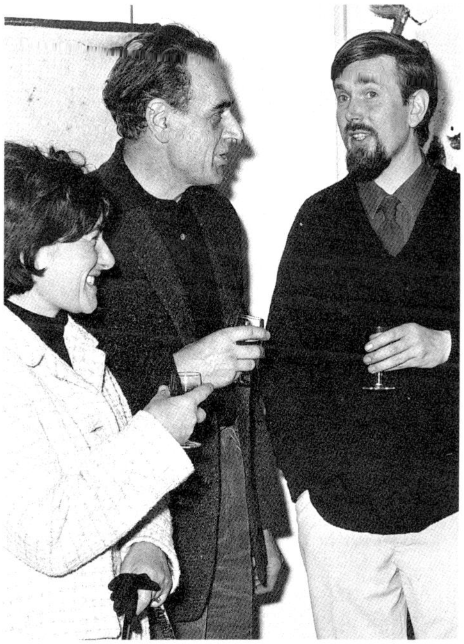

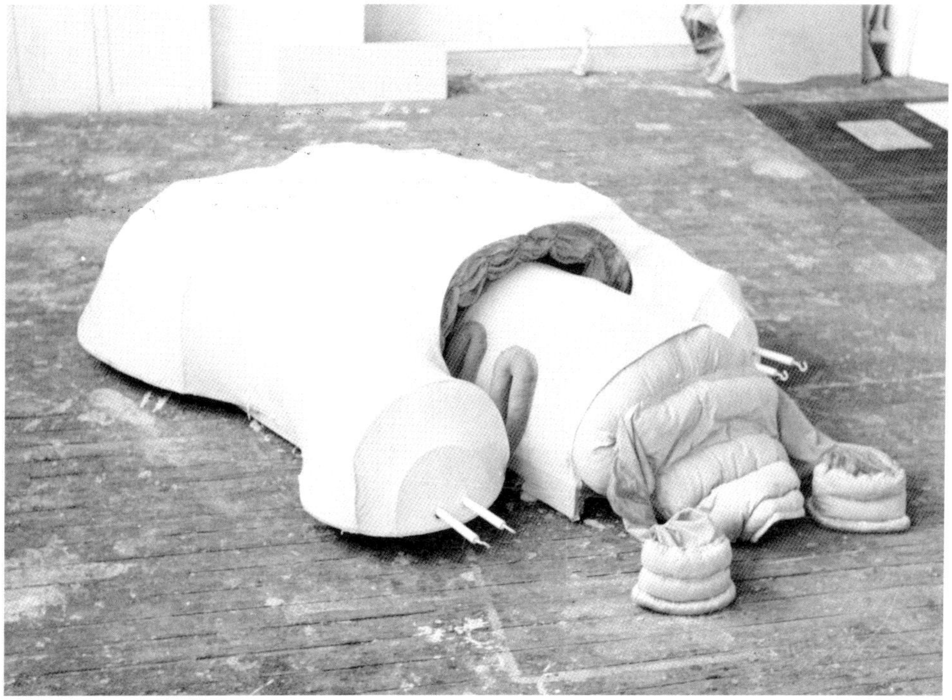

(top left) Patrick Hughes, member of staff, Leeds College of Art, 1964, at an exhibition at the Portal Gallery, July 1961

(above left) Eric Atkinson with Dr and Mrs W Tirr at the Molton Gallery, London, 1965

(top right) Third-year students' work, Fine Art Diploma Exhibition, Civic Theatre Gallery, Leeds 1968

(bottom right) Second-year Tent Project, 1967

students were forced to examine the social problems implicit in a co-operative undertaking as well as the structural difficulties in realising their creations, but the final dramatic exhibition of their 'Tents' exceeded the expectations of the staff as well as the students themselves.

No review of the work at Leeds during 1964–7 would be complete without some tribute to the 'Musical'. This was our first film production and involved the complete Fine Art Department in the creation of a satirical look at the Hollywood Musical with particular reference to Art History. It was the progenitor of 'Monty Python's Flying Circus', combining visual puns with farcical slapstick comedy. We had managed to acquire some 16mm film equipment and the production was directed by Russell Platt assisted by Peter Crass. The idea was originated by a group of four girls and was divided into four fifteen-minute acts. The opening sequence based on Botticelli's 'Birth of Venus' depicted a naked Venus floating ashore on a Shell Petroleum sign attended by a bevy of 'extras' in Victorian frockcoats and top hats. This was filmed on a deserted windswept beach on the North East Coast on a bleak day in early spring. Those students who did not succumb to pneumonia went on to make a sequence based on Poussin's paintings of classical Greek and Roman friezes. This was filmed on the steps of Leeds Town Hall, littered with amputated limbs and rolling heads and with a cloyingly sweet sequence based on 'The Swing' by Fragonard. The finale brought together the Fine Art Departments of all the neighbouring Art Colleges and was filmed at Knaresborough. Several boatloads of students chased one another up the river while a chorus of two hundred students in white sheets serenaded them from the banks with a rousing rendition of Handel's 'Hallelujah Chorus'.

There was a formal film 'Première' some weeks later. Who can forget Glynn William's splendid impersonation of the Queen presenting awards to the leading lady, Carol McNichol, who had arrived in a silver Rolls-Royce accompanied by two borzoi hounds? None of the films made later generated quite the same excitement although they were more skilfully made. One of the students involved in that first film project, a painter called Tony Scott, is now based in Hollywood. He and his brother Ridley Scott work as Directors on Oscar Winners with budgets far in excess of that allocated for the Leeds Film Unit! 'Musical' was then given its World Première on the Fringe of the Edinburgh International Festival where the critic J. R. L. Reyner called it 'a most delightful and irreverent film and a joy to watch'.

My next duel was with the graduating class of 1967 who flatly refused to wear caps and gowns to the degree ceremony! Our student body had become caught up in the wave of unrest that was beginning to rumble across the campuses of so many universities in Europe and North America. Eager to establish student rights and to have some voice in their own education they initiated a campaign of civil disobedience that swept into the 1970s, organising sit-ins and other class disruptions. Our dispute at Leeds was a relatively minor one. After several hours of 'labour/management negotiations' we reached an acceptable compromise. The graduates agreed to wear the gowns but not the 'goofy caps'! And they did look splendid ... the usually paint- and plaster-covered sweaters and jeans were replaced by bright mini-skirted dresses and drainpipe trousers topped by black scholar's gowns, transforming our usually shaggy and unkempt student body into a company of medieval pages. An overwhelming proportion of the graduating class received first-class honours and I felt that the changes in the programme were fully vindicated. Herbert Read readily agreed to present the Diplomas to the first graduating class and he accomplished this with his usual elegance even though his poor health prevented him from delivering his address which was read for him by Quentin Bell.

In autumn 1967 the distinguished painter Patrick Heron and my good friend John Warren Davis, the eminent sculptor, agreed to serve as external assessors for the second phase of the DipAD programme. Students on the one-year Postgraduate programme began to gather national awards like the Granada Fellowship in Painting, the Italian Government Scholarship, British Film Institute Award, Peter Stuyvesant Foundation Award for Sculpture and Fulbright Travel Awards. We had established exchange programmes for staff and students between Leeds and the Dortmund Werkkunstschule in Germany, the Corcoran School of Art in Washington DC (through my friendship with Dean Eugene Myers who had bought two of my paintings while serving with the US Military in England) and with Gray's School of Art in Aberdeen where my good friend and fellow RA student Derek Ashby was a member of Faculty.

Despite the brilliance of the independent art schools in post-war Britain or perhaps because of it there were moves within the Government to 'streamline' Further Education and establish a system of Polytechnics that would deliver a standardised education and save money in the process. The plans for the new Leeds Polytechnic had been approved and the days of the educational buccaneers were numbered. Initially the Chief Education Officer, John Taylor, and the Principal of the Art College, Eric Taylor, were enthusiastic about the merger but later came to regret their acceptance of the new regime without realising how devastating it would prove to be. In fact Eric Taylor resigned when the full implications of the College's loss of identity became apparent. I was very uneasy about the proposed changes but fully occupied in planning the new building. When I received an invitation to visit the Corcoran School of Art in the autumn of 1967 I was eager to accept but Leeds refused to release me because of my involvement with the building project so Roy and Rona Slade were asked to go in my place. James Twitty, a Professor of Painting at the Corcoran, came to Leeds on an exchange. Jim arrived at Leeds City station wearing a tartan cap and carrying a copy of *The Times* under his arm so that he would be more easily recognised but despite his British clothes he could never be mistaken for anyone but an American. By the time the Slades returned from the USA a year later I felt very strongly that the College was heading for disaster but was powerless to halt the mad stampede to the Polytechnic. Like Harry before me I had held the Department together for five years so when an invitation came to take a position in Canada I gladly accepted.

Patrick Heron, a frequent visitor to Leeds and a valued friend, became a vigorous campaigner on behalf of Art Education and the independent Art Colleges. Filling the vacuum left by Herbert Read's death, his was the voice of reason, intelligence and passion. In his article 'The Murder of the Art Schools' published in *The Guardian* in October 1971 he referred to the amazing brilliance of Leeds 'the most influential College in Europe since the Bauhaus' and to 'the quite dazzling multiplication of idioms that have generated at Leeds an unprecedented inventive powerhouse on the national scene'.

With love
Ricky

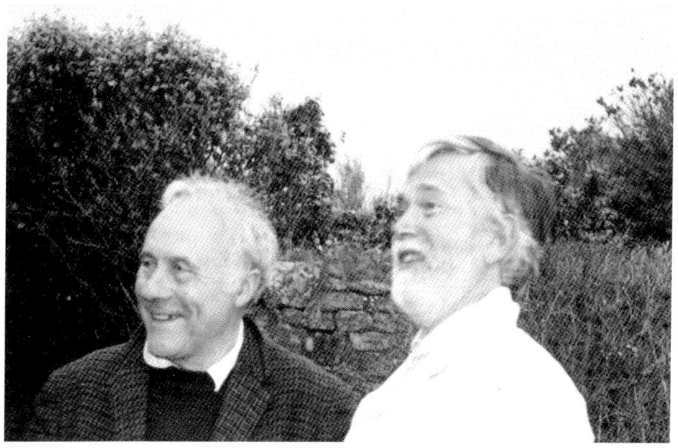

Patrick Heron and Eric Atkinson in the garden of Heron's home, Eagles' Nest, Zennor, Cornwall, 1988

Letter 8 George Hainsworth to Eric Atkinson

16 October 1998

Dear David

I wonder whether you remember George Hainsworth? He was a student at Leeds, but a year ahead of you. As a result he didn't go through the Basic Course with Harry and me. But Harry made special provision for him and his group, and he remembers clearly some of the fun we had on the Basic Course.

As you may recall, George won a Gulbenkian Scholarship for sculpture at the Slade. He is now a Professor of Fine Art, Design and the Built Environment at Leeds Metropolitan University.

I'm enclosing a letter I've just received from him.

With best wishes,
Ricky

10 October 1998

Dear Ricky

I started as a fine art student at the Leeds College of Art in September 1955. The principal was Edward Pullee. The nature of the course was academic, in the sense that there was a strong emphasis on life drawing, pictorial composition (one wasn't allowed to use oils for several years prior to going to college), plant drawing (ie botanical study under the tapestry tutor, Miss Auty), modelling in clay, carving in stone and wood, letter design, etc, etc.

Art history was dates, and a strong emphasis on 'movements'. All these components were part of a curriculum leading to the Intermediate Certificate in Art and Design. This was a two-year course which then led on to specialisation in painting, sculpture, graphics, dress design, etc.

The second phase, too, was a two-year course of study and culminated in the National Diploma in Design (NDD). The staff who taught the NDD didn't teach Intermediate students and vice versa; ie it was progressive and hierarchical. I certainly enjoyed the experience of starting at the College of Art, even though I was somewhat overawed by it. With hindsight one can see that it was probably provincial in outlook and insular in regard to the major art developments which had taken place in Europe.

Harry arrived as Head of Painting in Leeds about Easter 1956, that is about six or seven months into my course. My friend Barry Ward and I and about nine or ten other students were brought together with some staff, and Harry talked to us – a bit, I suppose, like a general to his troops or a football coach to his players.

The things that were implicit in his talk were that he had a vision, that we were going to help him to realise it, that it was exciting and we were privileged to be part of it, that we were important and were chosen, and that of course, Harry himself was important! He was charismatic (I think he was probably also chauvinistic). He needed to dominate.

The talk he gave us indicated the need to prove his educational vision within the period of the summer term, at the end of which it would either get further support or fold. To this end we, the chosen, were absolved from our previous timetabling. We were given the use of one of the big studios in the Painting School; I think it had previously been used for Still Life and the study of classical plaster casts – 'Drawing from the Antique'. When later I got a place at the Slade, the Slade still had such a facility.

At this stage, early in Harry's time at Leeds, the terms 'basic' and 'foundation' for courses were not in use. We, as the first group of his students, were given quite a large diversity of materials – paper, paint, metal, wood etc – and were encouraged to experiment with these materials creatively and without preconception or conditioning (insofar as this was possible) either separately or in collaboration with one another. The creativity (ie the 'Art') grew out of the relationship one built up with the materials. The Art was a by-product of accessing one's self: the rhythms, aspirations, sensitivities and insights which are part of an educative process. It was intended to help one understand 'form' and its importance to potent artistic expression.

I think that for a period of about a year prior to arriving at Leeds Harry had worked with primary schoolchildren and had been impressed and influenced by their innate creative potential; a potential which, if properly channelled, could yield unprecedented social benefits. I think this vision had strong parallels with the Bauhaus experiment, which later came to be the automatic and more obvious link with what Harry initiated at Leeds.

I think this link with the Bauhaus is very important for its egalitarian implications, especially when you realise that even at this late post-war period, education, despite assertions to the contrary and many advances, was class structured. I think that Harry was both egalitarian *and* elitist, and used the conflict between the two instinctively to avoid

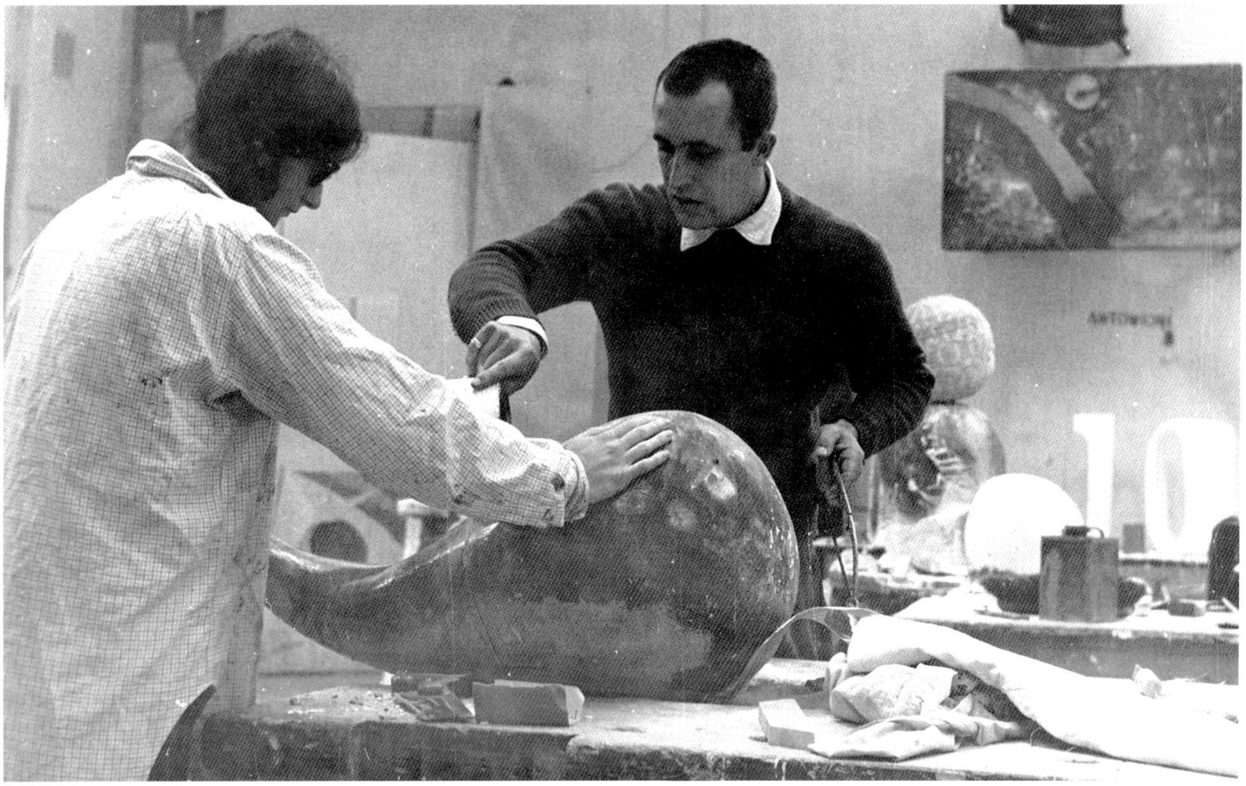

Professor George Hainsworth with a student in the sculpture class, Leeds College of Art, 1968

becoming academic, and to provide an imbalance which would drive his ideas on social change. He believed that Art could change things, not by its monetary value as is often now the case, but by the message it intrinsically carried.

In that term, from Easter up to the summer break in 1956, we worked quite pragmatically. We had crits, mainly from Harry, which sometimes were quite stringent. There wasn't a systematic programme. It was as though we, the students, were defining the programme. There were links being made with the Leeds University Art Department. The most interesting and dynamic Gregory Fellow at this point was Alan Davie. The Head of Fine Art at the University was Maurice de Sausmarez, who seemed to have a good rapport with Harry, and I believe may have been instrumental in helping to get academics such as Richard Hoggart (a language specialist and a Communist) to lecture to us in the context of Art History and Theory (only 'theory' was not a word in vogue then).

I think that the separation of we students from the rest of the student body did cause resentment and discord, particularly among the students in the years ahead of us. Established staff in the main seemed to respect Harry's ideas and were supportive. NDD staff became accessible to Basic Course students. It opened the system up.

At the end of this first term we put up an exhibition of our work, open to all the College to come and look at. Herbert Read came to the opening and enthusiastically lent his considerable support to the project. It seemed that Harry and Herbert Read were on the same intellectual wavelength and he became the project's patron, if not in name then in spirit.

I have no regrets that I was there at that time. It was an interesting experiment that would still be viable in the right hands today. Of course it is still there in foundation courses; we find it in the work brought to the admission interviews.

There's less emphasis nowadays on an understanding of form and formal concerns. But there is a much stronger emphasis on philosophies and ideologies of the nineteenth and twentieth centuries. The critical discussion side of things has expanded and students are much more aware of the wider spectrum of society and politics than in our time. But in their actual practice, they are forced to find a style too early, to crystallise their direction before they have arrived at it through exploration, research and discovery. And of course departments can no longer allow wide-ranging voyages of exploration: they are answerable to higher authorities who wield the knife.

Yours
George

Conversations between Sir Terry Frost and David Lewis

In July 1992 I taped a conversation with Terry in which we discussed the time he spent in Leeds as Gregory Fellow and its effect on his painting.

DL: In place of the rocking semicircles of your (earlier) Cornwall paintings, attenuated rectangular panels or trapeziums, separated by black lines, predominate in the paintings of the Leeds period. Some of these are known as the 'washing-line' paintings because the black lines soar upwards to a horizon at the top of the canvas.

Some of the canvases inspired by the (Yorkshire) Dales are hot dry summer paintings in brilliant orange and red with powerful black lines. Others are winter paintings in which the snow colours are cold and wet.

TF: Just sitting in a Land Rover with Kenneth Armitage and being in a vast cape of white and cold but brilliant space, the sharp air and smooth folds of white snow resting on fields, hanging on black lines.... Things like the Land Rover freezing up were useful because we had to walk to a farm and ask, quite early on a Sunday morning, for some warm water, and the walking was good because I went down and the white came up all around and yet it never touched me, so I was a black thing in a funnel of white with no space that I knew. I could not touch the sides, the space and the silence went with me, and I was so small.

In July 1993 I had another taped conversation with Terry. Here is an excerpt about how a series of painting and collages evolve from a drawing.

DL: It was exciting to us to hear (you) talk about such simple things as the sun and seeds, and lorries and clouds, and walking in the Dales, experiencing the almost vertical fields on each side rising to the brilliance of a white sky, or (your) description of Kath in a bathing suit laced up the back sitting on a rock beside a rushing stream in Nidderdale....

TF: I made a drawing of Kath from behind, as she was sitting with her feet in the cold rushing water of the stream, and there were these two semicircles of her buttocks coming in from the side of the paper with the crisscross of the lacing of her bathing suit, tied in a bow, in black charcoal – and that simple drawing had a lot of meaning for me. I remember as a kid I used to have to lace up my grandmother in the ivory-coloured stays, and how she had a bit of red flannel in the front where her cleavage was. And I remember how Ben used to talk about 'tightening up the form' as though he was talking about a spanner. And then when I looked at those semicircles in my drawing my mind went back to the boats, and I thought how the brown mizzen sails at the stern are laced taut to keep the boat into the wind. So I glued two raw hessian shapes onto the canvas and I thought I could pull them tight by knocking holes through and lacing them taut with Army bootlaces. That was 'SS9'. I wasn't happy with the lacing so the next time I got the proper tools for punching holes and grummets so the laces wouldn't tear up the canvas, and then as I was lacing up my shoes I saw that the trick was the triangular slit which you draw together when you tighten the laces; and all these things led to a series of paintings, collages, and lithographs with laces. Well, I took one of them up to London to show Leslie Waddington, and he said, 'Terry, it's too sexy; it's like a chastity belt'. Then he bought it for himself, so I knew it was OK....

In November 1998 I taped a conversation with Terry regarding Leeds, Thubron and the Basic Course.

DL: When the Basic Course was first introduced in 1956, what was the reaction of the Leeds College faculty to it?

TF: There was this Scottish lad, Tommy Watt, a good painter – he took the life class in the big room next to Harry's painting studio. He couldn't stand us. He was frightened that the whole thing was going to destroy the school. He didn't realise that Harry's idea of drawing was a damn sight more important and more alive and exciting than the old life-room style, which was stifling. By the time you'd done one of those things it was dead. But Tommy Watt got to like us in the end. Harry had a way of involving the old guard and making them feel like kings. There was Gavin Stewart – another Scot. If anyone wanted to discuss colour theory old Gavin could keep going for hours with no problem at all.

DL: What was so different?

TF: It was a fantastic period. Of course, none of the students have ever forgotten that time. I was lucky to overlap with two other Gregory Fellows. I went in once a week, and then Alan Davie would come in once a week and Nibs Dalwood would come in once a week. The whole thing was a studio with different attitudes and the same philosophical idea about it. We were all finding out how to get the best out of each other.

And the wonderful thing about Harry was that he'd give

a philosophical talk about creativity which would include diagrams on the blackboard, and about twenty cigarettes which he'd inhale right down to his big toe, and he'd finish up with a beautiful drawing of a lavatory bowl, then he'd add the chain, and then to the delight of the students he'd flush it to show what he thought of the Ministry of Education.

Anyway the thing was it was one of the best courses I've ever been involved in. I think we got it right.

DL: You worked for a time in Newcastle, didn't you? Was that very different?

TF: Yes, I went to Newcastle on a fellowship in 1964 and worked with Richard Hamilton. That course was much more intellectual than artistic, and quite linked with academic graphic art really. It's proved itself though because it's what all the Yanks were doing – and making a bloody fortune, weren't they? It was quite another attitude.

But I think Leeds got it right.

I've always been opposed to art history, but only the way it was taught. Harry pulled in Norbert Lynton from the architecture school and asked Norbert to do what art historians can't stand, a survey. All that art historians want to do is the period they've studied because it's the only bloody thing they know. That's disastrous for young students. Norbert introduced our students to Mondrian and Klee right from the first day, and he'd use historical examples to shed light on what contemporary artists are doing, and by God, in six months they looked at Duchamp as if they really understood what he was about.

DL: My great sadness was that the Basic Course was over too quickly.

TF: Yes, I know it was sad. But it did us all good. We were doing something we'd never done before. We had to shake things up and make everyone think.

When the old Ripley Museum folded Harry got some of their boxes and took everything out, eggs, skeletons, bones, archaeological stuff, and tipped it all out onto the studio floor for the first-year students to draw. That's how they learned their proportions and scale. And then Harry would send them out on scavenging expeditions to bring in stuff for collages and constructions. The challenge was to look at everyday things afresh and discover what you might call their accidental qualities and use them.

DL: You worked on some of the summer schools in Wales, didn't you?

TF: We did those with Harry and Ricky and Frank Lisle, the one-eyed painter from Leeds. We had a marvellous time with students from eighteen to eighty years old. They were up all night working with pure colour, and when they pinned the work up in the morning you discovered that everyone was personal and unique. That's why the course was so amazing, we were all learning, every man jack of us.

People from other art schools came to see us and they helped to break down some of the prejudices that still existed. We were at our best then, because we hadn't got buggered up when dear old Coldstream tried to streamline the standards. Once you put things into the hands of civil servants or ministers you're finished. They want everything to be bloody well the same.

Coldstream had a point when he suggested making the art schools part of the universities. But on the minus side you lose the energy and the impetuousness that comes from new ideas.

DL: Were the ideas generated by the Basic Course adopted by other art colleges?

TF: Yes. But it broke my heart to see how quickly the ideas became distorted. I look nowadays at students' portfolios and the work is all dead. Invention has gone. You look through, and no one has discovered anything for themselves. Bloody squares all over with no feeling at all. Ricky saw this starting to happen in Leeds.

DL: What do you feel about what Ricky was doing in Canada?

TF: O fantastic! There's a toughness there. You know that from his paintings. He employed so many good people – he always knew what to do with people. He got them excited. He opened up the whole thing into music and film and television. I saw the courses in action, and I thought they were first class. The students were happy, like they were in Leeds.

Ricky did a marvellous job, set the place alight. But then the academic bureaucracy tied his hands to play it safe. That's the tragedy – playing it safe. It means nothing exciting or innovative ever happens again.

In 1959 an exhibition, 'The Developing Process', was put on at the Institute of Contemporary Arts in London to show the teaching methods of Leeds and Newcastle. Terry Frost contributed the following to the catalogue:

TF: It was a very good starting point for the first-year students to study colour. In colour analysis students are faced with the fundamentals of colour related to form. The basic problem of alerting people's senses to colour can be demonstrated by using a flower as an example. The students are free to analyse and to synthesise as they will, and in doing so, they come to grips with certain basic problems.

The grammar of colour mixing gives an analogy in paint on paper of the colour of the flower.

Objective drawing: a description of the particular proportions and shape of the colour. The drawing (constructed) and the colour (felt) are both put into one's grasp at the same time.

The training of the eye in selection

The training of the hand

Training in seeing the part in relation to the whole

Then being involved to such a degree that one's senses are continually aware of colour and its relationship to a particular form at all times....

All of our students have found that with sufficient effort (I want to emphasise that it does not have to be the talented student only) the rhythm of growth can easily be observed, understood, and put down on the flat with the medium. This in turn enables the student to tackle the various problems of construction in any department of the School of Art. At the same time it gives them a sound foundation for their creative ideas, and they can make their own work grow, as in nature.

A student given, say, a 'thesis in yellow' will discover with complete freedom within the colour yellow organisation, harmony, and discord all allied to proportion and form, which would be very difficult to come by from the study of colour-theory alone. Simple things are noted, like the different greens on leaves or stalks which come with each different yellow. The amount of yellow or orange to blue and purple in a pansy. The cool and warm of colour. All these things are covered in an objective way in colour analysis, plus the surprise and reward of personal discovery.

From Colin Phipps

Architect, 1998,
student in the Basic Course, Leeds College of Art, 1956

Dear David

Coming straight from traditional grammar schools to the freewheeling nature and charisma of the people in charge was a wonderful transition between school and architecture.

It is now a matter of great regret among teachers, students and practitioners that architecture was taken out of the Art Schools. The interaction between architecture and art students has largely been lost, to be replaced by modular courses in architecture without an artist in sight. Instead we have architecture headed by engineers, computers and management.

The memorable thing about that first term at Leeds was sitting in those north-lit studios with Harry in jeans and crew-neck sweater, talking about painting, sculpture, Leonardo; he even talked about Mies, which was beyond the architecture tutors. He encouraged me particularly in my tentative efforts in painting and the whole concept of the relationships of objects and lines in space. Too soon we were back in the architecture school scratching around with a showroom for a glass company.

Others were around, of course: Terry Frost, Alan Davie, Gavin Stewart, Ricky Atkinson, Tom Hudson.

In addition to my burgeoning career as a major painter, I also sculpted a door handle which I like to think was cast in aluminium but was probably in plaster or alabaster. I also learned the then tricky technique of fibreglass moulding and I constructed a chair with a red shell sitting on a bent steel frame painted grey. I used it as my drawing board for several years to come.

Yours
Colin

From John Davies

Architect, 1998,
student in the Basic Course, Leeds College of Art, 1956

Dear David

I came to the Leeds School of Architecture in September 1956, having spent two years working for an architectural practice in Norwich and attending Norwich College of Art and the City Technical College. My father was an architect for Reckitt & Colman. The firm I worked for was mainly involved in the traditional council housing that blights our surroundings today and the course at Norwich was to borrow anything that came out of Sweden. My father had been a part-time student at Leeds in the 1920s and it was his idea that I should study at Leeds. I did A-level art at school and enjoyed painting, but my understanding of art did not extend beyond Impressionism.

After an introduction to Alec Lacy we were bundled off to the College of Art. Harry Thubron did not mince words and his earthy comments had the girls blushing. We started by dividing a sheet of paper into squares and filling in those squares with different tones and variations of blue. What was it all about? Then Harry pointed out that some squares came forwards and others backwards. The more we experimented the more we jumped about and the more exciting it all became. Then we tried using different colours. Then off to Timms where Vernon from Wards, who sold pencils, paper and paint, bought the pints. Anthony John Selby was always standing close to Vernon so as not to miss out on the next one. Back up to the top floor of the College with Harry talking about 'space' in art. We then got involved in shapes and the different impacts of the relationship of shapes in space and colour. This was all very tidy.

In walked Alan Davie. Throw the paint, walk on it, ride bikes over it. How exciting and all by accident. It nearly was when Malcolm Collins, whether intentionally or not when lighting his pipe, set fire to all the paper and turps.

Harry talked about Nicolas de Staël, who painted a picture of footballers using a spade instead of a paintbrush. It had a terrific impact and was busy and exciting. He spoke about how the paintings became non-figurative, peaceful, simpler with large areas of flat colour, the ultimate in space. We heard about de Staël's tragic suicide because he thought he was in reverse gear.

Following a period of cutting small cubes from a large cube of plaster, I had a go at metal sculpture with tuition from Tom Hudson and Laurie Burt. I burnt my fingers because I didn't realise that if a piece of metal was not red it could still be as hot as hell. We bent, twisted and welded, and I finally produced a form which I proudly displayed for Sir Hubert Bennett at the Intermediate Oral Exam.

Then we returned to the School of Architecture to practise Trajan lettering with Mr Swindells and design a doll's house for Mr Lacy. I had come to realise that there was more to architecture than copying the Swedes and putting diamond-patterned projecting headers on brickwork. Architecture had space and form; I was particularly interested in the development of the twisted curve or hyperbolic parabaloid of Naum Gabo. I think it was David Lewis who introduced me to Gabo.

I started to paint again in my spare time, enjoying action painting as a relief from the disciplines of architecture school. Two of these paintings became a deposit on the purchase of our first house. Harry Thubron was always pleased to give me a crit. Following my return to England from Hong Kong I started to paint very seriously. I had for some time been a friend of the late Michael Andrews and had consumed copious amounts of beer over many hours talking with Michael. Michael had a different approach to painting, being closely associated with Francis Bacon and Lucian Freud. I was running out of ideas with action painting and wanted more substance. I had developed a love for Trad Jazz from raving Ed O'Donnell, and was paying regular visits to a pub in Islington to listen to Johnny Parker's band. Michael suggested I should paint the band and develop paintings from there. I started by painting the whole band figuratively; then I started to abstract. I had been fascinated by the approach of de Staël and painted with a knife. I met Alf Dunn who had been at Leeds College of Art and who was then exhibiting kinetic sculpture and teaching graphic art at the Royal Academy. He suggested using a trowel! Like de Staël my paintings became simpler and more spatial, but I have no intention of committing suicide.

In conclusion, that term in Leeds College of Art was a fantastic idea. Harry Thubron and his team were instrumental in developing our architectural and artistic outlooks in a creative manner rather than just copying the likes of Corb, Mies and Gilbert Scott.

With best wishes
John

Letter 9 David Lewis to Peter Stead

November 1998

Dear Peter

Ben Nicholson encouraged my interest in Mondrian. It started with Ben's reliefs.

First there were his early ones, made in the early 1930s, circles and rectangles cut into cardboard and coloured. The circles were never circles and the rectangles were never rectangles. Their asymmetries were playful in the way they related to one another. Add the colour, and the playfulness became electric. Then came the white reliefs of the middle and late 1930s. They radiated a serenity of proportions so powerful that everything else in the room related to them.

Willie Barns-Graham and I had one in our little house on Teetotal Street in St Ives. Even on dark rainy days it radiated its serene energy. It was framed in a manner Ben described as 'reverse section'. The back of the relief was the same plane as the wall, so the relief pushed out into the actual space of the room. He said he learned this from Mondrian. There could be no illusory depths, no inner perspective. The white reliefs, like Mondrian's paintings, were intended to be part of the architectural space we live in, indeed its generators of proportion and scale.

I shall never forget seeing a Mondrian in Peggy Guggenheim's palazzo in Venice. It was 1954 and Willie and I were in Venice for the Biennale. We stayed on the Guidecca in a gloomy house once occupied by D'Annunzio and his mistress. A notice over the handbasin told us that the tap contained ruining water. We plied back and forth to St Mark's on a vaporetto with Max Fry standing at the prow. The British Pavilion was filled with a retrospective of Nicholson's paintings and reliefs. There were solo exhibitions of Arp and Max Ernst.

Ben's work caused a stir among the Europeans. It seemed to take them by surprise. They didn't expect such clarity and power from a British artist. The editors of Italian and French art magazines asked me to write on Ben for them. A new glossy magazine, *Aujourd'hui*, was still in the planning stage. Its editor was to be the sculptor-architect André Bloc. Bloc asked me to write the lead article on Ben for his inaugural issue.

In the hall of the Guggenheim palazzo you were confronted by a huge Ernst. Its message was nightmarish and menacing. Then there was a corridor with a Miró which offered a message of fun. And round the corner was a room with a French window overlooking the Grand Canal. Outside the window a bronze sculpture of a horse and rider by Marino Marini was a centre of attention, since the horse looked bored and sleepy but the rider was leaning back to expose his erection – which could be discreetly unscrewed and hidden whenever the Cardinal came by in his gondola. On a wall painted black beside the window was the Mondrian. Its reverse section radiated its equilibrium into the room. The world was all of a sudden silent and at peace.

I had been researching Mondrian for the little book I was doing for Faber. The French writer Michel Seuphor was a strong supporter. Sitting at breakfast in pavement cafés, he'd regale me with anecdotes about Mondrian, whom he knew well, including how poor Mondrian was, and how he'd chew raw peanuts and drink lots of water in the hope that the nuts would swell up inside him and he'd feel as if he'd had a decent meal. I had been to Amsterdam to see that warmest of art enthusiasts, Willi Sandberg, director of the Stedelijk, and I'd been to see S. B. Slijper, who was elderly and unwell, but had a large collection of early Mondrians. Through Ben I had introductions to several of his friends and colleagues from the 1930s in Paris, people he had exhibited with in Abstraction-Création or who had participated in *Circle*, Jean Arp, Herbin, César Domela, the writer Henri-Pierre Roche, and the Constructivist Antoine Pevsner, whose brother was Naum Gabo, all of whom had vivid things to say about the pre-war period.

These were heroic artists. They staked everything on what they did. They believed deeply in the directions they had forged in the 1920s and 1930s, and now that the war and the Occupation were over they went straight on without compromise. The more uncompromising they were the more scant was critical understanding or galleries to back them. I was lucky to get to know Pevsner quite well. He had spent the German Occupation of Paris in hiding – literally underground. He was everything the Nazis hated, a Russian Jew, an avant-garde Constructivist artist (therefore decadent), and a Leninist. He and Virginie survived because she, a one-time opera singer, could sing popular songs in the cafés.

I would go to his apartment in a district of Paris called Malakoff. I sometimes wondered whether he lived there because the name had Russian associations. On my way I would buy cheeses and a baguette. Pevsner would have me move up my chair so close to his that our knees touched. Virginie would serve us vodka in small glasses. In the apartment he wore the grey woollen skull cap she'd knitted for him.

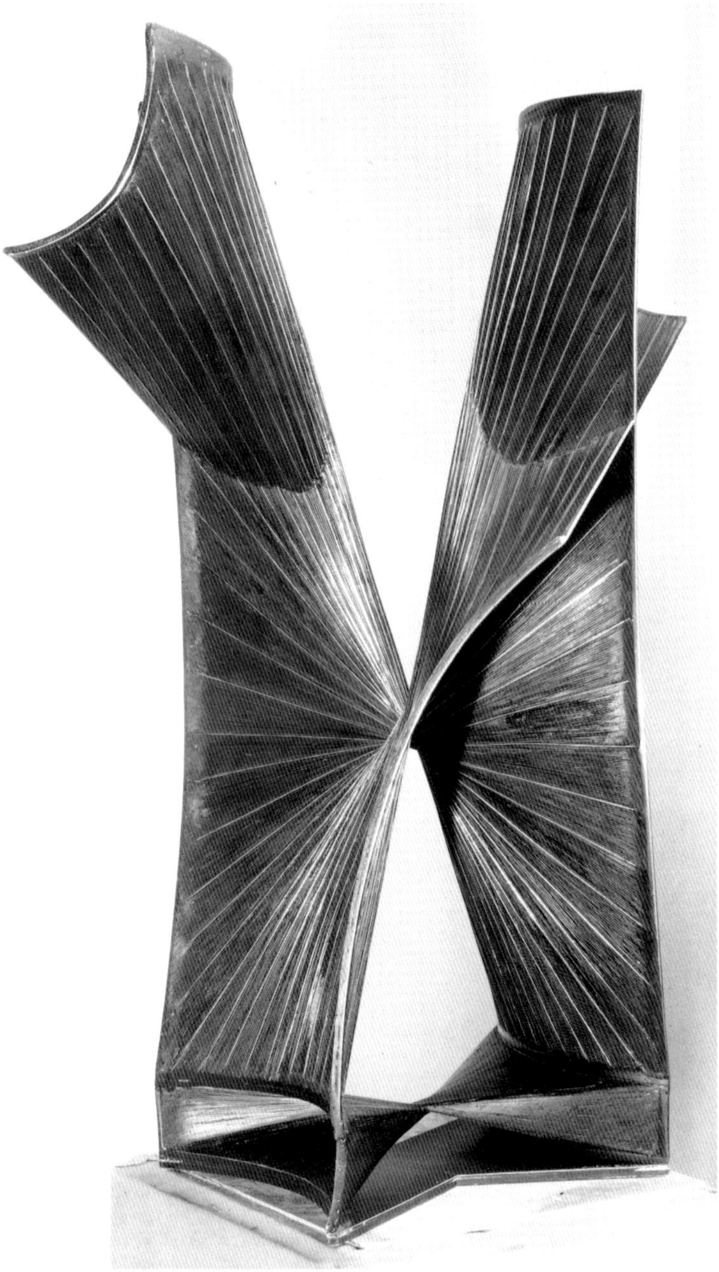

Antoine Pevsner
La colonne développable de la victoire
1946
height: *c.*48 in.
maquette, oxidised bronze

We would talk about Constructivism, about how curvilinear planes would make space as actual as mass, and about how the rhythms of line formed by the edges of the planes described time. He talked about the passage of light travelling through space and being whirled by the rhythm of a constructed sculpture. He talked about his training in Russia as a physicist and an engineer. Sometimes he'd illustrate what he was saying with drawings he'd done years before.

And he would talk about architecture too, but always in moral and heroic Constructivist terms, the rebuilding of cities using the technologies of movement and instant communications, and embodying socialist economic principles. We have fought a war for freedom, he would say; the freedom of the people. Although he and Gabo had had a falling out and didn't speak to one another, his voice would drop to a reverential whisper when he spoke about the curvilinear transparent planes in his brother's work as opening up the next stage in sculpture's evolution.

We would go to his studio. Once he gave me two photographs of sculptures. I happened to be going from Paris to Amsterdam. I showed the photographs to Willi Sandberg and described my visits to Pevsner's studio. Two weeks later Sandberg was in Paris. He called on Pevsner, and bought both the sculptures for the Stedelijk. Pevsner always maintained, against all my denials, that I had sold his sculptures. Of course I hadn't; but I like to think that I'd maybe been a small link in the chain that saved him and Virginie from a temporary financial despair – though never from loss of pride.

In his studio he had made a sculpture in the form of two great arcing planes soaring and intersecting upwards. He told me that when the allied troops marched into Paris, the crowds poured into the streets to welcome them. In the jostle of people he was standing next to an old woman who ecstatically pronged the air above her head with two fingers wide open. She had tears flowing from her eyes. He asked her why she was gesticulating like that. 'C'est la victoire, monsieur, c'est la victoire!' the woman shouted above the noise of the crowd as they cheered the armoured vehicles packed with waving soldiers. Eero Saarinen liked this sculpture so much that he commissioned a huge version of Victory for the General Motors Building in Detroit.

Perhaps the sculpture closest to Antoine's heart in these final years of his life was his maquette for the Unknown

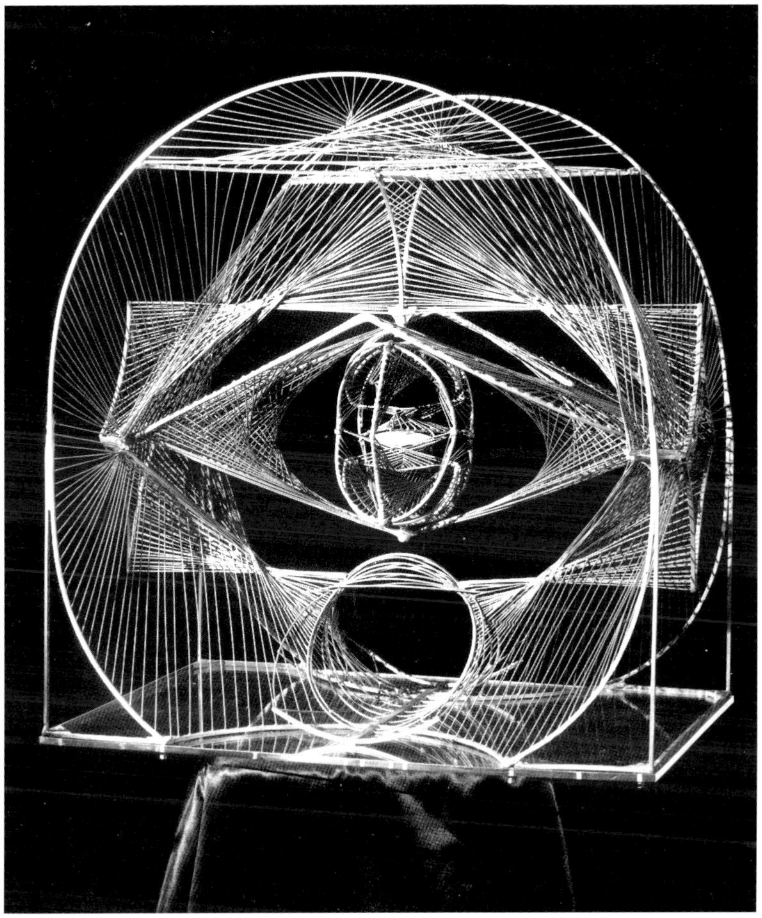

Antoine Pevsner
Le prisonnier politique inconnu
1952
height: *c.*24 in.
maquette, brass and marble

Political Prisoner competition. The maquette describes Pevsner's idea with wires representing the radii of intersecting arcing planes. The prisoner is an elongated oval of white marble, held by the forces of imprisonment in the centre. But the very planes which imprison him are also the forces that radiate his message out into space and freedom. Pevsner was premiated second, behind a static monument by the British sculptor Reg Butler. Perhaps the jury misunderstood the maquette and thought it represented a cage. Pevsner was mortified. He felt that the jury had misjudged the intelligence of the public in thinking that what people wanted was a statue, not a sculpture.

Forgive me, Peter, for spending so much time on Pevsner. Here was a man whose selfless courage amounted almost to madness. He made objects which for him had multiple meanings, but few people understood. He stuck to his focus through thick and thin. His persistence was coupled with a quiet modesty. Every day he went to his workshop, renewing, refining, clarifying his sculptural message. He believed that his constructions spoke of timeless physical laws at human scale. And he believed that if we can learn from the dynamic balances of these laws we will arrive at human social and moral behaviours which will synchronise with them.

I was drawn to Pevsner because, for me at least, he was not alone in his audacity. Haven't we come to expect the same lack of compromise from Mondrian, from Malevich, from Ben's white reliefs, and even from artists who were quite different, like Arp? But what about the younger artists?

In Paris I wandered into a gallery exhibiting Stephen Gilbert. He was making severe rectilinear and curvilinear constructions in aluminium. Some of these contained planes in black or white or primary colours, or highly polished surfaces which captured and reflected incidental movement, thus integrating the momentary within a construction of balance and serenity. I assumed Stephen Gilbert to be a Frenchman, and I asked the gallery owner whether it was possible for me to meet Monsieur Sheelbare.

Why he's here, said the gallery owner; and out from an office at the back of the gallery walked a small bony sparrow of an Englishman, and we became friends. He and his wife, who was also a sculptor, were very poor. They invited me to their studio for dinner. I came with a bottle of wine and a loaf of bread. Then Stephen and I got on a bus and got off at Les Halles. But we didn't go into the market. Instead we went round the back where the dumpsters were. Stephen had a string bag. We scavenged tomatos and lettuce, onions and cabbage and potatoes. What a splendid dinner we had that night!

By this time I was writing for a number of periodicals in Britain, Sweden, Holland, Italy and France. I was disturbed by the way most of my fellow writers on art and architecture wrote about style as *haute couture*, not as language or content. It was as if backing a particular artist and a particular style to become the next 'in-thing' was the point of critical writing.

I remember Victor Pasmore likening it to pundits at a horse race. He held up two glass tumblers to his eyes in imitation of binoculars. 'Poliakoff is roaring into the lead! Now Soulages is accelerating on the outside! Francis appears to be fading! Keep an eye on de Kooning on the rails! Poliakoff is falling back! Here comes Pollock pounding up the middle…!'

I was much more interested in the human aspect, in art as language and metaphor, in how one artist's language related to the languages of other artists, and in what makes artists devote their lives to languages most other people have difficulty in understanding. I was especially interested in how languages which seemed inaccessible to one generation became common currency to the next. I considered that I had a role to play as a bridge.

Houses at Peterlee

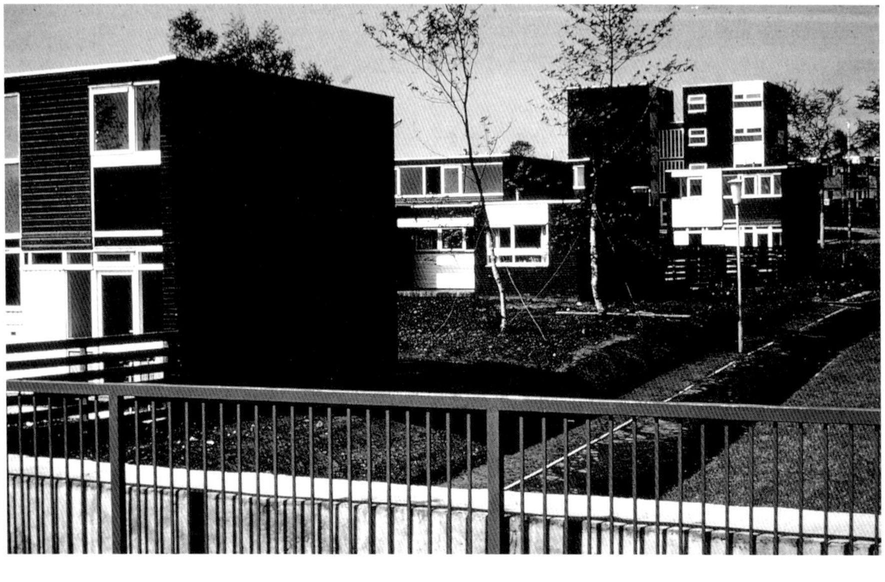

My writings about Mondrian and Pevsner and Nicholson's reliefs not only reflected on the abstract principles of proportion and scale, but on the creation of art-objects the balance and serenity of which related directly to architecture. And the proportions and scale of architecture, in turn, related to human interrelationships, community and environment. The way objects were put together, the evidence of the hand, the texture and tactility of brushstrokes in, say, a Mondrian, the physical quality of the metal planes in a Pevsner sculpture, were the grammar and syntax of language and sensibility. It didn't seem to be at all contradictory that I'd be writing about Pasmore and Robert Adams and Dorazio and Prampolini at the same time for different magazines.

You and I were in correspondence throughout 1955. I was excited to know that you and Stephen were working together on a synthesis of art and architecture, and that the model of a house you both had designed was to be shown at the Stedelijk in Amsterdam. The notion that you were also running the Symon Quinn Gallery, in, of all places, Huddersfield, and that you were showing a wide range of avant-garde artists, was very appealing. Things seemed to be happening in the North. There was an openness that was lacking in London. I had been working with Theo Crosby on the 'This is Tomorrow' exhibition, but the tawdriness of the infighting was frustrating.

The appointment of Victor Pasmore in 1955 to work as a consultant at Peterlee, bringing some of the principles of de Stijl to a community of coal miners, demonstrated bold social and design agendas. In April 1956 I came to see you, driving my pea-green van on its maiden journey, and I stayed at Dene Court. I wrote an introduction for Roger Hilton's exhibition at Symon Quinn; indeed I still have a small Hilton oil from that show. In July I enrolled to study architecture at Leeds College of Art; the spectrum of you and Stephen Gilbert, Terry Frost and Alan Davie, and Harry Thubron, Ricky Atkinson, Tom Hudson and Herbert Read, all made such good sense. I felt I was among friends.

With best wishes
David

Letter 10 Peter Stead to David Lewis

Dear David

Thank you for your letter. All the connecting elements leading eventually to my work with you started taking shape in the early 1950s when my life began to alter quite radically. I was learning to paint with the help of two friends from Huddersfield Art School and began to take this move so seriously that I designed and built myself a studio extension at Dene Court. I'm sure you will remember that as a place where we spent many happy hours talking, dreaming, and planning our future.

I also started my visual arts education by visiting the galleries in Leeds and Wakefield, with their wonderful collections of Hepworths, Moores, and Nicholsons, and an occasional visit to the Tate! My appreciation of Pevsner and Gabo came later.

I was learning how to use my eyes and express what I saw onto canvas and later in three-dimensional works. Thanks to Herbert Read, whose books began to have a major impact on my thinking, I realised that there was another important place I should visit where painting and sculpture and pottery could be seen 'in the flesh' – St Ives. But before I tell you that story I must recount the next most important stage in my working life.

This chapter could perhaps be titled 'Breuer and the Bauhaus come to Yorkshire', because that is the history of the house at Farnley Hey on the southern outskirts of Huddersfield. In 1950 John Womersley, a West Riding industrialist and an active supporter of the arts, decided to build himself a house using his brother Peter, recently graduated from the Architectural Association School in London, as designer. They asked me to advise on materials and details and use the skilled craftsmen in my family firm to produce a building of outstanding architectural merit. This experience was to be an important influence on my work. It taught me the value of collaboration in design and construction to achieve results of the highest quality and it gave me a better understanding of art and architecture up to the mddle of the twentieth century.

Peter Womersley's design was influenced by the houses built in the USA by Marcel Breuer in the 1940s and was probably the most important example of residential architecture in England immediately post-war. This was recognised by Nikolaus Pevsner in his book *Buildings of England*. For me Breuer's use of applied primary colours in his American houses was an important discovery. He must have been influenced by van Doesburg's lectures on de Stijl principles at the Bauhaus in the 1920s, even though he did not use coloured planar elements in his architecture until the 1940s. Peter Womersley was not interested in using colour and relied almost entirely on natural finishes. But I had started painting, and colour was all important to me, and as we started on site in 1952 I wanted to learn more about the influence of de Stijl on architecture. But more about that later.

So to St Ives, to continue the education adventure. In the summer of 1952, Elizabeth and I together with our eighteen-month-old daughter Lucinda set off for Cornwall to see what treats there were in store for us. There were plenty, we were not disappointed. It was a long car journey in those days, but the beauty of Penwith, the sea, the cliffs, the countryside, the marvellous colours and, best of all, the incredible light made it so worthwhile. So worthwhile and exciting that after two weeks I just did not want to leave. You know only too well, David, this has happened to dozens of artists so I'm sure you will not be surprised that I succumbed to the magic of St Ives!

The first contact made with the artist community was through a visit to Robin Nance's shop, a meeting place of renown. Next an invitation to Boots and Bill Redgrave's house, friends of most of the artists you knew and where we had a brief first meeting with you and Willie. Bill and Peter Lanyon were planning to start the St Peter's Loft school of art with Terry Frost, so this was my first conversation about art education with real artists and helped to open my eyes even more. Then a visit to the Leach Pottery; unfortunately Bernard was away but I met other members of the family. Then probably the most important meeting of all, with Patrick and Delia Heron in their studio cottage on the sea wall. Important because it started a friendship which lasted nearly fifty years and enabled me to start the Symon Quinn Gallery with the help and contacts Patrick gave me.

I left the magic and came back to Huddersfield feeling somewhat frustrated at leaving a dynamic centre to return to a place where the visual arts did not seem to be of any real importance. Football – Yes. Music and Brass Bands – Yes. Theatre – Yes. Painting and Sculpture – No. So, like our friends in Leeds and Wakefield and some other parts of Yorkshire, I began to think it was time to plant some seeds in the hope that they would grow to help develop a change in people's perception of the visual arts. How about helping to move the centre of things towards the county birthplace of two of our most important artists – Moore and Hepworth? Helen Knapp was working hard in this direction in the public gallery sector. And Alec Clegg had shown leadership and vision by establishing Bretton Hall as a college for training teachers in art, music and drama that had no counterpart in Western Europe. You will also remember, David, that in those days there were hardly any art reproductions, certainly not of abstract art; just a few postcards from the Tate. Not many people could see what was happening in painting and sculpture in Europe and America.

So a decision was made. I would open a private gallery in Huddersfield devoted mainly to exhibiting the genre that by this time was interesting me most – abstract art. I rented rooms on the first floor of a fine Victorian building in the market quarter of Huddersfield next to the market hall; both now demolished. So, not only little understanding of modern art but no sense of history either!

The Symon Quinn Gallery opened in August 1954 with an exhibition of British artists, most of them working from St Ives, titled 'Romantic Abstraction'. The *Huddersfield Examiner* reported: '… in many of the younger and gifted artists an enthusiasm that amounts to dedication, but, to the general public, abstract art is something either puzzling or repellent. The division between the public and the "modern" artist is greater than it ever was.' But the hoped for education process was about to start!

Over the next two years, thanks to the help and support of Patrick Heron, Charles Gimpel, and Helen Knapp, the director of the Wakefield City Art Gallery, I was able to show the works of over fifty of the most significant European-based artists, many of whom could be described as avant-garde.

Excellent reviews by A.C. Sewter in the *Manchester Guardian*, Bill Oliver in the *Yorkshire Post*, as well as continuing support from the *Examiner*, brought people to the gallery from all over the North. '… students in the North should make a special note of the existence of the Symon Quinn Gallery', wrote a reviewer in the journal *Architectural Design*. 'Peter Stead is to inaugurate a series of monthly lectures at the gallery entitled "Modern Art and Architecture".'

Lawrence Alloway's book *Nine Abstract Artists* was published and helped to spread the word. We started selling paintings, prints and pottery; and people still remind me, with satisfaction, of the works they purchased and still have in their homes. However, it was towards the end of 1954 that the next important development in the story took place.

I had gone to Roger Hilton's house in London to select the paintings for his show in the coming year and staying with him was his long-time friend the artist Stephen Gilbert on a visit from Paris. We found in conversation that we had a mutual interest in the possible realisation of a synthesis of painting and architecture and agreed to continue our discussion by correspondence. The year 1955 was a busy one for the Gallery; with one-man exhibitions by Patrick Heron, William Redgrave, Roger Hilton, and a show of a large group of artists working in Paris, many of them relatively unknown in England but many to become famous later: among them de Staël, Hartung, Soulages, Poliakoff, Vaseraly, Schoffer, Mathieu. Also one of my favourites, Sonia Delaunay, you have one of her pictures David, yes? Then later in the year another important show – Matisse, Picasso, Léger, Arp and Gabo.

I was gradually changing from painting to making sculptures; then at the beginning of January came the first letter from Stephen Gilbert and my life really did begin to change radically! I had sent him a photograph of Farnley Hey which he found interesting. But he was critical of the solid walls and use of natural materials and remarked that 'the present training of the architect makes it hard for him to grasp the essentials of structural space-form in colour'. This gave me an important clue to his way of thinking and in which direction we should be moving. He mentioned meeting you and Willie at the Nicholson exhibition in Paris together with Roger Hilton and John Forrester. A portent for the future, David!

I then wrote to him suggesting we design a house together for a sloping site I had chosen, and enclosed a plan suitable for a detached family residence. I also suggested various materials into which colour was integrated and not applied. We exchanged a number of drawings and by February the design was well advanced; to be built of steel, aluminium, and glass. He suggested naming the project 'House Neovision' after the name of the group he was collaborating with in Paris. And so it was.

A model of the house was made by Stephen and was exhibited at the Salon des Réalités Nouvelles in Paris and the Stedelijk Museum in Amsterdam. It was also published in the journal *Aujourd'hui: Art et Architecture*. Then in his

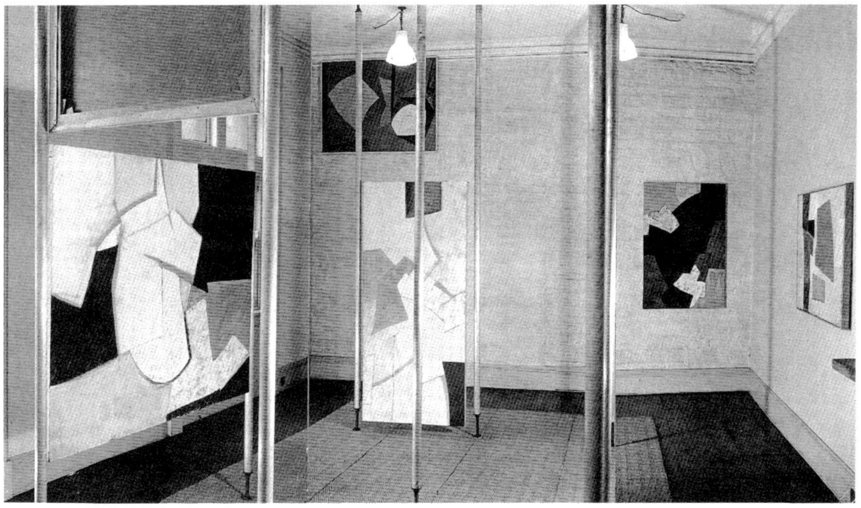

(above) Exhibition of paintings by Adrian Heath, Symon Quinn Gallery, Huddersfield, Jan–Feb 1956

(right) Roger Hilton
Painting, 1955, 10 x 10 in.
oil on canvas
collection: David Lewis

(far right) Stephen Gilbert
Construction, 1954

(bottom left) Stephen Gilbert
Neovision, 1955

(bottom right) Stephen Gilbert
Model, Y House, 1955

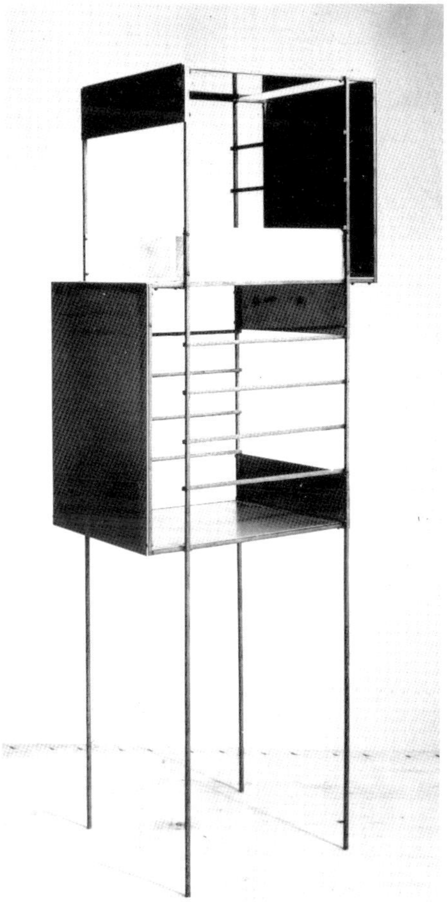

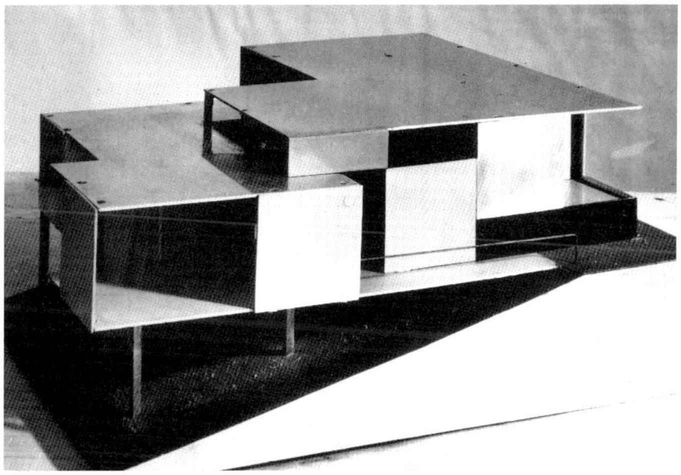

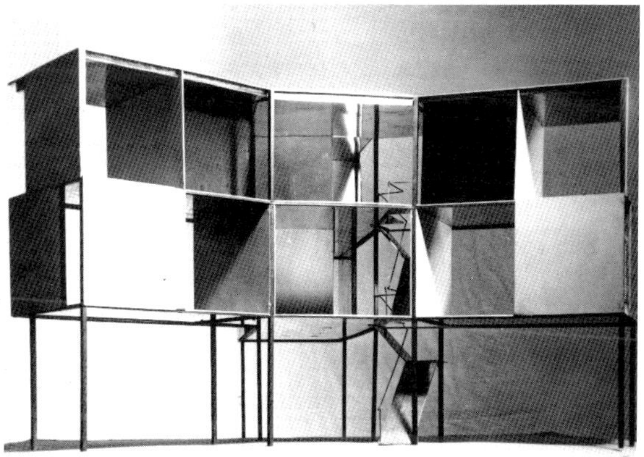

letter of 27 February the name Mondrian was mentioned for the first time and he went on to advise me to read Mondrian's essay 'Plastic Art and Pure Plastic Art'. He said that this essay had made a profound impression on him and enabled him to see the essentials as never before. He also sent me photographs of his orthogonal constructions with coloured planes and I read Mondrian's essay.

During the whole of the year we were in constant touch exchanging and developing our ideas. I had surveyed a flat site in Huddersfield and Stephen started to design a two-storey house for it; this became known as the Y-house. A beautiful model was made by Stephen and I consider this design to be one of the best and most original architectonic space-forms determined by planes of colour that had been created at that time. In August came the visit to the Whitechapel Gallery, then showing more of Mondrian's work than had ever been seen before in England. So now it was my turn to be profoundly impressed. It was my first sight of the work of the artist who has been the main influence on my own work for nearly forty-five years; not only his paintings but his prolific writings too. You, David, must have been one of the few people in England to have understood my excitement.

After the successful showing of Roger Hilton's paintings, for which you very kindly wrote the piece in the catalogue, I set off in the late autumn to stay with Stephen in Paris. He was very keen, by that time, that we should start working even more closely on the design of architectural projects originating from the constructions he had been making since 1954, when he joined Groupe Espace. I was introduced into a wonderfully creative atmosphere, seeing Stephen's work, and enjoying a long meeting with Vantongerloo in his studio nearby. My one disappointment was not being able to hear Sidney Bechet. He was so popular in Paris that there were long queues waiting to get into the club and we did not make it!

I was really lucky to be working with Stephen who probably understood Mondrian and the de Stijl movement better than any other artist at that time and was able to express this in his work. He was also able to describe their ideas with a clarity that they had found difficult and that was very important to me.

You and I had been corresponding during the latter part of 1955 and I had sent you extracts from Stephen's letters. Also you had helped me to make contact with Adrian Heath and in January 1956 I gave him a one-man show at the Symon Quinn Gallery, which received publicity. This was to be the last exhibition at the gallery because, by this time, Stephen Gilbert and I had started to design large urban-scale constructions and we needed suitable space in which to make them. So I decided to close the gallery and turn it into a studio. Stephen came to stay in Huddersfield in the spring and you came to visit us in April/May. You were one of the few people to understand what Stephen and I were doing. You were preparing a book on Mondrian and you had a close relationship with Ben Nicholson. He was probably the only artist in England who fully understood what Mondrian was doing and saying and had lived and worked with him in Hampstead in 1938–40.

Stephen had brought with him the models of the House Neovision and the Y-house, as well as drawings and writings. So we had lots to show you. I was visiting Terry Frost in Leeds, the beginning of a long and warm friendship, which meant the connections with that city were starting to build up and of course you played a major part in that. Then in June, Stephen and I were invited to exhibit the presentation drawings of House Neovision at the Hatton Gallery, in a show curated by Victor Pasmore and titled 'Abstracts'. Stephen went back to Paris, where by this time he was working on his first curvilinear constructions and had designed a house model with curved end walls. For the rest of the year I concentrated on the model of the house I was designing called the Prototype House based upon Mondrian's Neo-Plastic principles and influenced by the work Stephen and I had been doing during the last eighteen months.

You, David, began to make a significant contribution to all this work by using your considerable skills to communicate and propagate our ideas and theories. Then, of course, you made the decision to train as an architect and your enrolment at Leeds School of Architecture, a major item in this book, was the start of the work we were to do together over the next ten years.

The year 1957 came and went very quickly, we all of us had so much to do. You on your course; Stephen and I working to complete the large constructions; me preparing the drawings and starting work on the site at Branch Lane, Almondbury for my first house, the Prototype House. And making the model for my second house at Arkenley Lane. Lots of discussion, exchange of ideas, culminating in the lecture we gave together at Cambridge in November

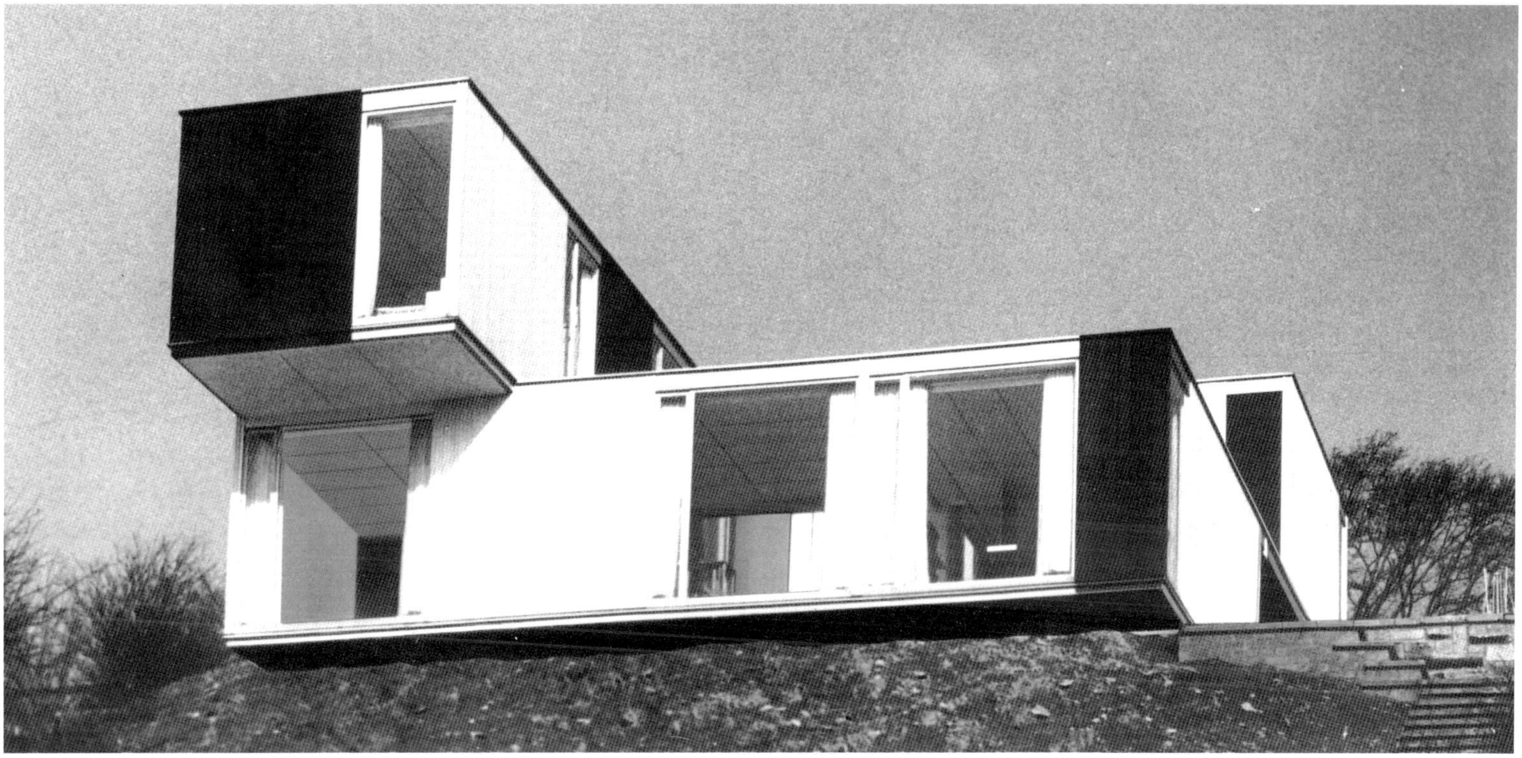

Peter Stead,
House at Arkenley Lane,
Almondbury, 1963

'Colour and Space and Architecture'. This was at the invitation of Simon Nicholson, Ben's son. In February 1958 we were spreading the word again, this time giving a lecture to Pasmore's students at the Arts Festival in Newcastle; then having discussions with Victor about a possible role in Peterlee New Town.

I completed my design for the Arkenley house and the structural consultant's drawings were submitted. I also designed two more houses for clients in Sheffield and Huddersfield. Then in November you and I published an illustrated article for Theo Crosby in *Architectural Design*, 'Colour Time Space'. Another busy year!

In the early part of 1959 I completed my Branch Lane house and it was sold to an enthusiastic buyer after a lot of favourable publicity. I started work on the foundations of the Arkenley house nearby and you were kind enough to make some beautiful presentation drawings of the detailing.

Because you were well on the way to becoming an architect, we decided to register ourselves as 'Design Collaborative' in May 1959. Collaboration is, I think, one of the central themes of your review of the events of the 1950s. And certainly it was the only way to achieve a synthesis of art and architecture.

However, and I think Mondrian would agree, the square is not yet complete.

Yours
Peter

Letter 11 Eric Atkinson to David Lewis

March 1999

Dear David

In this letter I hope I can clarify the reasons behind my emigration to Canada and my endeavour to start an art education programme here which would contain all I had learned from the Basic Course at Leeds and subsequently develop its own identity.

As I have already mentioned, I was very involved in planning the new studios for the proposed Leeds Polytechnic and the importance of this undertaking was the reason Leeds Education Authority gave for refusing me permission to visit the Corcoran School of Art in Washington DC. This refusal rankled as I became increasingly frustrated by the arbitrary decisions being made by some of the planning committees and I felt powerless to slow the breakneck rush to become part of a Polytechnic that by its sheer size would radically change the independent nature of the College of Art. Perhaps it was time to think about a new challenge?

By a strange coincidence Harry Thubron was staying with us when I received a letter from Peter Williams. Peter had at one time been an assistant to John Wood in the Department of Further Education in Leeds and was now the Chairman of the Faculty of Applied Arts at Fanshawe Community College in London, Ontario. He had written to ask if I would be interested in starting a Fine Art Department there. I had known Peter Williams in Leeds and so had Harry. When I showed Harry Peter's letter his immediate reaction was 'if you don't want to go, Sunshine … I wouldn't mind a crack at it!' I knew very little about art education in Canada and nothing about the Community Colleges but the possibilities intrigued me and so we set about preparing to emigrate.

During the early 1960s I had met two Canadian artists, Herb Ariss and John O'Henly – who taught at HB Beal Secondary School in London, Ontario – when they visited Leeds College of Art. One of the more provocative Canadian artists, Robin Page, had been on my Faculty at Leeds for several years. Robin, with his shock of black hair and full black beard, was an artist of great versatility. He was one of the first performance artists I had met and I assumed that any educational system that could produce such an ingenious and original character must have something to recommend it! I had been fascinated by the provocative work I saw at the splendid exhibition '100 Canadian Artists' sponsored by Richard Demarco at the Edinburgh International Festival in 1967. Richard Demarco, a passionate promoter of the arts in Scotland, travelled all over the world to bring exhibitions of new and exciting work to his gallery in Edinburgh. The 1967 exhibition was no exception and showcased work of great vitality displaying a wide range of expression. It was impossible to ignore the affinity between the work presented and the studio work being produced in Leeds. But these three connections were almost the sum total of my knowledge of the contemporary Canadian art scene.

The Province of Ontario established twenty-two Community Colleges during the late 1960s to bridge the gap that existed between the High Schools and the Universities and to provide students with another option for further education. Fanshawe College was the twenty-first to be built and opened its doors in 1967. The first President of the College, Dr James Colvin, appointed Mrs Mackie Cryderman to the Board of Governors as Art Consultant to advise on the establishment of visual art programmes in the College.

Mackie Cryderman was an exceptional influence on the arts in London. A graduate of Manitoba Art School and Ontario College of Art she had built the 'Bealart' programme at HB Beal Secondary School in London into one of the most imaginative and diverse programmes I have encountered. In 1934 she had attended a workshop run by Marion Richardson in Toronto and introduced some of Richardson's philosophy into her own department at Beal. Marion Richardson had written in her *Notes*, an influential booklet that was published in conjuction with an exhibition of Children's Art in London in 1938, that 'the artist discovers the world around him (that is to say in his raw material), relationships, order, harmony … just as the musician finds these things in the world of sound. This cannot be done by the conscious, scheming, planning mind. Art is not simply an effort of will but a gift of grace … to the child at least, the simplest and most natural thing in the world.' Mackie Cryderman never lost sight of this philosophy but expanded and developed it in her remarkable school programme. Mackie retired in 1963 but continued to foster the creative arts within the community.

In 1967 Mackie Cryderman saw an exhibition of work by staff and students from Leeds College of Art at the Corcoran Gallery of Art in Washington DC, organised by Fred Schwartz of the English Speaking Union, assisted by Roy and Rona Slade who were in Washington as exchange faculty from Leeds. Recognising the underlying pedagogical direction in art and design she decided that this was the

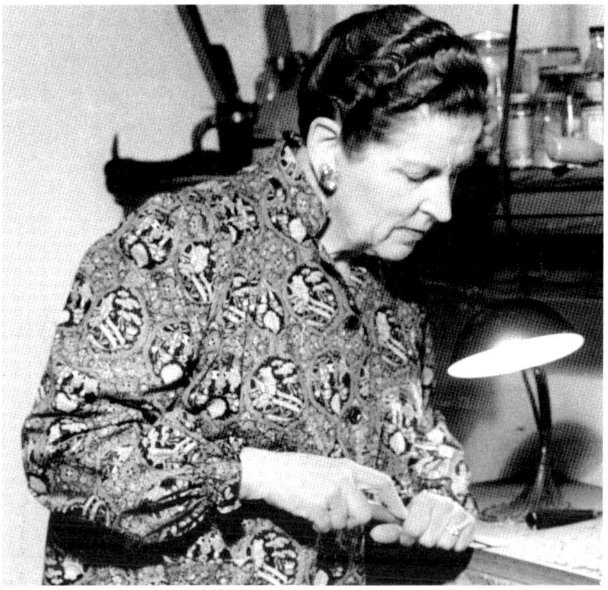

Mrs Mackie Cryderman, carving in her studio. She was Chair of Fanshawe College Advisory Board, 1967-69

approach she wished to encourage at the fledgling Community College in London and set about recruiting someone to implement it. When I eventually met her she was quite adamant that she envisaged 'something very different from anything else in town' and that she saw Fanshawe as an opportunity for a fresh approach somewhere in between the academic structure of the Visual Arts Department at the University of Western Ontario and the Bealart Programme at HB Beal Secondary School. When Mackie died suddenly in 1969 some months after my arrival in London, I lost a very supportive colleague and the Fine Art Programme lost a valued champion.

We arrived at Toronto International Airport on 17 April 1969 to begin the great adventure. Our five-year-old daughter Brigit burst into floods of tears because there were no beaver running about the tarmac and our seven-year-old son Sean was bitterly disappointed that there didn't appear to be any scarlet-coated Mounties there to meet us. 'Are you sure we have come to the right place? Is this really Canada?' After a short commuter flight to London and no sign of the promised College transport Muriel and I began to wonder the same thing!

When I arrived at Fanshawe College I found very few facilities. The Fine Art Basic Programme operated from two small rooms with no running water, although there was an extensive building programme for new studios and workshops underway. There were already some programmes in place, architectural art directed by Christopher Wallis and Merton Chambers and a photography programme under the direction of Bruce Moss and Arnim Walter. The design and communications programmes were in their formative stages but there was no integrated foundation programme. Expo 67 had generated an explosion of interest in the arts and one of the most positive results to emerge from this cultural blossoming was a more constructive approach to visual education. There was a genuine air of excitement within the College and we were blessed with a President who had the vision to explore the possibilities in any programme to 'find out what it could be rather than what it should be'. Even though I felt strongly that the time was ripe for new ideas to germinate and flourish I knew I faced a formidable challenge.

Like many immigrants 'parachuted in' to start a new venture I was assailed with advice from all sides. London, I soon discovered, was divided into small cliques of well-intentioned artists and art patrons all eager to promote their own candidates as members of the new Faculty, but after some soul searching I decided to recruit two Leeds graduates, Michael Durham, a painter and Robin Hobbs, a sculptor, as assistants. At least we understood the same visual language and I felt we would make more rapid progress if there was some common ground to build on. This move antagonised the local chapter of Canadian Artists Representation who objected vociferously to the appointment of non-Canadians. I knew that there would be obstacles to overcome if the fine art programme was to succeed but I had not foreseen such opposition from the arts community. There was already a glorious mix of nationalities teaching at the College. Teachers from Germany, the Netherlands, Greece, New Zealand, Australia, Japan and Italy as well as Canada, Britain and the USA were already appointed … many in the applied arts department. Why should three artists from Leeds pose such a threat? Nobody had ever objected when I appointed Canadians or Americans to the Leeds Faculty!

I soon realised that my Canadian students had attributes that differed from their British counterparts. This was emphasised when aboriginal students from the nearby Reservation arrived accompanied by a government-appointed agent to oversee their interviews for admission to the Col-

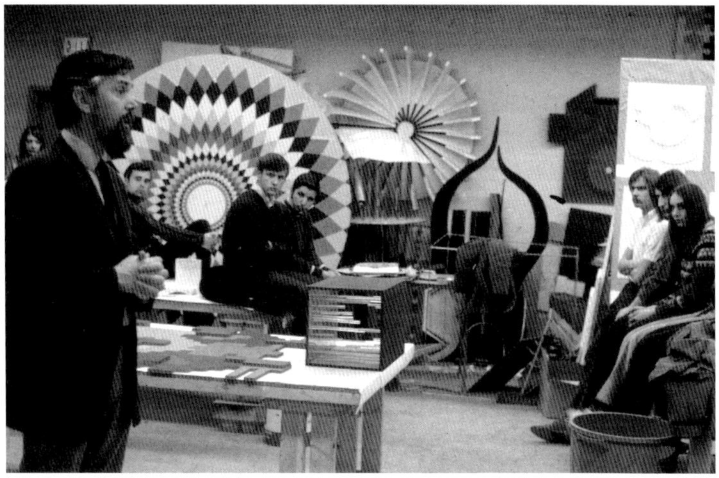

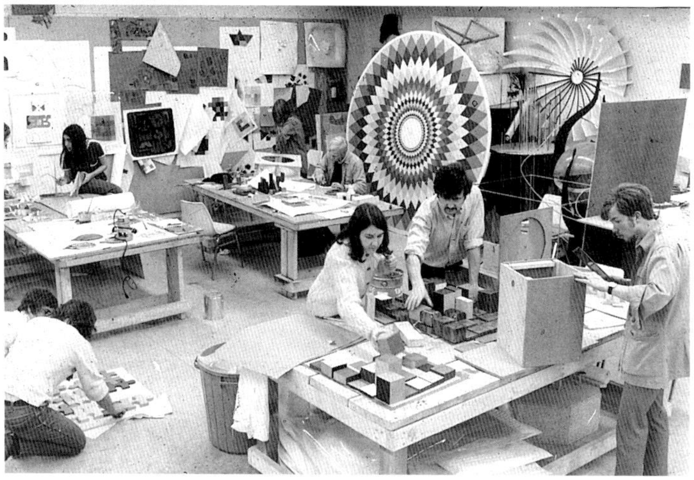

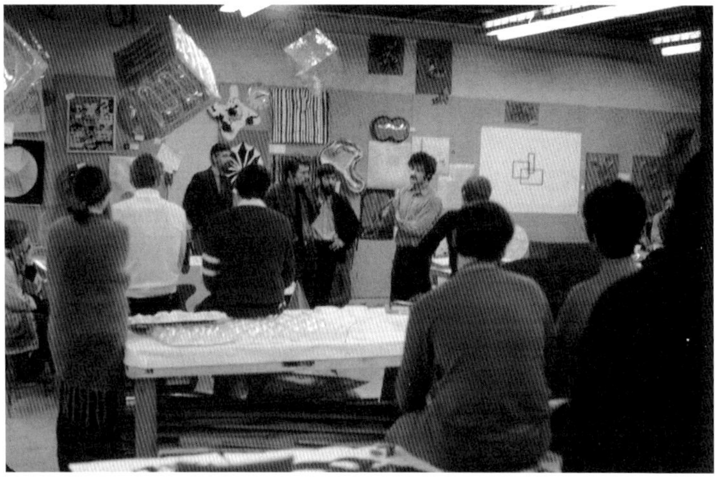

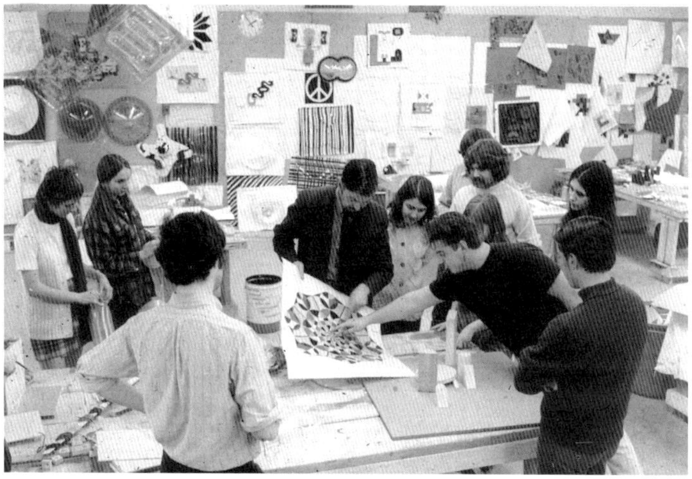

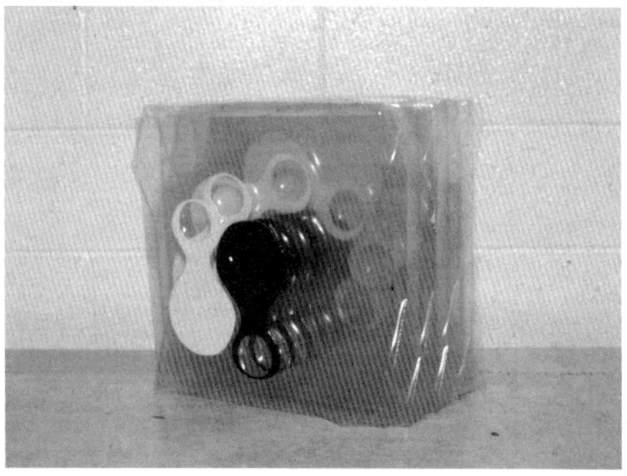

(top & centre left)
Studio crits by Eric Atkinson, Fanshawe College, 1970

(left)
Sculpture from vacuum formes, Fanshawe College, 1970

(top right)
Michael Durham in Machine Shop, Fanshawe College, 1970

(above right)
Eric Atkinson in studio with first-year students, Fanshawe College, 1970

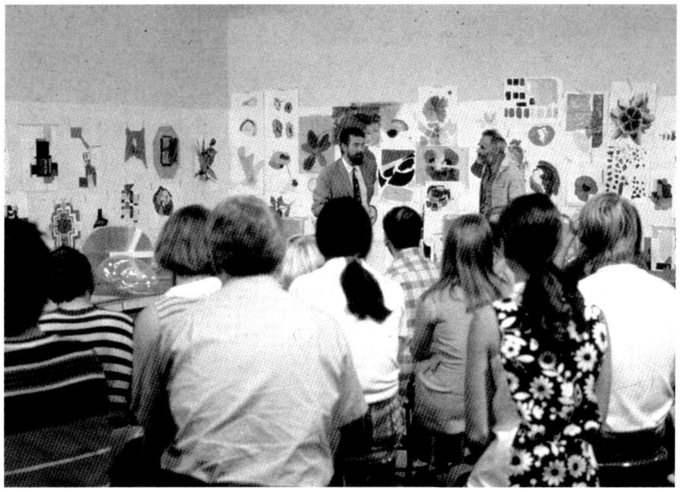

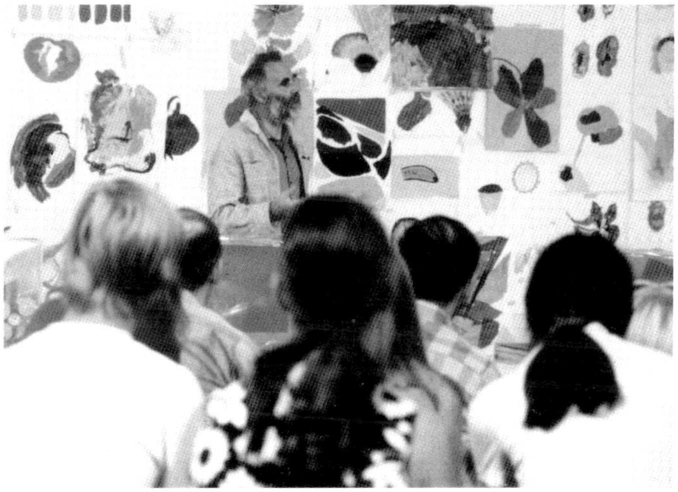

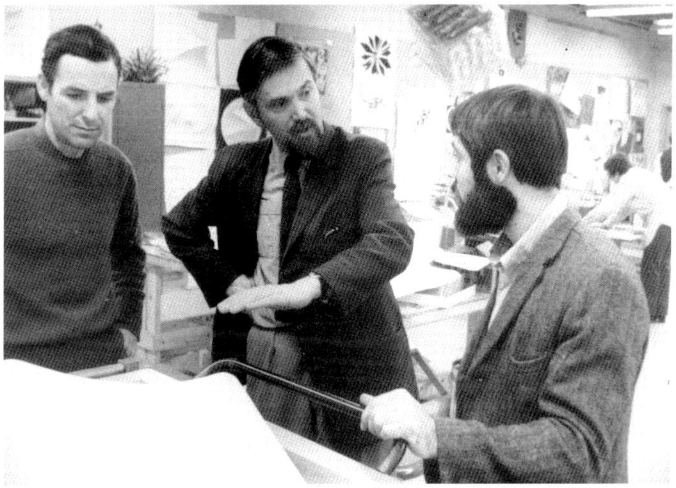

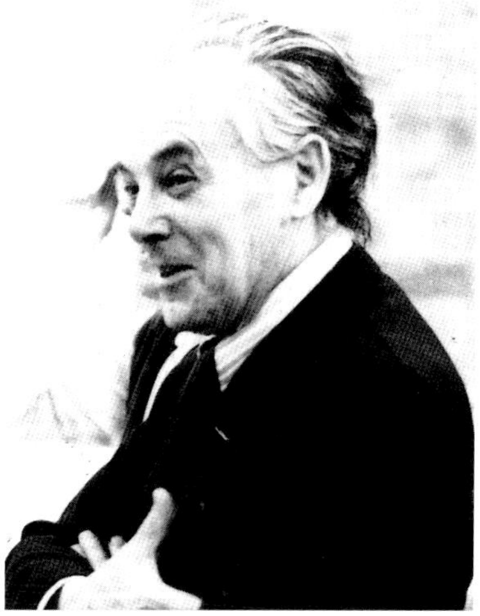

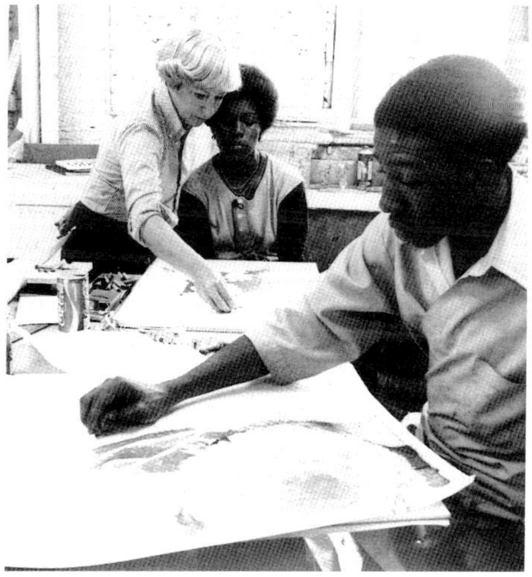

(top left)
Victor Pasmore and Eric Atkinson with students at Fanshawe Summer School, 1970

(centre left)
Victor Pasmore teaching at Fanshawe Summer School, 1970

(bottom left)
(standing left to right)
Jack Chambers, Eric Atkinson and Robin Hobbs in the Machine Shop at Fanshawe, 1970

(top right,)
Gyorgy Kepes at Fanshawe, 1979

(bottom right)
Rona Slade on the exchange programme with two first-year students at the Corcoran School of Art, Washington DC

lege, a practice that has now thankfully been abolished. Experiences in a different educational system had endowed Canadian students with abilities that could be guided in a different direction. In contrast to schools in Britain where only the lowliest group of students were sent for workshop practice all students in the Canadian school system had the opportunity to acquire technical skills. I discerned that their skills in workshop practice could become a foundation for turning technical training into a distinct art language. One of my first moves was to set up a machine shop within the Fine Art Department so that students could explore the possibilities of a wider range of less traditional processes and materials. These studies built upon the superior technical skills possessed by both male and female students. When we acquired a vacuum-former during my first year several local artists took advantage of the machine shop and we were able to build some much needed bridges in the community.

Another bridgehead was established between the community and the College when I presented a series of public lectures on twentieth-century art. These were initially part of a fledgling art history programme but when the President's wife, Mrs Eleanor Colvin, suggested that she and some friends would like to attend, it was decided to throw the doors open and invite the public. It was also my first experience with the local media. London, a city with a population of 250,000 in 1970, already had its own television station, four independent radio stations and published a daily newspaper. A sharp contrast to the situation I had left behind in Leeds. The rapid growth of the 'media industry' would later prove to be of inestimable value to Fanshawe graduates. During the summer of 1970 I felt sufficiently confident to invite Victor and Wendy Pasmore to come to London and run a two-week workshop for the Fine Art Department. This workshop generated intense media coverage across the Province and I began to understand the significance of Marshall McLuhan's dictum 'the medium is the message'!

The success of this venture became the foundation for an art history programme that enriched the experience of our students. It was complemented by an energetic 'visiting artist' series of lectures and workshops funded with the assistance of the Canada Council and by combining resources with the Visual Arts Department at the University of Western Ontario. When Stephen Joy joined the Faculty during the early 1970s he brought a richness of information and experience to the programme. Stephen, a tall, spare, bespectacled American who had worked at the Martha Jackson Gallery in New York, was working at the Dunkleman Gallery in Toronto when I first met him. I invited him to come and talk to our students. The positive reaction to his talk was an incentive to invite him to 'come on board'.... Stephen is one of those people that 'make the brew bubble'. He has an ability to embroil people in his ventures and to open doors to allow other people to contribute. He opened the Trajectory Gallery in London which became a showcase for our students and faculty and for the work of other young artists in Canada and the USA. Artists from across Canada, America, Australia and Europe came to lecture, perform and lead workshops and show their work. Anybody embarking on a lecture tour of North America was waylayed and persuaded to share their professional expertise with our students. Their names are too many to list here but some, like Gyorgy Kepes from MIT whose books had made such an impact on the Basic Course in Leeds, and the Scottish poet Sydney Graham stand out. Sydney stands out for quite another reason, too. Before his lecture I had taken him to lunch at the local Holiday Inn where he was staying and Sydney's lunch was all liquid! My trepidations grew as he imbibed enough scotch to fell an ox but when he stood up in the big lecture theatre in front of an audience of two hundred students he was pure magic. In his soft Scots voice he talked about his poetry and read us his poems in an atmosphere of unforgettable poignancy. He received a heartfelt standing ovation. Early the next morning I was wakened by a telephone call from the city police, 'Mr Atkinson, we have a gentleman here who claims you can vouch for him ... says he's a poet'. Sydney had gone out to celebrate his success at one of the local pubs and had spent the night with several fellow revellers from the Reservation in the 'drunk tank' at the local police station. Not all our guest lecturers were so entertaining.

During my term as Chairman of the Advisory Committee of the London Art Gallery I was able to organise two exhibitions that illustrate the extent of the cooperation possible between diverse organisations if there is sufficient will to succeed. In 1975 through my contact with Roy Slade, who had left Leeds and returned to Washington in 1970 and was by then director of the Corcoran Gallery, I was able to bring fifteen important works from their permanent collection to

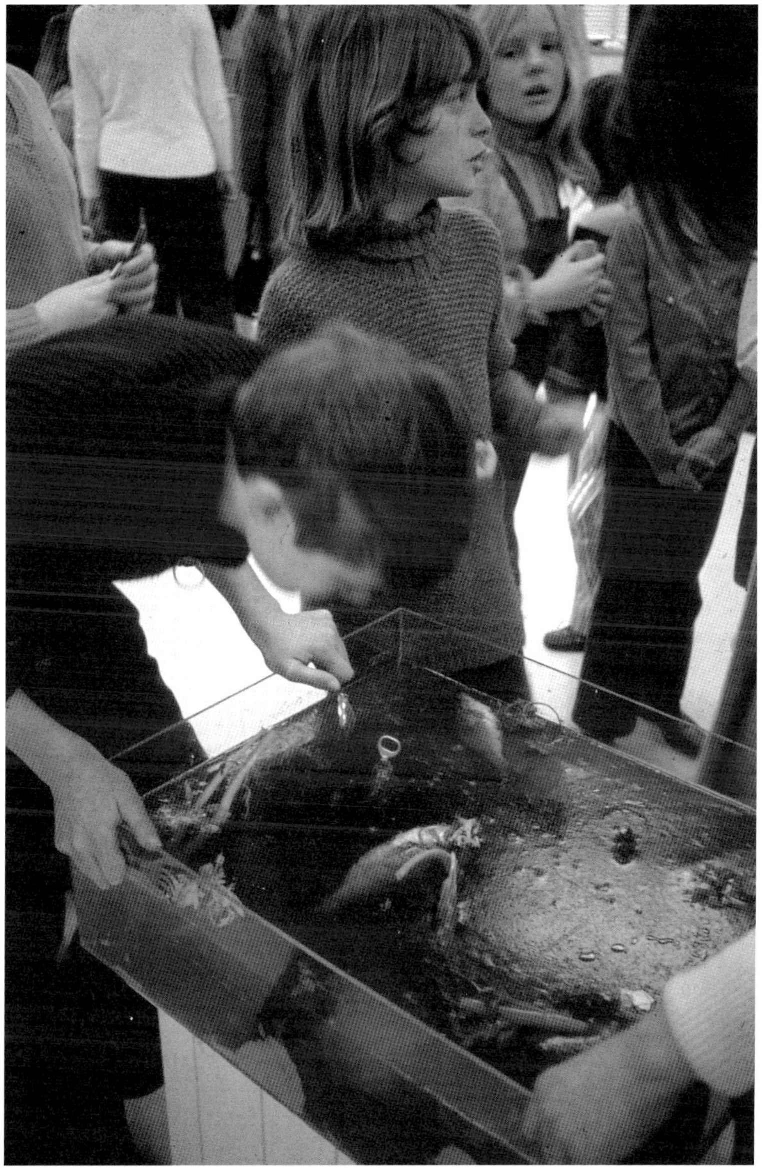

Edible sculpture exhibition, London Gallery, 1972

an exhibition in London sponsored by the Volunteer Committee of the Art Gallery. This was a unique opportunity for the art lovers of Michigan and SW Ontario to see works by celebrated contemporary artists like Josef Albers, Hans Hoffmann, Milton Avery, Adolph Gottlieb and Louise Nevelson without travelling to New York, Chicago or the Albright Knox Gallery in Buffalo. The second exhibition was a collaboration between Fanshawe faculty and students from the Fine Arts, TV and Radio and Culinary Arts Programmes and the children from the Saturday morning art classes at the Art Gallery. Every exhibit was designed to be eaten. The local Kelloggs plant provided one student with sufficient rice krispies to make a full-size coffin which contained a skeleton. The children from the Saturday morning classes created a luscious macramé hanging of black liquorice decorated with pineapple rings, glistening scarlet cherries and fat black olives. Barney Bree, who directed the Culinary Arts Programme, produced his masterly 'Homage to Lake Erie', a large fish tank filled with dark green jelly containing several dead fish, discarded pop cans and crumpled cigarette packets. This extraordinary exhibition of 'Edible Sculpture' was opened at 2.30pm and consumed with great delight at 4pm! Popular though it was with all the participants and the children who came equipped as instructed with plates and spoons it nearly provoked a strike among the caretaking staff at the gallery who had the unenviable task of mopping-up at closing time.

I had been Chairman of the Fine Art Department for three years before I became Dean of Applied Arts in 1972. During these years the building projects had been completed and there were now facilities to accommodate over a thousand students in the three schools – Fine Art, Design and Communications. During these years the Fine Art Programme had become the focus for all manner of interdisciplinary experiments within the College. The curriculum I had built around the premise that it was important to keep students in touch with their own creativity rather than teach them specific skills that stressed imitation was firmly established. It was these bridges between the disciplines that gave the Community Colleges their flexibility during their formative years.

We had well-equipped studios training students for careers in radio and television journalism and by 1976 we had our own radio station '6X' up and running. One of our greatest success stories grew out of the demands of the

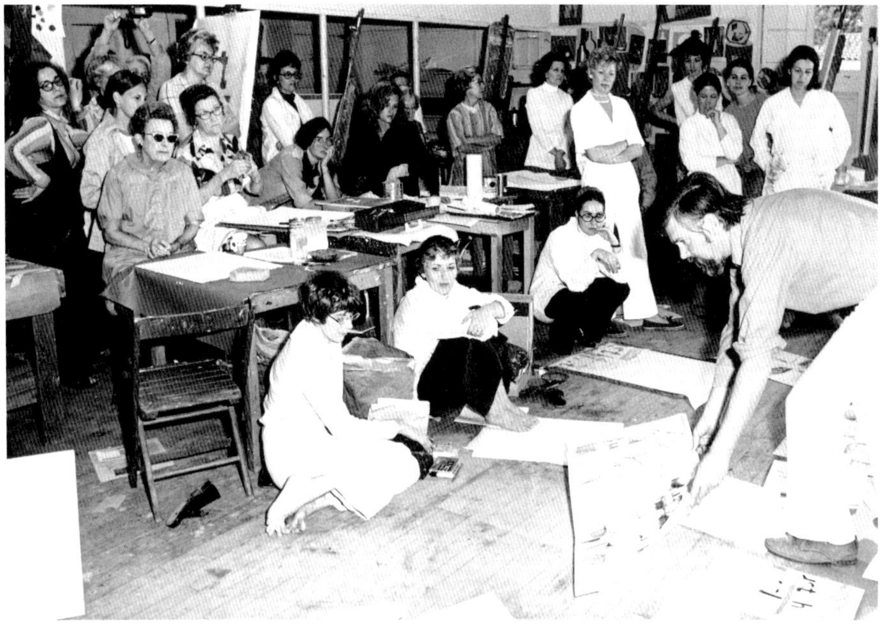

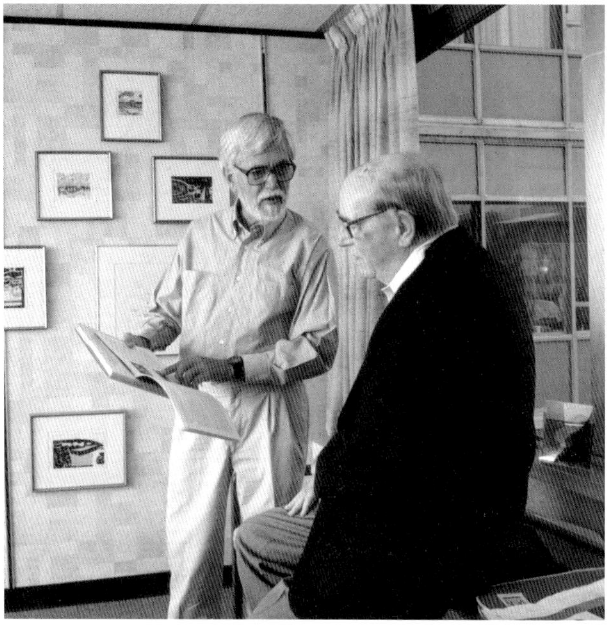

(above left)
Eric Atkinson with students at San Antonio Arts Center, Texas, 1973

(above right)
Eric Atkinson with Jake Moore, 1996

music industry for some form of training programme for musicians and engineers entering the recording industry. I had Tom Lodge on my faculty at that time. Tom was an extremely articulate, tall, red-headed entrepreneur who had been a disc jockey with Radio Caroline, a pirate radio station operating outside British waters during the early 1960s. He believed that the workshop should be a place for aesthetic experience and not just for imparting technical skills. He and Marshall McLuhan's son Eric, together with Michael Hayden, a sculptor from Toronto who worked with light and sound, directed a kinetic sculpture course that Muriel dubbed 'Creative Electronics' and from these small beginnings grew a pilot programme that developed into Music Industry Arts. MIA was the first of its kind in Canada and its graduates can be found throughout the North American film and music industry.

As the College grew in size and scope it inevitably became more structured. And as the liberal funding diminished it became apparent that the 'glory days' of pioneering were drawing to a close. I tried to stem the tide of encroaching bureaucracy but there were casualties as budgets were trimmed ... some programmes like the Fine Art Film Unit disappeared altogether. An incoming President implemented a plan to streamline the College structure and severely restricted the capacity of the Fine Art Department. Luxuries like team teaching became a thing of the past as the faculty decreased in direct proportion to available finances. The Fine Art Department I founded in 1969 still flourishes though on a much smaller scale than I had envisaged. The pendulum will swing back as pendulums do when economies improve but it will no longer be my concern. Another group at another time will accept the challenge and endeavour to complete a little more of the circle. Would I do it all again? Of course! Would I organise it any differently? I don't think so!

Fanshawe Fine Art Department would not enjoy the excellent reputation it has today without the help of a great many people. I should like to thank all those who helped to build it into one of the most unique departments in Canada. My thanks especially to Jake and Woody Moore who were unfailingly supportive and did so much to support me in the community. To all those who visited the Fine Art Department to share their experiences and to those who worked so hard in the studios as colleagues, faculty, technicians and students, thank you. And lastly to Dr Jim Colvin who encouraged me to realise a dream, my heartfelt gratitude.

Letter 12 Duncan de Kergommeaux to David Lewis

Dear David

Thank you for your letter. I'll answer as best I can. Like Ricky, I've spent fifty years in art education parallel to my career as a professional artist and I'll try to weave a story relating some of my experiences and observations.

As I'm neither an art historian nor a particularly rigorous researcher, I'm reluctant to elaborate on many crucial issues. Most of what I'll say will be coloured by selective memory and lack of personal diaries. However, it's the only story I can tell, so perhaps you can accept it with all the omissions and inaccuracies that retrospect inevitably leaves.

We're an immigrant nation and England has impacted strongly on every aspect of our culture, art education being no exception. There have been waves of influence and influx, one of which focused around Ricky Atkinson in the late 1960s. Like so many before him, he simply gave up everything and moved to Canada for the challenge of building something substantial in a community that needed his expertise. This is the continuing story of our development to which I'll add my perspective.

I grew up in Vancouver and then in northern British Columbia – as far away from the centre of art as it seemed possible to get. I'd no 'art' awareness. I liked to make marks on paper and I tried making oil paintings while in the air force. But there was never any thought in my mind that art could be a career. In those days and in that space, one would have had to look hard to find anyone who understood the meaning of the word 'artist'.

It was around 1950, when I was teaching at an Indian school near Prince Rupert, trying to get the students to look at their artistic heritage, that I started to consider the possibilities of studying art. I'd seen an exhibition of BC artists at the Prince Rupert Civic Center, circulated by the Vancouver Art Gallery, which piqued my interest. I still recall seeing in that exhibition a small abstract painting by Joseph Plaskett that completely confused me. Joe was the first recipient of the Emily Carr Scholarship in 1946, and moved to Paris in 1951 never to return full time to Canada. But as a coincidence he taught at Banff in the summer of 1975, the year that both Terry and I were there, and we have since then been close friends.

When I read some of the biographies from that exhibition I realised that 'a real artist' could come from a provincial background like mine. I dreamt of this possibility for many months. With a wife and two children to support there were few options open to me. I'd taken correspondence courses in art and naïvely worked at making paintings influenced by the Group of Seven and Emily Carr, an artist from Victoria who'd studied in London and St Ives at the turn of the century. But to go any further, I'd have to pursue this dream on a different level. I knew nothing about art schools except that the Banff School of Fine Arts offered summer courses in painting. Exactly what I wanted! So in the summer of 1951 I quit my job in Prince Rupert, moved my family to Victoria BC, and went off to Banff, where a new world was opened up to me from which I have never returned.

The English mountain painter A. C. Leighton started the Banff School as a summer painting camp in 1935. Although it was thought of as a summer school for hobbyists in the early years, it attracted as teachers such important artists as A.Y. Jackson, Jock McDonald, William Townsend, and William Scott.[1]

The summer I was there as a student, by absolute luck I opted to study with Jan Zach, a Czech artist, who'd come to Canada to escape Communism. He came via São Paulo where he'd been working on art projects for the Czech Pavilion at the World's Fair. He brought European culture, a keen intelligence, and a work ethic that he instilled in us. In addition to making us work hard at our painting during the six weeks, he introduced us to an overview of modern art up to Ben Nicholson and Henry Moore (who he believed was the greatest living sculptor). I did very well, won a small scholarship and the Banff School bought one of my paintings. Because of Zach, several serious young artists came to Banff that summer to study. This helped create a dynamic environment in which we spent most of our time believing we could resolve art issues.

Douglas Morton, who in later years was a member of the Regina Five and became Dean of Fine Arts at York University in Toronto, was a fellow student. Takao Tanabe had a job at the School as a maintenance man. He became an important Canadian artist and in 1974 was appointed head of Visual Arts at the Banff Center. Doug had studied in England with Martin Bloch and knew 'all about colour'. Tak had just come from the Hans Hofmann School in New York, full of wisdom and radical ideas. He was working with roofing tar on brown butcher's paper because he'd no money to buy art supplies.

In our discussions about where to go after Banff, it always seemed that, although there were art schools in Canada, one really had to go abroad for serious study. In 1953 Tak went

(right)
Jan Zach discussing work in progress, Banff School, 1951, with Douglas Morton (*left*) and Duncan de Kergommeaux

(far right)
Jan Zach discussing work in progress, Banff School, 1951, with Douglas Morton working on project

(bottom left)
Takao Tanabe with Joe Plaskett on the latter's seventieth birthday, Paris, July 1988

(bottom right)
Takao Tanabe
Envelope sketch
1967
13 x 17 in.
Serigraph

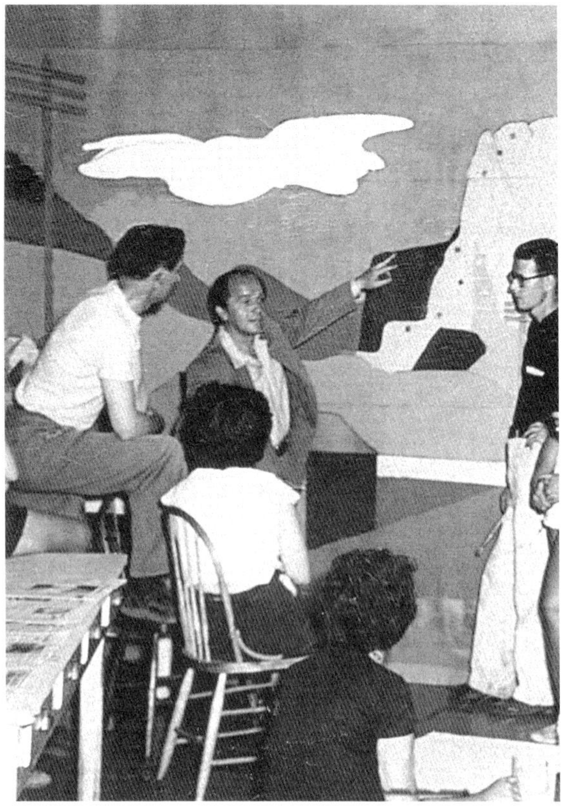

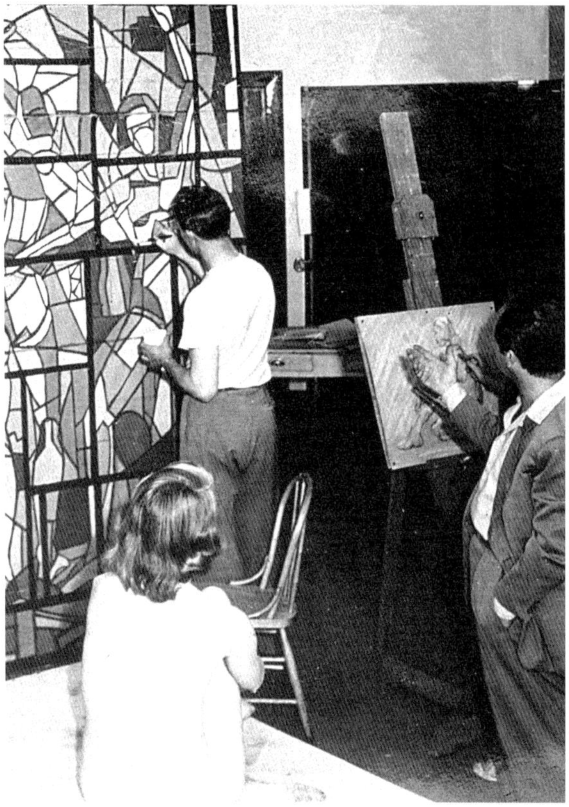

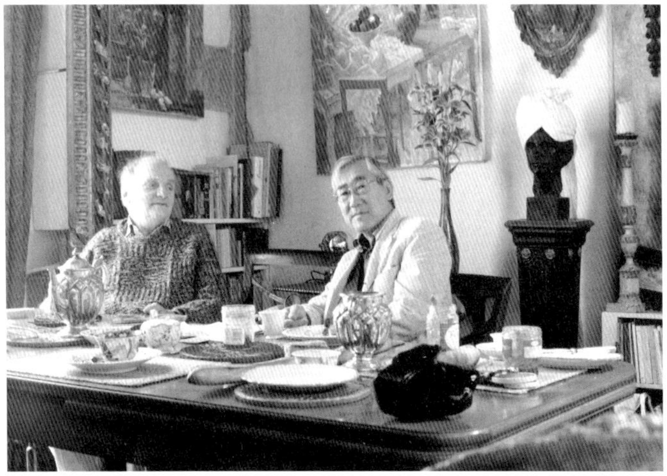

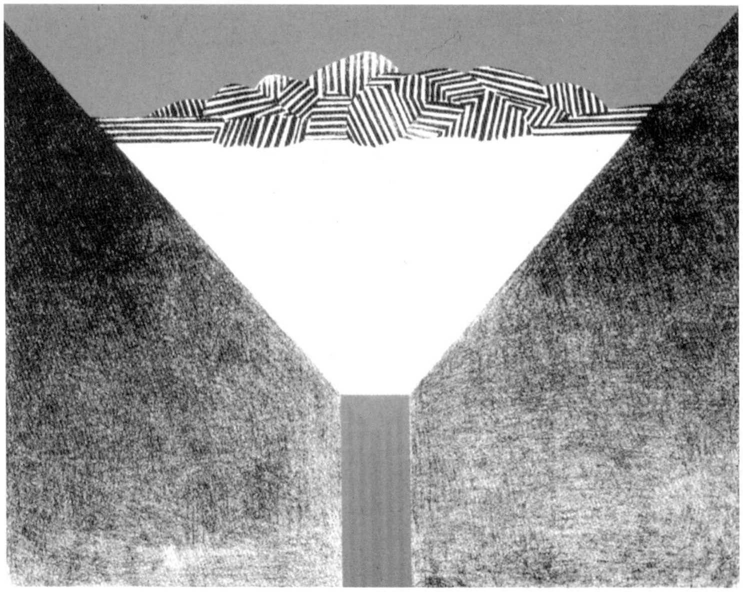

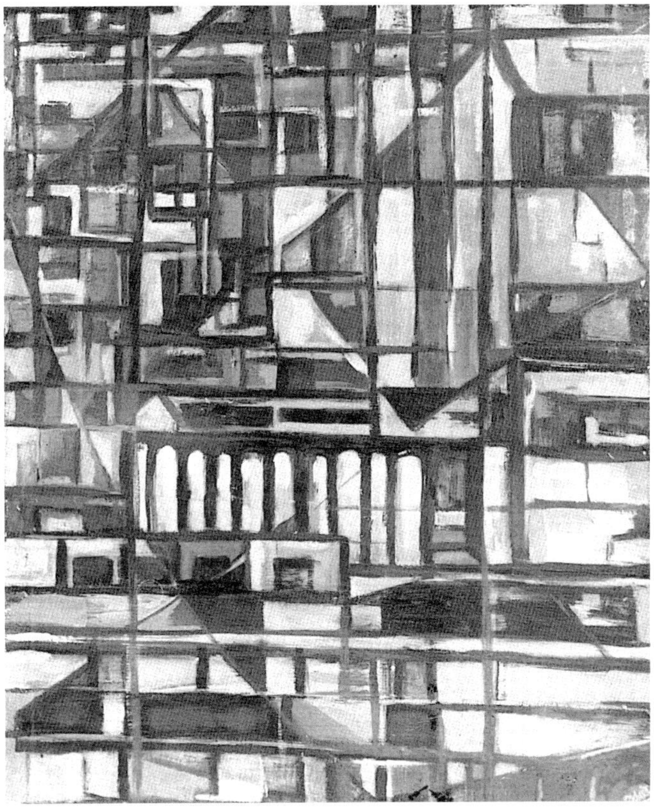

Duncan de Kergommeaux
Painting
1952
28 x 24 in.
casein on canvas
This was Duncan's first abstract painting

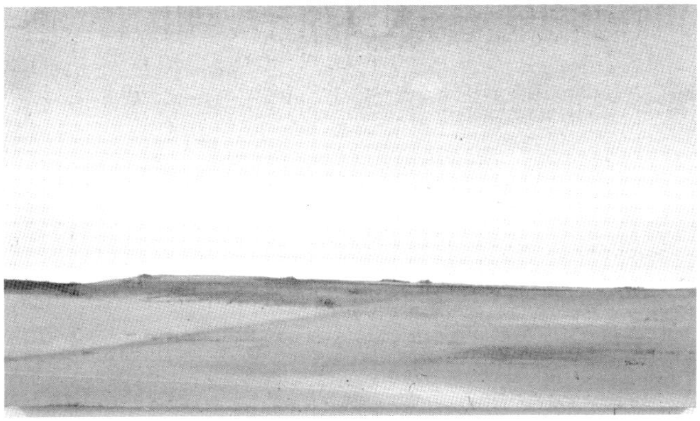

Takao Tanabe
The land 6/76
1976
26 x 44 in.
acrylic on canvas

to London for two years on an Emily Carr Scholarship, where he spent some time at the Central School of Arts and Crafts.

But there were things gestating in Regina that we were not aware of. In 1936, about the time the Banff School was started, Augustus Kenderine, a British artist who'd been teaching in Saskatoon, moved to Regina to start an art department at Regina College (University of Saskatchewan). He convinced the University to set up a summer school on his wilderness property at Emma Lake, north of Prince Albert. Like Banff, it became a six-week summer school.

In 1955, Kenneth Lochhead, a painter and Director of Regina College School of Art, with a colleague Arthur McKay, also a painter, convinced the University to add a two-week professional workshop to this summer programme. The first artists to lead the workshop were Canadians – Jack Shadbolt, a painter from Vancouver, and the following year, Joe Plaskett. In 1959 Barnett Newman led the workshop and became a major influence on the painters who would form the Regina Five and whose work was circulated across Canada by the National Gallery in 1961 – Ken Lochhead, Art Mckay, Douglas Morton, Ronald Bloore, Ted Godwin. In 1962 Clement Greenberg directed the workshop and left his large mark on the Regina painters as he had on the Painters Eleven in Toronto when he visited them in 1957.

By sheer coincidence, after my 1951 summer at Banff, Jan Zach opened an art school in Victoria where I was his student for the next two years. During that period I also took a summer course at the Victoria Art Gallery from Jock MacDonald.

By 1952, essentially a year after I'd started my career as a 'real artist', my work had been shown in juried exhibitions in Seattle, Vancouver and Victoria and I'd completed a large mural for the newsroom of the *Victoria Daily Times*. I felt like a professional. But Victoria was a small community with a group of artists who seemed to have too narrow a focus. I wanted more.

Zach went on to found the art department at Oregon State University in Eugene, Oregon, and in 1953 I moved to Ottawa to be closer to a major Canadian art community. I'd hoped to study in Europe on an Emily Carr Scholarship, but was ineligible because I was married.

Ottawa was good to me. I worked as a draughtsman at

Naval Headquarters and was able to set up a studio in a garage behind my house. However, Ottawa was quite parochial in the 1950s. It was a good place to live but as a community did little to foster the arts. With my work now being shown in national juried exhibitions, I'd a dealer in Montreal and was making the occasional sale. Montreal was a vibrant city in those days and just two hours away. A number of important artists had come from the province of Quebec over the years. Some like Riopelle, Borduas and Pellan had made international reputations. These French-Canadians were the artists I was most interested in when I moved east. For several years I exhibited in the Montreal Spring Show. Consequently I met and became friends with many of the Quebec artists, several of whom were members of the Automatistes who'd published the historic *Réfus Global* in 1948.

In the summer of 1955 I attended the Hans Hofmann School of Art in Provincetown, Massachusetts, and would continue to spend my summers in Provincetown for the next few years. This was my first introduction to American art other than from published illustrations. I've been asked many times what I learned from Hofmann, and have always seemed to struggle for an answer. Quite simply, he provided me with a confidence in my own work and a broader base for looking at art. As well as his own theories of 'push and pull', he introduced me to the writings of Piet Mondrian ('Pure Art and Pure Plastic Art'). From the theories of Hofmann and Mondrian, I consolidated and developed many of my attitudes towards painting. If one believes that when one is ready, the right teacher comes along, then our paths crossed at exactly the right moment. In 1956 I wrote a paper on my experience with Hofmann ('From Realism to Non-Objective') with numerous illustrations and delivered it as a lecture to a large group at the National Gallery in Ottawa. For years I used this material for my art classes. I felt firmly rooted as a force among the few contemporary artists working and teaching within the Ottawa community. I taught for the Civil Service Recreational Association and then for the Ottawa Community Art Center, which in later years became the Ottawa School of Art.

The National Gallery of Canada throughout its early history was closely linked to and developed with British expertise. When I moved to Ottawa in 1953 it was housed in the Victoria Memorial Museum, an old rather dismal fortress-like building. Their first major acquisition (1882) was a work by Frederick Leighton, then president of the Royal Academy in Britain. The first director, Eric Brown, was an Englishman, appointed in 1910. He developed a conservative collection policy with the help of Sir Edmund Walker and Robert Ross, appraiser of pictures at Somerset House. Fortunately there was strong support for the Group of Seven's large and powerful landscapes of the Canadian wilderness. In 1924, when Sir Edmund died, Charles Rickett, an English artist and critic, was appointed advisor for European paintings, a post he held until his death in 1931. Kathleen Fenwick, also born and educated in England, replaced Ross as curator of prints and drawings in 1928 and remained at the gallery for forty years.

When Brown retired in 1939, his assistant H. O. McCurry was made director. His collection policy was also conservative. The people I first met at the National Gallery and subsequently became friends with were the assistant director, Donald Buchanan; chief curator, Robert Hubbard; and curator of prints and drawings, Kathleen Fenwick. Although these three worked hard to enlarge the guidelines for the collection and exhibition of art it was still a pretty stuffy place when McCurry retired in 1955 and Alan Jarvis, a Canadian who had spent the last decade in London, England, was appointed director. He came highly recommended by Sir Kenneth Clark.

There are many versions of the Jarvis saga, but for me it was a period of hope and excitement. The National Gallery was moving out into the Canadian community and finally generating some real art energy. That's what I focused on and that's what coloured my vision. There is no question that, politically, Alan seemed to push all the wrong buttons and alienate a lot of people. He closed the Group of Seven wing to make office space, amputating from our vision a large part of our art history. Do you remember the rage and furore in Paris when André Malraux had the *Mona Lisa* put in storage? Well, there was that kind of outrage in Ottawa at hiding our 'icons'. Granted, Alan had a point – we were saturated with pine-tree imagery – but the Canadian public resented being told what they should look at. Despite some shortcomings, Jarvis was the art dynamo we needed to vitalise an old dinosaur. With a change of government and other complications involving purchases for the collection, which the new government would not approve, Jarvis was forced to resign in 1958. It seemed that we were back to square one.

When Charles Comfort, an artist-professor from the University of Toronto, was made the new director, the energy seemed to evaporate. But as a result of Alan's planning, the Gallery did move from the old museum to an office building in central Ottawa, a move that made the collection much more accessible. It wasn't until Comfort retired in 1966 and Jean Boggs, an art historian with broad teaching and curatorial experience, was appointed director that we noticed some radical changes in exhibition policy.

In 1957 the Canada Council was established, modelled on the British Arts Council. It encompassed all the arts in Canada. In the early years, before it became overly political and bureaucratic, it felt like a fresh breeze blowing across this barren land.

In 1958 I got a small Canada Council Scholarship to spend some time at the Instituto Allende in Mexico. The Instituto didn't have much to offer me after Hofmann, but it provided me with a studio space and a stimulating cultural environment. After a few months in Mexico we moved back to Victoria where I was going to teach part-time and spend the rest of my life making art. Immediately upon my return to Victoria, I knew I'd made a terrible mistake. What had in my memory been an ideal supportive setting for a young artist, was in reality quite a different place. The energy and sense of urgency I'd experienced around Ottawa didn't exist. The artists seemed smug and parochial, and my art suffered. Victoria didn't seem to have an active art scene while Ottawa was developing into a vital community.

So in 1960 when a friend offered me a job managing a Danish furniture store in an old blue barn outside of Ottawa, I jumped at the opportunity to return. As the business developed, what was to have been a part-time job turned into a major commitment. When we needed more space and moved to a new building, we started exhibiting local artists and the Blue Barn Gallery was born. As the only venue in Ottawa at the time to exhibit contemporary art we established a considerable reputation. When we moved again to a building with a larger exhibition space separate from the furniture business, we started showing work from across Canada. I continued with my painting and teaching at the Community Art Center and then at Carleton University where, for several years, I was advisor to the Fine Arts Committee and organised exhibitions and a programme of visiting artists. With works donated by my friends we founded Carleton's permanent collection which subsequently formed the nucleus of the Carleton University Art Gallery.

Expo 67 was in the air and everyone wanted to be a part of it. I got so involved in the Canadian Pavilion that I had several telephones on my desk and quite a few hard-hats – graphic designer, publications coordinator, arts and crafts coordinator, curator of the Karsh exhibition, and gallery director. As the Director of the Canadian Pavilion Art Gallery I was assigned the memorable task of greeting Charles de Gaulle at the Canadian Pavilion the day after he'd shouted 'Vive le Québec Libre' to a cheering Francophone audience. No Canadian of any political ambition was anywhere to be seen at the pavilion that day. There are so many stories to tell about this incredible time that it would take another letter. I thrived on being part of all the energy. Montreal, then at its peak as a vital cosmopolitan city, later suffered much from the entropy of nationalism.

After Expo 67 I opened Lofthouse Galleries in a converted house directly facing the old National Gallery. We continued a diverse programme of contemporary art exhibitions and I kept painting, and exhibiting my own work across the country.

In 1969 the Canadian Government Exhibition Commission asked me to design the Manitoba Centennial Caravan: a gift from Canada to the people of Manitoba to celebrate 100 years as a province. The concept was five tractor-trailers (each 10 ft wide and 100 ft long) that would tour the province, encapsulating different aspects of Manitoba's history from early settlement to the future. Although this challenge occupied a full year of my life, I kept painting. I kept teaching. I kept running my gallery. And I was getting bloody tired.

Also, like artists everywhere who were questioning the philosophical boundaries of art, my ideas were going through a major transition. I no longer wanted to deal with referential images and it was difficult for me to find work that excited me enough to subsidise its exhibition in my gallery. I felt I'd made what contribution I could to the Ottawa art community.

The new curator of contemporary art at the National Gallery, Brydon Smith, was organising major exhibitions of American Contemporary Art and had started to build a collection. The Gallery was alive again and under superb direction. The Americans had landed with their large-scale images and concepts. Canadian Art would never again be

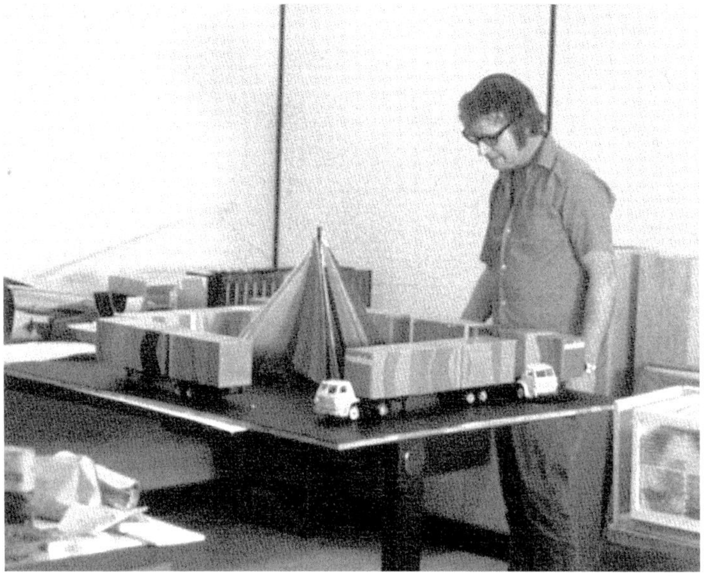

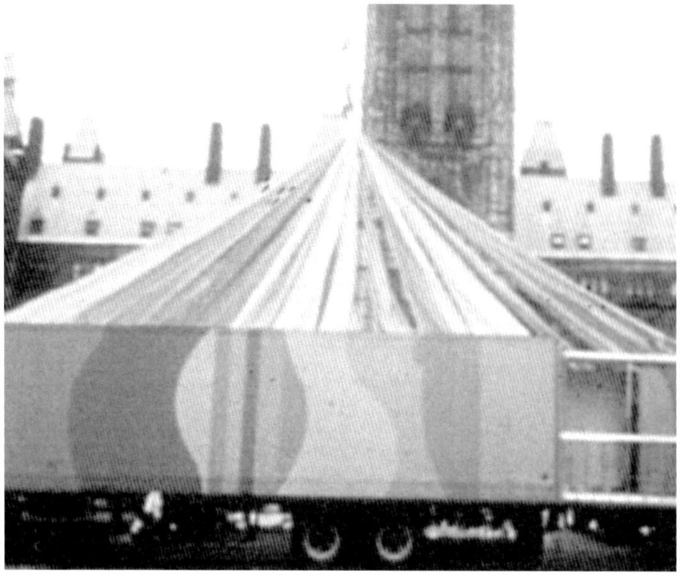

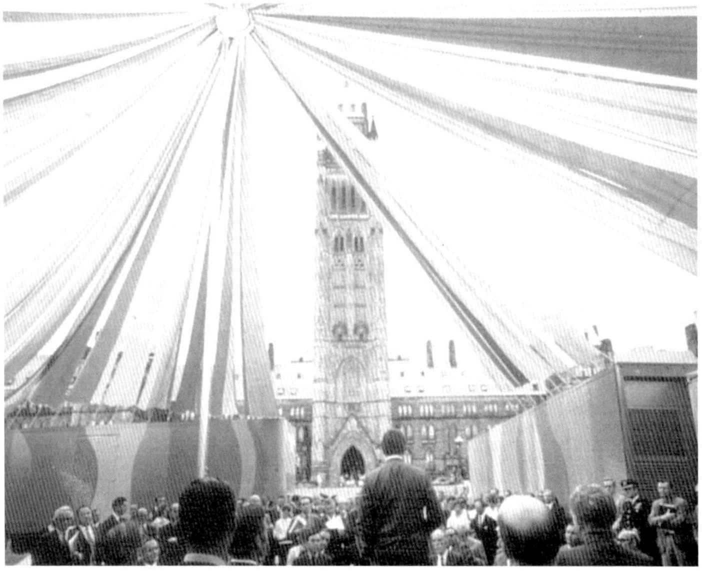

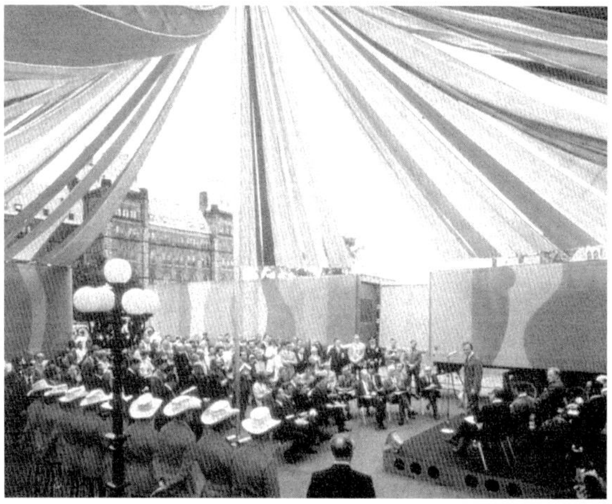

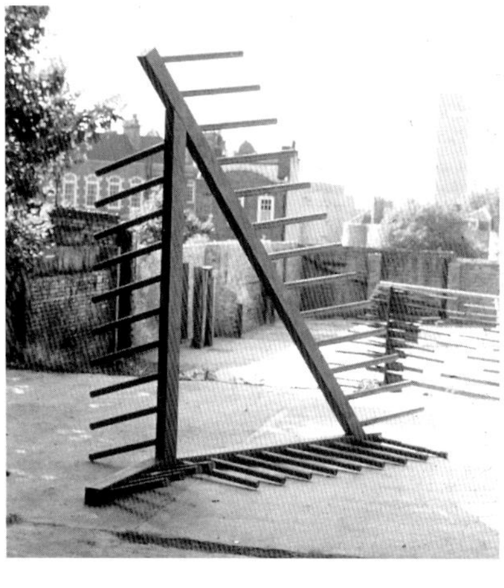

(top left) Duncan de Kergommeaux, Model for Centennial caravan

(above left) Dedication of caravan on Parliament Hill, Ottawa

(top right) Caravan on Parliament Hill, Ottawa

(centre right) Another view of the Dedication ceremony

(bottom right) William Tucker, *Track,* 1977

viewed through the same lens. I still had my large, perhaps romantic, vision of 'Canadian Artist' as one capable of adding something unique to our history. Perhaps it would be through art education.

I knew it was time for me to move on to other challenges. So in 1970 when Tony Urquhart, an artist I admired and whose work I'd exhibited several times in Ottawa, asked me to join the faculty of the University of Western Ontario (UWO) as a teacher of drawing and painting I thought about it long and hard. I'd been offered the resident artist position there in 1968, before the department was founded, but had turned it down. This offer seemed a bit more attractive.

In the late 1960s and early 1970s, with government money flowing, art all across Canada was finally being taken more seriously. Community colleges like Fanshawe were being built and establishing programmes in art. Many established universities were founding art departments. All this growth created a huge demand for competent teachers and administrators, which Canada simply couldn't supply. Many Canadian artists, who'd long been supported by Canada Council grants, felt it demeaning to teach. We simply had to look outside the borders of Canada.

In 1967 the Nova Scotia College of Art and Design, a prime candidate for educational revitalisation, got the message. They knew that if an institution wanted to compete in this new environment, it had to be prepared to offer courses that were more relevant and up to date, and hire teachers who were more relevant and up to date. Garry Kennedy, a conceptual artist and recent graduate of Ohio University, was hired as President. He was given a large budget and an open mandate to bring in excellent teachers in studio, art history and criticism. With a rich programme of international visiting artists and critics he managed to build a world-class institution. It was the most contemporary-thinking and literate art department in Canada – and perhaps in North America – at the time, a reputation it held for many years. Many of us in art education wanted to follow at least some aspects of this model.

In the Fall of 1970 I accepted the position at UWO and moved to London, Ontario. I hadn't heard of Fanshawe College or Ricky Atkinson and knew little about the new university art department that I was joining. W. S. A. Dale, an art historian and specialist in medieval art, was the department chair. I'd known him casually in Ottawa when he was assistant director of the National Gallery. Tony Urquhart, was head of studio. The department was a combination of history and studio with a mandate to prepare students for teachers' college – a rather narrow focus that I hoped we could expand as things developed.

After my hectic life in Ottawa, academic life seemed like a movie in slow motion. Within a couple of years I adjusted to this new environment where I could spend a lot of time thinking solely about art. Also, I liked the fact that we worked so closely with the art historians who provided another dimension to art that I'd never had the luxury to pursue.

Tony left for Waterloo University and I took his place as head of studio. When Bill Dale went on a sabbatical in 1973 I was made acting chair and during that year convinced the Dean that we needed a proper studio building with private studios for the teaching faculty. My rationale was that professional artists doing their own work in the department could make a significant contribution to our programme in many ways, one of which was by providing role models for students. For the next twenty years two other senior members of faculty, Roly Fenwick and Patterson Ewen, and I worked as professional artists in close proximity to the teaching studios. Students who were interested could be our assistants and get involved in the whole process. The effectiveness of this strategy was apparent in the performance of these students and in the fact that they were in high demand as teaching assistants when they went on to graduate studies.

In 1975, after the department was well established, Bill Dale resigned as chair to concentrate on teaching and research and again I was made acting chair. That year we were able to organise a rich programme of visitors with the help of Les Levine, an artist friend living in New York, and some extra funding from Fanshawe College and the London Regional Art Gallery. We recruited the British sculptor William Tucker to teach in our department. He used the large workshops at Fanshawe to make his own work. The same year we recruited José Barrio-Garay, then director of the School of Art at Ohio University, as chair. With a master's in painting and design from the University of Madrid and a PhD in art history from Columbia University, José brought to the department a broad cultural background and sympathy for contemporary art and artists. He supported and added to the visitors' pro-

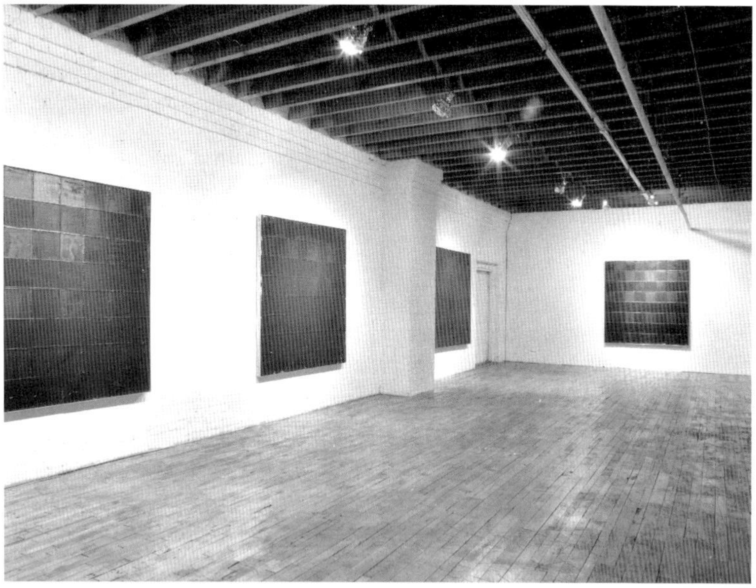

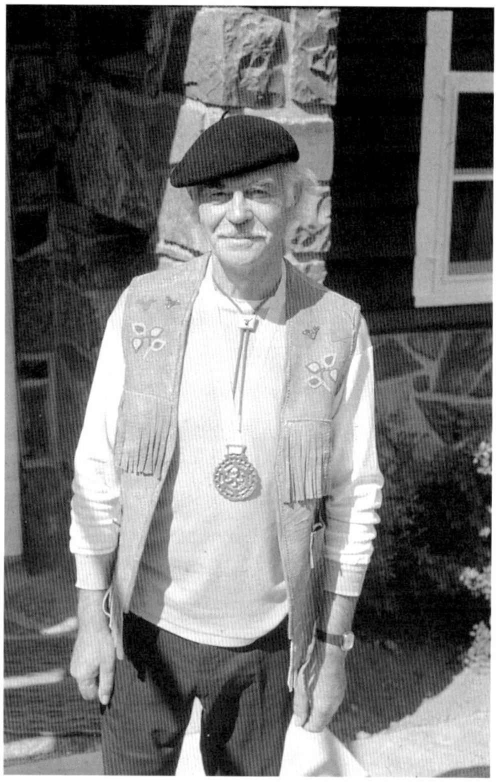

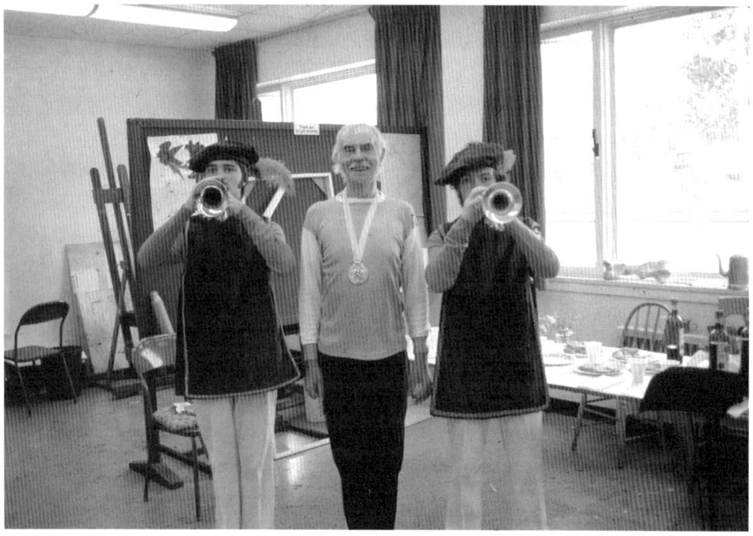

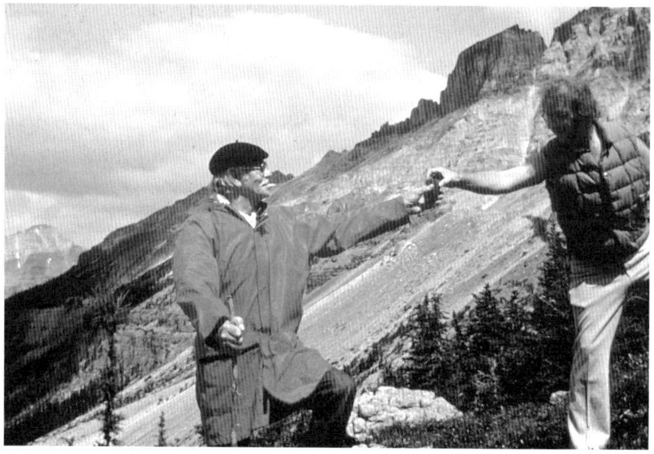

(above left) Duncan de Kergommeaux exhibition, Trajectory Gallery, London, Ontario

(above right) Terry Frost at the Banff Summer School, 1975

(above) Terry Frost and students at the Banff Summer School on Medal Day

(right) Terry Frost with Duncan de Kergommeaux at the Banff Summer School

gramme, which continued through my 1980–4 term as Chairman.

From 1970, when I first moved to London, until the mid-1980s, the city was an exciting place for an artist to live in. Downtown was a warren of artists' studios above retail stores and in old buildings waiting for demolition. It was like living in New York's SoHo. There was a contingent of good local artists who had passed through the hands of some enlightened teachers at Beale Technical School. These formed a group around Greg Curnoe, a Canadian artist who had attracted much national attention. They had a major exhibition at the National Gallery and were a force in the community. They founded an artist-run gallery (20/20, later called Forest City Gallery) for exhibiting their work, and for years got funding from the Canada Council for this and other projects. Jack Chambers, another local artist who had a lot of national exposure, was one of the founding members of Canadian Artists Representation (CAR), a union of Canadian artists fighting for artists' fees and other equities. There was a lot of politics but also a lot of energy. My only reservation was the 'politics'. Although I'd spent a good part of my life in Ottawa, I liked to believe that art was one thing that could be free of politics.

There was also a large group of very interesting and highly professional new arrivals, Alan Wood, Don Bonham, Michael Durham, Steve Parzybok, Robin Hobbs, Trevor Bell among many others from Britain and the USA who brought a broader vision to the scene. Several of these Ricky had recruited to support his programme at Fanshawe. Others taught at both UWO and Fanshawe College. I liked all the diverse energies this situation engendered. We had our fights; we had our fun; we had our camaraderie; we had amity and enmity and, sometimes, outright hostility. But I remember this as one of the most productive and happy periods of my life. When Stephen Joy, a professional gallery curator from New York, was hired to teach art history at Fanshawe College, he opened and personally funded the Trajectory Gallery in a large loft space in the centre of the city. Trajectory became another focal point for the art community, exhibiting work that would otherwise never have been seen. It was there that I had my local exhibitions for the next decade.

In the early 1970s the Banff School of Fine Arts changed its name to The Banff Center and redefined its vision. It became a professional centre for business management and the arts. In 1973 Takao Tanabe became Head of Visual Arts and it was under his excellent direction that a year-round programme was developed and the teaching focus became more professional. Publicised internationally, the Banff Center drew students from graduate programmes across North America. The School built several small studios for professional artists of varying disciplines to work in as visiting artists. Their only commitment to the school would be the occasional critique of students' work.

It was in Banff where I was teaching during the summer of 1975 that I first met Terry Frost. He'd been invited to replace William Scott as a teacher, who because of illness was unable to come to Banff that summer. All the instructors and students had gathered in a large classroom for a first meeting and the instructors were asked to provide slides of their work for the students to assess so they could decide with whom they wanted to study. It was a cumbersome process that took a couple of hours, at the end of which all the classes were, in theory, supposed to be democratically organised. Good in theory. Bad in practice! After reviewing all our slides, not one student opted to take a course from either Terry or me. We both thought this was hilarious, and it immediately established a friendship between us that we maintained throughout the summer and the years since. Despite the initial snub, we became popular teachers at the school.

Every day Terry and I ate our meals together. Breakfast and dinner in the dining-room, but lunch we prepared ourselves. We'd walk down the mountain trail to the village, buy our food, then climb back up and make lunch in one of our rooms. It was usually boiled eggs, sliced onions in vinegar, radishes, cheese, crackers and a glass of wine. In the evenings after dinner, we would drink in the lounge, play the occasional game of darts and read poetry, usually Lorca, to anyone who'd listen to us. On weekends we'd go on hikes up the many mountain trails and generally have a lot of fun. I'll never forget having dinner with Terry one night. He loved liver and onions. He wanted to take some back to his room for a snack so wrapped a piece up in a paper napkin and stuffed it in his pocket. We went on to a concert. In the middle of the performance Terry suddenly jumped up and exclaimed loudly, 'O my liver, my liver. It's leaking, it's leaking'. I was very startled until I realised what he was going on about. Among the audience he almost created pandemonium. But his was certainly the best performance that

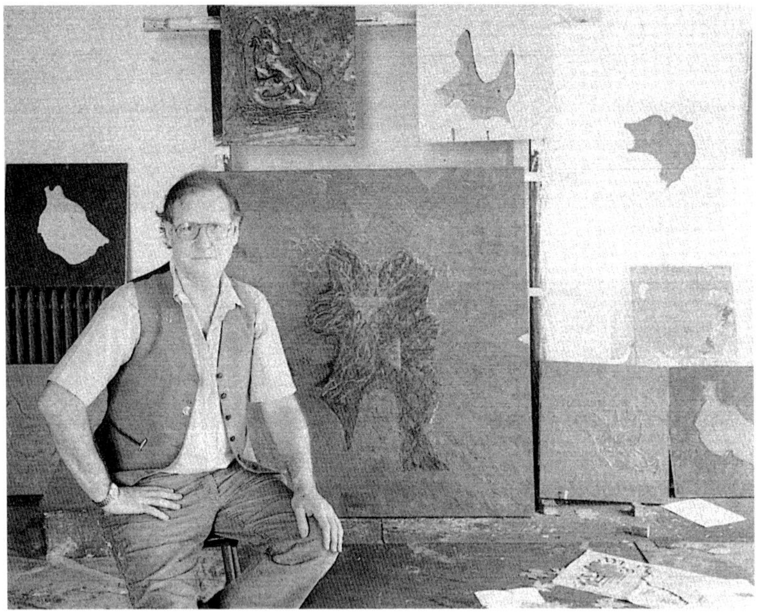

Duncan de Kergommeaux
in his New York studio, 1980

evening. Teaching with us were Joe Plaskett, back in Canada from Paris; Terry Johnson, Head of Studio at the Nova Scotia College of Art; Doug Morton, Dean of Arts at York University in Toronto; Graham Coughtry, a painter from Toronto, and others. It was a high-powered group that generated a lot of enthusiasm among the students. At the end of the summer when I returned to UWO I was determined to get Terry to come as a visiting artist, and with Ricky's help we were able to bring him to London, Ontario several times.

In 1979 students at the Nova Scotia College of Art were rebelling against conceptual art. I was invited there for the summer to give a course in painting. My work at that time was conceptual in terms of content. However, my materials were real paint on real canvas. Those were serious issues to deal with at the time. The college gave me a private studio and arranged for an exhibition of my work at the end of the summer. Being forced to produce an exhibition in six weeks that would sustain close scrutiny not only by students but also by a very critical faculty was a daunting challenge which fortified my belief about art education: challenge is the crucial ingredient for growth.

Directly after the summer at Nova Scotia College I spent a sabbatical year in New York. Occasionally students from Nova Scotia as well as UWO visited me and we could extend studio practice to looking at art, in the real neurotic world of the Big Apple. This was probably their most valuable lesson of all.

I was in Paris for a few months in 1985 so flew over to London for the opening of the St Ives Exhibition at the Tate and went from there to Newlyn where I spent a few days with Terry and Kath. Several years earlier my wife and I'd gone for Christmas to Zennor with Alan and Jenny Wood. It was then I met W.S. Graham (whom we later brought to Canada as a visitor) and was introduced to Patrick Heron. 'Well,' Patrick said, 'I've never met a Canadian who had anything useful to say about art,' and that was the end of our conversation.

And this is the end of our conversation, David; I hope some of what I've said is 'useful'.

Sincerely,
Duncan de Kergommeaux

PS: Today as I write this, I wonder where all the energy and rigour has gone. The buildings in the city block that housed Trajectory, the 20/20 Gallery, my loft and Ron Martin's above me, and so many other artists' studios have been levelled and turned into a parking lot. The industrial building close by that housed Michael Durham, Don Bonham, Trevor Bell, Alan Wood, Paterson Ewen, Robin Page, Jamelie Hassan, Jeff Gordon and many other artists over the years has been torn down and replaced by an apartment block. Many of the storefronts on our main street are vacant and the artists have gone. Greg Curnoe was killed in a biking accident; Jack Chambers lost his long battle with leukemia; other artists have left the city. Most of the major players at Fanshawe and UWO have moved on and those of us who have remained live in the suburbs surrounding a core suffering meltdown. It is a rather bizarre affair – almost as if the city needed to purge itself of an energy it could never understand or come to terms with.

When I heard recently that the Nova Scotia College of Art wanted to move out of the industrial buildings in the core of Halifax I couldn't help wondering if they might take a lesson from what has happened to the art scene in London, Ontario.

Duncan

1. A.Y. Jackson was a leading member of the Group of Seven; Jock MacDonald was a Scottish painter who moved to Canada in 1926 and taught widely; William Townsend was a painter and senior tutor at the Slade; William Scott was a well-known British painter.

Letter 13 Stephen Joy to David Lewis

Dear David

Let's start with Paris. Meeting with other, young, open-minded fellows, searching adventure. French, Spanish, Dutch, Italian. The idea of internationalism, of sharing, and informing has continued to colour all my activities since then.

My almost two years in Europe must have built upon something already within me for I became a sharer. If it is exciting, intriguing, if it opens doors and breaches horizons for me, I want to share it and hope that it has the same effect upon others. I have become a repository for massive miscellaneous information. I am, in fact, a kind of sponge. Squeeze me and out comes information about painting, sculpture, theatre, music, dance, architecture, anything. I suppose, more directly, I am a nosy bastard. Some people call it passion.

Feeling strongly that New York City was the place to be, I returned to New York with two hundred paintings I had done, and began the routine of showing these to galleries. I quickly learned the patter: 'Very nice. But go to the place down the street.' 'Good stuff, but take them to another.' Lesson one on how not to talk to artists, which has clung to me to this day. I also learned of the generosity of creative people. As a non-paying room-mate of an actor friend, as the recipient of a handful of money from a dancer because I was sitting in Washington Square, broke and despondent, talking with a working writer over dinner, which he paid for, I came to understand that the creative world is an interlocking ONE. I am excited as I write that.

I created a résumé and circulated it to all the major museums and galleries in New York. The only response came from Miss Jones of the Museum of Modern Art personnel department. We met for one hour, during which time she assured me that there were no curatorial positions open at the Museum, that my qualifications were top notch and she would not degrade me by offering the lowly position of sales clerk in their bookstore. This because of my experience as Chairman of the Arts Committee at the University of Wisconsin.

Needing a job, I answered an ad in the *New York Times* for a gallery handyman. The lengthy phone conversation with the receptionist-secretary ended with her saying that I was too good and sounded too intelligent for that menial work. She must have spoken to Martha Jackson. A week later the phone rang. 'Stephen, where are you? We need you. Come as soon as you can,' said the distinctive voice of Martha Jackson. I met her for the first time that morning when I began working, not as a handyman, but as part-time salesman of art. A new experience, a new world to explore. It wasn't a career move, but a chance event in a rabbit hole. This seems to be the manner of my movement in the art world – to say nothing of the real world. Six months later I was a full-time employee. A year later Martha asked me to become director. David Anderson, her son, worked at the gallery, but I was made director.

What happened to my painting? It suffered. In fact, I found that I could not shift gears from work to creativity. My focus was (and is) to do the best job possible in whatever position I find myself. An attitude which continues to colour all my activities to this day. I didn't realise, as I do now, that creativity could involve elements other than canvas and pigments or music and movement.

Martha Jackson's talent was to listen to artists, critics, curators, then make her own evaluations and juxtapositions. This led her into the vanguard of the world art scene. At a time when the role as shaker and mover in the art world was quickly moving from Paris to New York, Martha read the scene and became a major force in the New York world of art. It was my good fortune to become part of her team early in the history of the Martha Jackson Gallery when the New York scene was beginning to move under its own powerful head of steam.

New York in the 1950s was bursting with an American vitality which made an impact still to be felt upon the creative activities in every country. The Abstract Expressionists were wedging their way into art consciousness and changing the way we perceived 'art', taking over the scene totally by the mid 1950s. Martha Graham was changing the way dancers moved. Stephen Sondheim was re-creating the musical stage. Drama was being redesigned by Tennessee Williams and Arthur Miller. Steve Reich and Philip Glass were retuning our ears to music and opera.

It was this vortex in which I became involved, committed to the degree that I now realise it has formed my life since then. Dorothy Miller, Bill Seitz, from the Museum of Modern Art, Alan Solomon from the Guggenheim, Grace Glueck, critic for the *New York Times*, Emily Geneaur of the *Herald Tribune*, Rosalind Constable, *Time Magazine*, Thomas B. Hess, editor of *Art News*, Clement Greenberg, all became familiars. Gallery people Sidney Janis, Leo Castelli, Betty Parsons, all became coffee conversational-

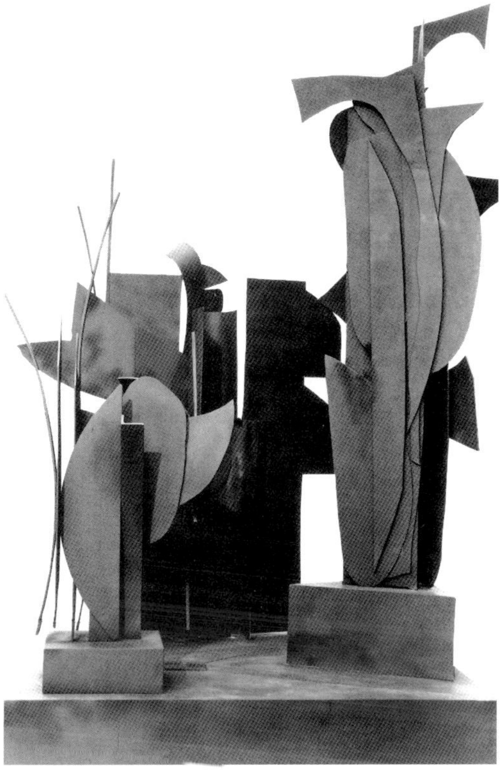

(above)
Louise Nevelson
Tropical Garden's Presence
1974, height: 99 in., painted aluminium
collection: Museum of Art, The Carnegie, Pittsburgh (gift of Mr & Mrs Charles Denby)

(above right)
Robert Motherwell
Castile (Espana)
1952, 47¼ x71¼ in., oil on masonite
collection: Museum of Art, The Carnegie, Pittsburgh (gift of Mr & Mrs Charles Denby)

(right)
Antoni Tapies
Untitled
1956, 36 x 20 in., sand, oil, pencil on paper
collection: Stephen Joy

(far right)
Antoni Tapies
Painting
1958, 76⅞ x 66¾ in., mixed media on canvas
collection: Museum of Art, The Carnegie, Pittsburgh

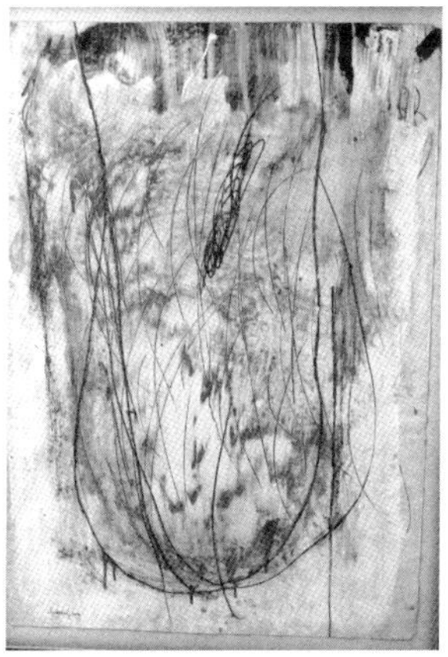

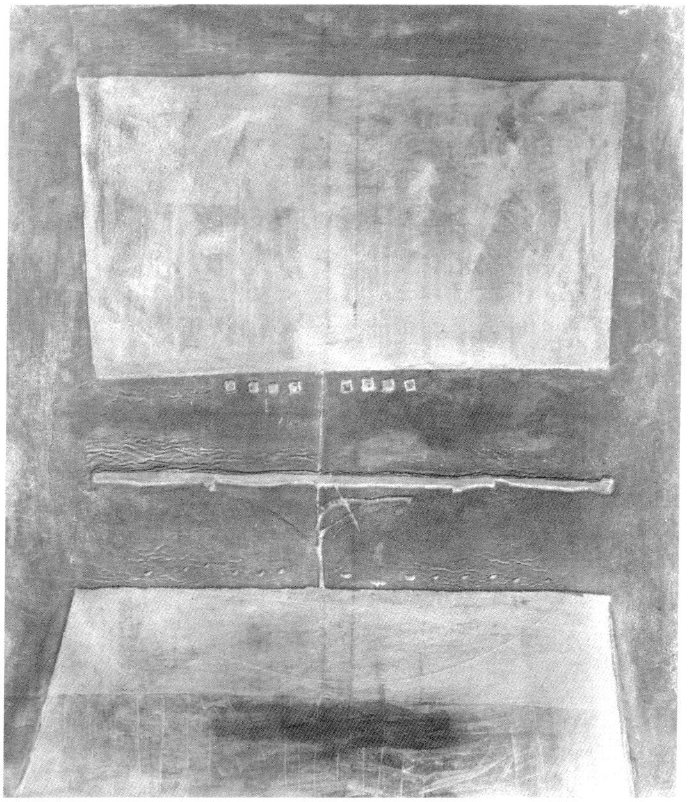

ists. Artists I was in contact with were more exciting: Willem de Kooning, Jim Dine, Lee Krasner, Louise Nevelson, Claes Oldenburg, Larry Rivers. Even Andy Warhol. Even Canadian Art. A gallery on 55th Street exposed us all to Guido Molinari, Marcel Barbeau, Claude Tousignant.

Parties, openings, lunches, dinners, drinks or rich studio conversations helped me realise that the crucial thing with all these creative people was the fact that they were pursuing a goal, an aim, even at a low level, a job, just as I was. Some had specific agendas, some floated with instinct, but they were intense about their activities. They were creative, complex and real. Elements embedded in all of us in various densities, but with the artist the density may be almost unbearable. Those of us on the periphery, being aware of this, held the artist's hand, lent a shoulder, opened an ear in the hope that this would ease the pain of the birth of painting, music, poetry or dance.

Working with Martha Jackson I found that my greatest function was to mediate between Martha and her stable of artists. Her manner of vague commitment/non-commitment tended to confuse the people with whom she dealt. Not only artists, but clients and press would meet with her, then turn to me for clarification. This liaison role brought me into close relationship with our artists.

For two summers I ran a gallery for Jackson in Provincetown, Massachusetts, which was at the time a community of major artists. Hans Hofman held open house constantly, Peter Busa built his glass-brick studio there, Robert Motherwell spent time there. I had met Motherwell before my European trip when he was pushing 'intrasubjectivism' as the name for what became known as 'Abstract Expressionism'. Walter Chrysler, Jr acquired and remodelled a church into his museum, where white-gloved minions served drinks and hors d'œuvres from silver platters. The Provincetown Martha Jackson Gallery was less pretentious. Trucking down works by gallery artists from New York, an international tone was introduced to Provincetown. I selected artists from the summer community for group and one-man shows. Lobster salad (lobster fresh from the sea), cheese and liquor were staples at our openings, but served from plates and platters buffet style and eaten from paper plates.

Visiting artists' studios was a built-in, given Martha Jackson policy. Martha and I were constantly at artists' studios, sometimes together and more frequently on our own. I was never too busy to look at an artist's slides and discuss his work which could lead to a studio visit. At the end of the season (May–June) we would hold a group show, a trial balloon to get reactions of clients, curators, artists. From this show a few artists were added to the 'stable'. Sometimes on a show-to-show basis, sometimes on a contract basis. Every effort was made to circulate all of our artists to galleries in other cities, including Paris, London, Tokyo and to include them in appropriate festival exhibitions and museum shows in the United States, South America and Europe. Jackson may have been the first New York gallery to have contracts with contemporary young artists and circulate them internationally.

Antonio Tapiès (Spain), Karel Appel (Holland), Teshigajara (Japan), Germaine Richier, George Mathieu, Yves Klein (France), Paul-Emile Borduas (Canada), William Scott, Barbara Hepworth (Britain) and Lucio Fontana (Italy) were all part of a programme of exchange exhibitions and studio spaces with some of the Martha Jackson Gallery artists. These artists from overseas would settle into a New York artist's studio and proceed to paint works for a show. Jackson's American artists included Sam Francis, Paul Jenkins, John Chamberlain, Al Leslie, Lester Johnson, Al Jensen, Louise Nevelson, Lee Krasner.

The Martha Jackson Gallery did not become involved with the various new thrusts in art during the 1950s. Martha did not seem to be tuned to Op Art, Minimal Art, Pop Art. The closest she came to recognising any of these was with the 'New Forms – New Media I–II' exhibitions. Works for the first version were collected with advice from critics, curators and artists. Martha left for her annual buying and contacting trip to Europe before the show opened. 'It's all yours now, dear,' she said as she entered her cab to the airport.

As the works came in for the show, we stored them in the guest room on the fourth floor of the building which quickly assumed the air of a storage room for some mad accumulator. Among the artists shown for the first time in a Madison Avenue gallery were Bob Indiana, Stan Vanderbeek, Charles Ginnever, Jim Dine, Claes Oldenburg, Robert Whitman, George Brecht, Chryssa, Alan Kaprow, Red Grooms (whose work we bought, on my advice, after he decided in a letter – which I have – that 'your gallery is not in the free spirit of my expression'). We borrowed

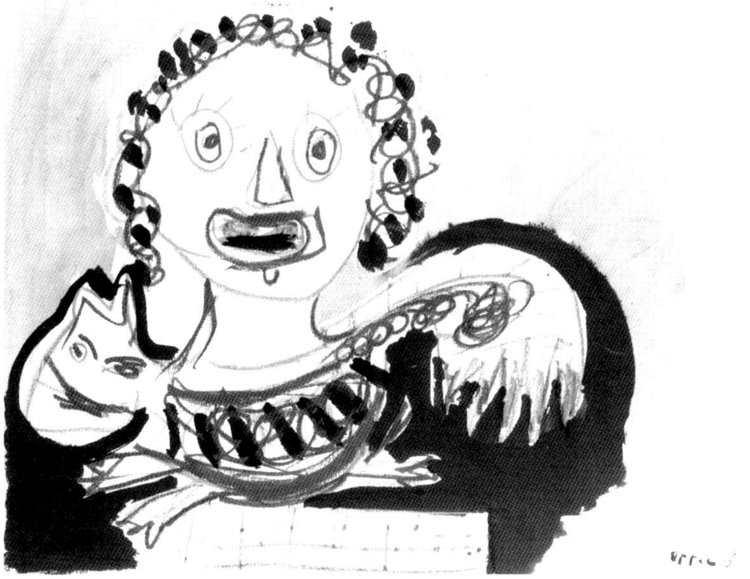

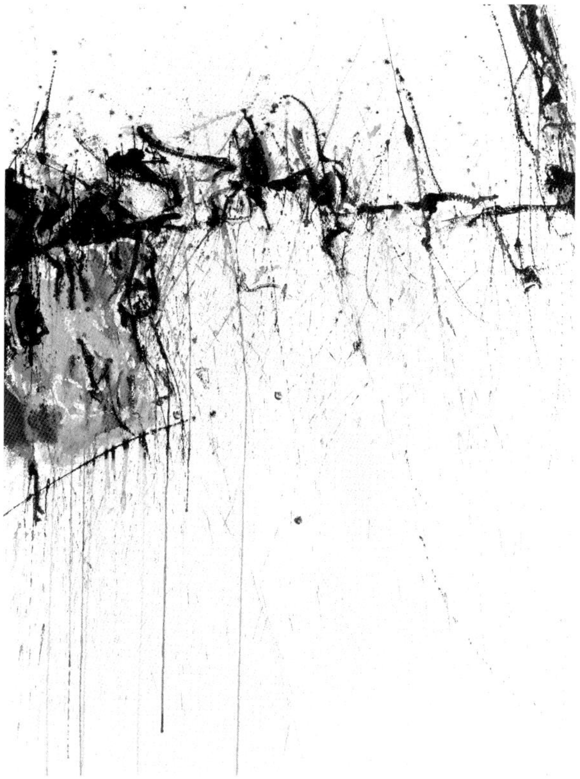

(above)
Karel Appel
Girl with cat
1966
19½ x 25⅝ in.
crayon, ink and wash
collection: Museum of Art, The Carnegie, Pittsburgh (gift of Benjamin D. Bernstein)

(above right)
Sam Francis
Yellow into black
1958
30¼ x 22¼ in.
watercolour and gouache on paper
collection: Museum of Art, The Carnegie, Pittsburgh

(right)
Jim Dine
Family
1959
50 x 30 in.
oil paint, string, crayon on canvas
collection: Stephen Joy

(bottom right)
Georges Mathieu
Painting
1957
72 x 48 in.
oil on canvas
collection: Museum of Art, The Carnegie, Pittsburgh

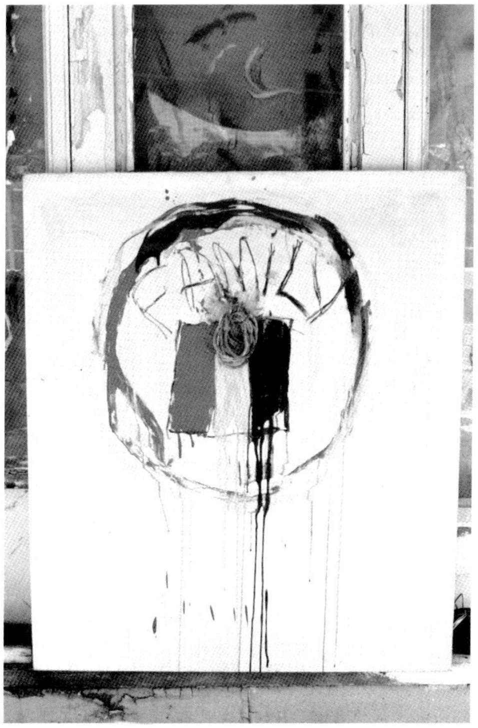

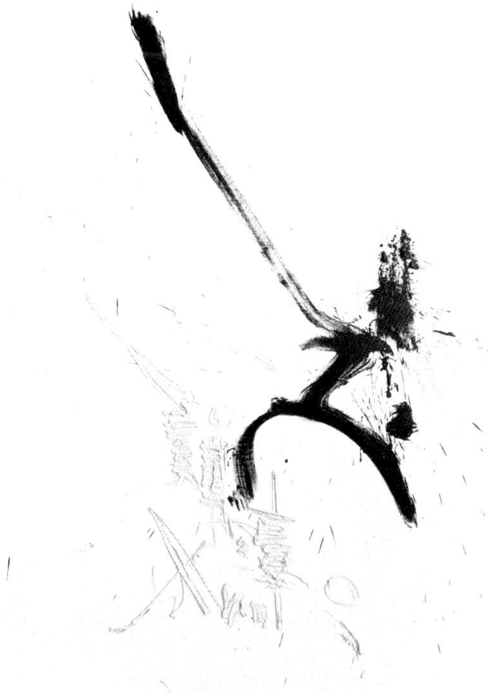

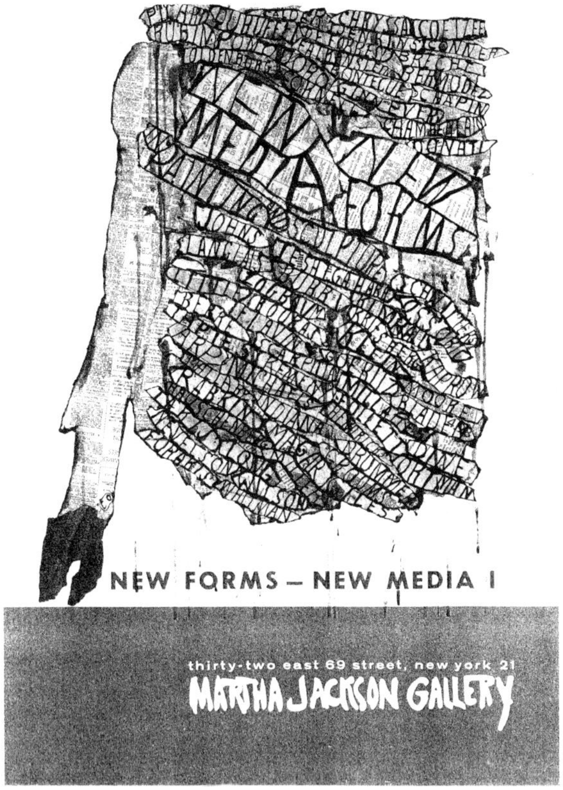

Catalogue cover for 'New Forms – New Media I' exhibition, Martha Jackson Gallery, New York, 1960

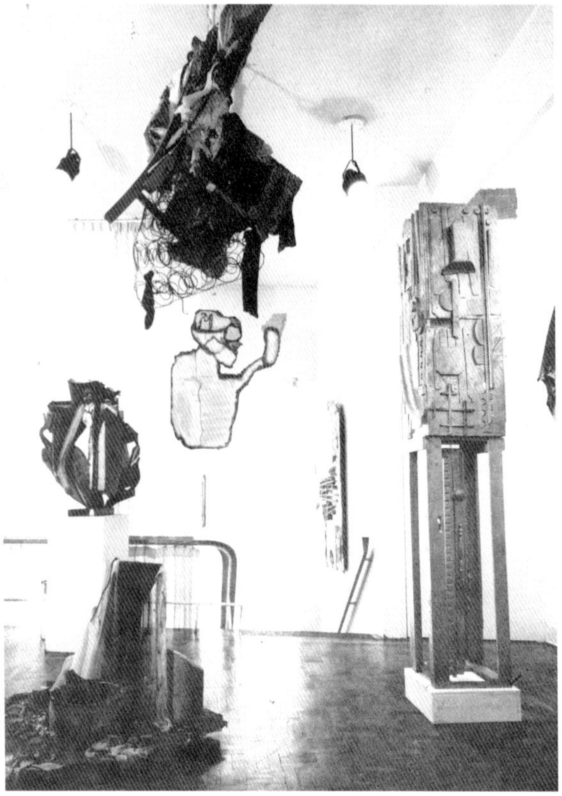

Some of the pieces exhibited at the exhibition, including works by Louise Nevelson, Robert Rauschenberg, John Chamberlain and Joseph Cornell

works by Jasper Johns and Robert Rauschenburg from Leo Castelli to create a kind of precedent for the newer artists. From this melange of totally discrepant works, it was my job to make a cohesive statement in the two-floor space of the gallery.

When the show opened, it was a sensation. It was the first time the works (later known as Pop) from the underground galleries, Hansa, Rubens, Judd were given stature by being seen on Madison Avenue. The opening involved a mob of people, questioning, discussing. Press coverage was immense. Newspapers, magazines, even CBC interviewed me for twenty minutes. I telephoned Martha in London with this information and she cut short her trip returning to become part of the brouhaha. It was decided to build on this success by putting together a second version 'New Forms – New Media II', for which Lawrence Alloway wrote an introduction to the catalogue.

At this time Martha made certain overtures and promises about my future at the Gallery. It quickly became apparent that these were not going to be fulfilled. After working with her for six and a half years we separated amicably. I told her in one of our last meetings that the exhibition I was working on 'Environments – Situations – Spaces', a follow-up to 'New Forms – New Media I–II', would be the last exciting show the Gallery would have. I selected five artists from the 'New Forms – New Media' shows for 'Environments – Situations – Spaces'. Claes Oldenburg, Jim Dine, Robert Whitman, Alan Kaprow and George Brecht were each given a specific area in the gallery to install, subject to consultation with me, whatever they pleased. Oldenburg hung his corrugated cardboard, scorched figures, Dine created his 'Spring Environment', Brecht placed a single cadmium yellow rocker under a spotlight in a dark room. Whitman filled his area with a car interior with a crash victim made of fabrics, glass, wood and cardboard, while Kaprow filled our courtyard with a massive collection of used tyres.

For one week Kaprow laboured over the form his space was to take. The tyres were a given, but he tried running clothes-lines from one end of the courtyard to another from which he hung bed sheets: no good. These were replaced by plastic sheets: no good. I was panicking as the opening day approached. In one of my many dialogues with Kaprow about what he was reaching for, he gave me a memorable statement: 'Stephen, you don't understand how difficult it is *not* to use all the imagination I have'.

Jim Dine was easier to work with. When I pointed out that the dripping paint cans he wanted to include in his 'Spring Environment' were a potential nuisance (paint dripping on the visitors' clothes), he agreed to simply have them hang there without dripping. He originally wanted an elaborate fan system to blow the painted fabric surrounding his installation, but he agreed to a more simple fan arrangement. The other artists presented less complex problems. My final feat was to don a mask and spray all the fabrics and paper with fire retardant, just in case.

Crowds poured in and comments were pro and con, but the dialogues were energetic. Martha asked me if I thought there was any talent in the show. I replied that I would take on Dine, Oldenburg, Brecht and Kaprow. She was noncommittal and these artists were taken on by Leo Castelli. Martha missed the Pop boat. At the same time, during the installation period, nearly every one of the artists came to me and said if Martha spoke to them again they would pull out of the show. They did not take well to her style and, perhaps, to her lack of understanding of what they were doing. And as I had predicted, it was the last exciting show the Martha Jackson Gallery ever had.

After I left the Gallery I freelanced, advising new galleries, dealing privately, none of which satisfied me. At one point, The Whitney Museum was having a small one-man show of Joseph Cornell's boxes. A client of mine asked if they were for sale. I found they were and he offered to buy the whole collection if the price could be agreed upon. I contacted a dealer who I knew was friendly with Cornell and asked her to speak with him. She came back with the reply that Cornell would sell the collection but his demands were so extraordinary that the deal fell through.

It was also during this period (mid 1960s) that I tried to implement an idea which I thought had potential. Since most of the galleries closed for the summer while their owners vacationed, or toured other cities (in Europe, mostly) looking for new talent or visiting important exhibitions, why not set up a summer exhibition (for summer tourists) with works which were normally in storage. I found along the Bowery, and West Broadway, below Houston Street huge spaces which could be had for very little rent. Many artists were living in the area in gigantic studio lofts for which they paid $50 to $100 a month. They took advantage of Canal Street, where they found cast-off, surplus materials, government over-runs, at very minimal cost and incorporated them in their sculpture, painting, constructions, stage sets or Performances and Happenings. The universal Madison Avenue dealers' response was that 'No one will ever go there. It is too dangerous an area. You can't get a cab there. There are no restaurants.' So the idea was not realised. Things have changed. The area is now chic, and elegant loft living spaces are renting for $1000 a month and upwards. Some of the smartest bars, restaurants and most interesting galleries in New York are now located there. That area is now SoHo.

In the late 1960s I visited a draft-dodging friend (as a conscientious objector during World War Two, I was sympathetic) in Toronto. Touring the city I dropped into the Dunkleman Gallery. As I talked with Yael Dunkleman, she remembered that I had sold her and her husband some sculpture while I was with the Martha Jackson Gallery. The phone rang, she answered it and her face went blank. 'Do you speak French?' she asked me. I said 'yes' and she handed me the phone. It was simple. A French-speaking artist wanted to know if he could bring in some slides to show her. I translated and an appointment was made. I still wonder if that small feat caused her to offer me a job at her gallery. The Dunklemans expressed a desire to bring in young artists, which by now I realised was my strong interest. I was not pleased with how the art scene was developing in New York, and Toronto intrigued me (any city that builds a city hall that looks like a clam captured between two plinths has got to have something going for it) and, as with my thoughts about New York while I was in Paris, I felt there was potential there. So I moved.

It was at the Dunkleman Gallery that I met Eric Atkinson, with whom I had an immediate rapport. Having just established the Fanshawe Fine Arts Programme, Eric invited me to visit Fanshawe as a guest speaker. Bumbling around Toronto I curated an exhibition at the recently opened theatre complex, The St Lawrence Center, helped coordinate an International Critics Conference, wrote reviews for *Arts Canada*, until Eric re-entered my life with the idea that I go to work teaching at Fanshawe. My only previous teaching experience was an informal stint at St Vincent's College near Pittsburgh when a Benedictine artist-priest friend had invited me to work there. It was there that we converted a rifle practice room into The Rifle Range Gallery and, with George Brecht's permission, staged his 'Automobile Event'. The Abbot said it was better than a panty raid. Roman Verostko, my priest friend, has now achieved an international reputation as a computer artist.

I realised that all my activities were of a teaching nature, although never of a formal, academic nature. I have always been available to whoever chose to tap me for information on any level or subject of which I have some knowledge. I have always felt that a gallery or museum must inform and educate as well as cultivate. The creative experience of one person may be the informational and educative experience, even an aspect of the creative experience, for another. With Fanshawe, teaching might help me share whatever understanding I had in this area. It was new, it was exciting. I could even broaden my perceptions. So I moved again, to London, Ontario.

Specific scheduling, staff meetings, so different from those required in running a gallery, became my new environment. I became part of a teaching staff which was almost as international as my New York environment. British, Dutch, American, Australian, we were all challenged by the idea of working with and informing students. Eric was the lynchpin, but we all had input in forming the programmes. He brought his Leeds experience to London and creatively adapted it to the Canadian situation. The scene change worked and Fanshawe Fine Arts became a dynamic educational force. The luxury of materials available to staff and students at Fanshawe opened explorations not possible at Leeds. Vacuum form machines, a fully-equipped wood shop, and photography studios expanded the students' ideas of what could be used to make personal expressions. Seemingly endless supplies of canvas and pigments at times led to prodigal waste. As head of the programme, Eric brought all this into a workable form.

At one point I asked the staff to make a series of notes on their concept of the programme: as philosophy, a pattern for relationships between students and staff, responsibilities of staff to students, students to staff. I then culled and melded this information into a policy-philosophy statement which we all agreed upon. It was never slavishly adhered to, but it was a reference core. Perhaps the most important concept to come out of this exercise was the idea that we were not in the business of *making artists*, but of the opening of perceptions, of minds and eyes to the colour and form around us, not just what was seen in museums. One of the favourite phrases bandied about was 'visual illiteracy', a phrase Eric continually peppered his talk with, whether lecturing or just conversing. Because of our varied and individual personalities and attitudes we tended to bend rules whenever they might interfere with imagination. This might well have been the unique contribution we made. We all went our separate ways, but respected what others had to offer.

When I joined Fanshawe Fine Arts, the programme was housed in a building which had been some kind of steel-working plant, a short walk away from the main campus. First-, second- and third-year students shared the huge single room. Each student saw what others were involved with, which created an atmosphere of cross pollination. They smoked pot, painted murals on the floors and walls of the building. The roof was not immune, for the students painted a warning for pilots designating the building an ART SCHOOL. They talked, exchanging their understandings of the various projects the staff assigned to them. This important stimulus and the staff's constant permissiveness opened us all to fresh possibilities.

In a project initiated by Eric the staff had the students design and create costumes which they were to wear on the public buses taking them to the downtown area. There they delighted and confounded Londoners with their imaginative other-worldly promenading; again, breaking down barriers between the world of imagination and the 'real' world.

At the old London Art Gallery, Eric instigated an exhibition called 'Edible Art'. Anyone could participate, the only stipulation being that all entries must be made of some edible material. At the opening (it was a one-shot deal) there were sculptures made of cookie dough, pools made of green jello, sea creatures made of vegetables, a rice crispie coffin housing a real non-edible skeleton, a curtain made of various flavoured life-savers, whip liquorice and gum drops, an abstract sculpture made of pancakes. Opening speeches completed, the guests plunged into the 'art' and devoured it. They had been asked to bring their own paper plates and forks and spoons. We were told later by the gallery director that the cleaning staff had issued an ultimatum: no more shows of that kind. The clean-up was a nightmare and took three times more effort than any other clean-up after an opening. But everyone had fun.

The number of people who felt comfortable with the idea of an art gallery after this experience can only be guessed at. Creating a gallery situation where people truly have fun and

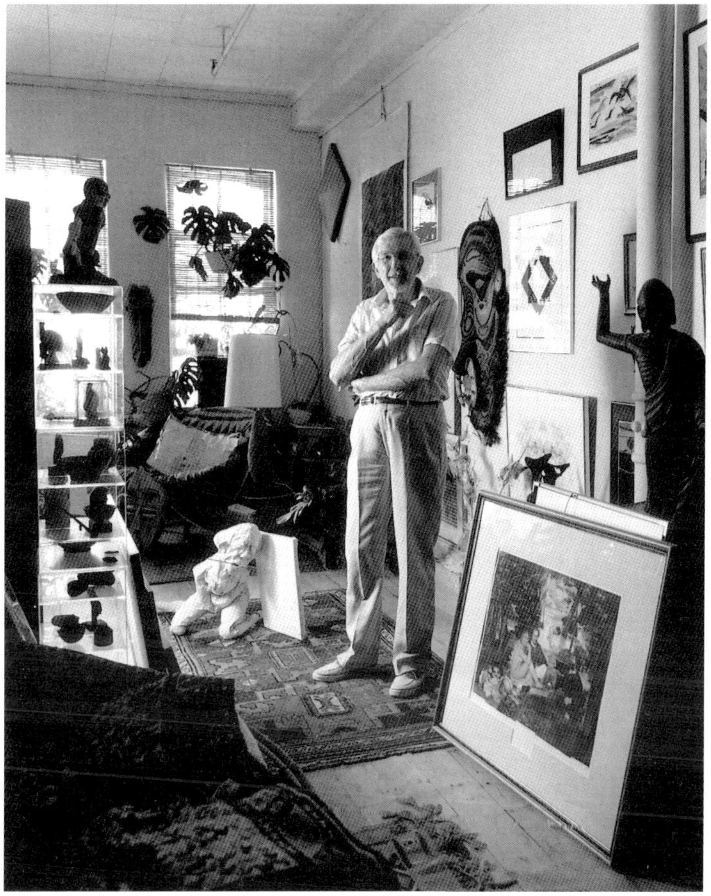

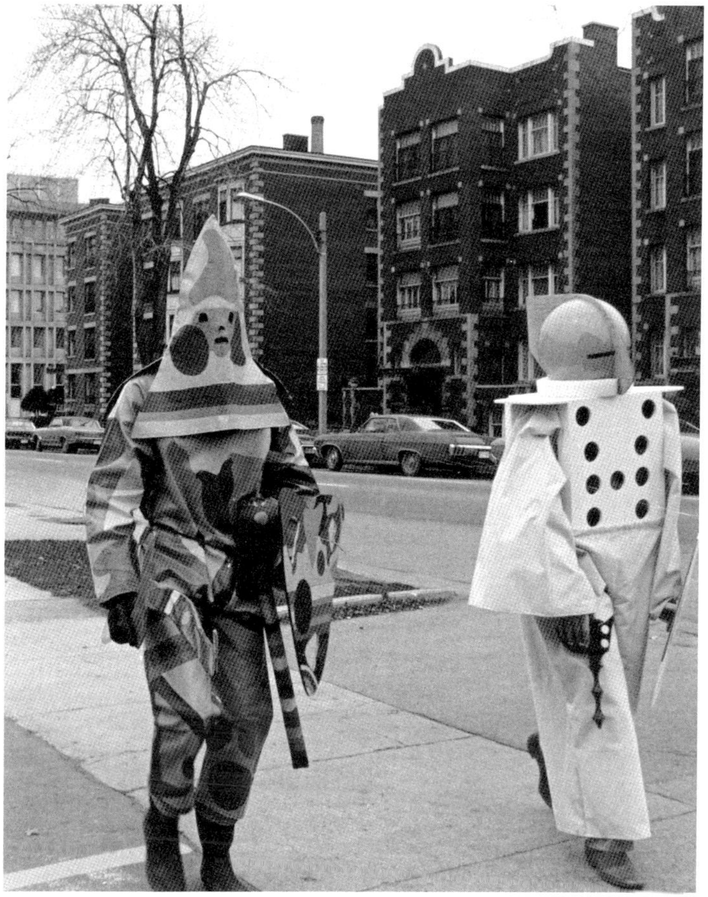

(above)
Stephen Joy at home, 1998
(photograph: Brian Hillier)

(above right)
Invasion of costume students in downtown London, Ontario, 1972
(photograph: Don Dunsmore)

(right)
Students preparing for Edible Art exhibition, London, Ontario, 1972

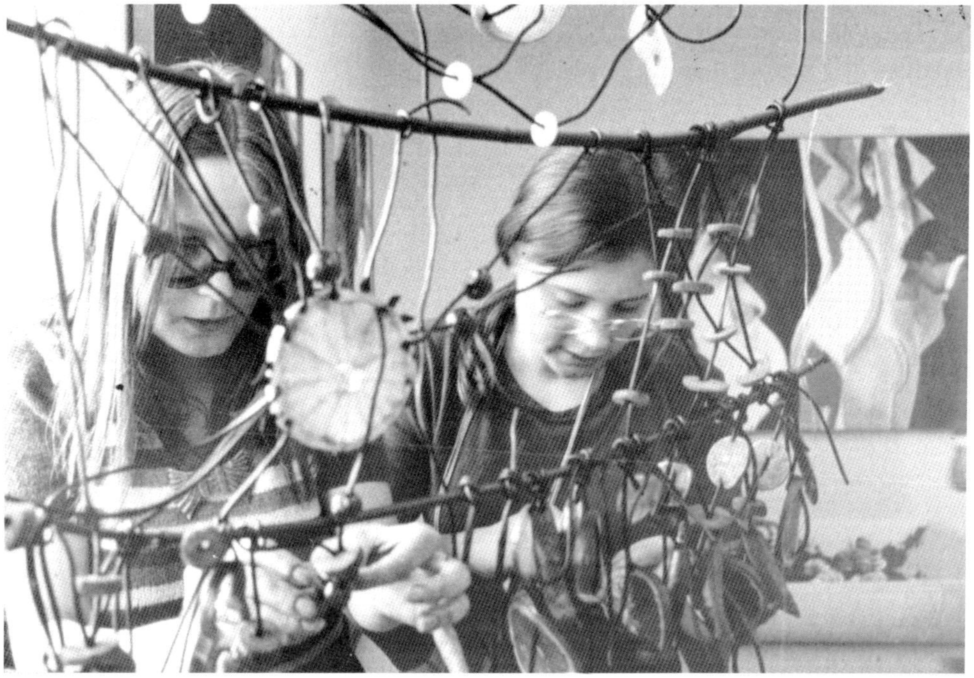

enjoy themselves is not normal gallery practice, but the experience of art as fun is important. Can we truly enjoy anything if we are intense and furrow browed? Pleasures should delight, open visions, leave reference marks to be revitalised in future reminiscences as well as stain all our lives.

Don Bonham, as artist staff member, involved the students in his personal projects. He supervised the students as they helped him create his racing cars and motor bikes, the bodies of which were fibreglass casts of nude women. Casting the forms, designing them to fit comfortably into Bonham's motor forms, creating the fibreglass torsos, gave the students insight into the craft and planning needed to realise a work.

Bonham arranged to take a group of his assistants to Salt Flats, Utah and present his racing cars as valid racers. There, the real racing men offered to put real motors into these artwork racers so that they might really compete. With thanks for the compliment, the offer was refused. The Bonham/student-made chasses would disintegrate under the power of a real motor.

Bonham created a fibreglass aeroplane, then wrote a script which involved the flight, crash, and rescue of the pilot from the burning debris. This became a project for the students. They arranged a barn (belonging to the parents of one of the students) for the re-enactment. They arranged to cast, act in and film the event. The logistics required to achieve this event demanded planning, organisation, rehearsal and documentation. These disciplines in an 'arts' activity can be carried over into any other activity with which one later becomes involved.

Fanshawe had a television training programme initiated by Eric's creative cross-breeding of the arts. At one point arrangements were made for the fine arts students to use the TV studios. They were shown the basics of camera control and editing. A nude model was brought in and instructed to improvise to the music played. As she danced, the students manipulated the several cameras with close ups/long shots/pan shots while other students edited the images. On the playback tape, this improvised event became one of the most exciting achievements of that year's student work.

Cross-breeding of media, and interplay of disparate materials was a vital part of what the students were exposed to. Any material, any objects were accepted by the staff as valid bodies to carry the imaginative message. This flexibility of mind was stressed in all studio work.

Rudolf Bikkers created and headed the print studio at Fanshawe in which he exposed the students to etching, lithography, aquatint, serigraphy. A technician par excellence, Rudolf insisted that his students, no matter how experimental, adhere to his standards. He established Editions Canada, a print facility where students not only helped him print his own projects, but designed and printed posters for their graduate exhibitions at Trajectory. Editions Canada had an excellent exhibition at Trajectory of the prints created under Bikkers' supervision. As well as the posters, third-year students designed the catalogues for the graduate shows held at Trajectory. The Fanshawe Advertising Programme, also part of Eric's overall vision for the Arts School, helped in these efforts, students assisting in the design and printing them on the presses they worked with as part of their training.

As further input we instituted field trips, which became a fundamental and (for the students) unforgettable part of the programme during the succeeding years. I planned trips to Toronto (The Art Gallery of Ontario, The Royal Ontario Museum), Kleinburg (The McMichael Canadian Collection), Detroit (The Detroit Institute of Art), Buffalo (The Albright-Knox), and, of course, New York City (The Metropolitan Museum, The Museum of Modern Art, The Guggenheim Museum, The Frick Collection, The Whitney Museum). I also programmed visits to the private galleries in all these cities as part of a plan to break the students' familiarity and dependence upon slides and reproductions and have them experience the power of original works. In New York we went to the theatre as often as we could, buying half-price tickets or standing room. During one visit to the Museum of Modern Art in New York a major Joseph Cornell show was about to open. I spoke to the MOMA membership office and the students and I were all admitted to the opening, an event of major excitement for us all.

To me this is what teaching is all about. To open doors, to break down barriers, to free the mind so that the person may more fully appreciate everything with which he can become involved. One of our philosophy statements was that the school/staff was not out to make artists, but to give the student the apparatus with which they might enhance their lives.

The Fine Arts staff and their programmes were frequently in conflict with the administration and physical resources

(top and centre left)
Two ink and wash drawings by Don Bonham for snowmobile project, 1973
collection: Eric & Muriel Atkinson, London, Ontario

(top right)
Don Bonham
Fibreglass and metal bike
collection of the artist
(photograph:
Don Dunsmore)

(bottom left)
Still of burning aeroplane from Don Bonham happening, 1973

(bottom right)
Wrapping an army tank, Victoria Park, London, Ontario, 1974
collection: The D. B. Weldon Library, The University of Western Ontario)
(photograph:
London Free Press)

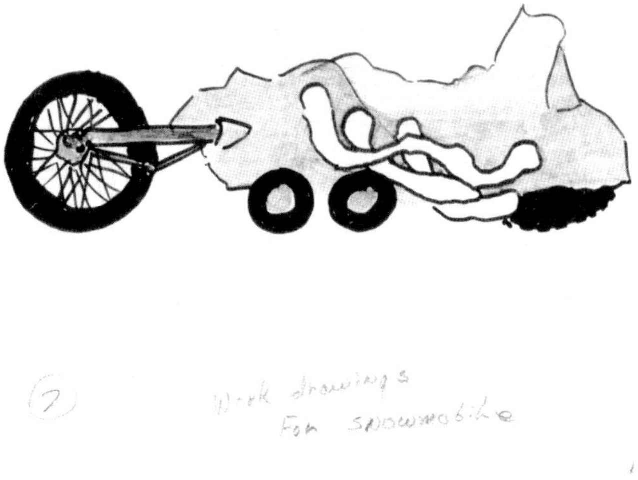

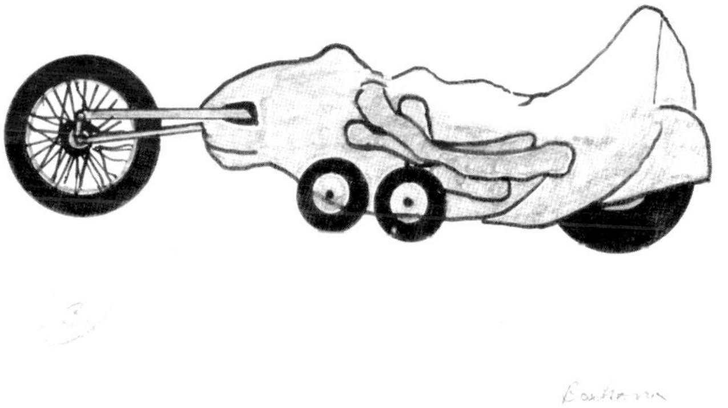

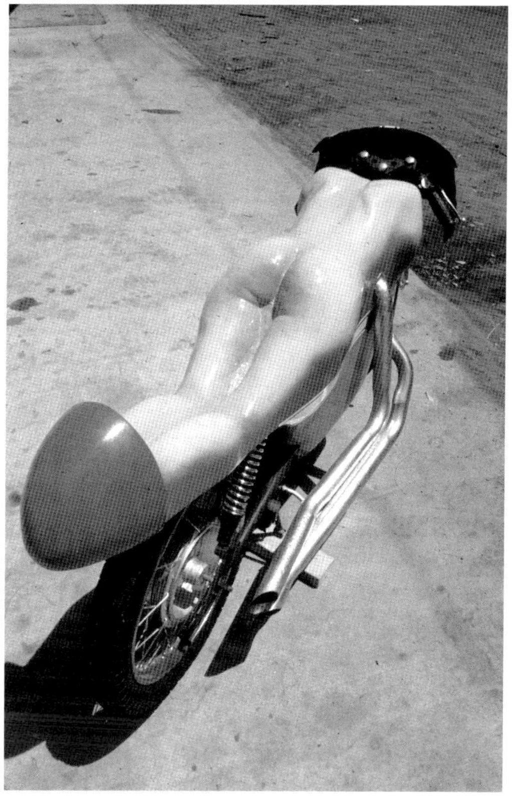

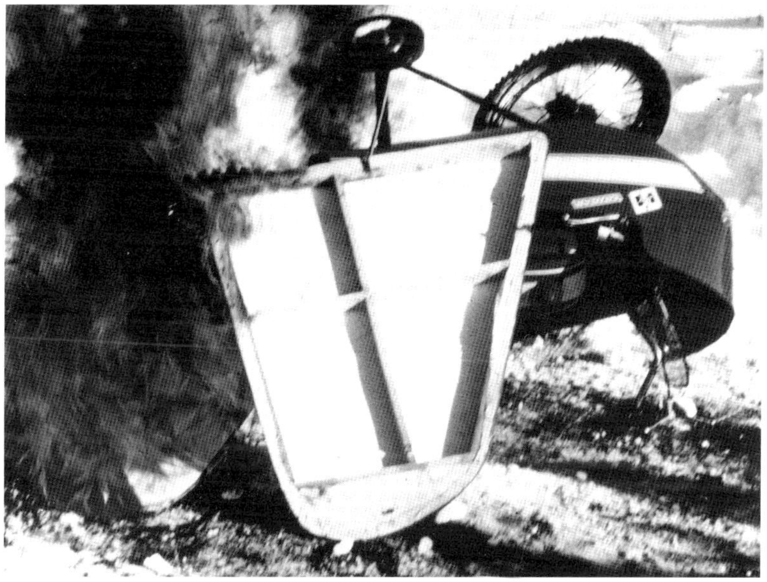

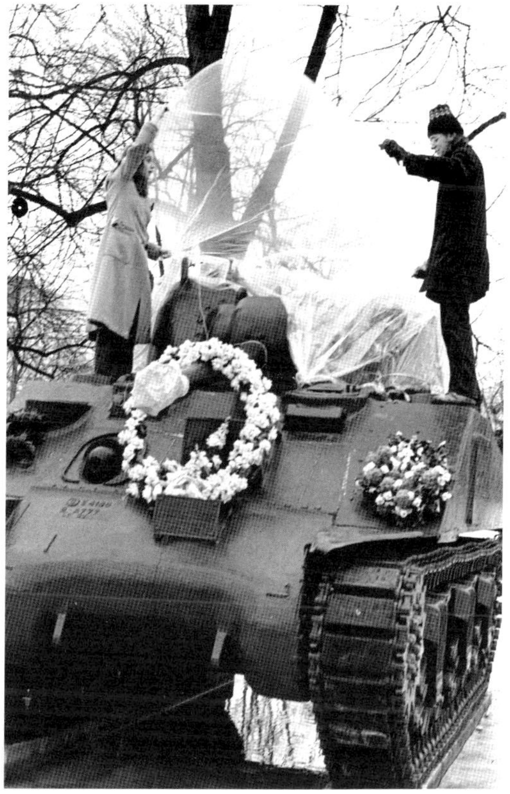

staff (responsible for building maintenance). In A Block works by students were constantly displayed in the halls. One such piece was made up of grass sod, wood and stone. (By the way, very well accomplished.) I was told by physical resources that they could not allow dirt in the hallways. Later, when we were in the new D Block, in studios especially designed for the Fine Arts programme, physical resources asked me to tell the students to be more careful about splattering paint on the floors and the furniture. The 'furniture' referred to was a collection of plastic moulded stacking chairs of the cheapest kind. I replied, saying that if I thought that more freely splattered paint on the floors and walls would make the students be more open and understanding, I would not only encourage them – I would help them splatter and urge them on to greater splattering.

A student parked his car near the 'pit', a room in the new D Block, where colour and its impacts were explored. He placed a four-by-eight plywood panel under the wheels of his car, loaded paint on the panel then spun the wheels. Paint flew everywhere. On the new pavement, on the car, on the building. The next day I received a memo from physical resources pointing out how wrong he was to have done this and the cost of cleaning it up, backed by Polaroid shots taken from their third-floor office. Again I confronted them, again I pointed out that this was a process of experimentation and learning. The student collected cleaning cost information refuting their quoted prices. I wrote a backup note. We never heard from them again. Until the next time. This student did not make masterpieces, but he told me, months later, that he really opened up to himself as a result of his wheel-spinning.

One of the students conceived the idea of wrapping things (Chrysto influences?). She began her wrapping in the studio using green trash bags. Other students became involved and they proceeded to wrap doors, pillars in the halls, then wound up wrapping the hall TV monitors. They were excited, involved and unified. Physical resources contacted me but were less stringent than before. The students ended up in Victoria Park in downtown London which contains three war memorials: one for the Boer War, a Veterans Memorial, and a World War Two tank. The students proceeded to wrap the tank with yards of transparent plastic sheeting. They then decorated the wrapped tank with a mass of artificial flowers. Somehow the *London Free Press* became aware of this activity, photographed it and published the story. Forget physical resources. It was almost the villagers attacking the villain with pitchforks and torches. Now we had the townspeople condemning the students, Fanshawe Fine Arts and its staff for permitting such a sacrilegious act to take place. With his usual tact and diplomacy, Eric, head of the Fine Arts Programme, fended off all negative comments and almost persuaded the Veterans group that the students, in fact, were honouring the men represented by the tank by the flowers that had been placed upon it. What was not reported was that I encouraged them in this activity to the extent of supplying the students with rolls of plastic sheeting from the Trajectory Gallery and driving them to the park. After which I informed the newspaper of their intent to commit this 'sacrilegious' act.

We brought in provocative artists as speakers. Dennis Young, the director of the Art Gallery of Ontario in Toronto, David Lewis, Lucas Samaris, Victor Pasmore, Gyorgy Kepes, Roman Verostko all stirred the pot with their energies and open-ended thoughts.

With all this burgeoning of vision, perhaps the most significant event was the setting up of the Trajectory Gallery, a programme created to train students in gallery procedures for which I acted as faculty advisor. (I had been chairman of the Gallery Committee at the University of Wisconsin, with a faculty advisor, so the wheel had turned full circle.) The building we found was located in the middle of a block of fine Victorian-style structures. Street-level shops were a cleaning establishment, a recycled clothing store, a print gallery and a restaurant called Say Cheese. (Hilary Alderson, who owned this excellent cheese emporium, at one point commissioned ten London artists to create serigraphs around the theme of Say Cheese. This portfolio is now a collectors' item.) Trajectory found a home in a five-floor building dating back to before the turn of the century. Painted on the outside was 'D'Arches', the name of the original builder and occupant. Still in its original state the building had been a leather goods manufacturing establishment, mainly putting out harness and other needs of the horse-drawn age. At various times of its existence it had been a warehouse, and a factory of sorts. There was a rumour that a theatre group had had its base there as well. Student volunteers painted over the two-toned cheap hotel green walls, sanded and varithaned the dark green floors. An electrician friend surreptitiously installed our track lighting since getting a licence from the city would be costly. So we had a gallery.

The first exhibition ('Views', 1971) was planned by the student committee under my supervision. After much discussion and brainstorming we came up with the concept of including as many local artists as would be willing to participate and so establish the scope and breadth of the gallery's policy. The student committee and I visited studios for weeks on end and the artists' response was always enthusiastic and cooperative. Of those who exhibited in 'Views', Jamelie Hassan, Tom Benner, Richard Bonderenko, Brian Saby, Becky Burke and Gill Moll have all moved into the forefront of the Canadian art scene.

From here on the students planned the Trajectory one-man and group shows as well as any other activities taking place in the gallery. They were responsible for publicity, press releases, installing the exhibitions, designing posters and mailers and seeing that the gallery was constantly presentable. Some who were involved in the programme have gone on to work in galleries or become curators in museums.

After a year and a half the Student Union withdrew its sponsorship, stating that they were not satisfied with the recognition and publicity they were receiving for their (minimal) investment. In a study done at this time on cultural activities in London, Trajectory was mentioned with the London Art Gallery and the art programmes at Beal Secondary School, Fanshawe and the University of Western Ontario as important contributors to the cultural community. With this encouragement, I assumed total personal responsibility for running Trajectory. All costs, from rent to hydro to costs of openings, printing, shipping were covered by myself. My Fanshawe income was fed into Trajectory, but it was no longer a Fanshawe-sponsored project. It was a shoestring operation, but I would never allow it to look like one. Designing posters, flyers, using surplus paper stock to cut costs took effort, but the results were top notch.

This completely new and deeper involvement with the London arts community caused my work at Fanshawe, and my various board memberships, to pale beside the demands of visiting studios, selecting and rejecting works for exhibition, programming the changing shows, coming up with provocative ideas for group shows. A great deal of this work was achieved with the help and voluntary effort of artists and students. In all my arts activities in London they have been incredibly supportive.

Trajectory became a focal point for a variety of activities: happenings, performance art, jazz concerts, exhibitions of local artists (no money to import), including staff members from Fanshawe Fine Arts, Beal Secondary School, and University of Western Ontario Visual Arts. There were art and experimental film programmes, performances, poetry readings, and Halloween costume parties. I even gave a series of talks on the history of contemporary art, a variation on the lectures I gave at Fanshawe.

When Eric agreed to a one-man show at Trajectory, I was very pleased. I knew his work, thought highly of it, and felt painting of that calibre would be exciting to show. Susanne Tausig, reviewing the exhibition for the *London Free Press*, remarked: 'Atkinson probes the world underneath the surface, the interaction of molecules. Colourful particles dance on the canvas, creating areas of concentrated energy. This is what a good artist does.'

Running Trajectory and working at Fanshawe opened up a number of opportunities for myself and the students. The St Thomas Psychiatric Hospital wanted to decorate their drab halls and rooms with art work. The director of the hospital and I developed the idea for a group of students to paint murals in these spaces. Volunteer students worked in this environment in free and open contact with the residents-patients. A certain rapport developed and soon the patients were working with the students who, working with the hospital staff, encouraged them to make paintings of their own.

There was one memorable event. One of the patients was given a four-by-eight panel and some paint. With great intensity he proceeded to cover the panel on the floor with red, black and blue. He stood back to observe what he had done. His intensity became passion and he stepped onto the panel smearing the paint with his feet, creating a strong mass of movement in the colours. After a few minutes, he stepped back and said: 'That was my mother'. Later I brought the patients' works into Trajectory for an exhibition. The students found this exciting since they had been instrumental in creating the works by their involvement with the patients. The public found the show interesting and the reviews were very positive.

Trajectory was used by the students to create banners for the Site Party held on the location designated for what was to become The London Regional Art and Historical Museums at the Forks of the Thames. The banners hung from the two bridges at the Forks, as well as from the several tents which housed painting and sculpture projects, using Styrofoam, and street painting. Some Fanshawe students undertook to wrap the old iron bridge in aluminium foil.

Some of the other exhibitions I booked into Trajectory were one-man shows by Jeff Willmore, Michael Durham, Doug Mitchell, Tom Benner, Joseph Hubbard, Dan Crawford, Graham Wright, Peter Borowski, Harry Mountain, Becky Burke, Don Bonham, Jim Gillies, Pat Thibert, Walter Redinger. Alan Wood not only had an exhibition, but gave a group of students a picture to transfer into a seven-colour serigraph on canvas, which was successfully sold during his show. Duncan de Kergommeaux showed his black square explorations in a memorable and challenging exhibition. All these artists have become established in Canada and a few have reached beyond. The best of the group shows was 'Continuum' in which ten artists were given spaces to do with whatever they pleased (shades of 'Environments – Situations – Spaces') and 'Recap' which reviewed five years of one-man shows at Trajectory.

Attendance was always good and our opening receptions invariably crowded. Some of the students and artists said they came to the opening for the cheese and fresh bread, their only chance to have a semblance of a meal. Perhaps the greatest compliment I had for Trajectory was the comment by a lady I met at the Farmers' Market. 'Stephen,' she said, 'I don't always understand what you are showing, but I always visit Trajectory. It is exciting.' In other words, she was open to experiencing and discovering for herself. To me this is the crux of education. To be open, to be willing to taste new experiences, to reach.

On occasion I would show my own accumulation of prints, paintings and sculpture ranging from European, American, Canadian, Oriental artefacts gathered from my travels to a collection of posters and mailing shots of exceptional design from New York galleries dating from the 1950s and 1960s. An exceptional exhibit was my set of George Rouault prints from his illustrations for Alfred Jarry's *Ubu Roi*, augmented with some borrowed pieces. Tamayo from Mexico and Kakagamic, a Canadian Indian, were two of the professional artists shown at Trajectory. When the second or third rooms of the gallery were not being used for exhibitions, I allowed students to use them as studios.

To properly heat the five thousand square feet of space would have doubled the cost of running the gallery. The rent was $300 a month and was never increased by the two Italian owners during the twelve years that Trajectory existed. They had the same policy toward the artists occupying the upper floors. To me these men were true patrons of the arts. Forget the collectors, the museums, the government and corporate funding; these men quietly and firmly sustained a gallery and the artists who had studios in their building.

Our reviews in the *London Free Press* were always good, even at times glowing with excitement. I was accused of having an affair with Leonore Crawford, the reviewer, to ensure good reviews. The fact was that she had a real passion for the arts and she called them as she saw them. Fortunately for Trajectory, she saw the shows as groundbreaking and exciting. Without the presence of Sheri Clift as receptionist and gallery assistant to set the inviting atmosphere, Trajectory would not have been the success that it was. Artists and visitors gathered for coffee and gossip around her desk and so created a meeting place where they could exchange information about their work, exhibitions to enter, exhibitions to criticise.

When I retired from Fanshawe I had to redesign my world. New patterns had to be created since there was no longer the academic world to shape the days. I had closed Trajectory, having become somewhat disillusioned with cocktail party comments about what a wonderful thing I was doing with Trajectory coming from people who had not visited the gallery for the last year or more. There is a kind of fraudulence that exists within people who talk art and culture, but do not really participate in or contribute to it, although they make empty gestures of doing so. Somewhere along this road the Mayor's award for cultural contribution to the city was given to me. A very nice recognition which I promptly returned as a protest, since the Mayor and City Hall in general were being ambiguous and totally lacking in imagination and understanding of what theatre, music and visual arts could contribute to the community.

I continued my cultural participation as a member and chairman of the City of London Arts Advisory Committee, and my board membership at the London Regional Art and

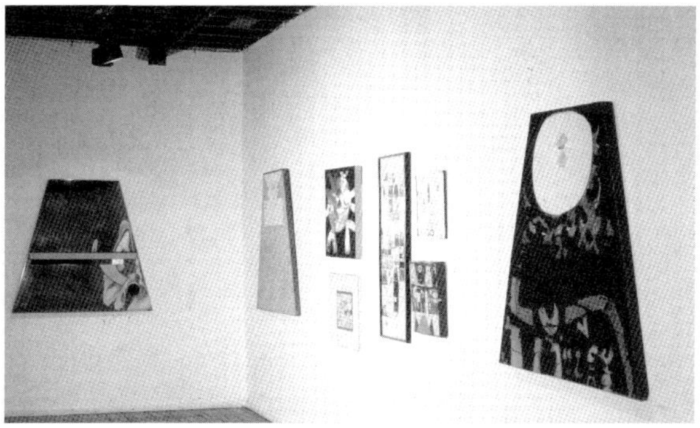

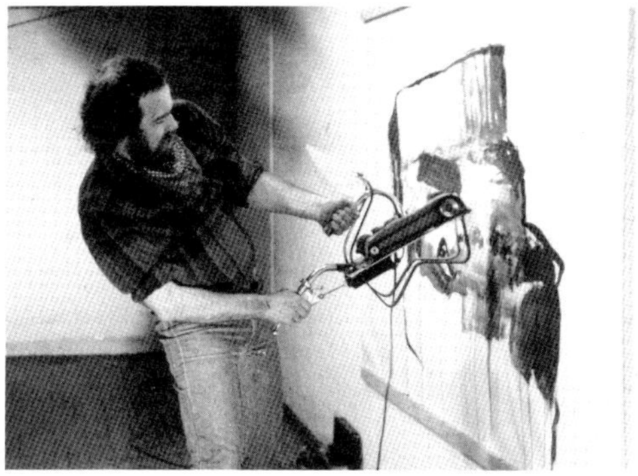

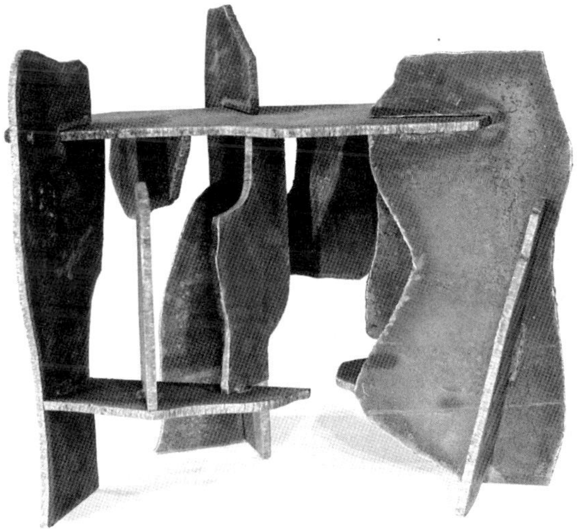

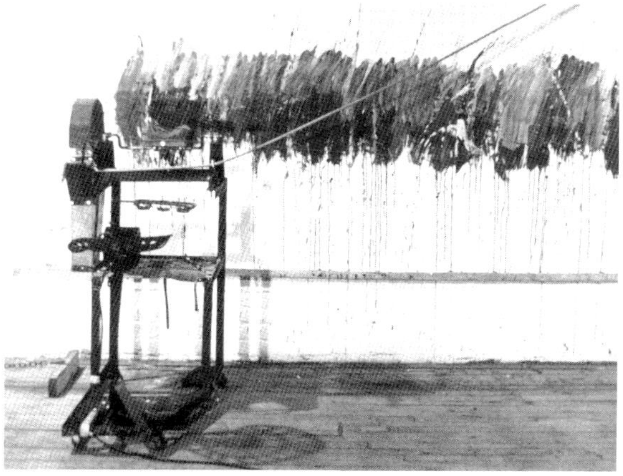

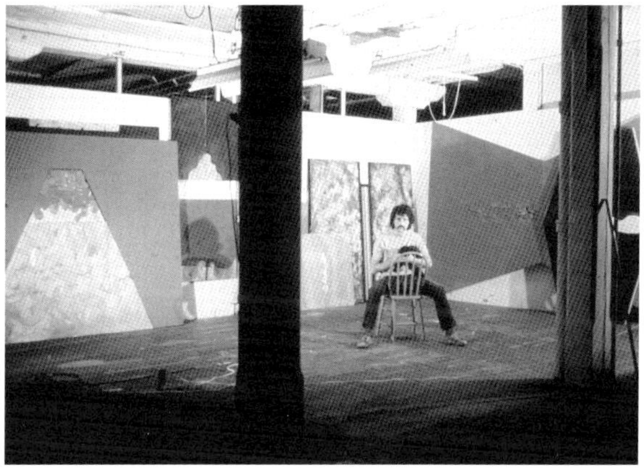

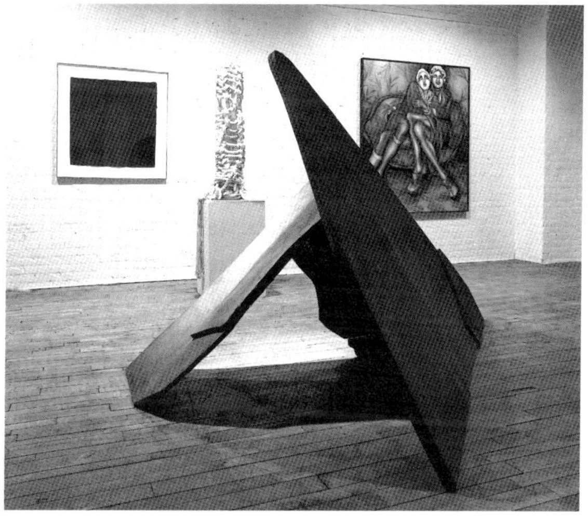

(top left)
Eric Atkinson retrospective exhibition, Trajectory Gallery, London, Ontario, 1979
(photograph: Stephen Joy)

(top & centre right)
Graham Wright's 'Machines that Paint' exhibition at the Trajectory Gallery, London, Ontario, 1975

(centre left)
Patrick Thibert
Intra – Structure No.20
1977
length: 20 in.
welded mild steel
collection: Eric & Muriel Atkinson, London, Ontario

(bottom left)
Michael Durham in his studio, London, Ontario, 1973

(bottom right)
RECAP installation, Trajectory Gallery, London, Ontario, 1972–77, showing paintings by Duncan de Kergommeaux (*left*) and Rebecca Burke, and sculptures by Jeanine Lodge and Patrick Thibert (*foreground*)
(photograph: Stephen Joy)

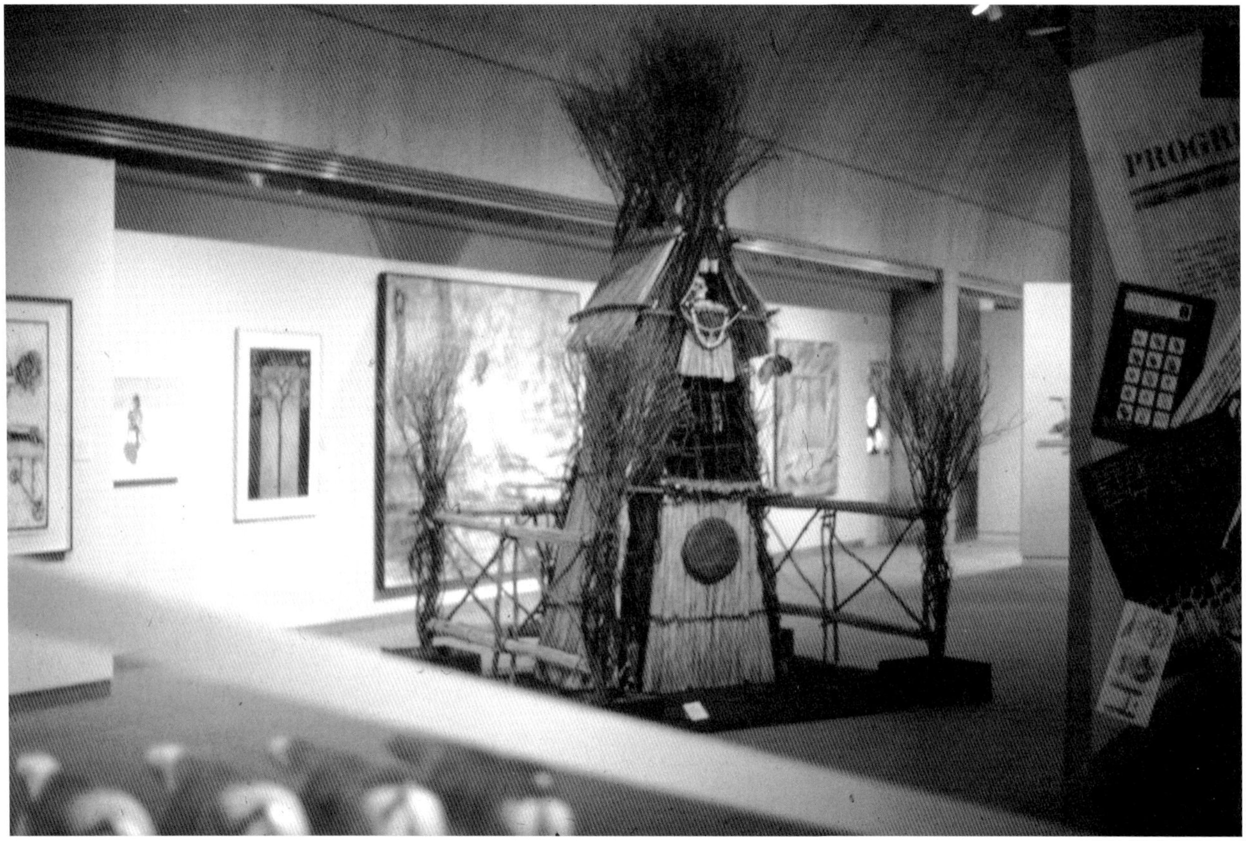

Catalyst exhibition at London Regional Art Gallery, Ontario, 1994 (photograph: Stephen Joy)

Historical Museums. I wrote art criticism for *Scene Magazine* and letters to the *London Free Press* commenting on cultural affairs in London. I curated a massive and successful exhibition using local artists as part of an art centre experiment in St Thomas when nine hundred people came to the opening. Another arts centre project for downtown London dissolved after a few months. I curated a retrospective for Fanshawe Fine Arts at the London Regional Art and Historical Museums called 'Catalyst' which brought together artists who had graduated from Fanshawe in the past twenty-five years and one thousand people came to the opening. I became producer for a series of artists' interviews for Rogers Cable, the London community television channel. I was a founding board member of the London Arts Council, which was indirectly responsible for my creating and publishing the *London Arts Directory* and the *Directory of Public Art in London*.

Joseph Campbell writes of 'The Journey' and 'The Adventure' as being the core and function of one's life. Applying this concept to my own Journey, the innumerable stops beginning with Paris, then New York and St Vincents and finally Toronto and the conjunction of my journey with Eric Atkinson's, for gathering knowledge and information have merely led me to new stops for new information and knowledge and understanding. The Adventure is not the accumulation, but the projection from these stops into new bases from which more projections occur. It has been a great – and yet to be – traversed road. There is no end in sight.

Letter 14 Fred Steinmetz to David Lewis

21 June 1999

Dear David

I am delighted to add my personal comments and observations in recognition of the many contributions Eric Atkinson has made in the field of art education. The past thirty years have been such a rewarding and significant experience, that I feel excited just talking about it and recalling some of the most notable highlights.

I arrived on the Fanshawe College scene in 1969, fresh out of a ten-year career as a television producer. Ricky was already on board, chairing the Applied Arts division, and Fine Art programme. He was soon to become the Dean of the School of Applied Arts. It was a wonderful and crazy time in the history of the country and, indeed, the world. The time of Timothy Leary, Vietnam, polyester pants, drugs, free love, rock and roll, counter-culture, and Woodstock. Indeed, my own rejection of the established, overly commercialised 'TV Biz' in favour of education, was an expression of the mood of the day. I thought that, through the education of the young I could maybe make a difference. Perhaps through the graduates I could help turn the industry around to the true meaning of communication, entertainment, and education, back indeed to the original mandate of television. Education had become one of the many institutions that no longer served the needs of the 'now' generation. According to the radicals of the early 1960s, it had to change. Home schooling, alternative schools, schools without walls, all became quick fixes for what many felt was a system that perpetuated old concepts, stood in the way of progress, and was no longer relevant. My personal efforts were concentrated on providing an education that was as close to the real life situation as possible. You see, I too was caught up in the revolution and I wanted to make a difference that would save us from the 'establishment'. The world around us was to become the classroom, and the events of the day a significant portion of the curriculum. I recall taking my students to the Peace Bridge in Sarnia (at the border with the US) where we protested at the Vietnam War, and became involved in actual 'sit-ins'. In this way students experienced the reality of protest and confrontation and, as future journalists, could draw on the experience and comment with some authority. We produced documentaries for and against drug use, examined the role of the military and police in civil rights demonstrations, and found ourselves questioning the very rules and procedures that were imposed on us by our own college. Many of my colleagues were of the same mind; some failed in their forays into education, some got sucked into the education mill and could not extricate themselves, and some, myself included, were lucky and found in education a new expression for our creative energies.

It was also the time to have new wonderful things happen, even in conservative London, Ontario. Mackie Cryderman, a painter and teacher at a local high school, and member of the Fanshawe College Board of Governors, became the driving force behind the creation of the Fine Art division at the new college which was established, along with nineteen other Ontario colleges, in 1967. This massive endeavour on the part of the Ontario government was unprecedented both in scale and vision. Through her contacts in the art world Mackie became instrumental in convincing Ricky to leave behind nearly twenty years of successful art education in Britain and bring his family and experience in art education to London, Ontario. Ricky's experience in art education was based on creative personal exploration and the establishment of new languages, languages that grew out of the traditional art education of England, but also incorporated concepts of science, the new literature and the rapidly expanding field of electronics. Behind him lay people such as Herbert Read, Victor Pasmore, Henry Moore, and many others. This rich background gave him the grounding to tackle this assignment with the necessary confidence. Over the years, Ricky had developed a very personal belief about education. This was to be his opportunity for a fresh start, a chance to create an art school which would reflect his personal vision.

Contemporary events can have profound effects on us if our receptors are in tune with them and if we can read their true significance. The emergence of the Beatles proved to be such an event for Ricky. He was certain that the fact that their talents were spawned in an art school environment was significant for the unprecedented success of the group. This event cemented for him the belief that all art forms were inextricably entwined and that, with the right alchemy and the proper environment, one could set free 'Beatles' in all the disciplines. As if to prove his belief, he gave our television students and our fine art students an opportunity to enrol in an experimental programme that allowed them the freedom to create art using such tools as the Moog synthesiser (more about this instrument later), television and audio devices, and anything else that made a sound or produced an interesting image. The curriculum of this experimental programme was only loosely structured. Part of the curriculum required students to participate in a series of 'sensitivity sessions' to stimulate them and to awaken new ideas in their heads. One of these sessions took place on a farm, one of Marshall McLuhan's interesting experimental venues. Here they had to perform all normal day-to-day functions while blindfolded. This exercise lasted for two full days and nights and brought about some startling revelations for the participants. Incidentally, it also resulted in blistered feet for most, due to the extreme attention the blind transfer to their feet.

The Moog synthesiser was an electronic keyboard instrument that exemplified the spirit of the day because it gave the performer the opportunity to create music in a totally individual manner. The performer could produce sounds that, to all intents and purposes, had never been heard before. It was an electronic marvel of transistors and patch-cords, that used the basic concepts of the 'theramin', an earlier, single-sound electronic instrument that was played by altering pitch and volume using the hands, and allowed the player to create a limited range of electronic musical sounds.

Armed with the Moog and some other state-of-the-art technology, a cohort of 'hip' students began the new programme, while we, the college administration, asked the government for permission to offer it a full year later. These students, in Creative Electronics (as the programme came to be known), eviscerated television sets, radios and all manner of electronic paraphernalia, used the bits and pieces in wondrous combinations, and created a new form of electronic art. While the outcome of these experiments was sometimes less than pleasing to the listener who had been brought up on Mozart and Haydn, it nevertheless was seminal, for it gave birth to a very important programme within the fine art setting, the Music Industry Arts Programme.

I am getting ahead of myself, so let me briefly reflect on the Fine Art programme as it was in the late 1960s and into the 1970s. Ricky and his staff knew that, although new and experimental in nature, the emphasis had to be on providing a solid base of pedagogically sound art training, guided by a team of instructors who had experience in delivering such an education. Thus the curriculum carried a significant theoretical content, with the studios and equipment as the main focus for the students. I say that because it is important to realise that the type of student we attracted in the 1960s and 1970s wanted to do things, not talk about them. Painting, sculpture, printmaking, environmental art, ceramics and glass, sound, performance, mixed media and photography provided the students with a rich offering of activities. Always the emphasis was on a team teaching approach. As Ricky was so fond of proclaiming, 'create synergy, everyone's input counts, the result will be greater than the sum of the parts'.

Our workshops contained the latest equipment, including a pair of vacuum moulding machines, print presses, even a kiln, built and operated by our ceramic artist Tom Coulter. Shortly after we built it, the city made us remove it, claiming that it would eventually set the college, if not the entire eastern part of London, on fire. I also understand it was feared that the fire in the kiln could cause aircraft headed for the local airport to mistake it for a runway light and ... well you can imagine a DC9 landing on a two-way city road. Tom had a fierce temper and he released it by reducing the kiln to a pile of bricks in less time than he took to build it.

Art history was a significant aspect of the curriculum and it was taught by Stephen Joy, an art historian and artist from New York. He has since retired and become an important member of the London art community where he has owned and operated a successful gallery, has written numerous articles on art, and exerts considerable influence on the local city art gallery.

It is difficult to recall the names of all the teachers from the past thirty years, but I must mention Chris Wallace. Chris is a Canadian artist who handled the environmental art portfolio. Together with technician Bill Woodman, who himself had produced fine stained glass works in England, he drew on the materials, processes and disciplines that produced art that would enhance and complement the appearance of the environment. Chris did not view environmental art as separate from the actual environment, but as part of it. As an example, using the combination of glass and concrete he created windows that were visually spectacular, and became a part of the actual structure. Walls took on shapes that were exciting and surprising, made possible by the introduction of plastics and the vacuum mould equipment. The quest was to make life and the environment the very material of art, the way paint and the canvas used to be.

Artists wanted to be a part of our experiment and joined

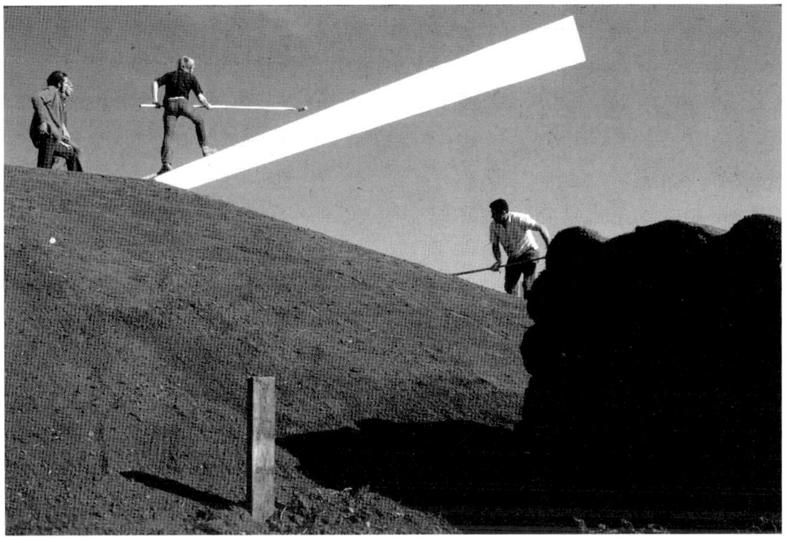

Two views of environmental sculpture by Kosso Eloul

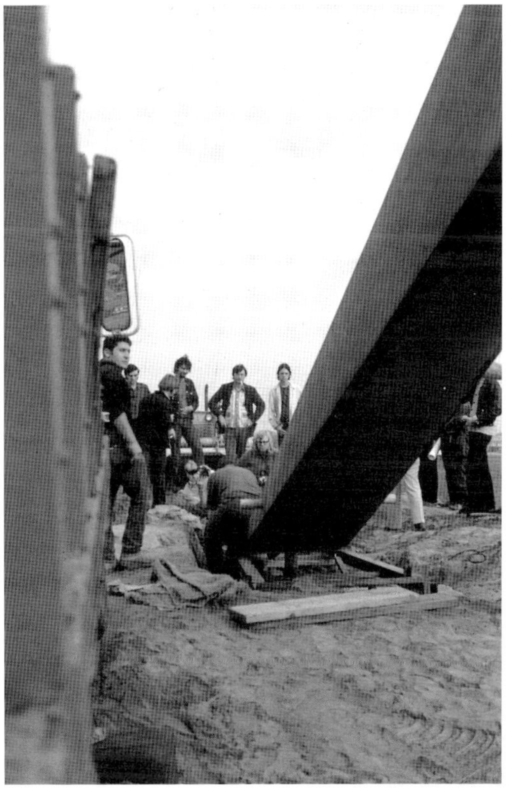

our students from time to time. Such an event happened when sculptor Kosso Eloul collaborated with our fine art students and a willing heavy equipment operator, to produce London's first and only truly environmental sculpture. Together they planned and created a bright yellow shaft that projected some fifty feet out of an earth mound into the sky like some huge phallic symbol. Often ridiculed, sometimes loved and sometimes hated, but never ignored by Londoners and visitors alike. It was a pity, David, that this wondrous thing had to come to an untimely end (although it did last almost twenty years). The broad base formed a launching ramp and an open invitation to a new breed of bicycle daredevils. Their attempts to drive up the shaft and to see how close they could come to certain death, resulted in a plan to have a safety fence erected. This fence would have surrounded the entire mound and would have acted as a major distraction from the actual sculpture. I met with Kosso and told him of our plans to erect the fence – his comment was, 'kill it' (the sculpture, not the plan). So we killed it. It is now a nice flat section of our parking lot, and the complaints have stopped.

What was it that made Ricky's approach to art education so different? I think it was that it provided us with a bridge to move from yesterday to today, and from one pedagogy to another. It was also important because Ricky tried very hard to make the education relevant to the needs of the day. You can well imagine that drawing ears and noses and beautiful hands was not uppermost in the minds of this new generation of students. They were throwing out the old and bringing in the new. Music was their God, drugs became the new sacrament, and musicians were their heroes. If we wanted to be successful in art education, we had to broaden the definition of the beast. Art education had become more than what we had previously defined as art education. The new and improved 'applied arts' included radio, television, film, graphic art, photography, theatre, music, and especially modern, recorded music. Something we had not done previously was to address these activities in a new vocabulary, a vocabulary that brought with it a revised meaning and approach. Language became the catalyst that altered the quality of the activity through the vocabulary employed to describe it. This change was an attempt to elevate activities that were often very technical in nature, beyond the technical, into the realm of art. In addition to providing us with this new language, Ricky constantly reminded students of fascinating historical relationships of art and everyday life, common threads of purpose, and interesting anecdotes that helped students understand the important relationships of art and life, of yesterday and today. I have always enjoyed comparing this approach to the life cycle of the nautilus. As it grows within its shell it seals behind it the previous chamber and builds a new, larger one. This process of addition continues until it finally passes on at a ripe old age. What is so fascinating is this. While the body abandons each old chamber in favour of a new, larger one, it leaves behind it a thread of living tissue … all the way to the beginning. A living history and a constant reminder of the connection of yesterday and today, of here and back there. Oh yes, this wonderful function also ensures that the nautilus remains balanced in the proper depth of the sea, thus ensuring its survival.

In the early 1970s, the CRTC (the regulatory body of the Canadian broadcasting industry) legislated that the music content of Canadian radio stations must include thirty per cent of Canadian music. This was to have a profound effect on the music industry in Canada. It meant that we had to develop our own talent, music, marketing concepts, producers and engineers, in short … a homegrown music industry. What it did for the college was to provide us with the opportunity to shift the emphasis from experimentation (the creative electronics programme I talked about earlier), to a full-blown Music Production and Engineering programme. The Music Industry Arts (MIA) programme began in earnest and soon there followed recording studios, sophisticated state-of-the-art audio equipment, and skilled teachers such as producer Jack Richardson, Terry McManus, Bill Seddon, and Don Geppert. To this day, the MIA programme is the only one of its kind in the country and, under the present guidance of Jan Greene, enjoys an unequalled popularity with budding rock stars and aspiring music producers. The strong link to fine art, and the continuing collaboration between fine art and television production training, encouraged Ricky and his staff to bring some fascinating media moguls into our midst. Marshall McLuhan and his son Eric spent time with us. McLuhan had given the world a new language that was at once elucidating and, at the same time, confounding. He was often as confusing as the environment which he attempted to define. This fascinating teacher-philosopher forced us to question all of our previous assumptions and beliefs. McLuhan became one of the most important icons of that period and, though often misunderstood and misquoted, his insights and predictions are visible around us today.

During the early 1970s there was an energy and an audacity that was refreshing and invigorating, something that has never been repeated in my thirty years with this institution. It was not uncommon for our students to disregard the walls of the college and produce art and activities that flowed out of the confines of their studios and into the halls among the college community. The place buzzed with activities: ceramic exhibitions in the entrance foyer of the college, spontaneous TV programmes video-taped in the halls, impromptu theatre anywhere there was an audience. Of particular note was a collaborative venture between the students in the food preparation programme and fine art. Now, David, you must know that this was going to be the event of the year. Even with all of Ricky's best attempts to turn this into the ultimate cooperative art extravaganza, food and more food is what it was. It also resulted in the best attended and the tastiest art exhibition the city had ever witnessed. As Ricky always insisted, 'if it's in the name of education, and the end result is good for the students, nothing in education should ever be seen as inappropriate'. Armed with this philosophy our school ventured ahead, created the most vital and innovative art department in the country – and got into hot water from time to time.

Through his action and not just his words, Ricky demonstrated that art education must be allowed to 'happen'. It must not just be talked about or needlessly constrained by rules, concepts, traditions, and those meaningless structures that we find so easy to define and defend in traditional academia. Of course, such a philosophy does not come without risk, and many times we had to defend those activities that seemed to clash with accepted practices. Thankfully Ricky was always very skilled at finding the right words, and if he couldn't find the right words, he would baffle the administration with fancy footwork. As often as not, that worked.

In 1973 our College gained a national reputation with the acquisition of an FM radio licence. Radio CIXX-FM or 6X as it is known to everyone in London and a forty-mile radius around. I had always believed in the unfettered use of all of the technology at our disposal. Radio not only gave us a voice into the community, it also allowed us to break down the walls of the institution and offer education via the airwaves. I believe it was my most important achievement while at the college. The planning phase of 6X-FM brought us into a working relationship with author and head of the CRTC Harry J. Boyle. Harry was a wonderfully articulate and crusty chap whom I got to know well during my years as a television producer. After several discussions, Harry challenged us to develop innovative programming, and to offer the community something that no other private station could give them. Tom Lodge, former programme director of Radio Caroline (a pirate radio off the coast of England), and grandson of Sir Oliver Lodge (of Spiritualism fame and one of the inventors of radio), came on board and helped us meet the challenge of 'innovative programming'. Tom was to become the first coordinator of the Music Industry Arts programme. We offered programmes that involved the experimental 'creative electronics' students and their funky music. Artists were given air time to develop their own creative expressions, and Ryerson, a polytechnical institute based in Toronto, provided us with the first credit courses to be offered on our FM station.

From Radio to Cinema … let me tell you about our attempt to offer a film programme. We hired Jan Turek, a film director from Czechoslovakia, who became the driving force behind this exciting venture. Students wrote the scripts, produced, directed and operated all of the equipment required to create a film. The idea was great but the cost of such a programme was to eventually threaten the existence of the entire fine art programme. Since we did not have our own film labs, every roll of film had to be shipped to Toronto and processed at great cost. The whole episode was particularly exciting for Ricky who now had to learn a whole new vocabulary filled with words such as 'gaffer', 'grips', 'Siemen double bank flatbed editors', 'rushes', 'prints' and … big bucks. The film programme became a roller-coaster ride, cruising between success, failure, surprises, and forever … big bucks. Perhaps the time was not right for such a programme. Television was still in the process of evolving into the medium we know today, and its immediacy made it the attractive programme for the majority of students. Ultimately Ricky decided to pull the plug on this one and park the 'Siemen film editor' in a safe, cool spot. While the loss of the film programme was lamented by some, Tony McAulay, the present-day coordinator of fine art, and the Chair of the day, Sam Krizan, saw a useful place for film and video in the fine art programme and, to this day, it still plays an important role for students who seek to express themselves in this medium.

During the 1970s, our curriculum design and maintenance philosophy was based on a simple formula, the parts that worked well were kept, those that did not, were discarded. Always there was the underlying principle – don't force it, let it happen. Dialogue and criticism was an integral component of the process and Ricky made certain that standards were kept very high. Students were not allowed to get away with 'success by chance', the thought process was more important than the finished project. 'Learn the rules before you break them.' Even to this day Ben Linnsen, Patrick Thibert and Michael Durham, all longtime teachers in the fine art programme, reflect this philosophy in their teaching.

What was it about the time and the place that made education so exciting, energetic and spontaneous? It certainly had a lot to do with 'new beginnings'. Our staff was young and idealistic and eager to make an impression. Teachers in related and applied arts programmes were fresh out of industry. Ricky was starting a new life and career in the New World, his second chance to do it all again. Change was in the air; change that was fuelled and sustained by the energy of artists, political and social activists, students, and most importantly, politicians who were willing to hand out buckets of money to build a new kind of education in this province. Ricky, and the staff who worked with him, sensed the excitement and possibilities before them and seized the moment. Supported by a seemingly endless supply of money, and a benevolent leadership, unencumbered by the potential limitations of a blueprint for art education, we had found the freedom to build an exciting art school at Fanshawe College.

Where are we today? The dynamics that create great and wonderful things are often not the dynamics that can sustain them over the long haul. A different kind of energy seems to take over. Today's education seems to be following industrial models of operation, a process obsessed with delivery and control. A process that determines procedures, defines activities, determines success or failure by numerical outcomes, and ultimately operates by rules instead of intelligence and instinct. This process kills ideas, sucks spontaneity and creativity out of creative individuals, and paralyses art. There is no doubt that we have evolved into a mature and responsible art school. Our students are pro-

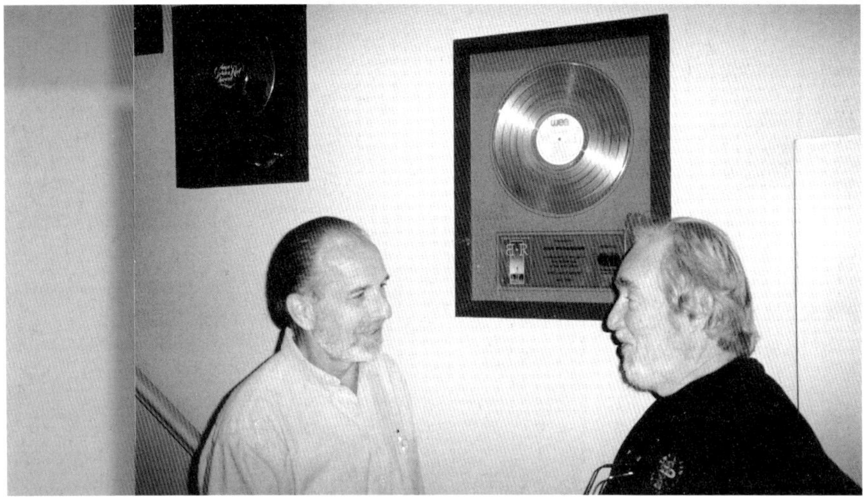

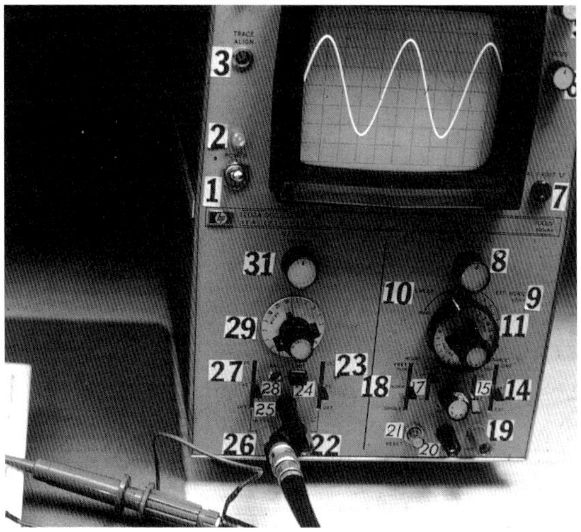

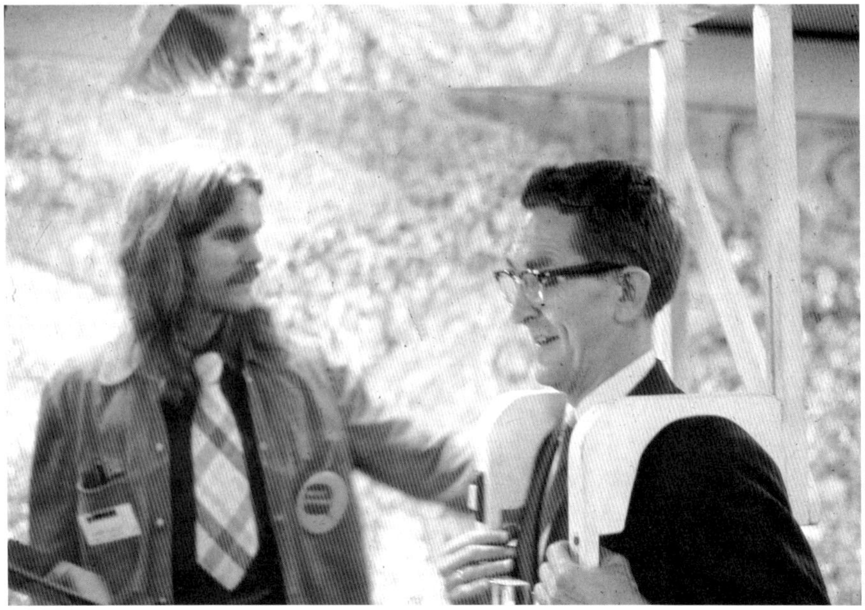

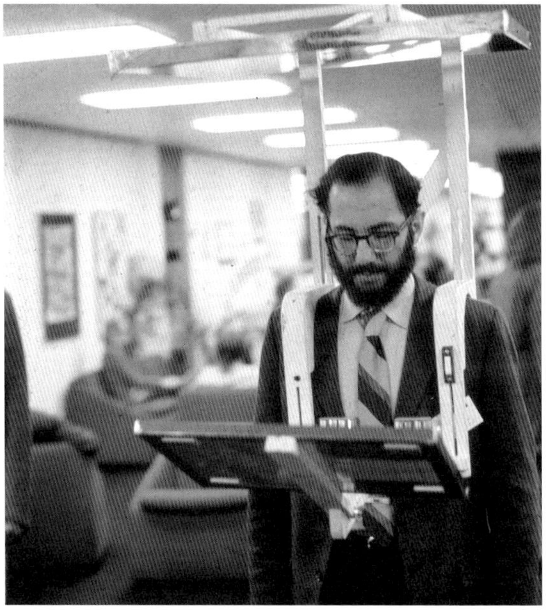

(top left) Music Industry Arts recording studio. Jack Richardson with Fred Steinmetz (*left*)

(top right) Creative electronics, 1972

(bottom left & right) Two views of walking sculpture project, with Michael Hayden, 1973

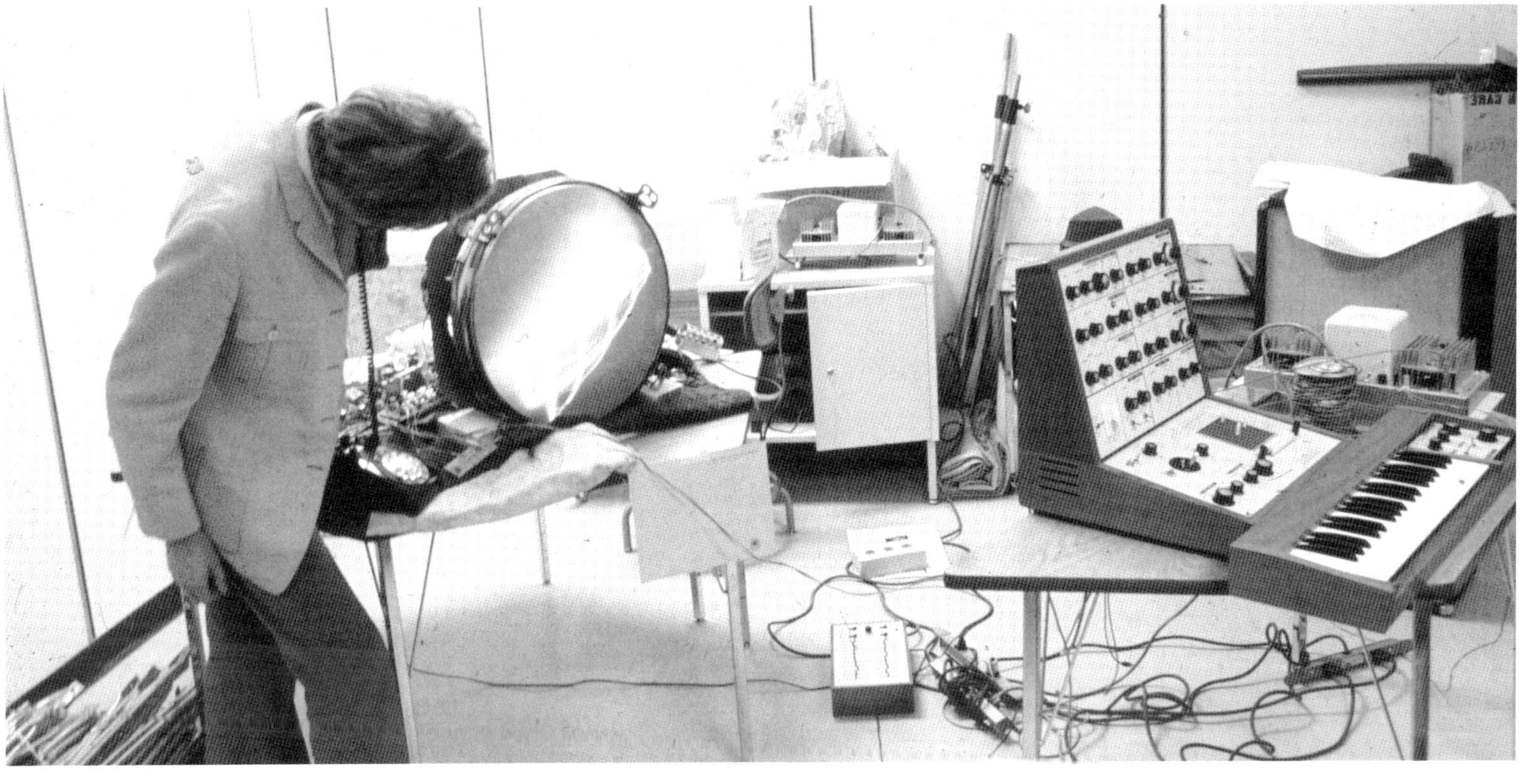

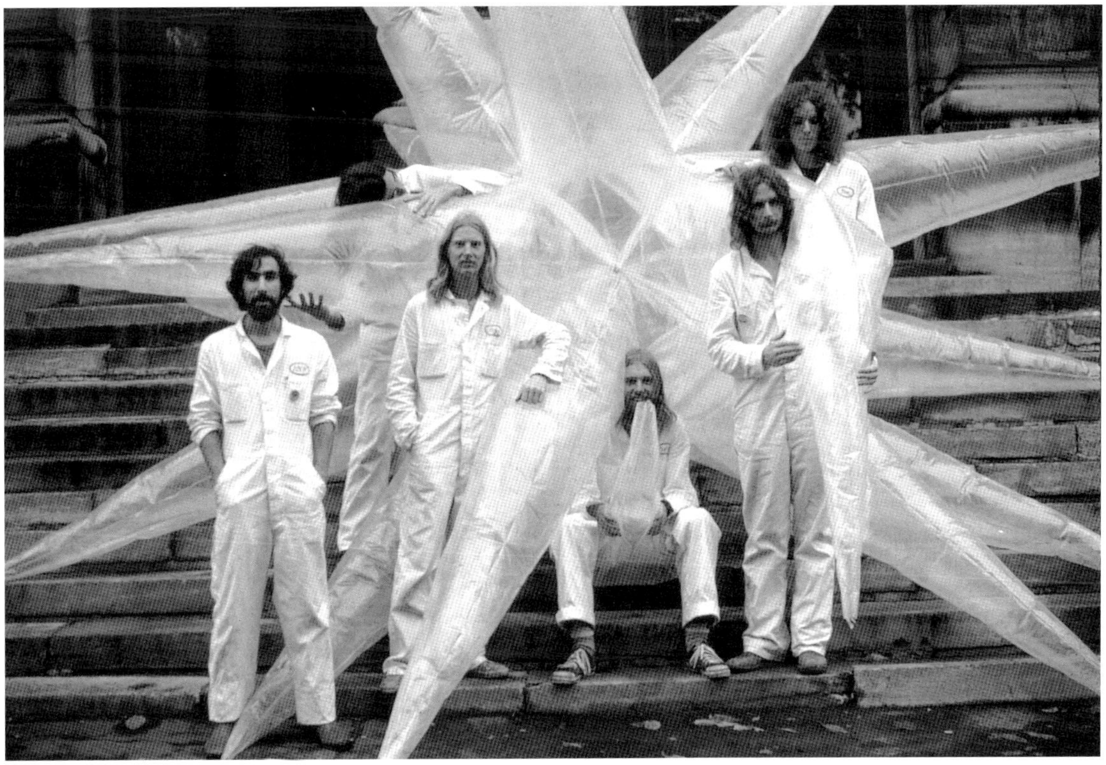

(above)
Tom Lodge with MOOG Synthesiser, TV and music, 1972

(right)
Music Industry Arts students: plastic sculpture project, 1973

ducing some excellent work and the community has finally recognised us as legitimate. Is that good, or have we slowly learned to follow bureaucratic rules, to bend against opposition and pressures? It seems to be terribly important for us to be recognised, and we are willing to pay a considerable price to achieve that state. Many universities out of province and country have given us the desired recognition. We are still trying to convince our local university, the University of Western Ontario, that our students should be given two years advanced standing for the three years at Fanshawe College. The university degree is still seen as the Everest of education and the college diploma as little more than an acknowledgment of participation. Art education, more than any other education, must be able to stay fresh, with frequent infusions of new ideas, presented by active practising artists. A chronic lack of funding prevents much of this from happening. Insufficient funding is today's major problem, and I blame a succession of short-sighted governments for this gross neglect of the educational system. Since the 1960s our funding has been cut by more than fifty per cent, while our operating costs have gone out of sight. In addition, few college heads are truly interested in the wellbeing of each individual programme. They are too busy with the excessive bureaucracy of their jobs and therefore their chief interest must be for the overall health of the institution. For the 'front line manager' this invariably means meeting the bottom line, following policies, appeasing the various constituencies in the college community, and appearing to be fiscally responsible to the taxpayer.

Ricky envisaged an art programme that was similar to our supermarkets. A place where you could roam about with your cart, pick up some music training, some film, some painting and so on, then use these raw materials, cook a tasty dish, an education for a rewarding life. Instead, what we have evolved into is a series of well-defined, self-contained packages of fine art, music, television, etc. Packages that are well designed and look attractive to the consumer; to a great extent, we have lost the freedom to experiment and to allow nature to take its course. Why is it that we so often turn wonderful ideas into stagnant entities without blood? In an age of generalists we have become specialists … out of step again.

So, David, here we are, and through it all we owe much to Ricky's leadership and vision, no matter how structured we have become, how much we feel we have betrayed his ideals and dreams of the 1960s and 1970s. Seeds of that experience are still lingering in the system, and someday, somewhere, those seeds may find another fertile environment, will germinate, and will again infuse art education with the vitality, originality and sheer joy that reflect the creative energy and vision of Eric Atkinson. I am hopeful that these matters go in waves, hopefully waves at thirty-year intervals.

I would like to end on a personal note. In 1993 I was asked to create a Communication Arts programme for the Higher Colleges of Technology, in the United Arab Emirates. This assignment gave me the opportunity to start an educational programme from the ground up. For three years I experienced what Ricky must have experienced here in London. The almost daily adrenaline rush that one experiences when all systems are in synch, and the creative process is in high gear. My thirty years of experience operated in the background only, giving me the confidence to go on. What was so exciting were the calculated risks I took with every move I made. Perhaps we should all move on from time to time, to feel the thrill and experience the terror that comes with new beginnings.

So long, David, and thank you for this opportunity. Best of luck to you Ricky, my friend and mentor. Have a long and productive life. Love to Muriel.

Fred

Letter 15 Arlene Kennedy to David Lewis

24 March 1998

Dear David

I wanted to write to tell you about the long and rich relationship we at the McIntosh Gallery have enjoyed with Ricky Atkinson. As both artist and educator Ricky is a significant force in the London community and a catalyst in linking Fanshawe College with the McIntosh Gallery and the University of Western Ontario, particularly in our partnership with the Faculty of Engineering Sciences.

Art education in Canada has always been an interesting hybrid between British and American trends and practice. Nowhere has this interaction been more clearly visible than in London, Ontario over the last three decades. There is a potent art education matrix in London of a major Canadian university that began a visual arts degree programme in 1967; a special art programme at H.B. Beal Secondary School (founded in 1912); a feeder system of primary and secondary school art programmes; and an innovative environmental arts and fine arts programme at Fanshawe Community College.

Since the early 1970s Ricky Atkinson has driven the Fanshawe programme and initiated partnerships with the wider community including the McIntosh Gallery, Canada's oldest university gallery. With a tradition of engaging The University of Western Ontario's academic departments in interdisciplinary investigations, and the participation of the wider community, the Gallery was fertile ground for Ricky's overtures.

Maurice Stubbs, the first full-time professional Director of the McIntosh Gallery (from 1969 to 1989), responded to the challenge. An art educator himself, trained in his native Australia, Maurice Stubbs had been influenced by a seminal British conference in 1952 that featured the renowned art educator Herbert Read. He shared in the ferment of reform engendered by educators such as Dewey and Lowenfeld and embodied in the programmes at Leeds. Stubbs also discovered that these ideas were supported by Clair Bice, Director of the London Art Gallery, and a member of the committee that hired Ricky Atkinson at Fanshawe College.

Professors of Engineering at Western also espoused the innovative pedagogies and projects Ricky Atkinson proposed: Bob Swartzman (who later developed a business around solar energy for, among other things, a solar-powered refrigerator in India); Mel Poucher, a materials engineer who was also a Chair of the advisory committee for the Fanshawe Fine Art department and gave lectures on engineering for art students (just as Ricky gave lectures and seminars on art to engineering students at Western); Alan Davenport, head of the Boundary Layer Wind Tunnel (which tested designs for structures like the CN Tower, bridges, buildings and North Sea oil rigs, including your designs, David); and Ian Duerden, among others, all investigated the interrelationship of art and engineering for the creative individual.

McIntosh Gallery projects that arose out of this productive collaboration included the following: a film series; Gzowsky Engineering Society guest speakers such as Phyllis Lambert, architect and founder of the Canadian Center for Architecture in Montreal; joint exhibitions such as 'Steel: the Engineer and the Sculptor', 'Wind and Wave' and 'Art and New Technologies' (which included joint hands-on laboratory explorations by artists and engineers); an Engineering Artist in Residence programme (Jan Shepherd), through Dean Mohan Mathur and the current Director, Arlene Kennedy, in effect since 1991; kite design and flying contests for the community, Ricky's drawings for the 1977 *Engineering Student Handbook*; public art installations in the Engineering department, such as Walter Redinger's wall mural and Ed Zelenak's outdoor steel sculpture; and occasional art exhibitions of the Fanshawe faculty, both as a group and individually.

Your appointment, David, as Visiting Professor Emeritus of the Faculty of Engineering is a prime example of the opportunities Ricky provided at Western for the discussion of topics like the engineering-related problems in architecture.

Since 1973 Ricky has initiated annual graduation exhibitions for Fanshawe College fine art students. Initially, these were to demonstrate the value of this kind of event with a view to Fanshawe eventually creating its own art gallery. Like the annual student exhibitions of Western's Visual Arts Department held at the McIntosh Gallery, these exhibitions have served as a window for the wider community and the individual academic communities to observe the distinct and unique character of each art education programme as evidenced in the work of students and teachers. For the last nine years the Curator of the McIntosh Gallery, Catherine Elliot Shaw, has presented a formal lecture at Fanshawe College on exhibiting professionally at a public art gallery and the business of being an artist. She has then conducted the equivalent of a 'studio visit' with those students interested.

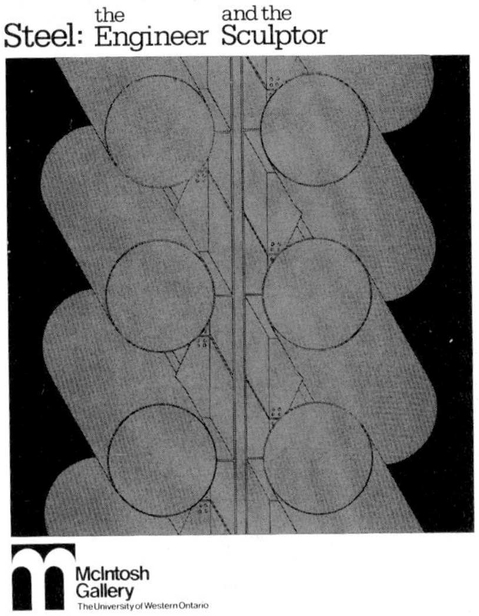

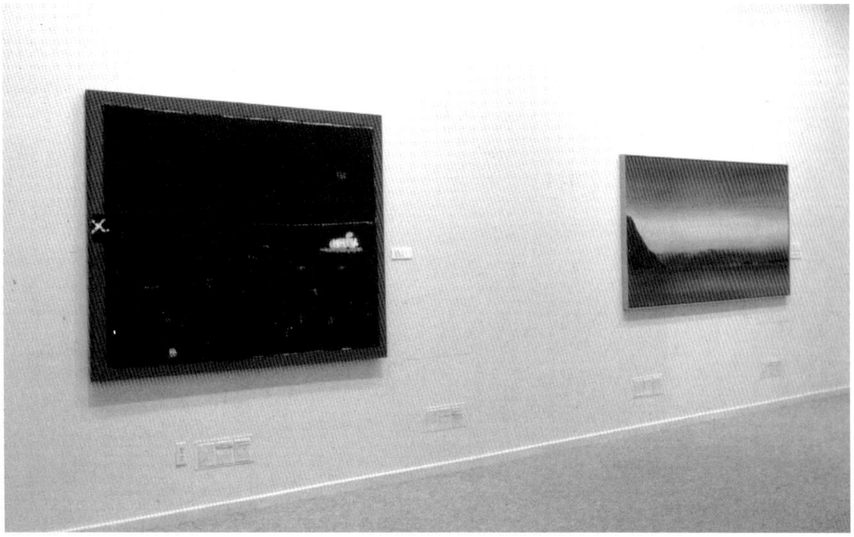

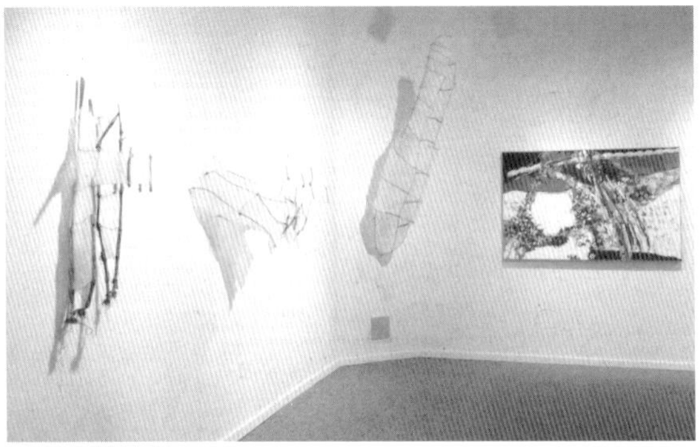

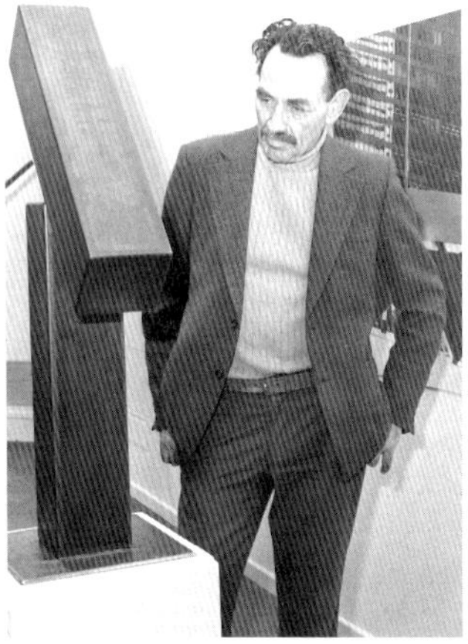

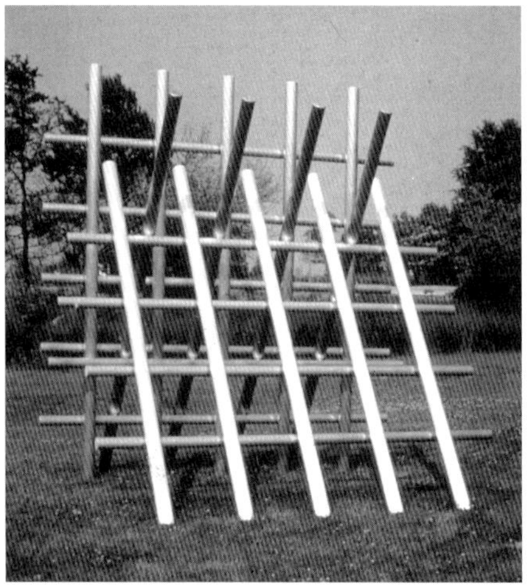

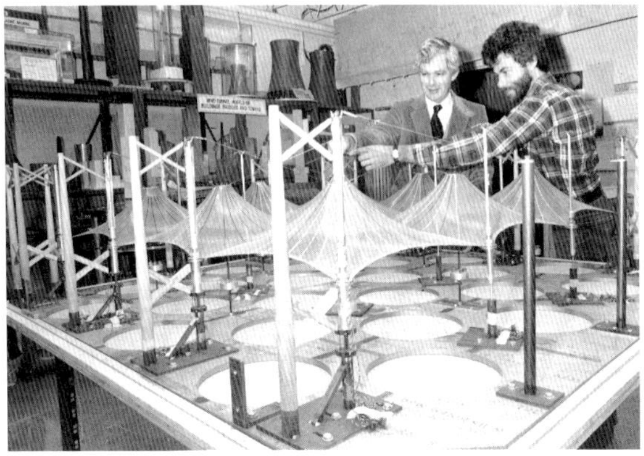

(top left) Catalogue cover, 1980

(top right) Eric Atkinson, *Pelican Island,* 1994, (at the McIntosh Gallery)

*(centre left)*Fanshawe graduation exhibition, McIntosh Gallery, 1981

(centre above) Kosso Eloul at the exhibition 'Steel: The Engineer and The Sculptor', 1980

(centre right) Patrick Thibert, *Laws Field,* 1983, 10½ ft x 10 ft x 8 ft 3 in.,
collection: University of Western Ontario

(left) Professor Davenport (*on left*) with model for 'Steel: The Engineer and The Sculptor', 1980

Combined with a powerful regional influence from London artists such as Greg Curnoe, the internationalist influence of Ricky Atkinson has injected a dynamic tension into the art education scene that remains unabated, the legacy of an excellent art educator made available for the entire community.

I wish you every success with your documentation of this remarkable era in art education.

Warmest regards,
Arlene Kennedy
Director

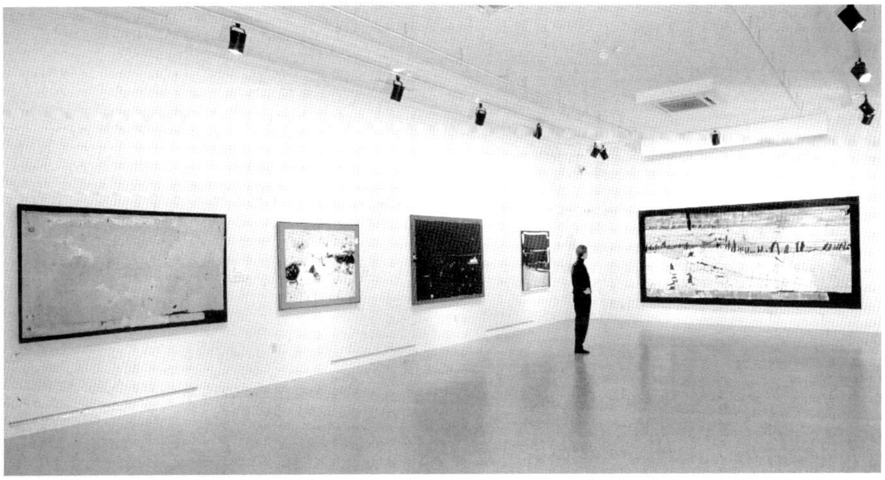

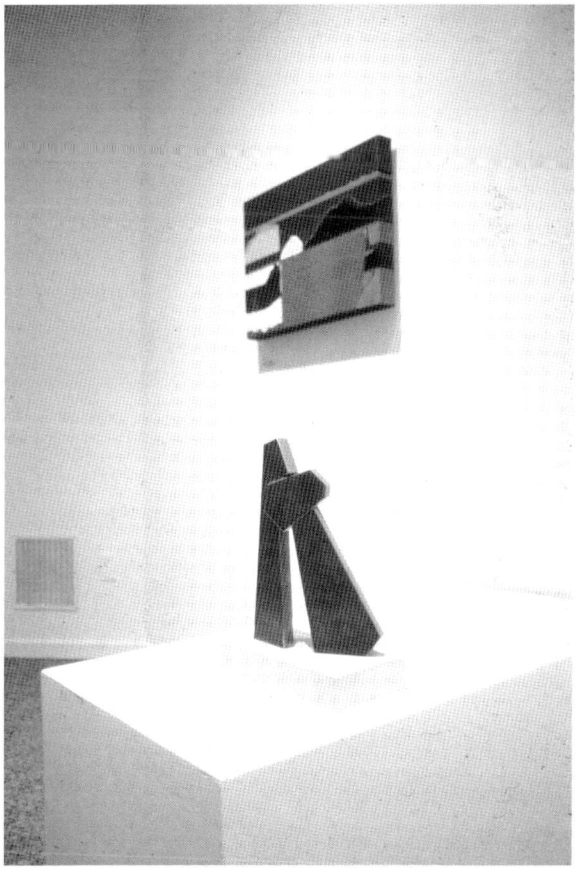

(above) View of 'Landmarks' exhibition, McIntosh Gallery, February 2000

(right) Works by Eric Atkinson and Gino Lorcini at the McIntosh Gallery, 1981

The Incomplete Circle: The Paintings of Eric Atkinson

David Lewis

'My paintings are records of journeys through the landscape – the forms echoing the geological structure of the land and the calligraphy left by man and nature upon its surface.' These words were written by Ricky Atkinson in 1994.[1] As a statement they seem to be straightforward enough. We understand exactly what he's saying. Or do we? What if the landscape he is referring to is not only that of the world out there – but is also the landscape of our interior world, the world of the mind?

Everywhere we go, we carry interior landscapes with us. These are the landscapes of our memory – the beaches we have walked along at low tide; the meadows of our childhoods, rich with the scents of grass after rain; the silence of snow, glimpsed through the bedroom window in the silver light of a winter dawn. There are the landscapes of our knowledge (for example, 'the geological structure of the land'). There are the landscapes of history ('the calligraphy left by man and nature upon its surface'). And let us not forget the landscapes of dreams.

In many ways these interior landscapes are much more powerful than the exterior ones. We do not remember every step of our walk along the beach. We remember vivid fragments, which we store away: the view of the horizon, with a freighter no larger than an insect balanced on its rim, the crash and hiss of waves, the cries of gulls, the texture of sand, the scent of sea breezes. We carry these with us wherever we go, along with countless thousands of other fragments of memory.

And there they are, locked away, semi-forgotten and private, until suddenly we call on them, at a moment's notice, during a conversation at a cocktail party, or when we are reading a book, or when we are looking at photographs with a friend, to be assembled into sharply focused composite images, and described with vivid qualities – the lonely elderly fisherman at dusk whose line is cast far into the surf, the sting of the sun on the back of one's hand, the dancing colours of mother-of-pearl in the recessed spiral of a wet seashell.

These are personal interior landscapes, stored away. But what makes them powerful is that they have features in common with the interior landscapes of other people all around us. And as soon as we establish this commonality we have the makings of our shared language of landscapes.

Our museums and art galleries, and even our own houses, are full of examples of languages of landscape which we share with other people. We do not have to experience at first hand the heat of the cornfields of Arles to appreciate van Gogh, nor do we have to have lived in Renaissance Italy to appreciate the landscapes in a Bellini or a Raphael.

Ricky's early paintings and drawings – the ones of his native Hartlepool, where merchant ships are berthed at the dockside, and the gaunt lattices of cranes are fretworks against the sky, and a wind is shimmering the water – were a success at his first exhibitions in London, not because the visitors to the gallery knew Hartlepool especially, but because the paintings and drawings spoke a common language.

The gallery-goers were emerging from a war in which major port cities like London, Glasgow, and Liverpool had been heavily bombed, yet merchant ships carrying supplies and munitions and troops got through. Ricky's images of the Hartlepool docks operate at a number of levels. There is a quiet, modest heroism. There is a sense of a return to normal. Yet there is also an innocence and joyfulness in the freshness and flurries of the wind on the water of the harbour, which tell us that the for-everness of nature transcends the temporal. Even the small size of these paintings and drawings (12x6in, or 14x8in), and their materials – paper, watercolour – were components of the language of modesty, innocence and freshness.

Discovering and establishing one's personal language, and being able to translate one's personal language into common or community language through communication, is the essence of the art education which Ricky was so intimately involved with at Leeds and later in Canada. In Ricky's case, as his statement tells us, his personal language is landscape. Once he moved to Leeds and became involved in teaching the Basic Course, his work changed. Gone are the specific images of ships and docks and cranes. Why?

One of the paintings reproduced in colour in this book is 'Silver Grey'. Its date is 1962, in the middle of his Leeds period. Unlike the Hartlepool paintings 'Silver Grey' is large and shorn of specific images; yet if anything, in spite of its abstract language, it is more specific. Although there are no overt representational references to Hartlepool, Ricky's birthplace is still very much the subject of this painting. So too are the landscapes of Yorkshire.

Hartlepool is an old seaport. It goes back a thousand years, to the times of the invasions and settlements of the Norsemen and beyond. Many of the stones of the seawalls are handcut granite from the quarries in the hills above the town, and incised into them are occasional cyphers cut by long-forgotten hands – and now so eroded by tides and rain and wind and sand as to be almost illegible.

Similarly, ancient stones – possibly marking the places of the dead, like the gravestones in our later churchyards – stand around on the hills overlooking the sea. Is the enigma of these stones to remind us of the particular dead, a king or a hero, whose existence has long since faded from personal memory, or are they, like the stones of Avebury, part of a collective ritual, the enigma of which still echoes in our collective memories because of the stones?

Around Leeds is the landscape of the Yorkshire moors. This is a landscape of hills and valleys, sometimes gentle, sometimes steep, shaped over countless centuries by nature and by man. It is grazing country. The fields are bounded by walls of hewn granite blocks to keep the flocks of sheep contained in pastures, and these walls run over the contours and into the valleys like black baling bands.

But it is not only a country of surface landscapes. It is also mining country. Deep into its seams run the galleries of the miners, boring like termites into the bones of the land. It is a landscape of grandeur and depth, yet intimacy. Hardly surprisingly, it has bred sculptors as well as painters, artists like Henry Moore and Barbara Hepworth, whose images relate directly to this land.

In the winter snow covers the land. The black walls, and sunlight and shadow, give definition to its swellings, and the tracks of animals and humans in the snow, revealing the soil below, are visual punctuations, but they are also punctuations no more permanent than the next thaw.

'Silver Grey' deals with all of this subject matter at once. In his statement Ricky talks about his paintings as 'journeys through the landscape'. A journey can, of course, be a mental journey. But a journey is also something made, a physical journey. This painting is both. The surface of the canvas is built up thickly with pigment, sand and cloth, and the artist has laid colour on it and scored into it. Some of the marks in the painting are like transitory footsteps in soft snowy slush; others could be ancient cyphers in the process of being eroded; and as we look at this painting we become aware of richnesses of metaphors and meanings far beyond the capacity of his earlier realistic paintings to reveal to us.

In one of his letters printed here Ricky recounts a visit to the small farmhouse Kurt Schwitters lived in in England's Lake District after his escape from wartime Europe. He writes about how amazed he was as a young art student to find that Schwitters made such powerful art using scraps of trash, as Picasso and Braque had done in their Cubist years – shreds of newsprint, bus tickets, rags, and so forth – revealing a wealth of visual richness in the stuff we throw away every day. How could that be?

For Ricky, that visit was a journey into uncharted territory. It broke the mould that art had to be oil paint on canvas or watercolour on paper. It told him that one of the main purposes of art is to awaken in us new dimensions of language. In 'Silver Grey' Ricky incorporates gauze and sand in much the same way that our spoken languages renew themselves by incorporating new words and phrases drawn from science, sports or slang.

Today Ricky is an immigrant in Canada. There is nothing particularly unusual in that. We are all migrants in one form or another. We like to think that, when we travel, the most important things we have with us are our bags. They are not. Wherever we go, even if it is only to the next town, the most important things we travel with are our cultures and our memories.

Every country in the world has been enriched by the influences of other cultures. We have already noted how, in the landscapes of Ricky's boyhood, we can find the stone markers of the Danes, and the defensive earthworks of the Saxons; and going to a later period, we find that the seventeenth-century architecture of his home town has a rich heritage of curvilinear gables resulting from trade and cultural exchanges with Holland. These are small but precise evidences of cultural migration.

In a similar way the earliest immigrants from Europe to the eastern seaboards of America and Canada brought only the most elementary tools, saws, axes and adzes. But they also brought their skills and memories of the built environments of their birthrights – the churches, the houses, the shops, the furniture, the ceramics, and even the town plans. Out of these materials the basis for the sophisticated values and aspirations of our culture was laid and the strands of our collective memories were woven.

The places Ricky left behind when he emigrated to Canada were, for all their grandeur, intimate and small in scale – the farms and villages tucked into the contours, the narrow roads winding over hilltops and down into wooded valleys and across stone bridges over rushing streams.

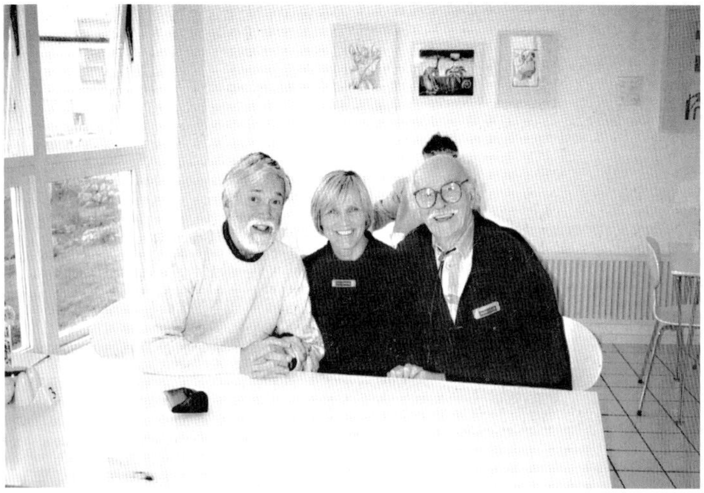

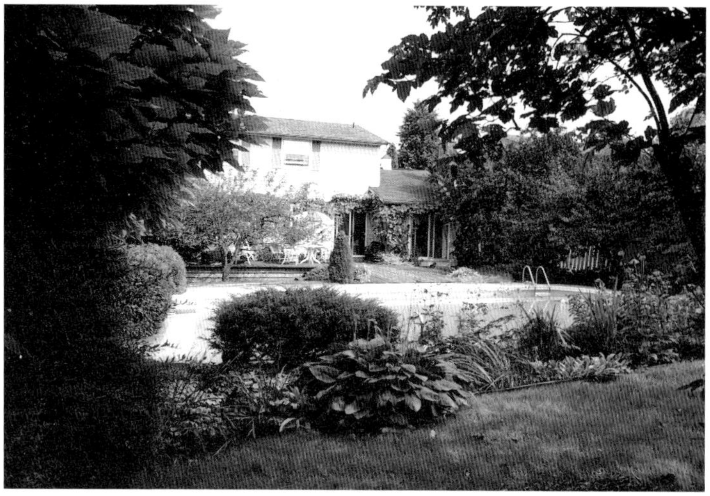

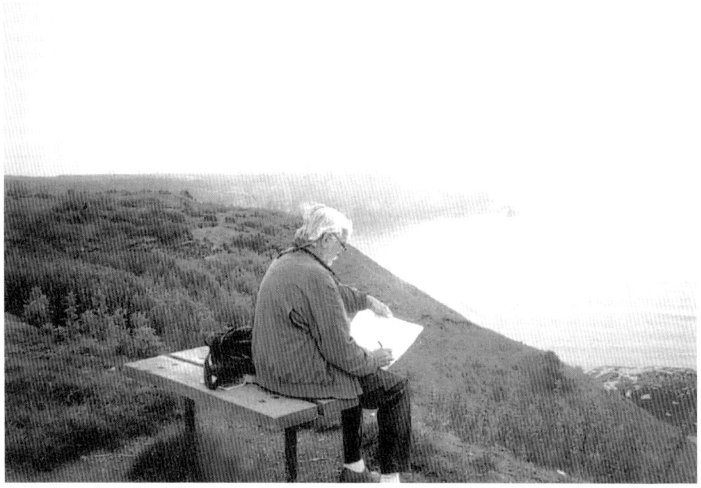

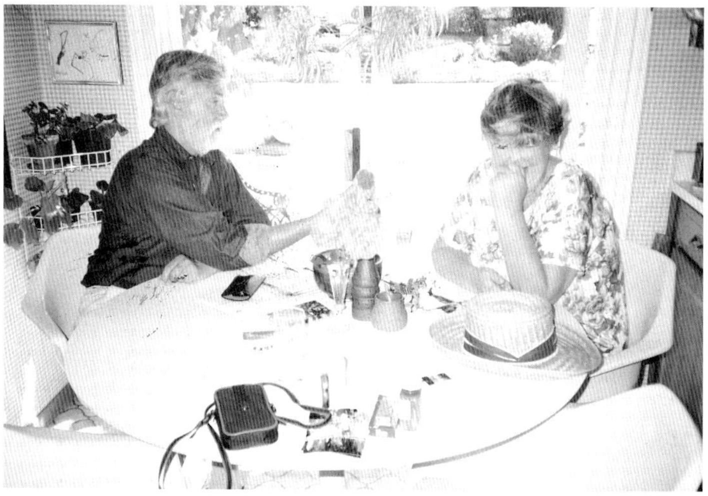

(top left)
Ricky with Penny Brown and Terry Frost at the Tate Gallery, St Ives, Cornwall

(above)
Ricky sketching in Scotland

(top right)
Ricky and Muriel's home, London, Ontario

(centre right)
Ricky and Muriel in their kitchen

(bottom right)
Eric Atkinson chatting with the Hon. Brian Tobin (Prime Minister, Newfoundland) and Joe Fontana, MP for London (*centre*), at the exhibition 'Painting Tour to Cornwall', London Regional Art Gallery, 1995

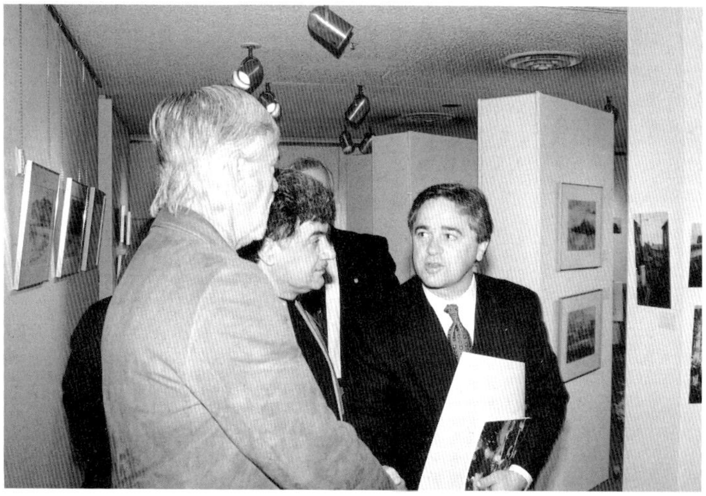

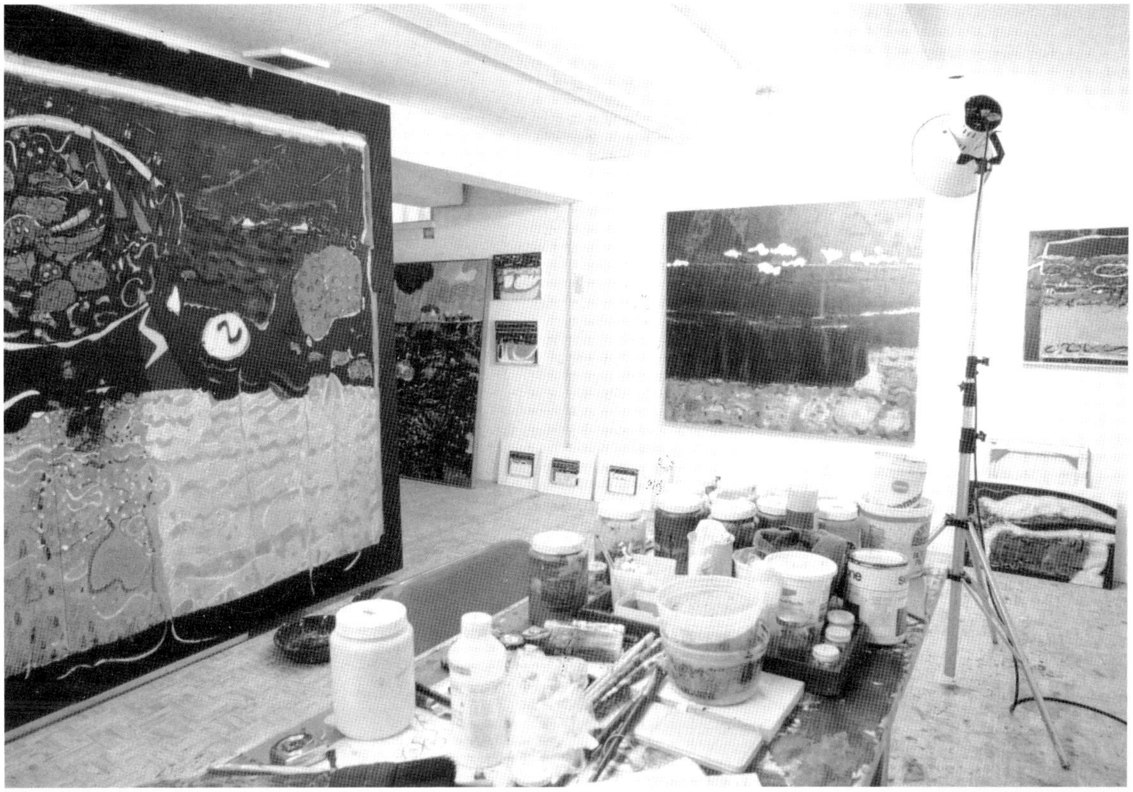

Two views of Eric Atkinson's studio at his home, London, Ontario

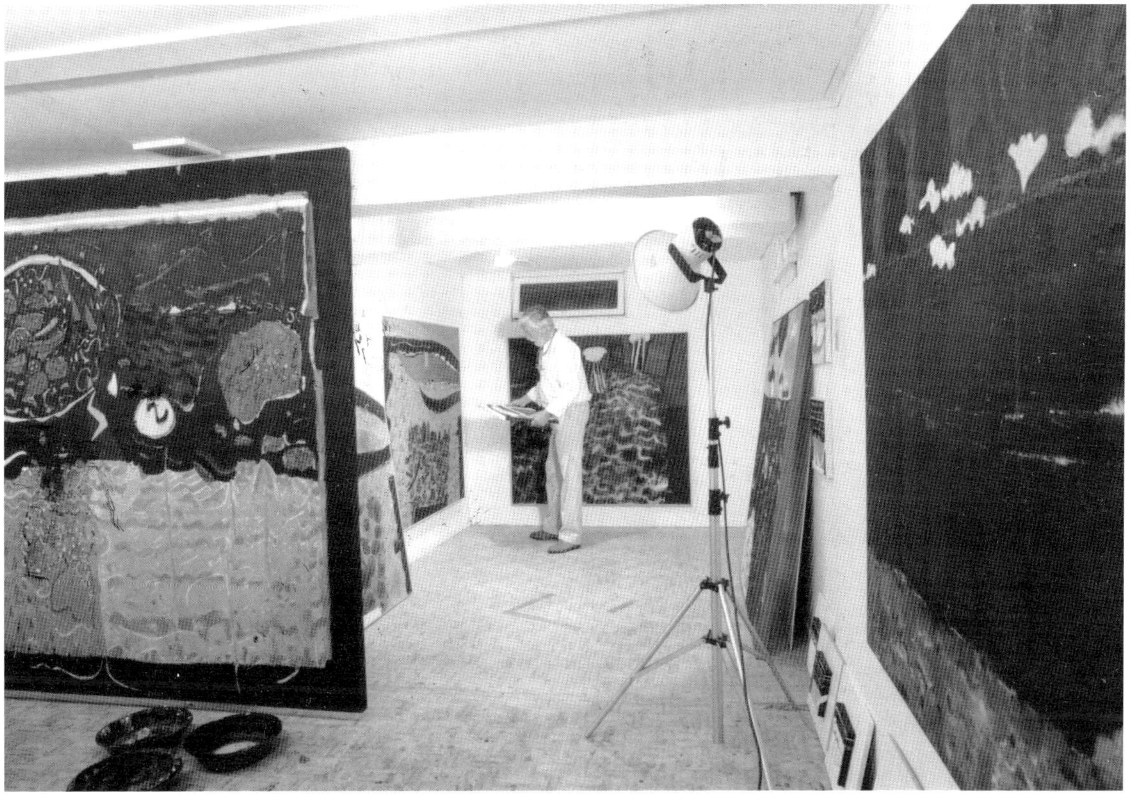

But when he came to Canada he was confronted by a wholly different scale. Here was a huge country, thousands of miles from east to west, encompassing rocky coasts, deserts, lakes, tundra, prairies and mountains. And here in Ontario, just one province as large as several European countries put together, roads went north and south and east and west from horizon to horizon; here were Lake Huron, and Lake Erie, and Lake Ontario, each as large as an inland sea; here in the winter was an unbroken plateau of whiteness; here, in the summer, dark thunder clouds rolled like giant dark waves across the land. And here too was a depth of time, not measured, like Europe, in human-history terms, but in terms of vast spans of natural time, ice ages, folds in the earth's crust, and the slow formation of sedimentary soil and rock.

Human scale is different too. Here huge cities and airports have been built and interstate highways and railroads span the continent. But compared with the land, these man-made things are new. Our cultures are still shallow. Our futures are more vulnerable to technological change than we care to admit. In every direction all around us is nature, continuing its ageless rhythm. Over the past twenty-five years Ricky has been concerned with this dichotomy. Are there no marks, no incised stones, no petroglyphs, anywhere in this vastness to mark an earlier human and cultural presence?

What of the generations of Native Americans? In the far west, nomads from the Mongolian steppes are said to have island-hopped across the Bering Straits and fanned out to claim the forests, the prairies, and the valleys of gaunt mountain ranges, all the way south to Mexico and beyond where they created jungle and mountain cities. But what of Canada? Did the Norsemen who invaded the north of England cross the Atlantic as well and reach Newfoundland and Prince Edward Island? Did they voyage into Hudson Bay? How far did they penetrate into eastern Canada? And what about the cyphers of the passage of our own civilisation?

These questions have become the dominant themes of Ricky's paintings. One series is based on the islands around Manitoulin in the north-eastern waters of Lake Huron. These islands become extraordinarily mysterious when the mists hang over the lake's smooth leaden surface, and the inland sea and the sky merge into one endless permanent plane of diaphanous grey. It is in the late afternoon that the islands – or are they maybe clouds? – hover at the horizon as though suspended motionless in space and outside time, waiting to drift into twilight's slowly enveloping darkness, and we hover with them, wondering about the transitoriness of human existence as one more day slides into night.

In another series of paintings, a beach (or is it the underwater bed of a sea or lake?) is littered with bits and pieces caught midway between having been something and being transformed into something else. What are they, these bits and pieces? Are they the cogwheels of machines, or the shards of pots, or human bones, or the fossils of extinct species? And will the cycles of transformation ever stop? If we listen, as we stand in front of these paintings asking these questions, we can begin to hear the silences of time beyond time.

In another series, vast dark thunderstorms roll across the paintings, creating rage in the waters of Georgian Bay, stirring sand and wind and rain with air currents of giant strength, and we – in our frail houses and cities in which these paintings are exhibited – can only watch from the outside, powerless in their presence; and yet in all of them there is a light beyond the storm, sometimes yellow, sometimes a cold blue-white, the messengers of a rhythm of natural change. And in yet another thunderstorm series, a dark river leads us towards (or away from) giant upright stones, which could be the monuments of past ice ages, or gravestones, or the abandoned shells of buildings from a forgotten civilisation.

There is a series of four canvases, in which Ricky engages the same outer landscape of Lake Huron with his own inner self, and by implication with ours, in four different scenarios. In the first there is the eternal calm of night turning into dawn, with hints of islands, or maybe boats, in the ethereal light. In the second, a whipping storm has risen, with winds shredding the clouds in the blue sky. The shore is turned to froth as waves pound, churning up what seems like sand, feathers, bones and shells. In the third the storm continues; the sky is cold and white, the froth from the waves is like snow, and the sea-lake is laced with flashes of reflected sun like battle blood. In the fourth, the lake is stacked with rune stones, maybe the enigmatic markers of past migrations.

But, more importantly, are these not the markers of our own personal migrations – our thoughts, our dreams, our personal cultures? The fact that we do not know exactly what they are makes them starting-points for our own per-

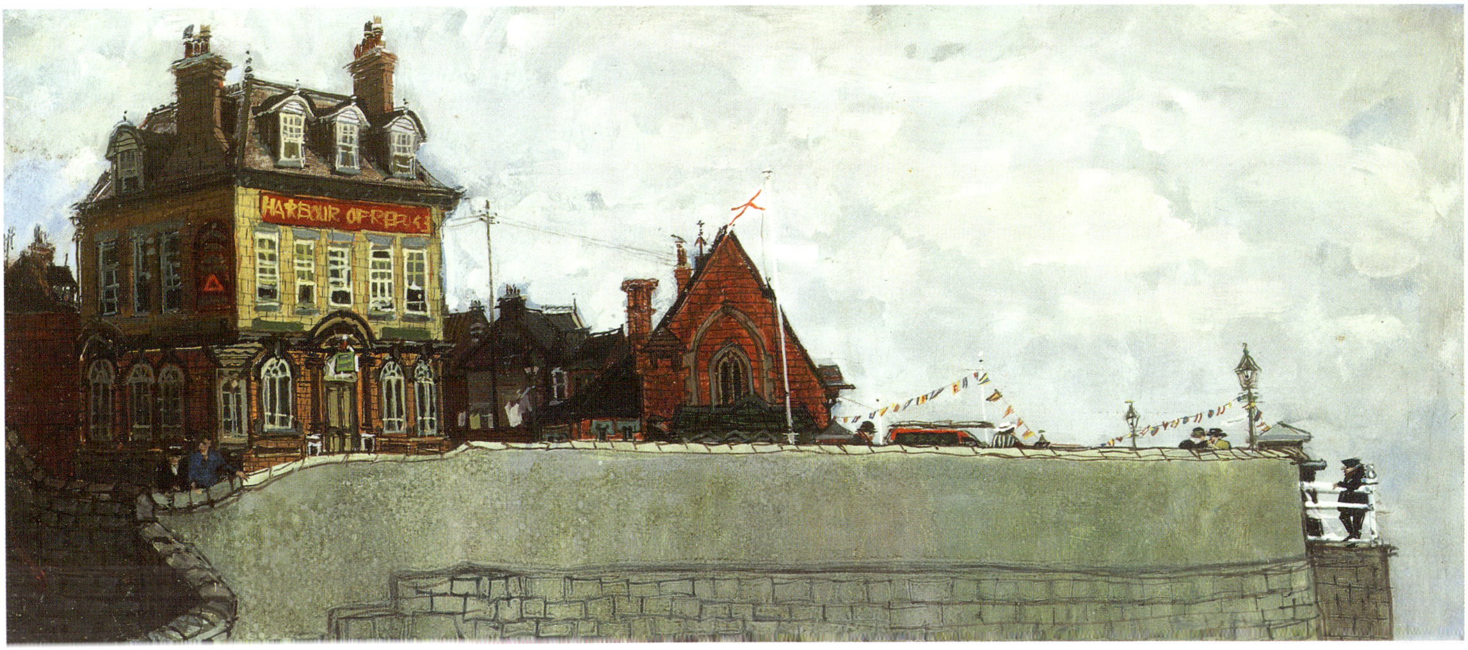

Eric Atkinson
Harbour of Refuge
(public house, sea wall, Hartlepool)
1952
15½ x 36½ in.
oil on board
collection: Sean and Jill Atkinson,
Lake Francis, Ontario

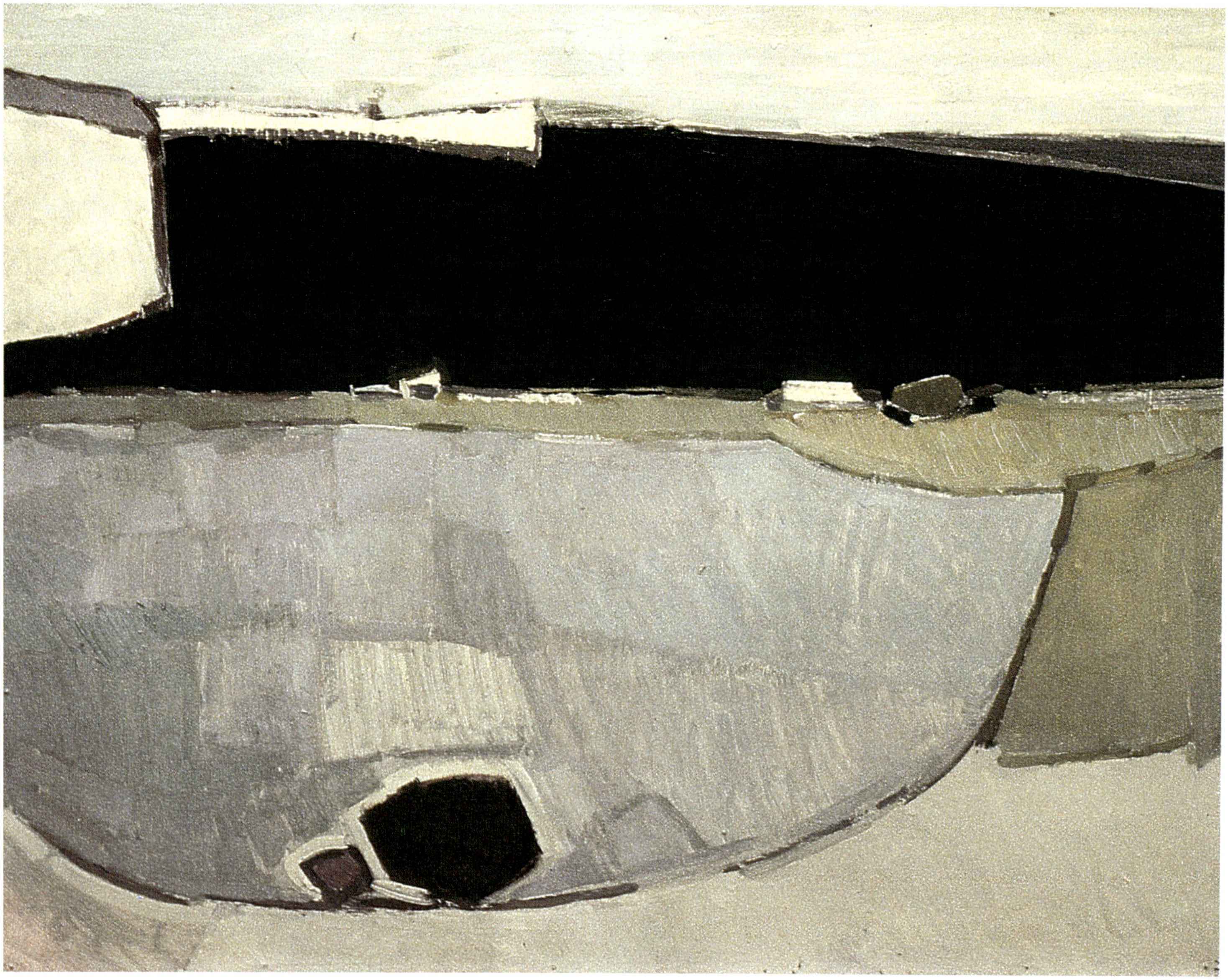

Eric Atkinson
Pembrokeshire Coastline
1963
28 x 36 in.
oil on board
collection: Leeds City Art Gallery

Eric Atkinson
Silver Grey
1962
63 x 54 in.
mixed medium, sand
on canvas with gauze
collection of the artist

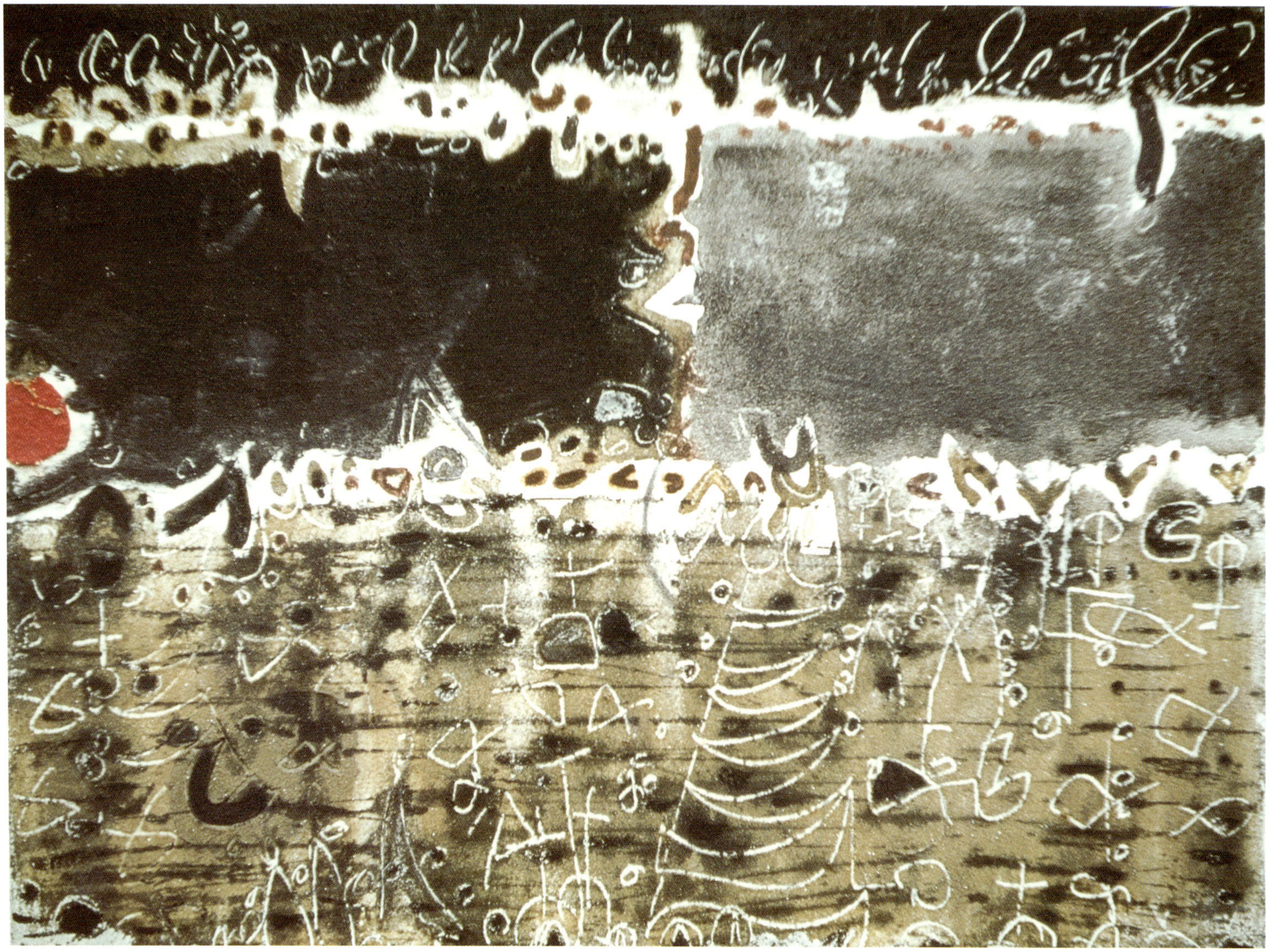

Eric Atkinson
Finistere: Celtic landscape
1967
28 x 36 in.
acrylic, sand, cloth on canvas
Private collection

Eric Atkinson
Landmarks
1972
20 x 30 in.
collection: David Lewis

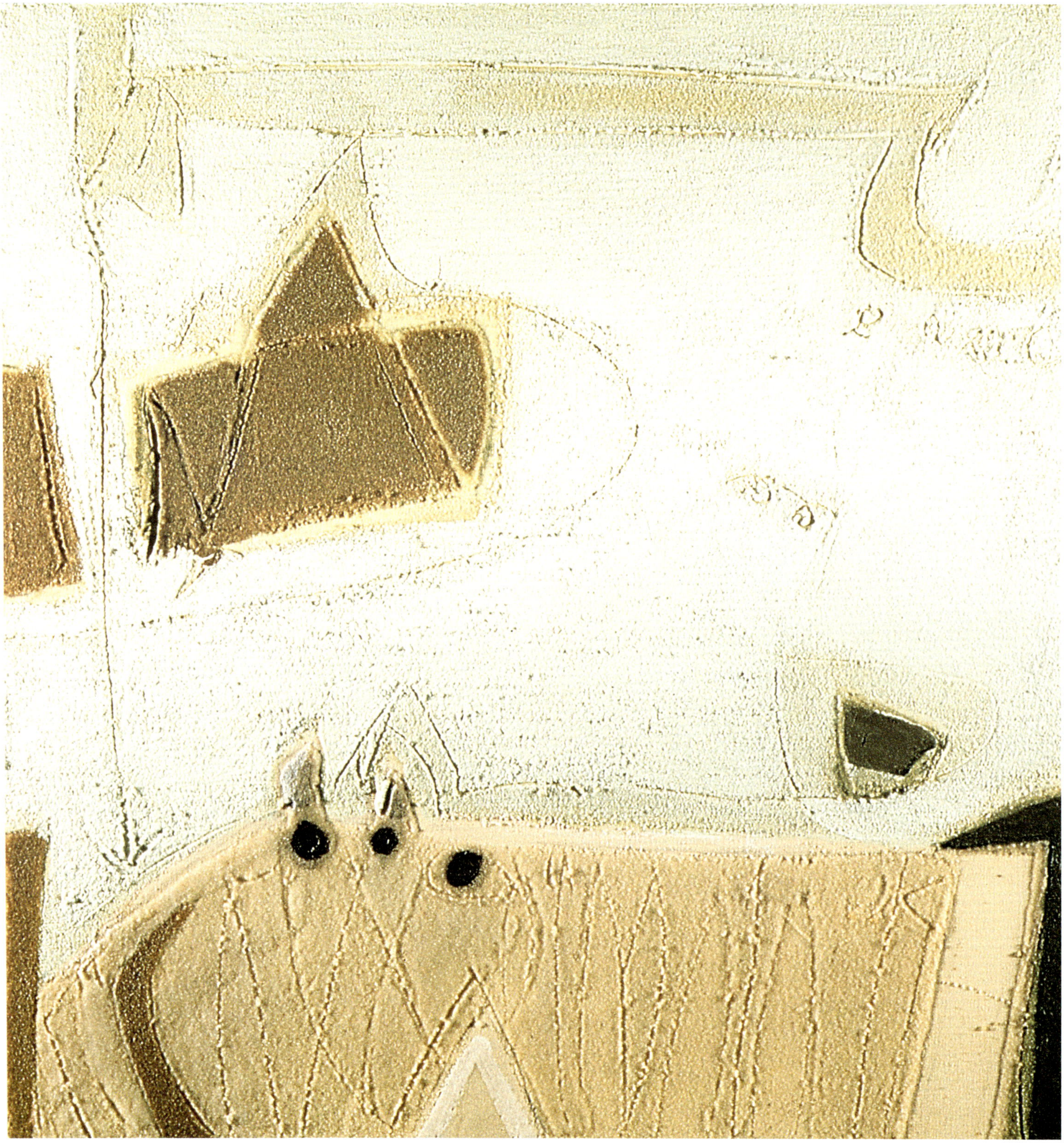

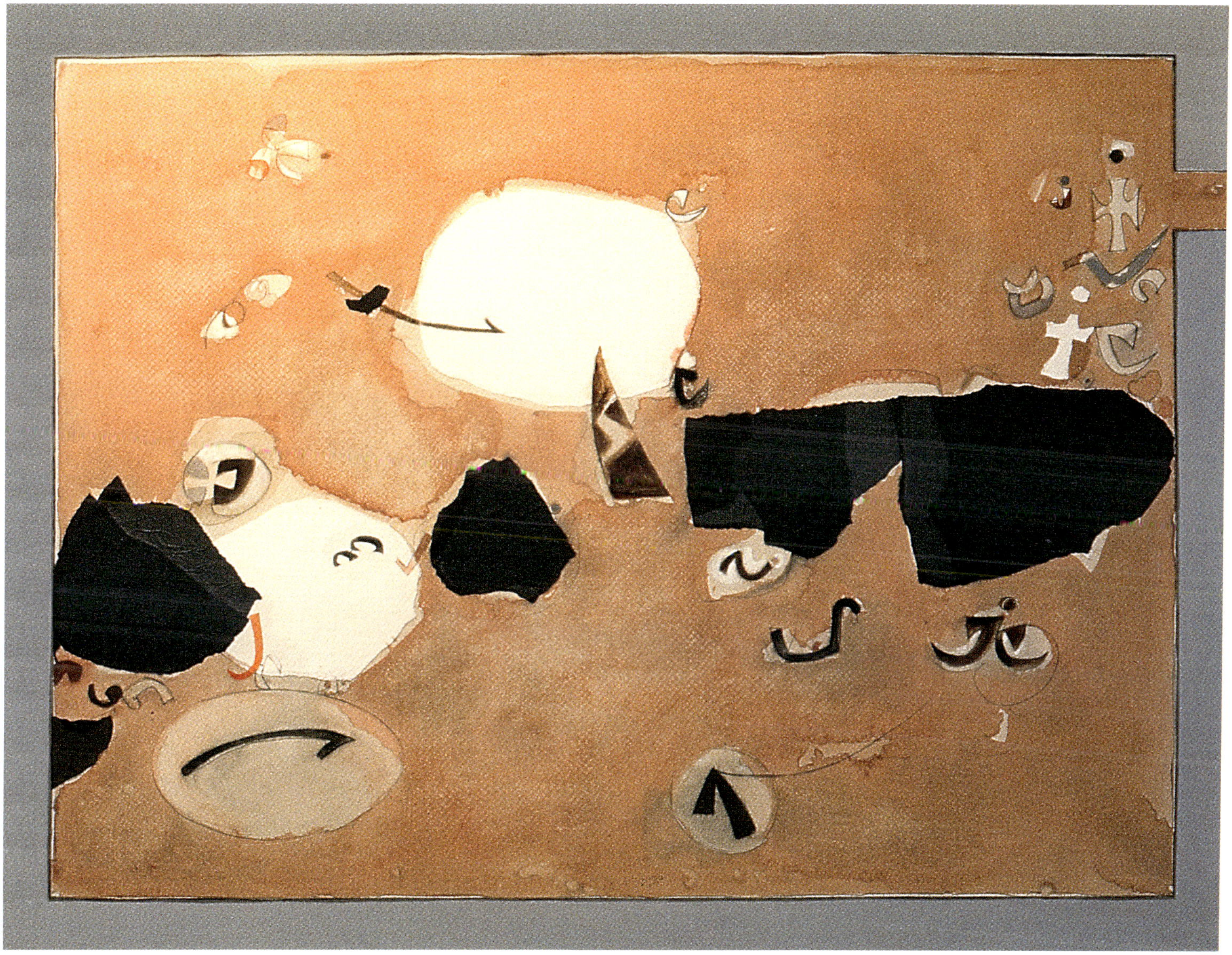

(above) Eric Atkinson
Synergy landscape
1978, 42 x 54 in., acrylic and paper collage
Private collection

(left) Eric Atkinson
White Indian Head
1984, 20 x 20 in., acrylic and sand on canvas
collection: Dr & Mrs T Brown

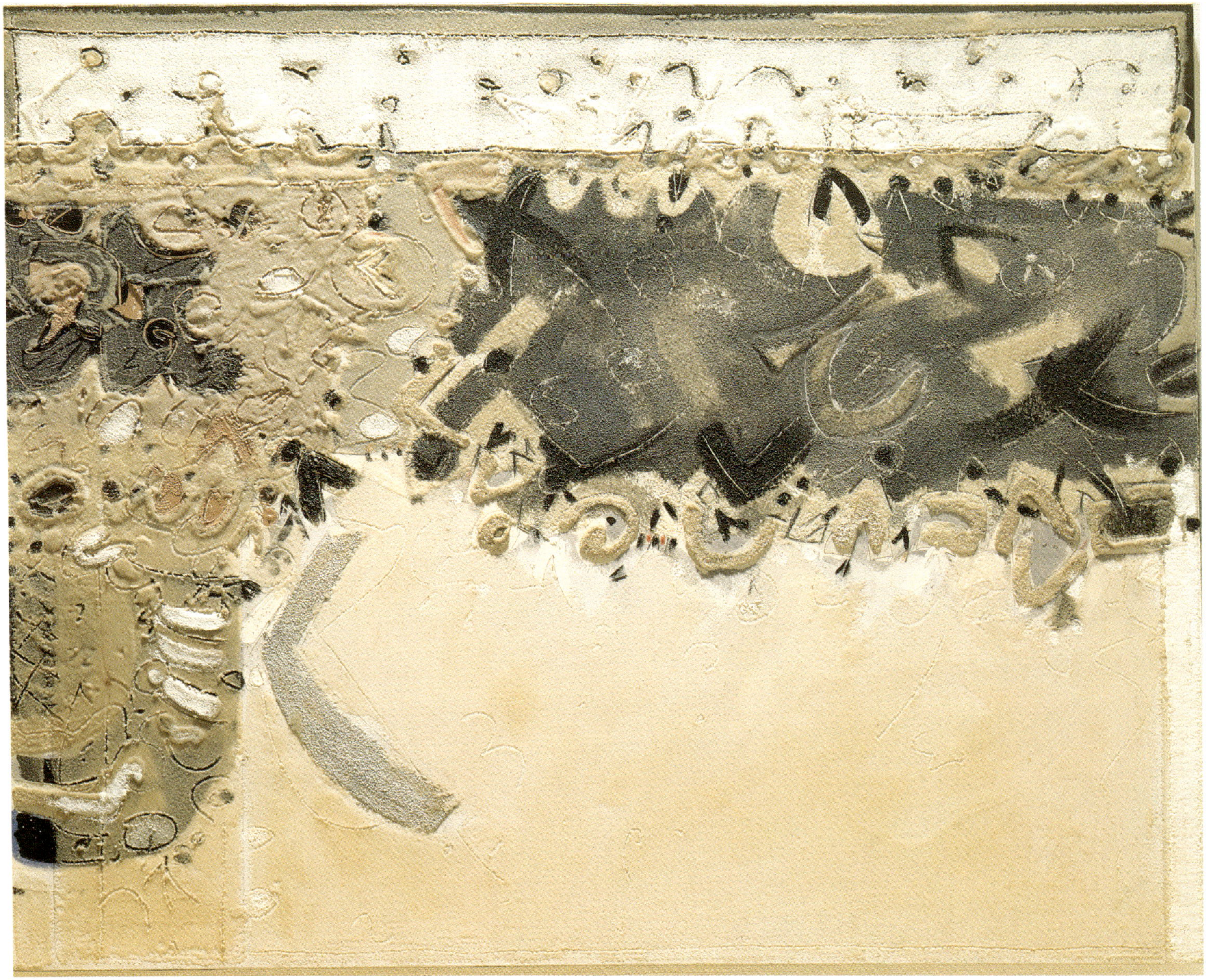

Eric Atkinson
Writing on stone park
1984
42 x 54 in.
acrylic and sand on canvas
collection: International Ocelot
Collection, Calgary, Alberta

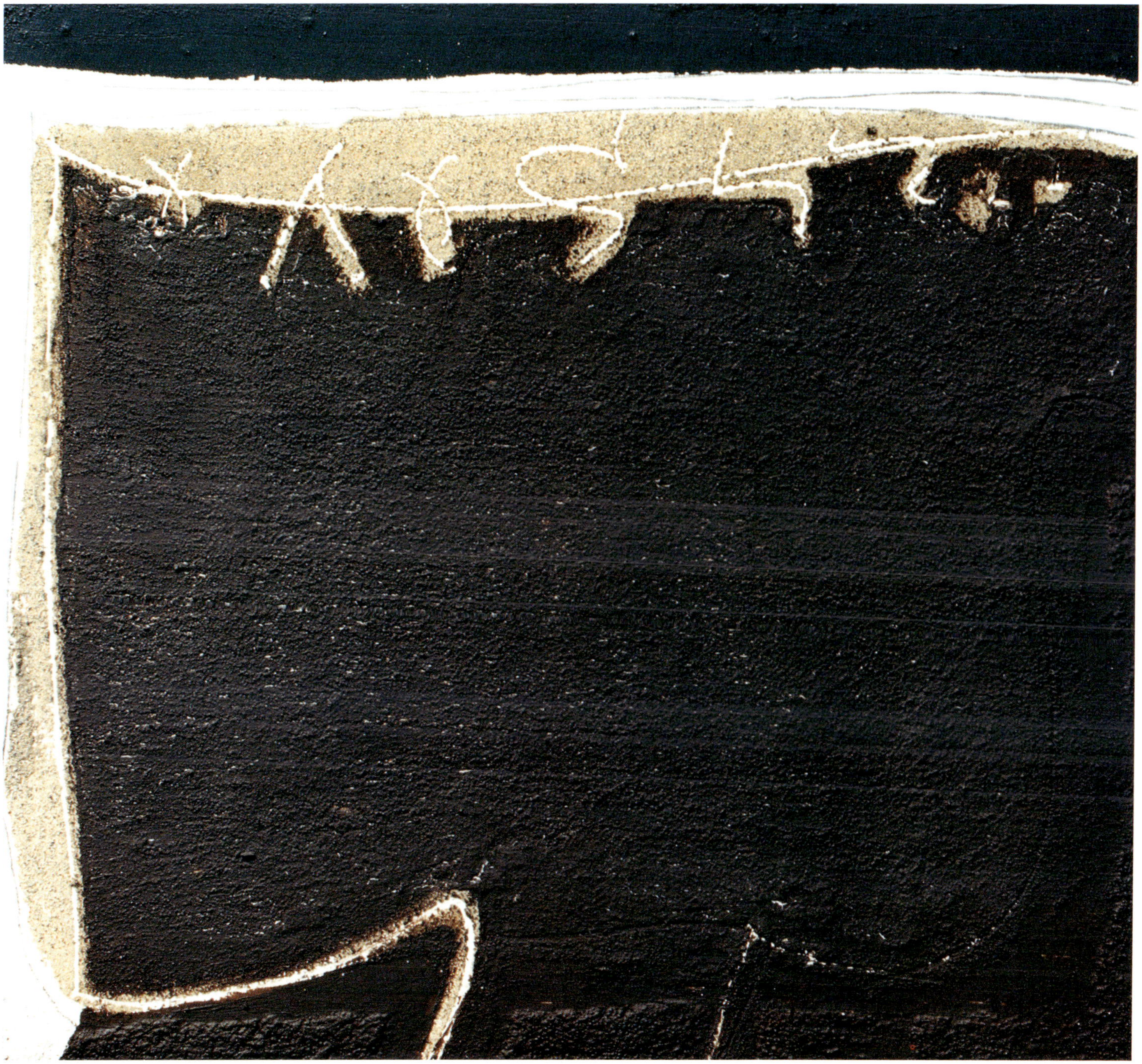

Eric Atkinson
Landmarks
1988
21 x 24 in.
acrylic and sand on board
collection: Mr & Mrs Gino Lorcini,
Greensville, Ontario

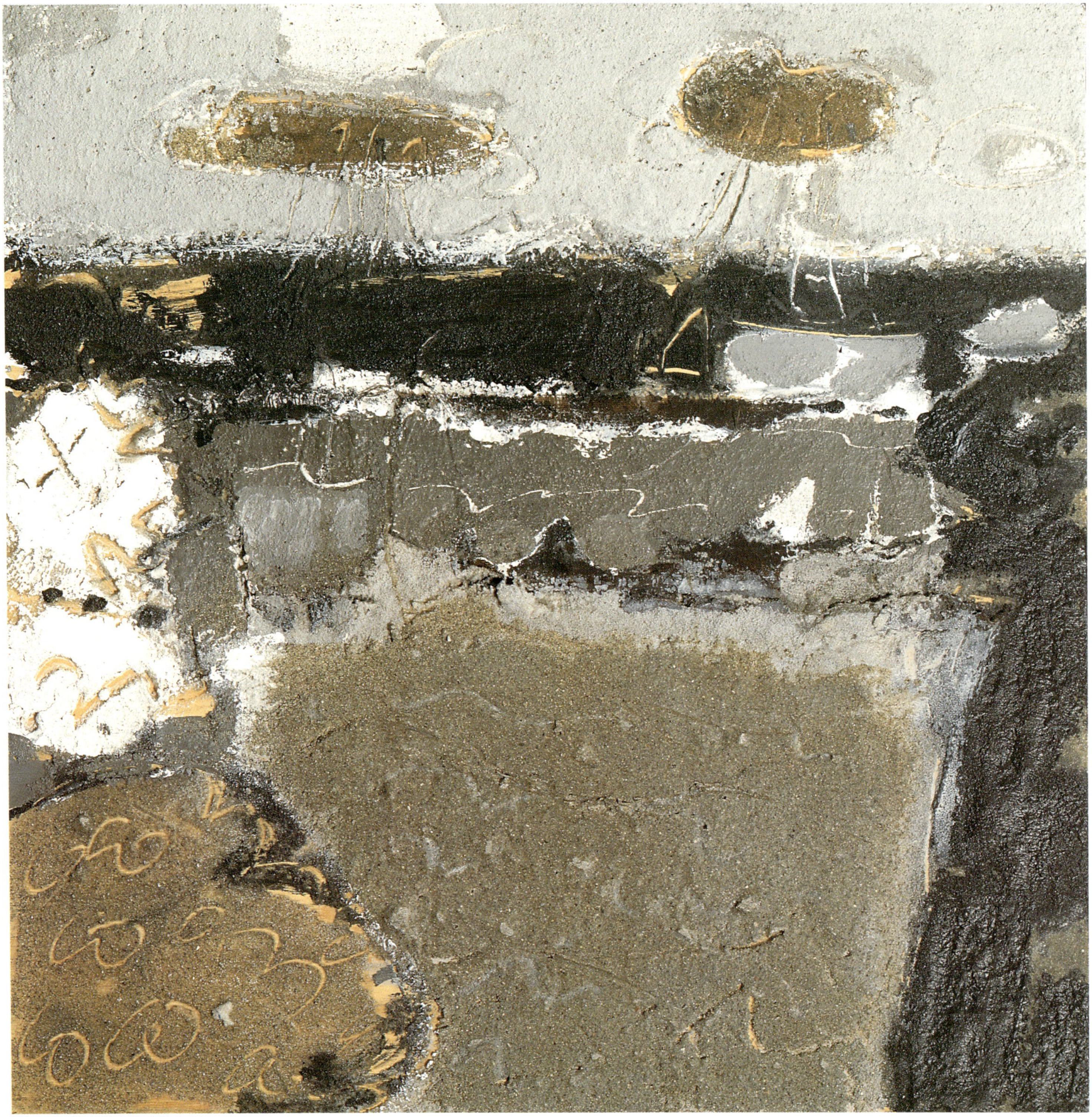

Eric Atkinson
Lake Huron, Ontario
1992, 16 x 16 in., acrylic and sand on board
collection: Mr & Mrs Ian Tripp, London, Ontario

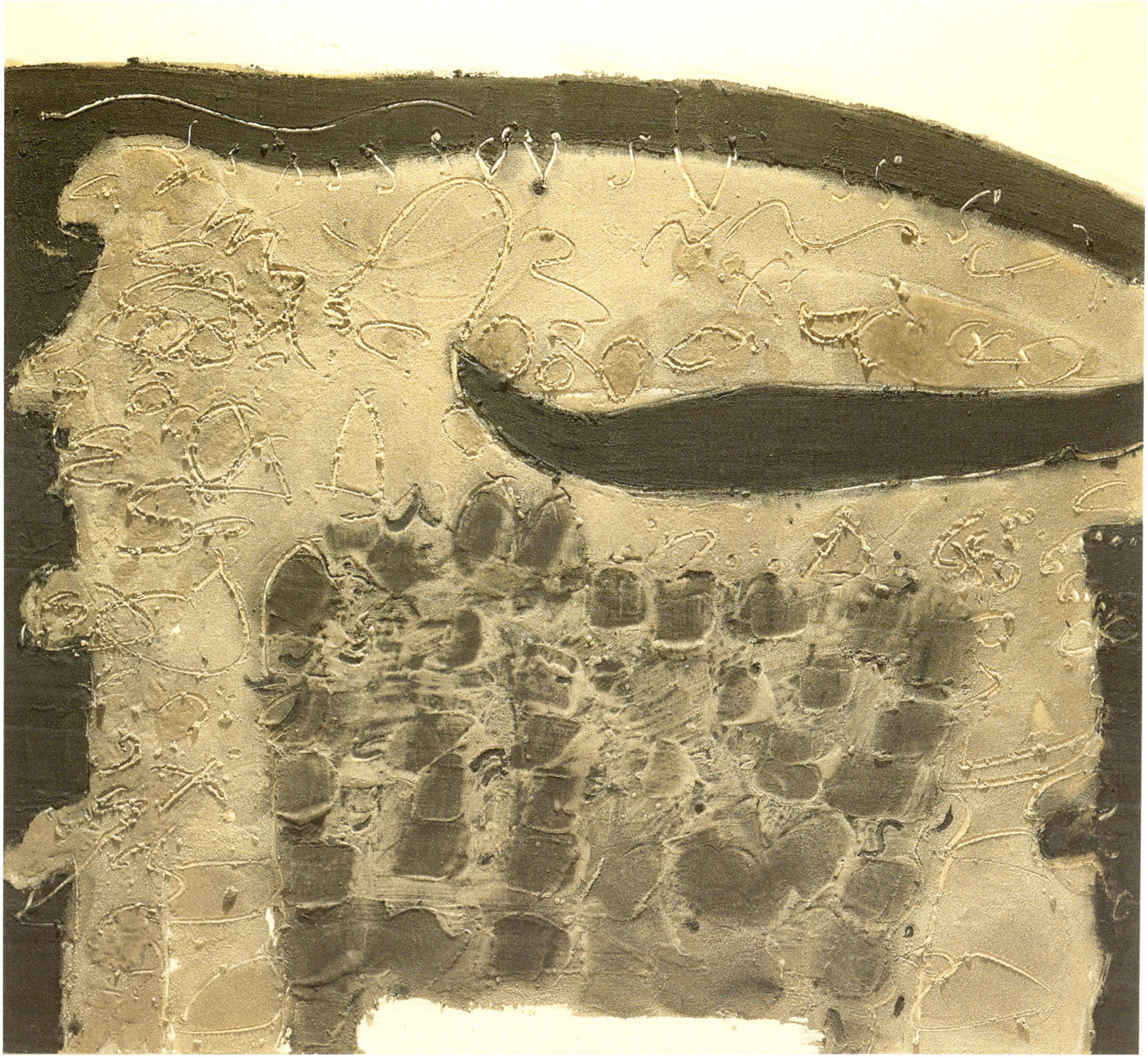

Eric Atkinson
Vikingland
1993
54 x 60 in.
acrylic and sand on canvas
collection of the artist

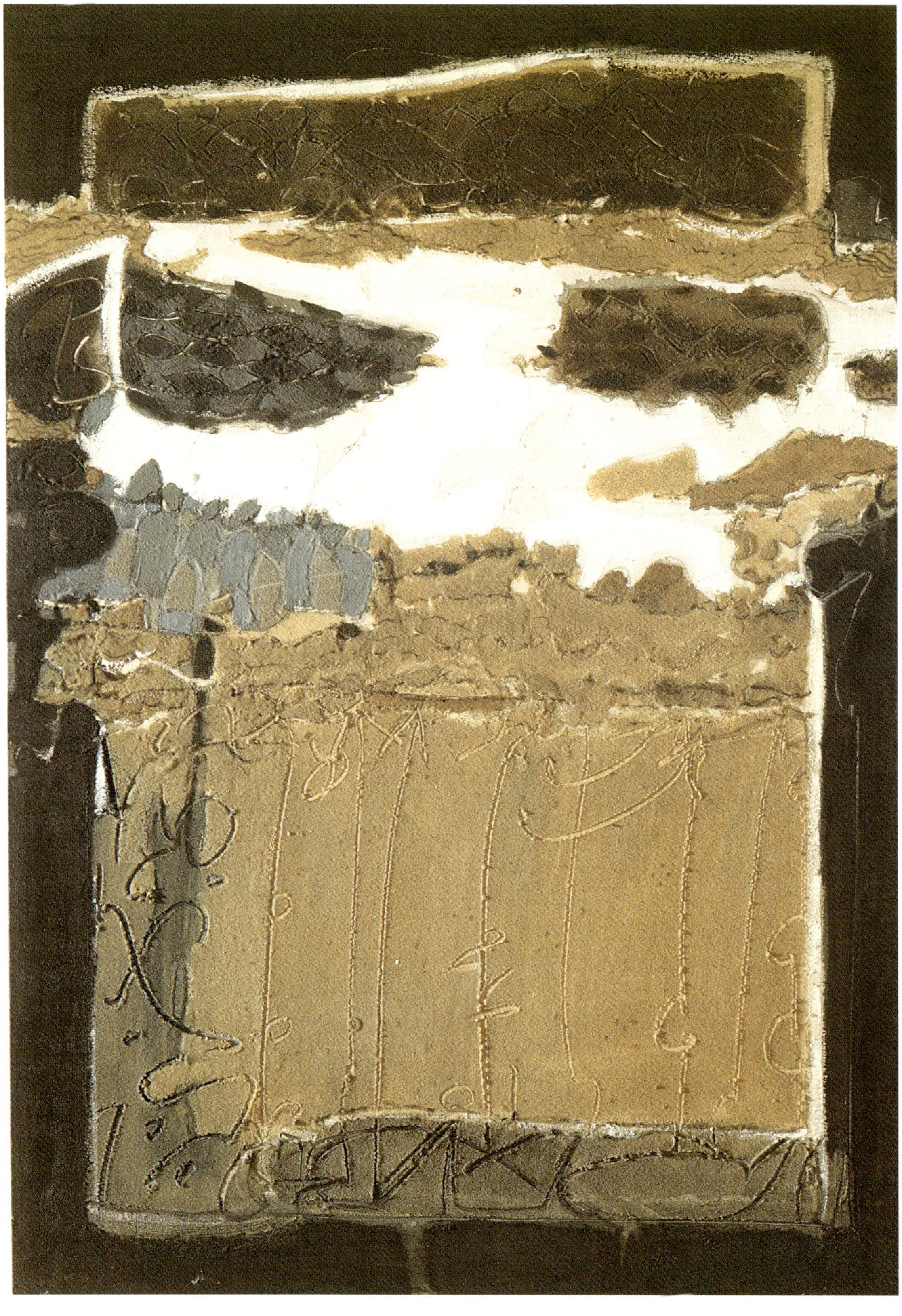

Eric Atkinson
Songlines II
1992
50 x 36 in.
acrylic and sand on canvas
collection: Mr & Mrs Ian Tripp,
London, Ontario

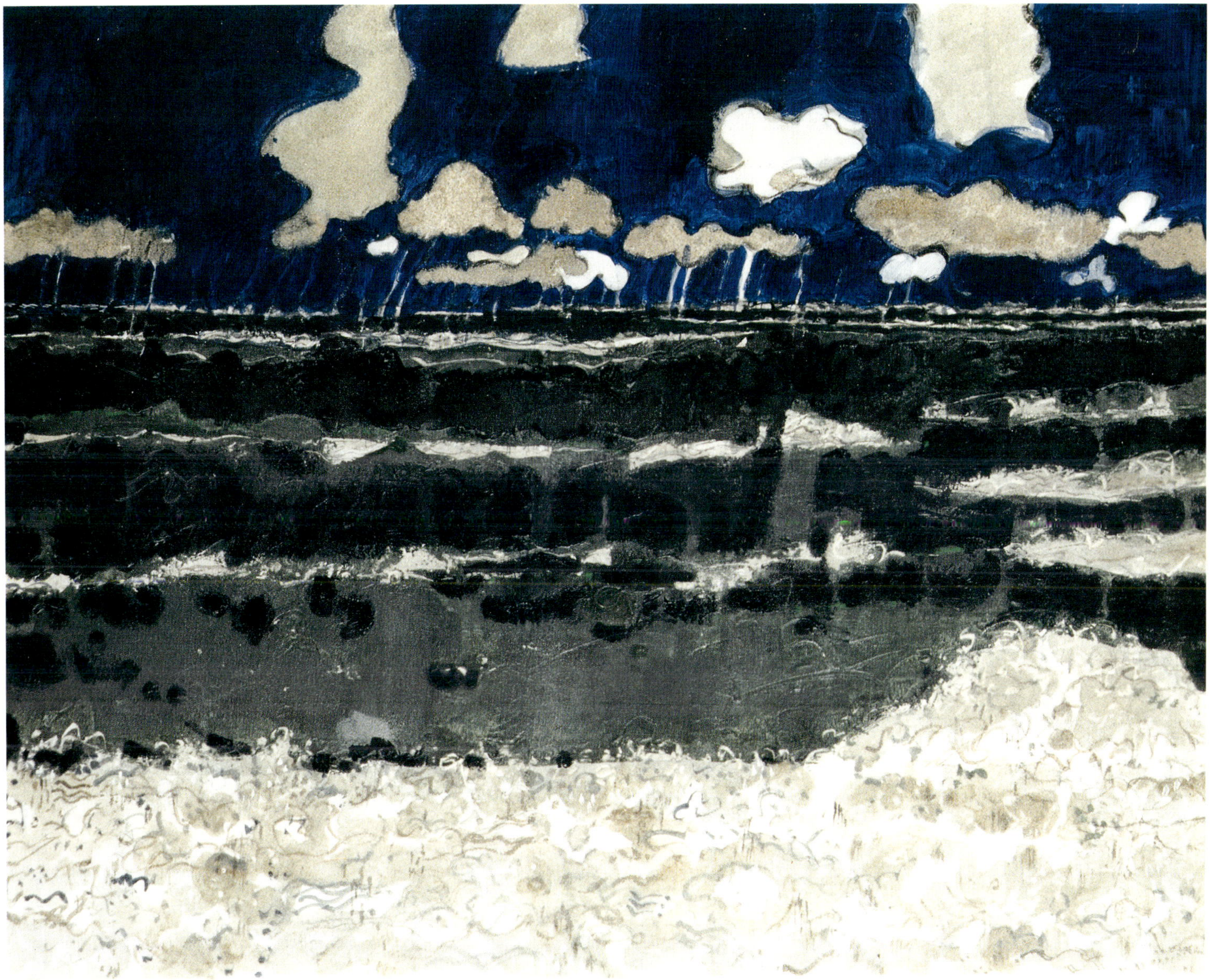

Eric Atkinson
Whipping Storm, Huron
1998
28 x 36 in.
acrylic and sand on canvas
collection: Thielsen Galleries,
London, Ontario

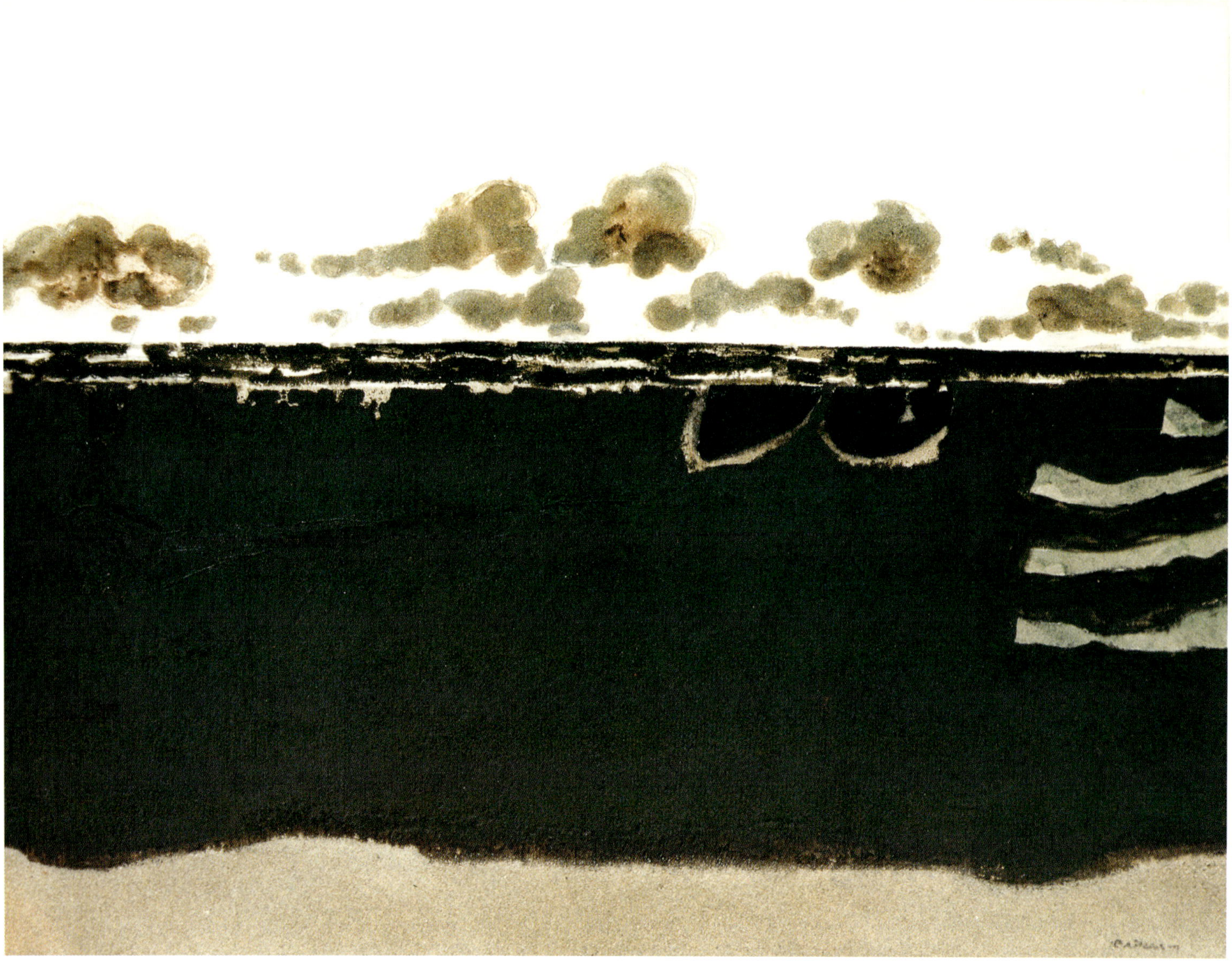

Eric Atkinson
Dawn, Huron
1998
28 x 36 in.
acrylic and sand on canvas
collection: Thielsen Galleries,
London, Ontario

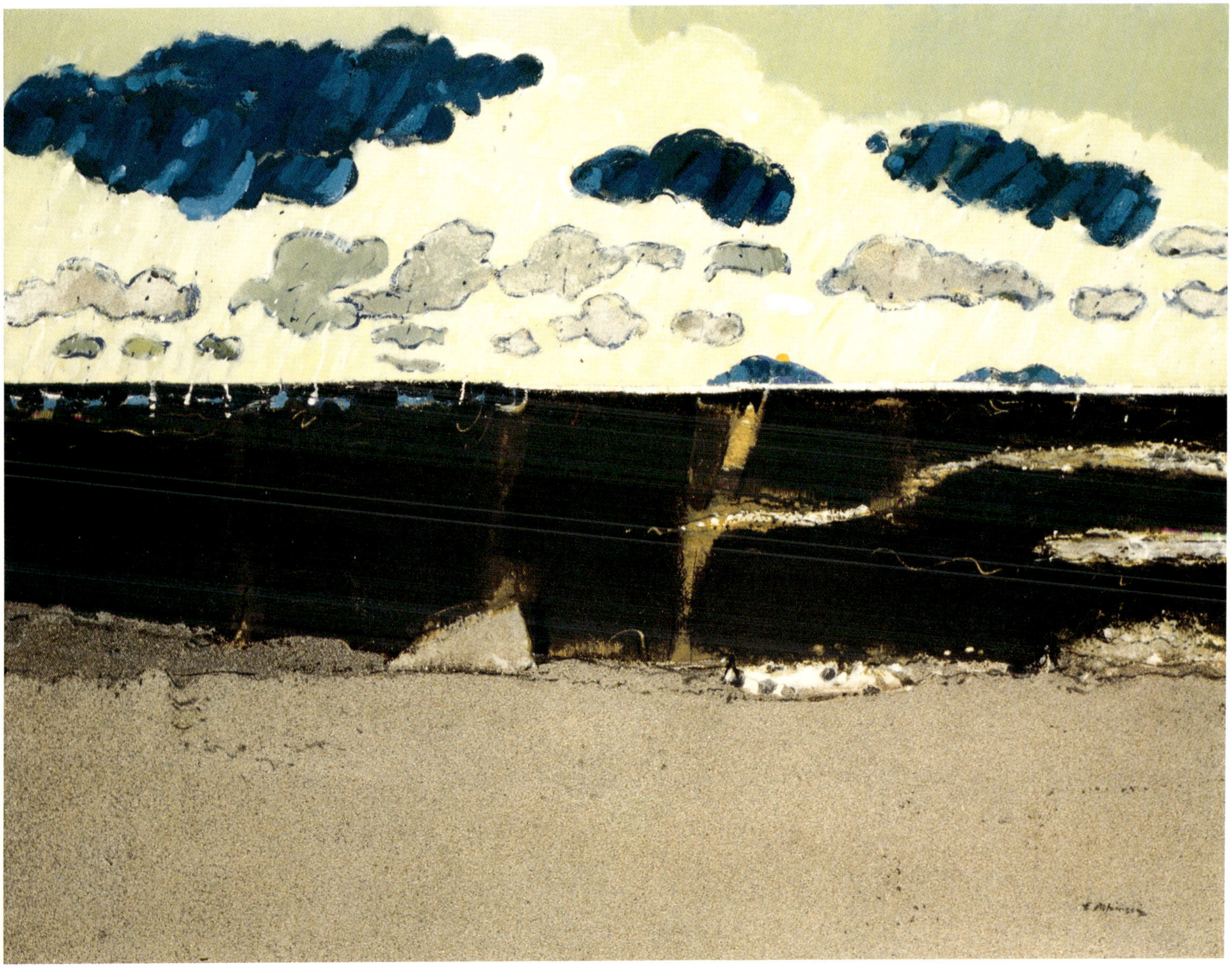

Eric Atkinson
Sunrise, Huron
1998
28 x 36 in.
acrylic and sand on canvas
collection: Thielsen Galleries,
London, Ontario

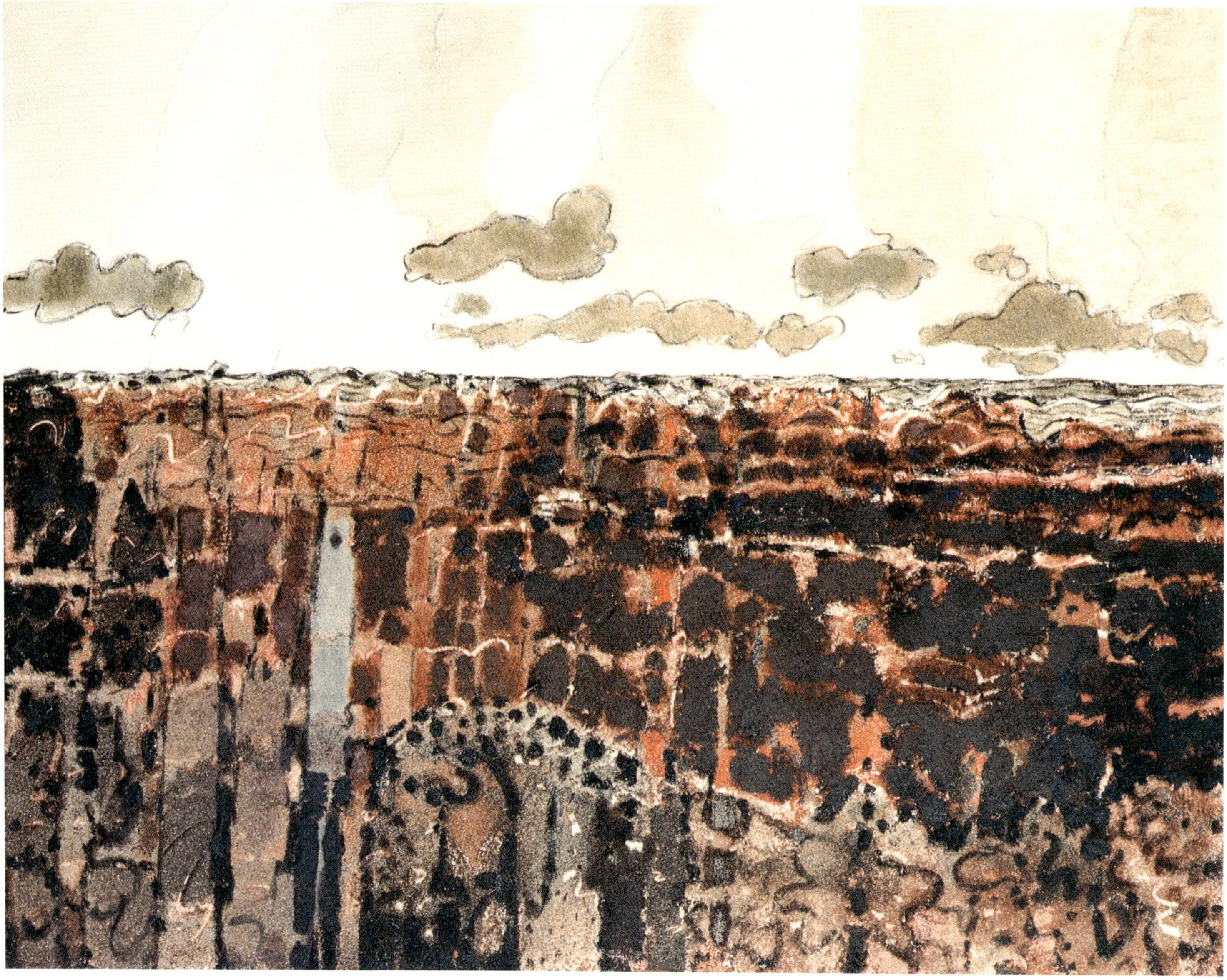

Eric Atkinson
Wind and Rock, Huron
1998
28 x 36 in.
acrylic and sand on canvas
collection: Wallace Gallery, Calgary, Alberta

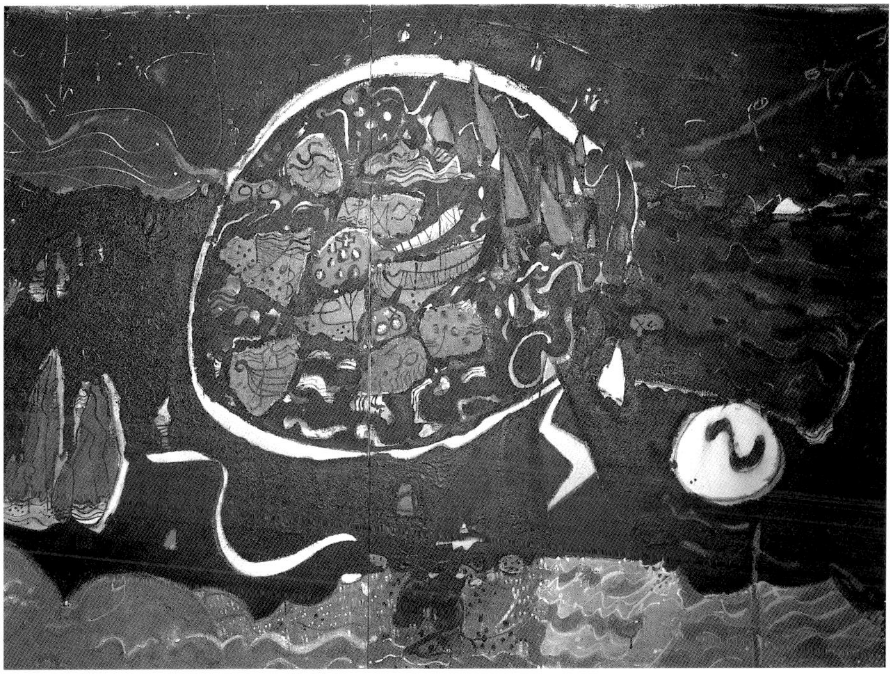

Detail from Eric Atkinson
Floating to Valhalla
1994
80 x 168 in.
acrylic and sand on canvas
collection of the artist

sonal journeys. The irony of these paintings is, of course, that they are presented, not as explanations, but as enigmas waiting for our individual interpretations. By asking questions, Ricky asks us to find answers within ourselves; for here we are, in the midst of our culture of mass communications, e-mails, faxes, webs, and whatnot, which carry us instantly to every corner of time and space – while at the same time we are confronted by powerful and perennial landscapes, telling us about the endless rhythms of nature, about time outside time.

Five years ago Ricky made a vast triptych, 'Floating to Valhalla', rich in poetic allusion. Here are sky and lake dark as winter's night, and a lake-bed rich with fossils and the trails of water-snails and urchins. In the lake is a naked man. Is he floating, or is he submerged, drowned, suspended in the water's pressure? Is he our contemporary? Or is he from some old and mysterious culture, like the Wiltshire man, or from the Lascaux caves, or from the almost contemporary but vanished Bushpeople from the South African karroo? Near him as he floats or drowns is an incomplete circle, open on one side. Is it an ovum – or a womb – abounding in the beginnings of life yet to be born? Or is it the mounded settlement of a past civilisation? Or is it a fractured limestone, filled with fossils? Fragments of what? Fossils of what?

To the right of the canvas stand vertical stones, like the stones of Avebury or Stonehenge, or the gravestones of our own forebears in our churchyards and cemeteries – while below in the lake are the sediments of what may be our contemporary world, in the process of being compressed into fossilised rock, possibly to be inherited and wondered about by far-off future generations.

What are the meanings of all of this? They are the artefacts of interior landscapes, his and ours. They bring to our consciousness the languages and visual poetry of landscapes we all share. But parallel with these paintings is Ricky's life-work as an educator, encouraging students to explore their inner selves through the media of art and also through the vehicles of the latest technologies. His paintings remind his students, just as they remind us, of how vulnerable we are to accelerating technological change in a natural universe in which the pace of evolution is for the most part so gradual as to be barely perceptible.

1. Artist's Statement, *Landmarks*, catalogue to a retrospective exhibition of paintings and drawings by Eric Atkinson, London Regional Art Museum, Canada, 1994.

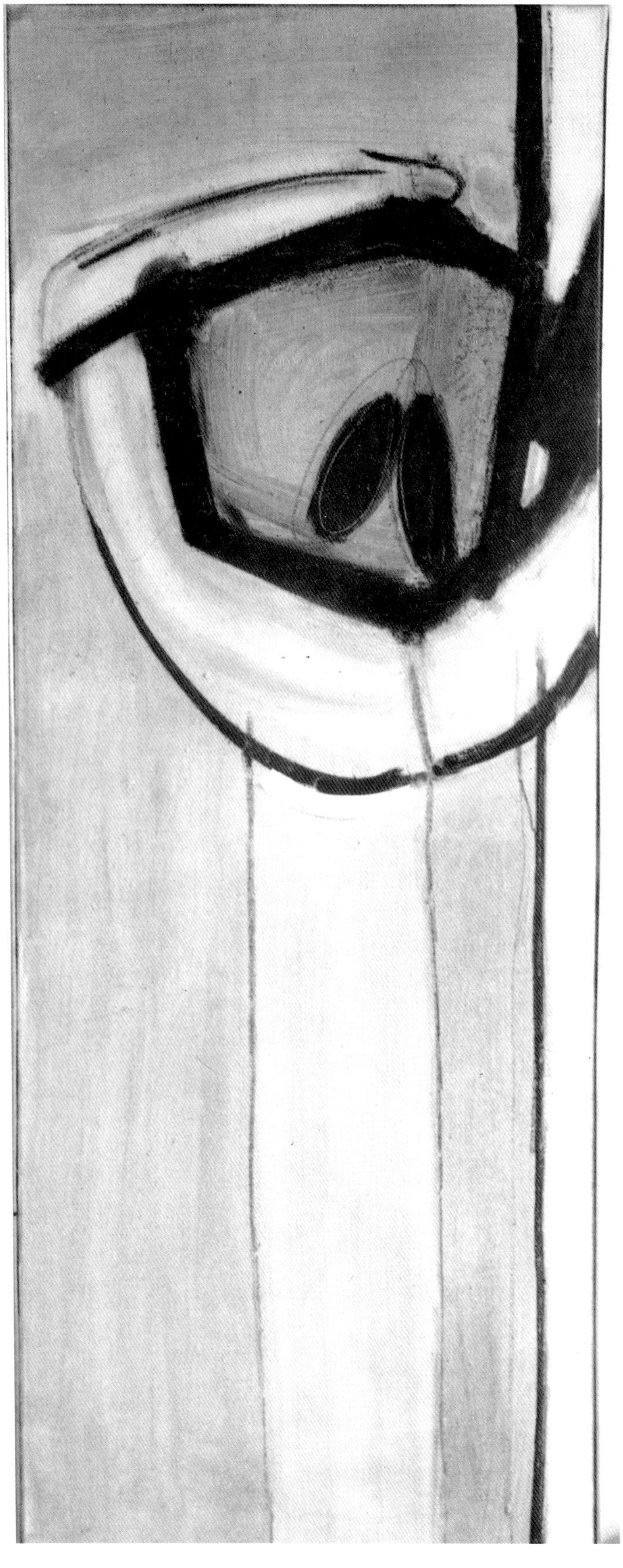

Eric Atkinson
Moonfruit
1961
62 x 25 in.
acrylic on canvas
collection:
Mr & Mrs D. Sleight,
Geddington,UK

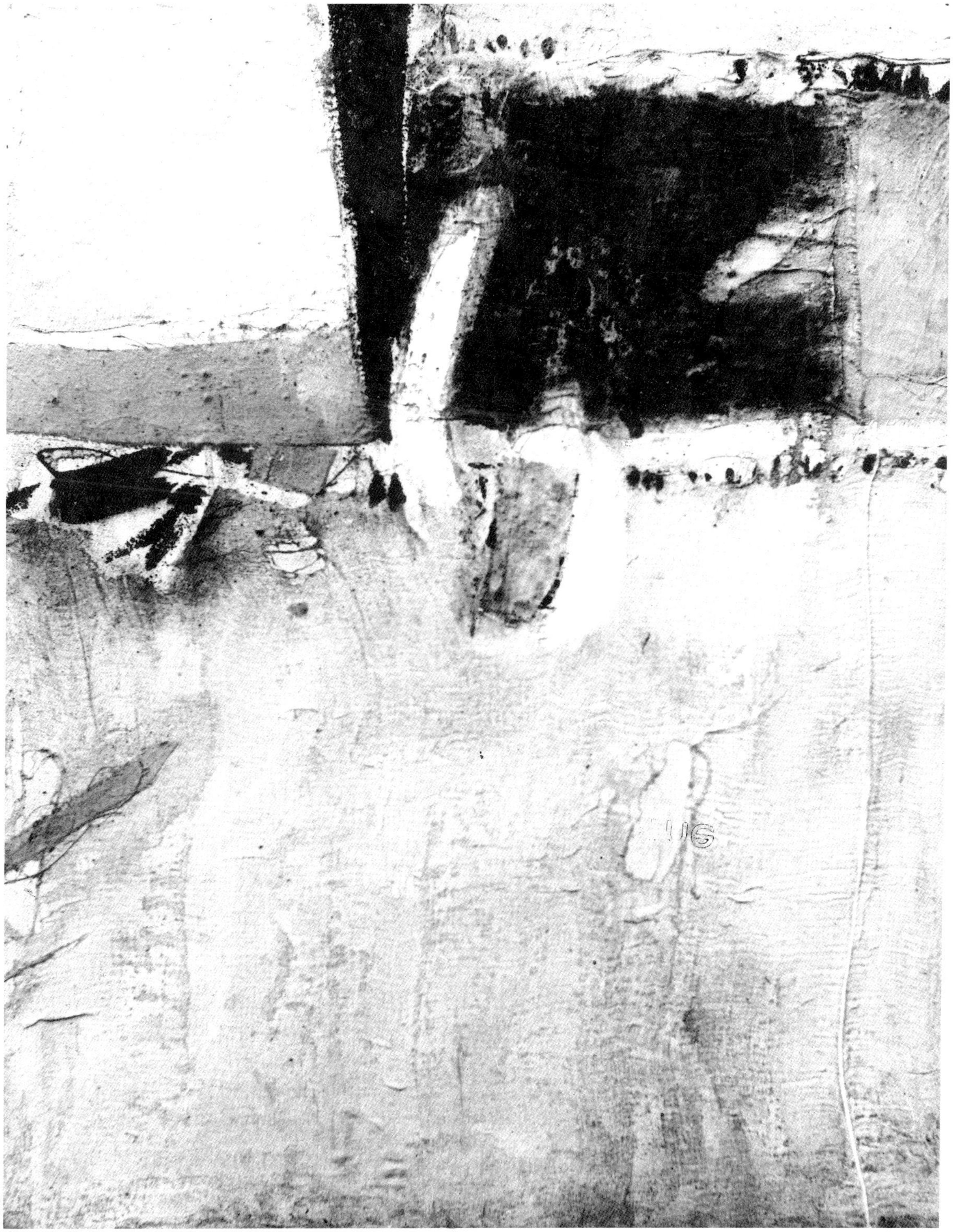

Eric Atkinson
White winter Z
1963
32 x 28 in.
collage, sand on canvas
Private collection

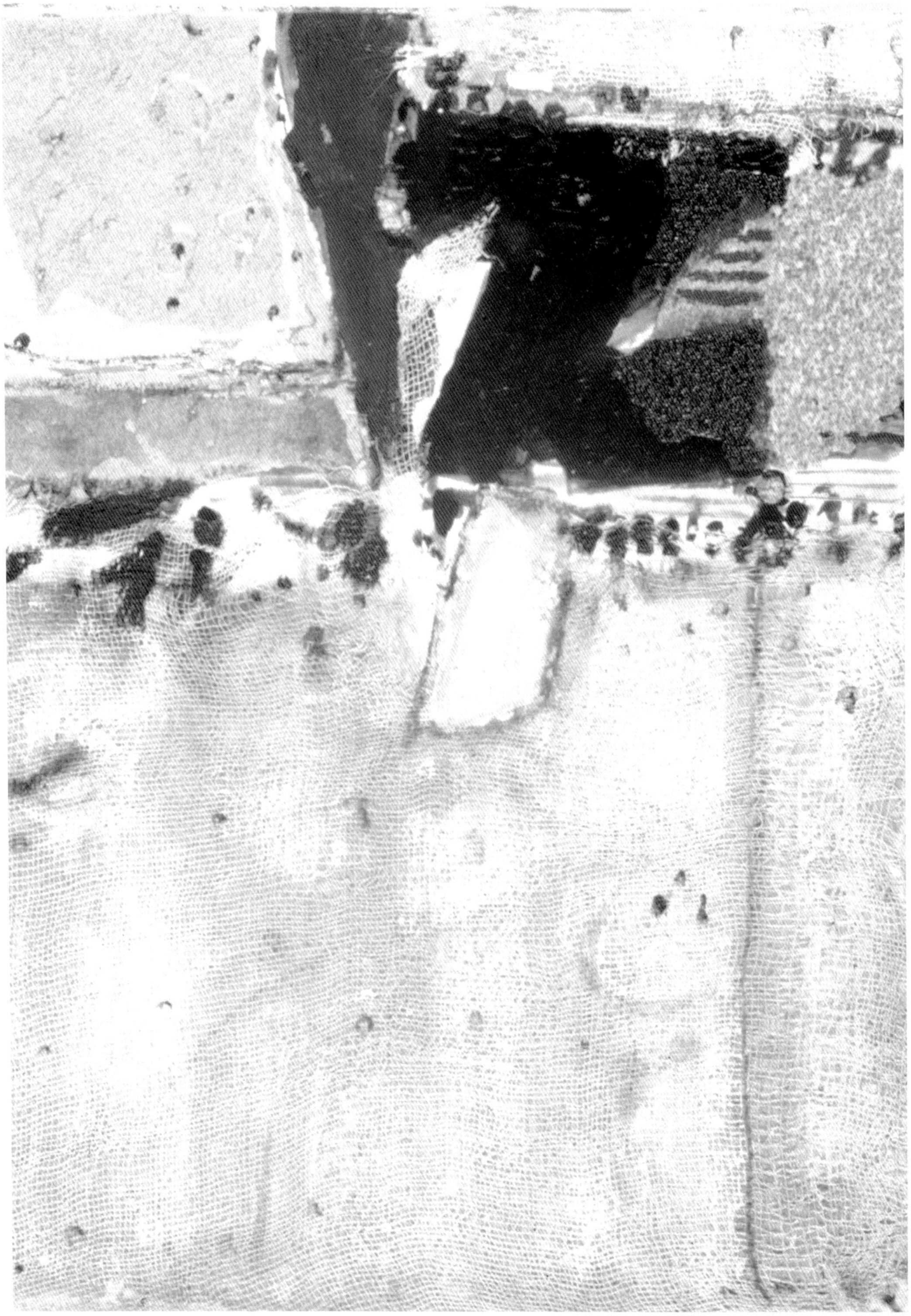

Eric Atkinson
Sketch for Silver Grey
1962
10 x 8 in.
collage
collection: Mr & Mrs
Patrick Thibert, Ontario

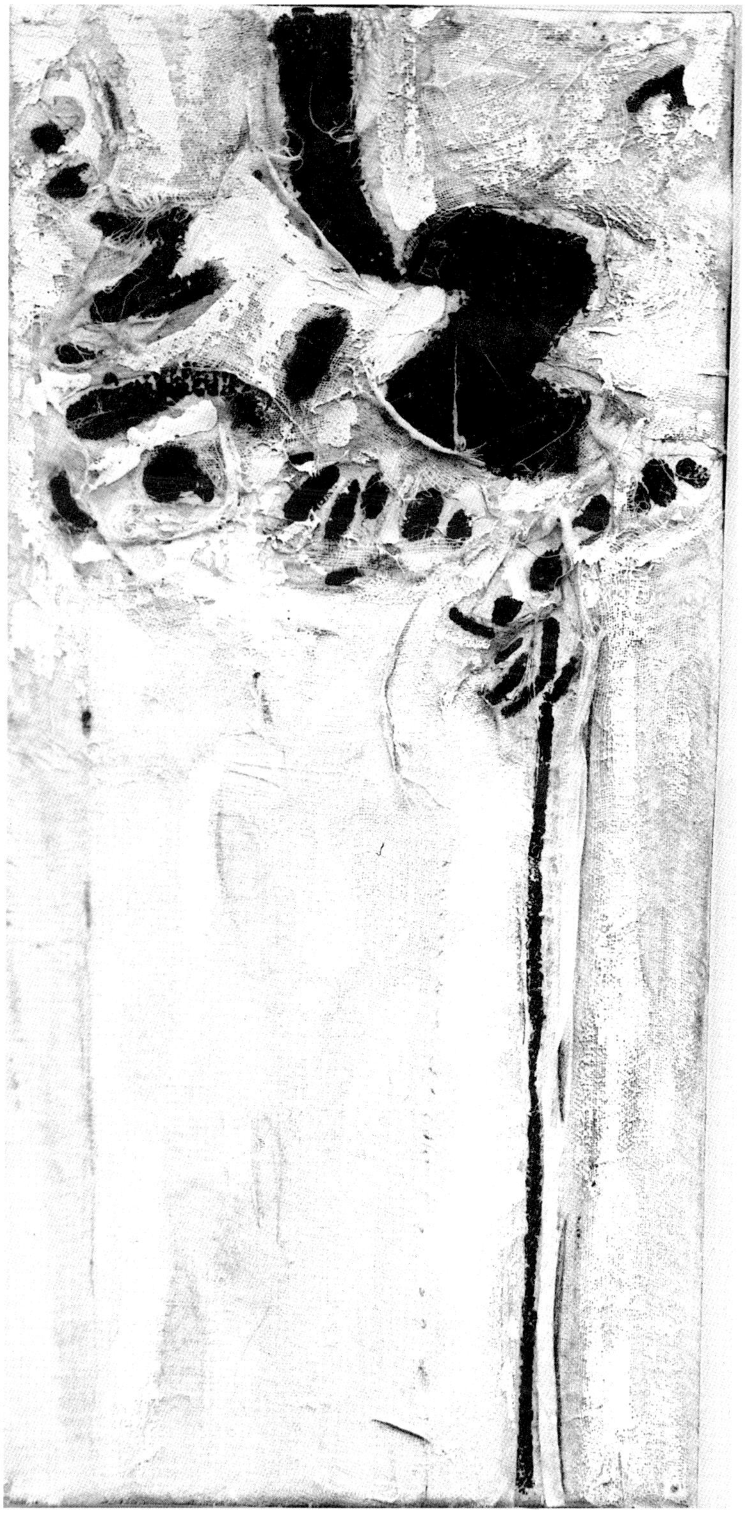

Eric Atkinson
Small Silver Grey
1963
10 x 4 in.
cloth, collage on
canvas
collection: Mr & Mrs P.
Williams, Vancouver

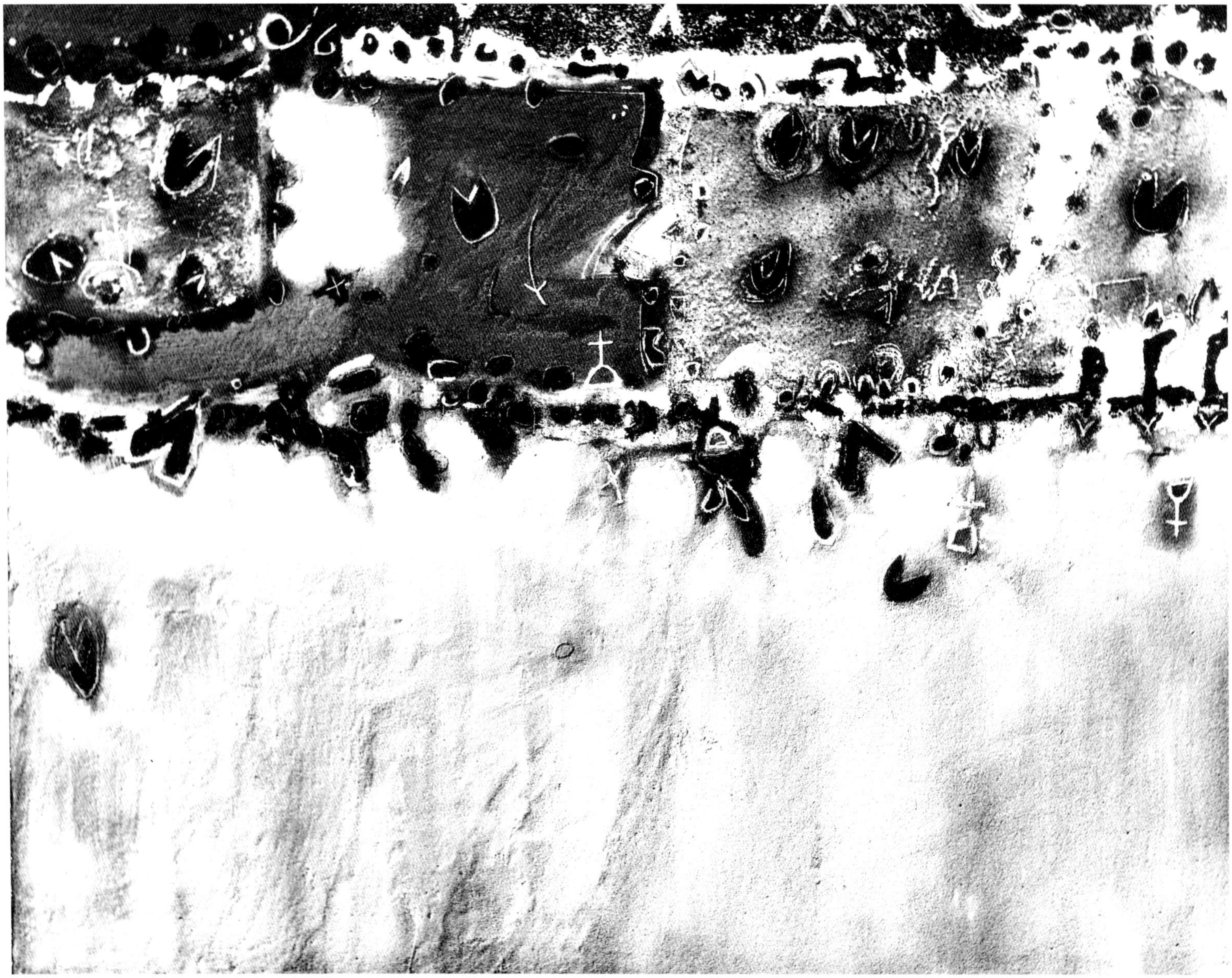

Eric Atkinson
Finistere Coast
1967
28 x 36 in.
acrylic, sand on canvas
collection: Mrs Audrey Burton, Harrogate

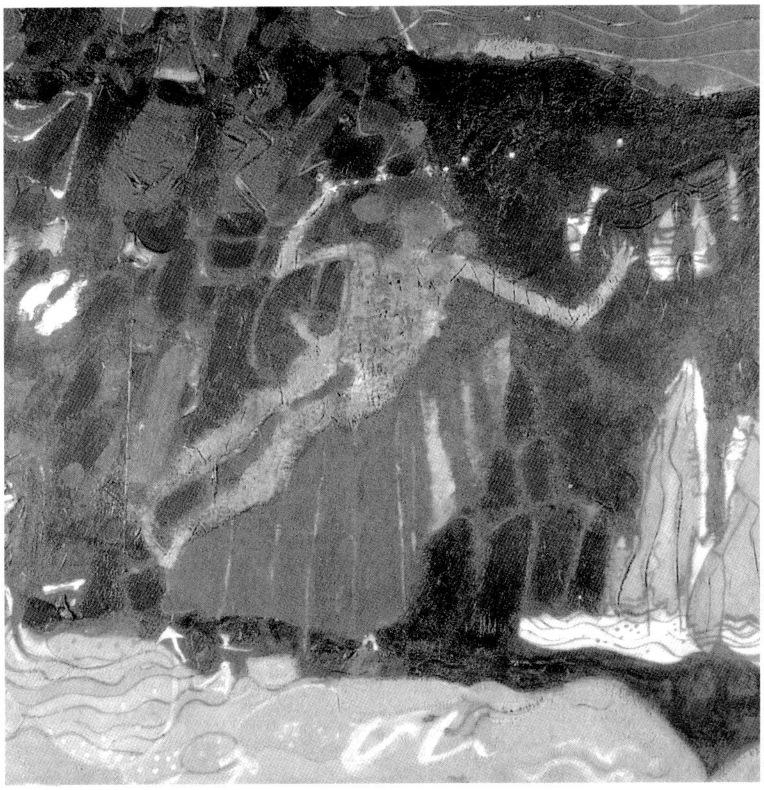

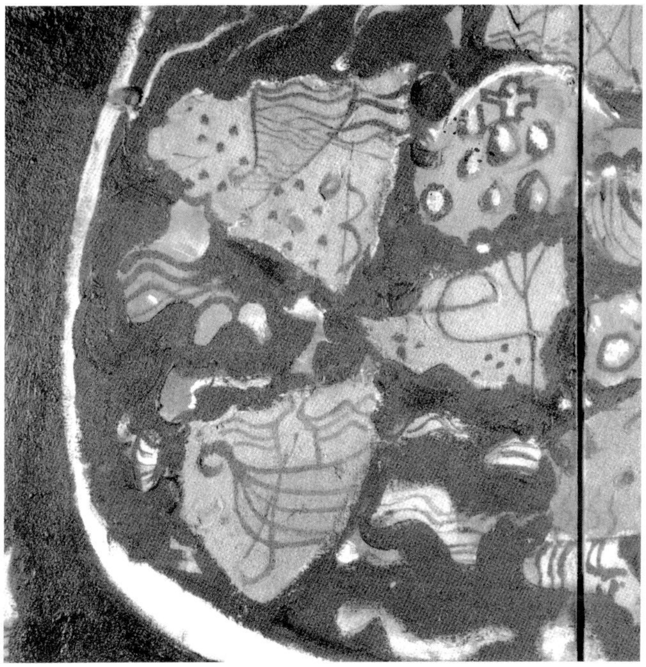

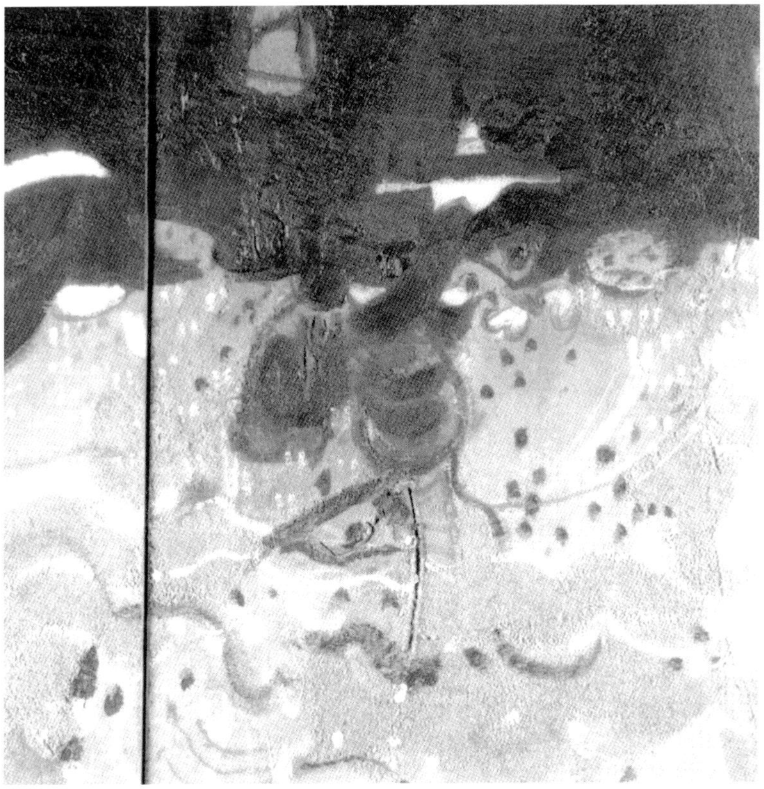

Details from Eric Atkinson
Floating to Valhalla
1994
80 x 168 in.
acrylic and sand on canvas
collection of the artist

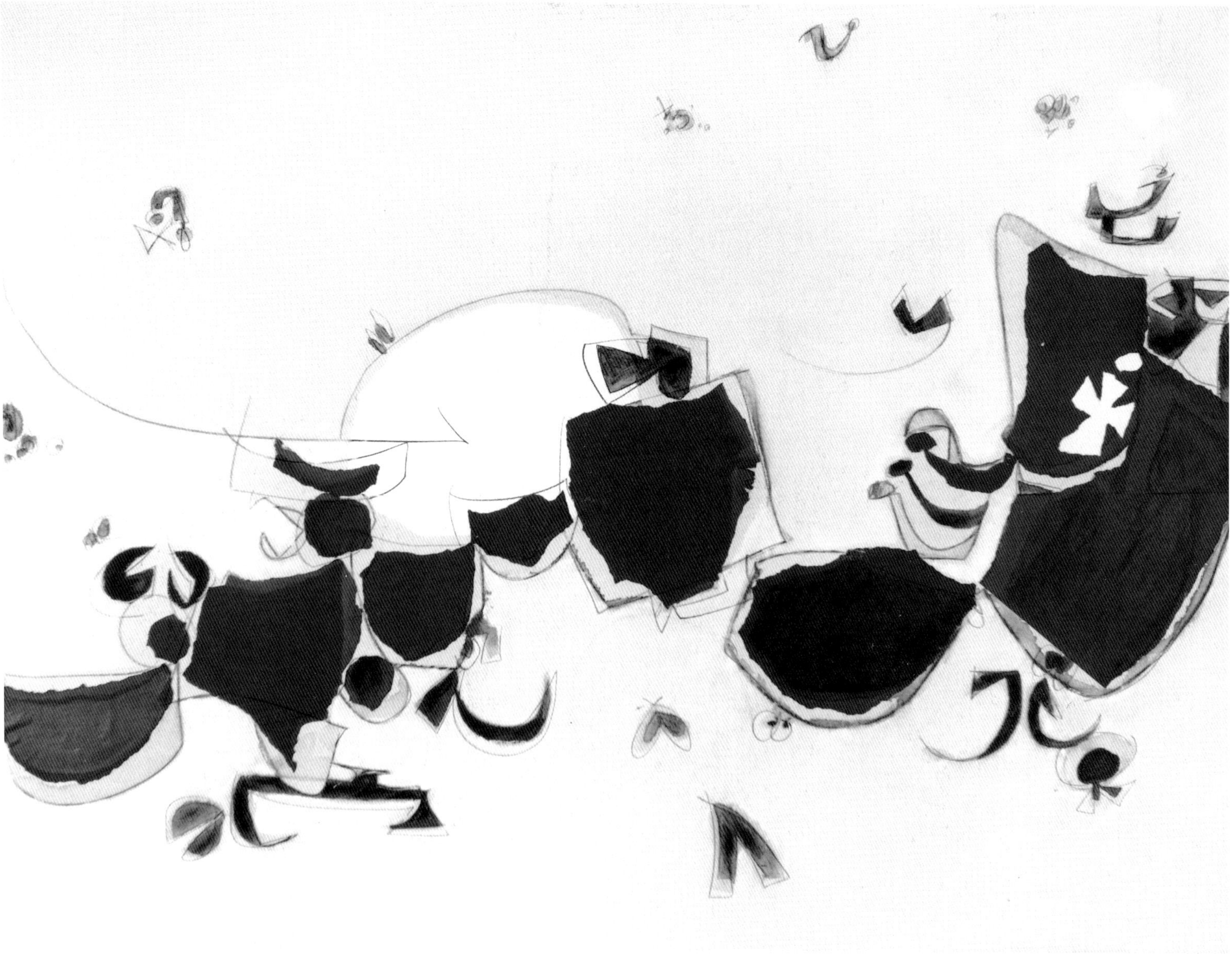

(above) Eric Atkinson, *Synergy Landscape Mexico,* 1978, 42 x 54 in., acrylic and collage
collection: Dr & Mrs Tom Brown, London, Ontario

(facing page) Eric Atkinson, *Floating Violet,* 1979, 54 x 60 in., acrylic and paper collage on canvas
collection: Kelly Mancari, London, Ontario

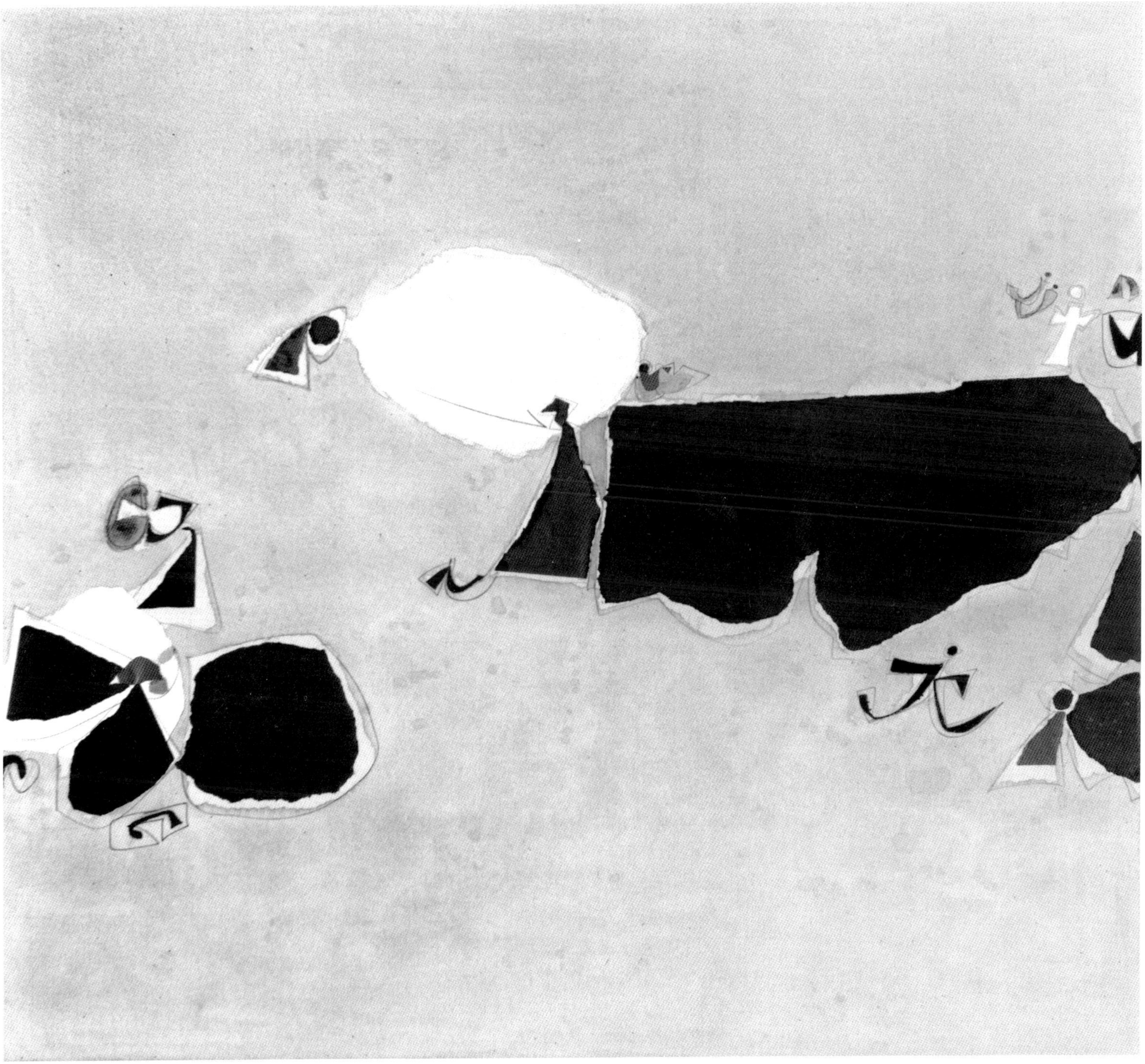

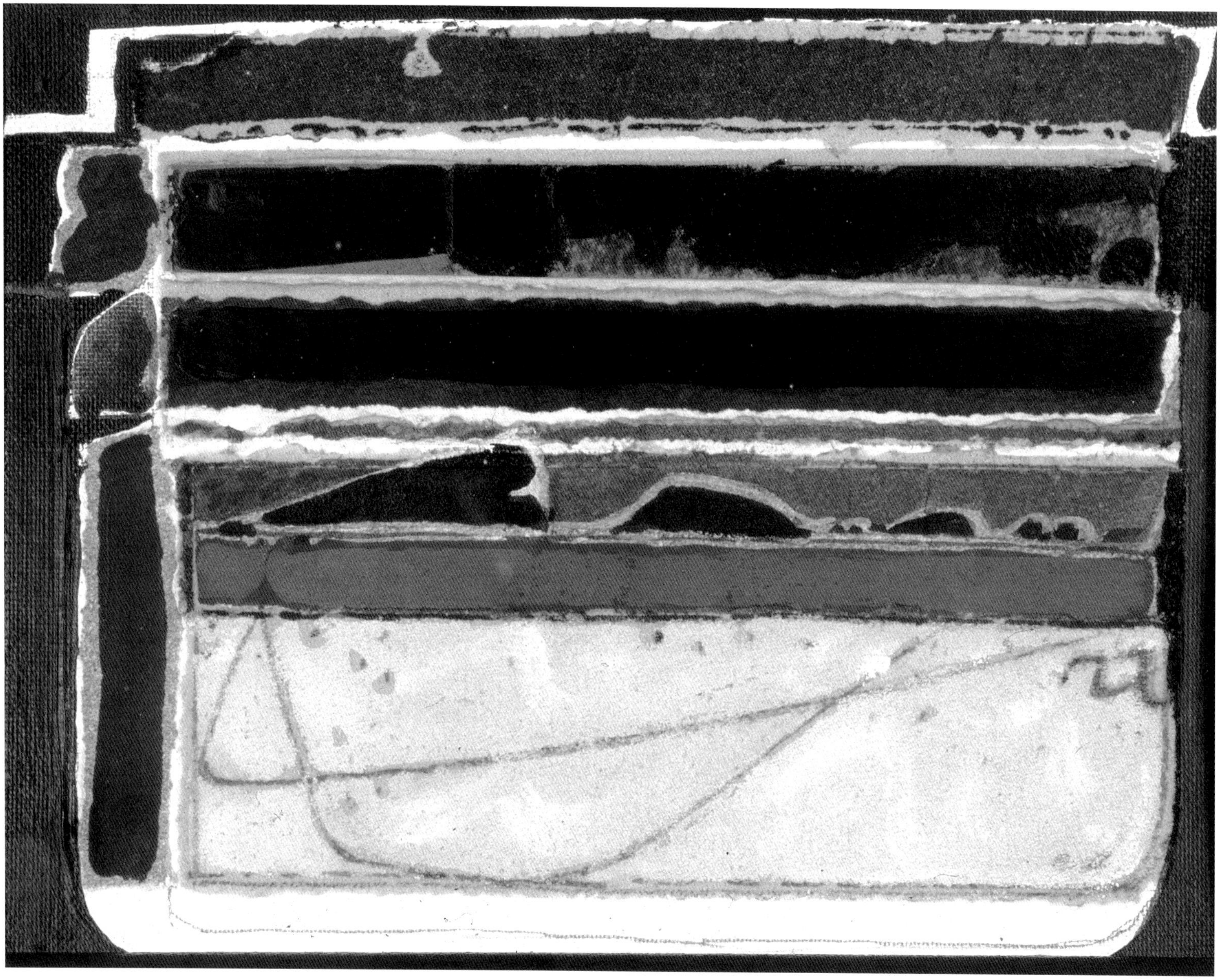

(above) Eric Atkinson, *Huron Series,* 1986, 7 x 9 in., acrylic and collage
collection: David Lewis

(facing page) Eric Atkinson, *Waves & Rainstorm,* 1991, 14 x 16½ in., watercolour, pen, ink, wax acrylic on paper
collection: David Lewis

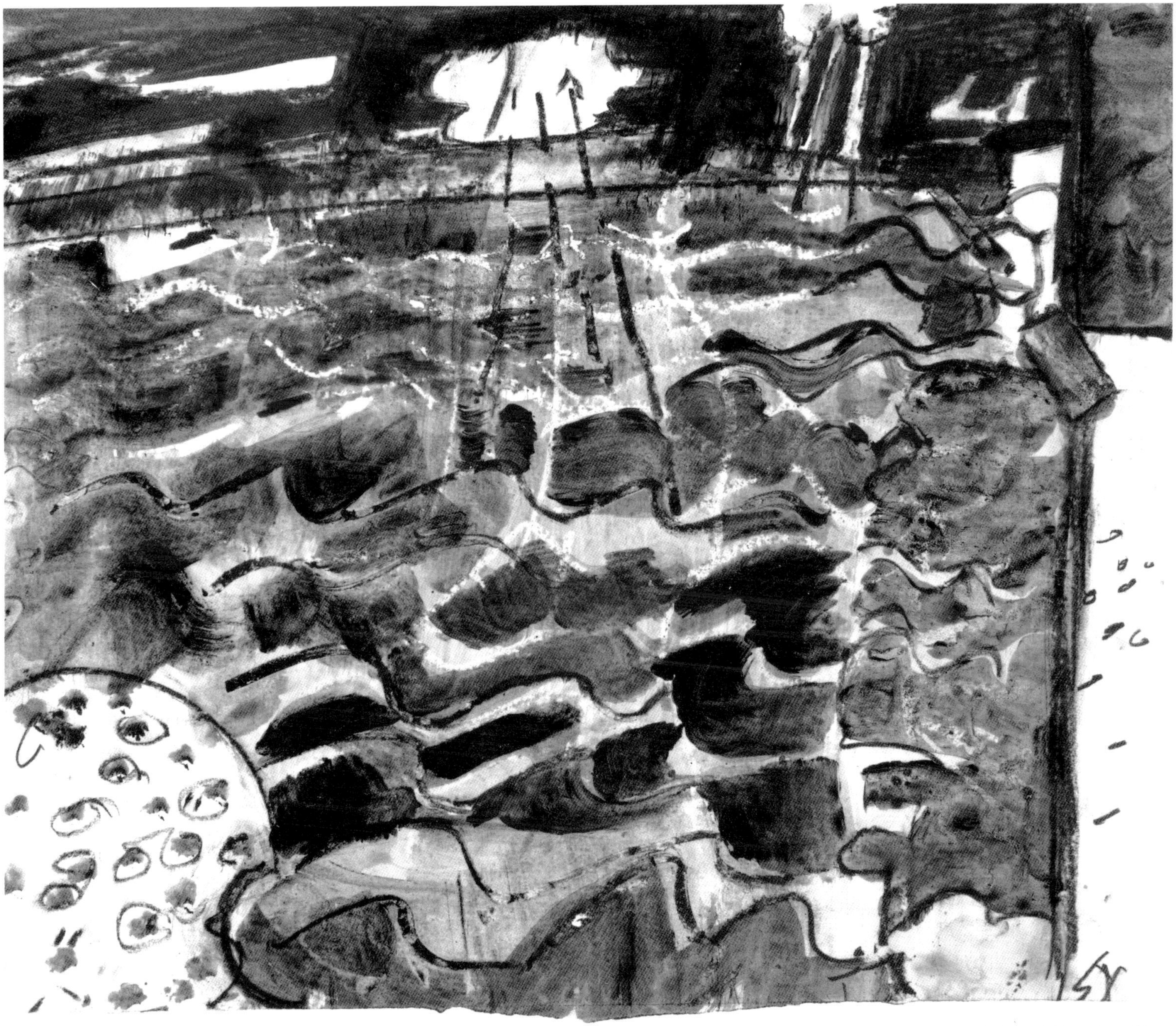

ERIC ATKINSON: BIOGRAPHICAL NOTES

1928 Born, Hartlepool, County Durham, England
1935 Watched a display of Aurora-Borealis: luminous streamers on the northern horizon.
At Hartlepool Headland: introduced (with father) to the dramatist George Bernard Shaw
1938 Visited the Empire Exhibition at Bellahouston Park, Glasgow, and saw display of modern architecture
1941 Coventry medieval city and cathedral badly damaged by German Luftwaffe: visiting relatives there at the time
1942 Recruited as Civil Defence Messenger, Hartlepool
1943 Hartlepool College of Art
1946 Ambleside, Lake District: meeting with Kurt Schwitters
1947–49 National Service
1950–55 Royal Academy Schools: London, England.
Married Muriel Ross, 1954, in Edinburgh, Scotland
1955 Elected member of New English Art Club
1956 David Lewis, first lecture: Leeds City Art Gallery
Lecturer, Leeds College of Art, Yorkshire
1963–69 Head of Fine Art Department, Leeds College of Art
1969 Moved to Canada
1970 Chairman, Fine Art: Fanshawe College, London, Ontario
1972–82 Dean, Faculty of Applied Arts, Fanshawe College
1973 American Endowment for the Arts, visiting professor, University of Texas; judge, San Antonio Biennale Exhibition; visited Mexico
1978 Elected Member Royal Canadian Academy
1982–94 Professor, Fine Art Department, Fanshawe College.
1994 Retired from teaching.

PUBLICATIONS AND FILMS

1964 'Alfred Wallis, Cornish Primitive Painter', *Accent Magazine*, Leeds: reprinted in Tate Gallery Exhibition catalogue, *Leeds Revived*, 1968
1970 'Art Education', *Mash Magazine*, Chicago Art Institute
1982 'Forum: Imaginative Use of Space', *TKO Magazine*, London, Ontario
1986 'Visual Education on the Back Burner', *Bulletin Magazine*, Canadian Community Colleges, Toronto
Artist's Proof, Eric Atkinson and Art Education, 30 min. film narrated by Jack Pollock, Toronto, for Rogers Cable Television
Paintings featured in Pan-Canadian production *The Amateur* with John Savage and Christopher Plummer, MGM Films
1991 Drawing featured in the American-Japanese publication of the works of American potter Warren MacKenzie
1994 Video, *Landmarks* exhibition, London Regional Art and Historical Museums, Rogers Cable Television
1997 Some notes on the *John H. Moore Collection of European Art*, curated by Eric Atkinson, London Regional Art and Historical Museums
1998 *Recollections*, Hartlepool Art Gallery, England.
Exhibition on Internet: Website, Owton-Rossmere Partnership, UK, 30 mins.

SELECTED SOLO EXHIBITIONS

1954 Redfern Gallery, London, England
1956 Redfern Gallery, London, England
1960 Redfern Gallery, London, England
The City Art Gallery, Wakefield, Yorkshire
Howard Roberts Gallery, Cardiff, Wales
1961 Municipal Art Gallery, Middlesbrough, Yorkshire
1963 Zwemmer Gallery, London, England
Royal Oak Gallery, Higher Bebington, Cheshire, England
1964 Midland Group Gallery, Nottingham, England Lane Gallery, Bradford, Yorkshire
Queens Square Gallery, Leeds, Yorkshire
1965 Molton Gallery, London, England
1969 Queens Square Gallery, Leeds, Yorkshire
Galerie Rottger, Lunen, Germany
Galerie Heid, Marberg, Germany
1970 Nancy Poole Gallery, London, Ontario
1972 London Regional Art Gallery, London, Ontario
1973 Morse Capponi Gallery, Detroit, Michigan
1974 Thielsen Galleries Ltd, London, Ontario
1975 *Mexican Series*, Park Square Gallery, Leeds, Yorkshire
1977 McIntosh Gallery, University of Western Ontario, London, Ontario
1978 The Pollock Gallery Ltd, Toronto, Ontario
1979 Trajectory Gallery, London, Ontario
Pollock Gallery Ltd, Toronto, Ontario
1980 Mendel Art Gallery, Saskatoon, Saskatchewan
University of Wisconsin, Kenosha, Wisconsin
1981 Pollock Gallery Ltd, Toronto, Ontario
Franz Bader Gallery, Washington, DC
1982 Barbara Fiedler Gallery, Washington, DC
Zenith Gallery, Pittsburgh, Pennsylvania
1983 McIntosh Gallery, University of Western Ontario, London, Ontario
Woodstock Art Gallery, Woodstock, Ontario
1987 The Concept Gallery, Pittsburgh, Pennsylvania
1989 Thielsen Galleries Ltd, London, Ontario
1994 *eric atkinson landmarks* (catalogue), London Regional Art and Historical Museums, London, Ontario
1997 *Scottish Journey*, Thielsen Galleries Inc., London, Ontario

SELECTED GROUP EXHIBITIONS

1952 Irving Galleries, London, England
Leicester Galleries, London, England
Tooth Gallery, London, England
1953 *Artists Under 30*, RBA Galleries, London, England
Annual Contemporary Exhibition, Wildenstein Gallery, London, England
Artist's House, Manette Street, London, England
Figures in Their Setting, Contemporary Art Society Exhibition, Tate Gallery, London, England
1954 London Group Exhibition, New Burlington Galleries, London, England
Contemporary Art Society Collection, Tate Gallery, London, England
Royal Academy Summer Exhibition, London, England
1958 Austin Hayes Gallery, York, England
British Painting, Whitechapel Art Gallery, London, England
Parkinson Gallery, Leeds University, Leeds, Yorkshire
1959 St John's College, York University, York, England
John Moore's Liverpool Exhibition No. 2, Walker Art Gallery, Liverpool, England
Yorkshire Artists Exhibition, City Art Gallery, Leeds, Yorkshire
Nine Painters From N.E. (selected by Victor Pasmore), Hatton Gallery, Newcastle upon Tyne, England
1960 *Ten Younger English Painters*, Redfern Gallery, London, England
1963 John Moore's Liverpool Exhibition No. 3, Walker Art Gallery, Liverpool, England
Galerie Charles Lienhard, Zurich, Switzerland
1964 *Atkinson and Slade*, Lane Gallery, Bradford, Yorkshire
1965 Leeds International Exhibition Exchange Stadthausgalerie, Dortmund, Germany
Leeds Staff Exhibition, University of Alberta, Canada
Then and Now, Leeds Institute Gallery, Leeds, Yorkshire
1966 *Form and Image*, Leeds Institute Gallery, Leeds, Yorkshire
Susan Bolard Gallery, Zurich, Switzerland

1967 *Edinburgh 100*, Richard Demarco Gallery, Edinburgh, Scotland

1968 *Alliance in Art: Contemporary American and British Art*, Sotherby Gallery, Washington, DC

Leeds Ten, Midland Group Gallery, Nottingham, England

Leeds Ten, Park Square Gallery, Leeds, Yorkshire

1969 British Council Touring Exhibition, Arts Council of Great Britain, Tel-Aviv, Israel

1970 *British Painting*, Corcoran Gallery and British Embassy, Washington, DC

Seven Artists, Althouse College, University of Western Ontario, London, Ontario

Fanshawe College Basic Year Exhibition, Rothman Gallery, Stratford, Ontario

1971 Kitchener-Waterloo Art Gallery, Kitchener, Ontario

Kingpitcher Gallery, Pittsburgh, Pennsylvania

1974 *Collectors Choice*, Playhouse Gallery, Leeds, Yorkshire

1977 *Viewpoint, Atkinson, Forrest, Jansy*, McIntosh Gallery, London, Ontario

Saskatoon/London Exchange, Mendel Art Gallery, Saskatoon, Saskatchewan

1978 *London/Banff Exchange*, Whyte Gallery, Banff, Alberta

1980 *Lewis Collection*, Museum of Art, Carnegie Institute, Pittsburgh, Pennsylvania

Area Artists Part I, London Regional Art Gallery, London, Ontario

Atkinson, Frost, Thubron, Chadwick, Thielsen Galleries Inc., London, Ontario

1981 *Atkinson-Lorcini Preview*, McIntosh Gallery, University of Western Ontario, London, Ontario

1981–82 Fanshawe College Arts Faculty Exhibition, University of Windsor and Woodstock Art Gallery, Gallery Stratford, Stratford, Ontario

Exhibition with photographers Edward and Cole Weston, Zenith Gallery, Pittsburgh, Pennsylvania

1984 *Associations, Zelanak, Atkinson, Paterson Ewen*, London Regional Art Gallery, London, Ontario

1991 Concept Gallery, Pittsburgh, Pennsylvania

1993 *Down By The Riverside*, London Regional Art and Historical Museums, London, Ontario

1995 *David Lewis, Eric Atkinson*, Mendelson Gallery, Pittsburgh, Pennsylvania

1995 *Land Escapes*, London Regional Art and Historical Museums, London, Ontario

1996 *Forty Years Friendship, Terry Frost, David Lewis, Eric Atkinson, Warren MacKenzie*, Mendelson Gallery, Pittsburgh, Pennsylvania

1997 Summer Exhibition, Wallace Galleries, Calgary, Alberta

1998 *Recollections*, Hartlepool Art Gallery, Hartlepool, England

Scanning the Contemporary Landscape, Atkinson, Fenwick, Stubbs, Gallery Lambton, Sarnia, Ontario

1998–99 *Links Between Artists in Cornwall and Leeds University*, The Tate Gallery, St Ives, Cornwall, England

2000 *Landmarks*, McIntosh Gallery, University of Western Ontario. Eric Atkinson and Dr Grant Young: an artist and a geologist respond to the landscape

SELECTED BIBLIOGRAPHY

Andreae, Janice 'Season in Review', *Arts Magazine*, Toronto, March 1987

Berger, John 'London Galleries', *Time and Tide Magazine*, November 1955

Bone, Stephen 'The Art of Eric Atkinson', *The Times*, 6 September 1956

Burdett, Bob 'Canadian Artists in Exhibition', *Roundstone*, Toronto, 1974

Crawford, Lenore 'Mexican Theme Dominates', *The London Free Press*, March 1974

Crawford, Lenore 'Big Works Count in Atkinson Display', *The London Free Press*, 20 October 1970

Demarco, Richard *1st Edinburgh Open 100* (catalogue), Demarco Gallery, Edinburgh, 1967

Fair, Barry *Down By The Riverside* (catalogue), London Regional Art and Historical Museums, 1993

Gibbons, Phillip 'The Work of Eric Atkinson', *The Studio Magazine*, October 1956

Halpern, Sonia *Land Escapes* (catalogue), London Regional Art and Historical Museums, 1995

Johnson, W.E. 'Hartlepool Artist', *Northern Daily Mail*, 6 November 1952

Kitchin, Myfanwy 'Atkinson and Warren-Davis: Midland Group Nottingham', *Manchester Guardian*, 18 March 1964

Kritzwiser, Kay 'Artist Atkinson, Happy Wearing Two Hats', *The Globe and Mail*, Toronto, 25 October 1980

Laurie, Peter 'Atkinson A Love For The Landscape', *Interrobang* Magazine, Fanshawe College, 15 March 1979

Lewis, David 'Collecting, A Personal Affair', *Carnegie Institute Magazine*, Summer issue, Pittsburgh, 1981

Lewis, David *Scanning the Contemporary Landscape* (catalogue), Gallery Lambton, Ontario, December 1998

Lewis, David 'Canada and White', in *Terry Frost*, Scolar Press, Aldershot, 1994

Maddox, Conroy 'Atkinson, Molton Gallery Exhibition', *Manchester Guardian*, 16 April 1965

Miller, Donald 'Painting and Photography, Atkinson, Edward & Cole Weston', *Pittsburgh Post Gazette*, 28 September 1982

Moppett, George *London/Saskatoon Exchange* (catalogue), Mendel Art Gallery, Saskatoon, 1977

Moppett, George *Eric Atkinson* (catalogue), Mendel Art Gallery, Saskatoon, 1980

Newton, Eric 'The Painter's Intention, Eric Atkinson', *Time and Tide Magazine*, 13 February 1954

Newton, Eric 'Atkinson at Zwemmer Gallery, London', *Manchester Guardian*, 12 February 1963

O'Brien, Paddy *London Collects* (catalogue). London Regional Art Gallery, London, Ontario, 1972

Oliver, W.T. 'Zest and Sense of Fun Shone Through', *Yorkshire Post*, 23 June 1975

Purdie, James 'A Battle for Name Over Number', *The Globe and Mail*, Toronto, February 1978

Rans, Goldie 'A Passion For Creativity', *London Magazine*, March 1988

Read, Sir Herbert *Malerei und Plastik aus Leeds* (foreword to exhibition catalogue), Dortmund/Leeds Exchange exhibition, Dortmund, Germany, 1961

Reaney, James 'Huronia Series, A Trip to the Beach', *The London Free Press*, 2 June 1984

Robertson, Bryan 'British Painters of Today', *The Listener*, February 1953

Russell, John 'Mixtures, London Group', *The Sunday Times*, September 1954

Sandle, Douglas *Forms and Image in Contemporary Art* (catalogue), Leeds University, March 1966

Secrest, Meryle 'An American in Leeds', *Studio International*, May 1969

Secrest, Meryle 'The Performance is Now in Progress', *The Washington Post*, 18 May 1969

Silverstein, John *Fine Art Department Faculty Exhibition* (catalogue), The Gallery/Stratford, 18 April 1982

Stubbs, Maurice *Canadian Art Collection* (catalogue), McIntosh Gallery, The University of Western Ontario, 1983

Tausig, Susanne 'Probe Beneath Realities Surface', *The London Free Press*, 17 March 1979

Taylor, Alfred 'His Art is in His Job', *Yorkshire Evening Post*, December 1965

Sunderland, - 'Atkinson Striking Work', *The Scotsman*, February 1954

Sylvester, David 'Round the London Galleries', *The Listener*, 12 February 1954

Wallis, Neville 'Sincerity of Purpose: A Private Universe', *The Observer*, 6 November 1953

Whittet, G.E. 'Atkinson and Ceri Richards', *The Studio Magazine of Contemporary Art*, May 1956

PUBLIC COLLECTIONS

Abbot Hall Art Gallery, Kendal
Alcoa Collections, Pittsburgh
Arts Council of Great Britain
Balaszeskul Collection, Berlin, Germany
Bayer Foundation Art Collection, Pittsburgh
Bishops Stortford College
The Blackburn Group Inc., London, Ontario
Boots College, Nottingham
Bretton Hall Collection, Wakefield
California Art College, Print Collection
Cassels Brock Ltd, Toronto
Clarendon College, Nottingham
Contemporary Art Society, London, England
Fanshawe College Collection, London, Ontario
Ford Foundation, Detroit, Michigan
Glaxo Laboratories Collection
Government Heritage Collection, London, England
Hartlepool Art Gallery
Hereford City Art Gallery
Herefordshire Education Authority
Imperial Chemical Industries Collection
Imperial Oil Ltd, Calgary, Alberta
Keele University Collection
Kent Education Authority Collection
John Labatt Limited Collection
Lambton Art Gallery, Sarnia, Ontario
Lear & Siegler Ltd, Toronto
Leeds C.A.S., Leeds University
Leeds City Art Gallery
Leeds Schools Collection
Leicester Art Gallery
Leicestershire Education Authority Collection
London Life Insurance Company Ltd Art Collection
London Regional Art and Historical Museums Collection
London Regional Cancer Center Art Collection
Marburg University, Germany
McIntosh Gallery, University of Western Ontario, London, Ontario
McNay Art Institute, San Antonio, Texas
Ministry of Works, Great Britain
National Hospital Collection, UK
National Museum of the Performing Arts, UK
National Portrait Gallery, London
North Riding of Yorkshire Education Collection
Nuffield Collection
Ocelot International Collection, Calgary, Alberta
Ontario Heritage Foundation, London, Ontario
Oxford University Collection
P & O Steamship Company Collection
Pan Canadian Corp., Calgary, Alberta
Pittsburgh Metals Collection
Rothman Foundation, Ontario
Royal Academy of Arts, London
Siskind, Cromarty, Ivey & Dowler Art Collection, London
Smash Editorial: Feature Film Editing, Toronto
Southern Pacific Hotel Ltd, Toronto
Touche Ross Collection, Pittsburgh
United Steel, Pittsburgh
Urban Design Associates, Pittsburgh
Victoria and Albert Museum, London, England
Wakefield Art Gallery and Museums
Whitbread Brewery Collection

Index